200

LEAST OF ALL SAINTS

LEAST OF ALL SAINTS

The Story of Aimee Semple McPherson

by Robert Bahr

PRENTICE-HALL, INC., Englewood Cliffs, N.J.

Least of All Saints:
The Story of Aimee Semple McPherson
by Robert Bahr

Printed in the United States of America

Prentice-Hall International, Inc., London
Prentice-Hall of Australia, Pty. Ltd., Sydney
Prentice-Hall of Canada, Ltd., Toronto
Prentice-Hall of India Private Ltd., New Delhi
Prentice-Hall of Japan, Inc., Tokyo
Prentice-Hall of Southeast Asia Pte. Ltd., Singapore
Whitehall Books Limited, Wellington, New Zealand

10 9 8 7 6 5 4 3 2 1

Library of Congress Cataloging in Publication Data

Bahr, Robert.
    Least of all saints.

    Bibliography: p.
    1. McPherson, Aimee Semple, 1890-1944.   2. Evange-
lists—United States—Biography.   I. Title.
BX7990.I68M273   289.9 [B]   78-26530
ISBN 0-13-527978-X

To my mother
Katherine Louise Kuebler Bahr
and
to my friend
Alice Harrison Bahr

FOREWORD

Officials of the Church of the Foursquare Gospel still insist, at least formally, that Aimee's kidnap story is true, apparently believing the church's future stands or falls on the issue—a view as absurd as it is untenable. The Roman Catholic Church is not shaken by the fact that Peter, the Rock upon whom it is built, denied Christ three times at Gethsemane; Judaism has made no effort to deny that David, from whose line the Messiah Himself shall come, was both a murderer and an adulterer.

The church's attitude is certainly understandable—we the public maintain a peculiar attitude toward ministers of the Gospel. While an entertainer might make a million dollars a year providing some temporal distraction without raising an eyebrow, a Billy Sunday or Aimee Semple McPherson dare not acknowledge a fraction of that income, even though they provide, in addition to the entertainment, mass psychotherapy, a renewal of spirit, and who knows but salvation in the bargain.

This judgmental attitude toward preachers goes beyond the question of money; we also view them as having less right than the rest of us to be human. For example, we would find it far more provocative to learn that the local minister has taken a mistress than to hear the same of the barber. The barber is naughty, the minister a hypocrite. That's a stupid attitude, to say the least—while the minister may have a special gift for preaching, he enjoys no more dispensation from temptation than the rest of us.

Some people have outstanding gifts. Like Aimee, they preach with unique power and vitality; and, like Aimee, we cannot but expect them to sin with some vitality as well. The Church of the Foursquare Gospel needn't defend Aimee. It seems to me the story of her life is a far more meaningful testimony in this day and can have much more impact, even for the Gospel, than the superficial and unreal image that has thus far been projected.

I have mentioned all this for several reasons. First, it explains why Dr. Charles Duarte of the Temple's Heritage Department refused me the use of the church's archives—only those pledging to write the story the church has been telling since 1926 may utilize these facilities. It explains why Aimee's own autobiographies are unacceptable as final sources. It also explains why some of my best sources, among them relatives and others still active in the Church of the Foursquare Gospel, require that I do not use their names and thereby jeopardize essential relationships.

Moreover, it is why, if pressed to define this work, I would term it a speculative and dramatic re-creation of Aimee Semple McPherson's life. It is my opinion after traveling the length and breadth of the country, conducting scores of interviews in Ontario, Florida, Providence, Los Angeles, and elsewhere, scouring hundreds of published and unpublished records, letters, and other sources, that this book is an authentic version of her life and work. All the episodes and much of the dialogue are based on the above sources, many of which are listed herein. Where evidence is conflicting, I have drawn conclusions in harmony with the heavier weight of facts, and where I have found it necessary to speculate, I have said so and to what extent in the Notes and Comments in the back of the book.

But I have never entertained the thought of writing a definitive biography of Aimee Semple McPherson. In this best of all possible worlds, I envisoned Aimee as the greatest of all possible heroines, and that is the story I set out to tell. I have omitted decades of her life, although sketching in the highlights of those omitted periods in Notes and Comments. I have created, particularly in Part Four, both dialogue and scenes which are suggested by recorded testimony, but have never been proved. Thus, the book's most controversial aspects express widely held and documented opinions as well as facts that have been presented in a court of law.

So, a speculative biography it is. The richness and truth of this woman's life can be told in no other way.

Unto me, who am
less than the least of all saints,
is this grace given,
that I should preach among
the Gentiles the unsearchable
riches of Christ.
—*Saint Paul, Ephesians 3:8*

But praise be to God,
He has used even me, the
least of all saints.
—*Aimee Semple McPherson*

PART ONE

CHAPTER I

Early Friday morning, October 6, 1944, the people descended upon Angelus Temple. By noon they blocked traffic in the streets, hovering around the tabernacle's huge glass doors, cluttering the sidewalks for two blocks along Lemoyne Street to the north and Park Avenue to the east. Glendale Boulevard, which paralleled the temple's grand semicircular facade, was congested all the way to Sunset Boulevard, and across the street in Echo Park, crowds milled beside the lake.

Ushers quietly formed the people into lines two abreast. The aged, the crippled, and military servicemen went directly into the sanctuary; the others waited. Some had brought stools or folding chairs and a few had packed lunches, but thousands stood stoically sweltering under the Los Angeles sun. Special attendants silently whisked the few who collapsed to a first-aid station on the temple's second floor.

Those who passed through the great doors found an expansive vestibule, cool and serene and dimly lit, with sweeping stairways rising to the balconies. The fragrance of blossoms filled the air, and through the doors leading to the sanctuary the mourners could see the myriad floral displays. The proscenium—for it was no ordinary church platform—was laden with flowers. The arrangements spilled over into the orchestra pit, cluttered the far aisles. Some hung from the walls.

To the left towered a nine-foot harp of gold chrysanthemums, orchids, and gladioli. On the wall to the right hung a huge globe of multi-colored carnations. A gold chalice of flowers stood on an altar pedestal. There were floral pearly gates, floral crosses everywhere, a

2

floral replica of the throne on which for two decades Sister Aimee had reigned.

Entering the sanctuary along the central aisle, the mourners first noted the chandelier suspended from the blue dome, its crystals twinkling in the soft sunlight of the stained-glass windows. Then, inevitably, their eyes went to the stage, the apex of the funnel-shaped auditorium. There a blanket of purple orchids and red roses draped the bower of the bronze coffin in which Aimee Semple McPherson lay in state. Still attractive and appearing decades younger than her fifty-four years, she rested on pleated white satin, a white suede Bible in her hands. A simple white satin gown and a navy blue cape draped her body.

Some, gazing at the face, commented that it did not appear at all like Sister Aimee. Certainly she had remained handsome, with wide mouth and high cheeks and large, well-spaced eyes. But without the striking smile, the magnetism and effusive energy, she seemed hardly a figure capable of swaying millions, moving the imagination of an entire nation, entertaining celebrities and royalty, and wielding enormous economic and political power. In fact, she appeared in death rather ordinary.

Yet, as newspapers around the world recalled that October, Aimee Semple McPherson had been one of the most powerful and influential women in American history—and certainly the most controversial. She had been hailed by her most devout followers as Queen of Heaven—and simultaneously condemned by her detractors as the perpetrator of fraud, hypocrisy, perjury, misappropriation of funds, grand theft, physical assault, alcoholism, and adultery. Years earlier, a widely respected minister, well acquainted with Sister Aimee, had written: "Christianity, as a whole, has suffered from the wound this misguided woman has inflicted in its very heart, to say nothing of the corruption that her power has worked in public office."

Yet, even in the heat of the most vehement verbal assaults, most of her disciples never wavered in their loyalty. As Aimee herself once said, "I have the passionate devotion of thousands. If the papers tomorrow morning proved that I had committed eleven murders, those thousands would still believe in me."

Their loyalty didn't end with her death. The Los Angeles *Times* estimated that 45,000 people filed past her coffin between October 6 and 8, and on that final day of the viewing the lines were still so long that temple administrators waived the 4:30 closing time. Long into the night, somber followers shuffled down the center aisle of Angelus Temple.

From all over the world they continued to send flowers. The sanctuary overflowed with them, until finally the administrators pleaded through radio broadcasts and newspapers that no more be sent. Ultimately it was learned that five railroad cars full of flowers addressed to the temple had never been unloaded. Even the death of the immortal Will Rogers had not stirred such a floral outpouring.

Among Sister Aimee's followers were those who insisted she had not died, that the body in the coffin was not hers, and that she would return as she had once before in all her grandeur, brilliant and sweeping, leading them through laughter and tears, holding ten thousand people to her side. Others accepted her death, but rested in the confidence that long after the backbiters and gossipmongers who tortured her memory were gone, Sister Aimee's fame would live on, and she would reign with the saints in heaven. For them, Monday, October 9, 1944, was a day of rejoicing, for to be absent from the body was to be present with the Lord, and Sister Aimee had moved on to Glory.

At 1:00 P.M., the funeral service began. Cars were double-parked for half a mile in every direction from the temple. More than five thousand people crowded into the building, filling both balconies, the foyer, and stairways. Another fifteen hundred filled the L.I.F.E. Bible College auditorium next door. Several hundred pressed into the Five Hundred Room on the temple's second floor, and more than two thousand jammed the surrounding streets and sidewalks, and gathered in Echo Park.

Dr. Howard P. Courtney, general field supervisor and director of the temple's foreign missions, said, "Today we are here to commemorate the stepping up of a country girl into God's Hall of Fame. Along with Zwingli, Huss, Wycliffe, Savonarola, Luther, Wesley, Whitefield, Knox, and Moody, Aimee Semple McPherson rightly takes her place with the greatest of spiritual leaders.

"Hymns, instrumental numbers, and sacred operas, all the product of her genius, gave her a musical name which ranks her with the immortals. Civic authorities will long remember her for her outstanding charitable efforts when, during the time of need, hundreds of thousands were fed and clothed regardless of creed or color. She has fought a good fight. She has finished her course. She has kept the faith."

Five thousand voices were raised that October afternoon in Angelus Temple, not in dirges of death, but songs of triumph. Her people sang as in former days, with the fervor she herself had inspired, strong with the assurance that she and they would be united again one day. It was to her, the living Sister Aimee, they sang the promise:

4

When the trumpet of the Lord shall sound
And time shall be no more,
And the morning breaks eternal bright and fair,
When the saved of earth shall gather
Over on the other shore
And the role is called up yonder,
I'll be there!
    When the role is called up yonder,
    When the role is called up yonder . . .

CHAPTER II

. . . When the role is called up yonder
When the role is called up yonder I'll be there.

Hurling herself up the steep cellar steps, Mildred Kennedy sang in a shrill, vigorous voice. She carried a pan of milk in one hand and with the other she clutched the railing for support.

It had been a tiresome day for Happy Minnie, as she was known in this isolated corner of Ontario, and although she sang heartily, and smiled to herself, there was beneath the smile a bullish hardness. Mentally she ordered her feet to march. There would be no lagging on those steps, not the slightest hint of it. For, if there was anything that troubled Minnie Kennedy, it was the idea that she was approaching middle age. Not by a long shot she wasn't. In fact, she felt every bit as sprightly as her seventeen-year-old daughter, and would have acted it, too, except that in so small a village as Salford, all the neighbors would soon be gossiping about her.

Just as Minnie reached the kitchen, Aimee burst into the room from the barnyard, hurling her school books onto the table.

"Dear Lord, you scared the daylights out of me!" Minnie exclaimed.

Gasping for breath, Aimee stared at her mother. Her large brown eyes peered from beneath lowered lids, focusing on the wall behind Minnie's head. She made no comment, no movement, while her breathing slowed. Then she turned back toward the barnyard and, throwing herself against the doorframe, gazed across the field deep in thought.

"You know, I don't believe there *is* a God," she finally muttered.

Minnie had long ago grown accustomed to her daughter's flair for melodrama, but for these words she had been entirely unprepared. Hastening to the nearest chair, she dropped into it, quickly setting the pan of milk on the table. "What on earth are you saying?" she demanded.

"Hm?"

"You said—you said *you don't believe in God,* child!"

"I did? Well, I don't. Why *should* I?"

"Now that's just the silliest thing I ever heard. How can you break your poor mother's heart and say such a foolish thing? My sweet little Aimee!"

Aimee stared into Minnie's weary eyes and wondered how she could explain to her the teachings of Darwin and Voltaire, Paine and Ingersoll. It was all well and good for Minnie, a hardworking, simple farmer's wife, to believe every word of the Bible was inspired by God, "cover to cover," as they said at the Salvation Army meetings. Certainly such innocent faith filled a need. But how could any intelligent, educated person swallow that? How could Aimee herself have believed it for so long? The earth created in six days, a human male formed from clay, Eve shaped from his rib, tempted by a talking snake! An infant born of a virgin! A man who raised the dead coming back to life three days after being crucified! Yes, it was fine for the simple folk who could accept such things, people like Minnie. But to Aimee it was, if not preposterous, certainly unlikely.

"Why, Aimee, who made the world?" asked Minnie plaintively. "Who made the sun and the moon and the stars?"

"I'll tell you." Aimee swept to the table and, grasping a pencil, began pacing. "It all started out a molten mass of lava. And the heat made it spin. That made it fall apart, and the moon and the stars and the sun and the earth all flew off. On the earth, as things began to cool down, fungus started to grow, then cell life, and after millions of years fish in the sea, and then birds and the earth animals. And then man evolved from the monkey."

She had spoken with an air of self-assurance, but of course it wasn't quite so cut and dry. The science teacher had mentioned the missing link—or links. He even used such terms as "it is generally accepted," "most scientists believe," and "we speculate." But the scientists and teachers didn't ask for blind faith in the impossible. They said, "You've got your senses—your sight, hearing, touch, and the rest. Use them. Trust them. And use your virtually infinite human intelligence to interpret what your senses are telling you. You can believe in your senses. You can believe in your reason. Man is his own God."

7

Aimee felt it was true. Still, just the past night, sitting at the window in the darkness of her room, gazing out across the corn to where the fields met the farthest stars, she admitted what she could never tell Minnie or anyone: that the truth was made of ice and dwelled alone like a barren planet in an empty place. It heard no voice, only the hollow echo of itself.

Why did she persist so stubbornly to prove there was no God, that no life was immortal, and that beyond this mere instant we call life there exist only the grave and the worms and eternal death? How insane that all we ever do, all we learn, the heights of fame and fortune we attain, all come to nothing at the end. All the animals and even the insects do as well, and there is just no sense to anything.

While James and Minnie had slept. Aimee felt the absurdity of life more deeply than ever. She imagined those who had lived a life of righteousness heaped in the same graves as those who had robbed, raped, and murdered, those who'd suffered to defend truth and goodness buried beside liars and deceivers. What had Solomon written? She reached for her Bible, paged to the second chapter of Ecclesiastes, verses 15 and 16, and in the moonlight read:

> Then said I in my heart, As it happeneth to the fool, so it happeneth even to me; and why was I then more wise? Then I said to my heart, that this also is vanity.

> For there is no remembrance of the wise more than of the fool for ever; seeing that which now is in the days to come shall all be forgotten. And how dieth the wise man? as the fool.

Aimee read Solomon's concluding words several times: "Therefore I hated life."

Although she'd never have told Minnie, the night before at the window she had whispered a simple prayer: "God, if there be a God, reveal yourself to me."

But there had followed no miracles, not even the smallest one. On her way home from school that day she'd told the Salvation Army captain about her prayer, and he'd replied, "Now, dearie, the Bible's *full* of miracles! You wouldn't be needing more than them, would you?"

"They're no good," Aimee protested. "Nothing two thousand years old that I have to take on faith. Maybe that was a miracle for the disciples when Christ walked on water, but for me it's hearsay. And none of the old-hat stuff about stars and trees and mountains. Sure they're miracles if you believe in God in the first place. But what if it all just happened by the evolutionary process?"

Another pastor, Ingersoll's most learned theologian, had explained a week earlier that the day of miracles was over. "The drugs, surgeons—those are God's miracles today, my girl. Man himself is the agent through which God does the impossible."

So it was as she had thought, a choice between a cringing, cowardly, indefensible faith and the cold, empty face of absurdity.

"Oh, my poor baby," Minnie moaned, breaking into Aimee's thoughts. "I just can't believe it. No, I can't. Can this be the same little angel I dressed in her own darling Salvation Army suit when she was just a little pip in the third grade? With the navy blue jacket and red trim and your own little cap. How you led your little friends to the penitent's bench, so they could be saved and go to heaven someday. And now—look what's happened to you!" She dropped her head, nodding. "I'm just ashamed. So ashamed."

Anger flared in Aimee's eyes. "Well, you just *go on* being ashamed! You can't be any more ashamed of *me* than I am of *you*. Standing on street corners asking for money like some poor *beggar*."

Minnie's face reddened.

"God forgive you, Aimee Elizabeth. If your dad and me wear rags, it's so we can send you to the high school, buy you the best clothes and all. If I wear funny clothes, it's so you won't have to, Aimee Elizabeth. And what has it got me? A daughter who says, 'Thank you, Momma, I know how many times you and Daddy sacrificed for me and I'm so grateful'? No. Just an arrogant, selfish, headstrong, God-forsaking, spoiled child."

Aimee started to speak. Then, bursting into tears, she ran into the living room and up the stairs to her bedroom.

"Shut up!" she screamed, slamming the door and throwing herself onto the bed. She felt buried in an avalanche of guilt again, and she knew that, as always, suppertime would find her apologizing to her mother. Minnie would insist upon it.

"Now, say you're sorry, Aimee, sweetie. Go ahead, say you're sorry to poor Minnie."

"I'm sorry, Momma."

"Now, *that's* my girl. I forgive you. And God forgives you. I bet you feel better already."

But perhaps she wouldn't apologize, not this time. And maybe never again. It wasn't always her fault, as Minnie insisted. She was tired of cowering like a baby under the continual assault of guilt. She was cowering even now. The thought made her angry, and she leaped from the bed, brushing the tears away, and raced down the steps to the piano. She began pounding out a ragtime rhythm, the worldly music Minnie described as sinful. Realizing that, Aimee played with particular pleasure.

After Thanksgiving that year of 1907, Aimee's life became enormously active, which was just as she wished it. She had read about Sarah Bernhardt, the world's greatest actress, and immediately hurled herself into a theatrical career by cajoling teachers into giving her a lead in the school's Christmas play. The program director of the Salford Methodist Church, where her father James sang in the choir, asked her to play a part in the holiday extravaganza. She even won a role in the Ingersoll Presbyterian Church's Christmas Pageant. Racing from school to rehearsals to supper at the farm, back to Ingersoll for more rehearsals, and finally back home for bed kept Aimee's head spinning and her spirits high, and it was all very exciting. She simply could not endure boredom, and would rather have died than live the humdrum life to which most people seemed destined. More clearly than anything, she knew her life would somehow be special. She would *make* it special. She would never, ever be bored.

"Did ya see what they're doing to the old grocery store there on Main Street by the depot?" asked one of the girls after school one day.

"The vacant one?"

"It ain't vacant no more. The Holy Rollers got a hold of it. They're making it into a church."

"Not a church, silly," said another. "A meetinghouse. And they're Pentecostals."

"Well, I don't know what you call it, but they get God and go flip-flopping all over the floor and everything. Momma says they're nuts, or else the devil gets after them."

Aimee turned on the girl who was speaking. "And just how do you *know* what goes on there," she demanded. "Have you been there?"

"Not on you life," she said. "You wouldn't get me in there for nothing. But Momma went last year when that same preacher was in town. When he set up that tent by the swamp there on Main Street, and they just *had* to get up and flop around or the mosquitoes would've eaten them alive!"

The Holy Rollers—fanatics, touched in the head, as Minnie had phrased it. But driving home from school that afternoon, Aimee had a startling thought. The Holy Rollers behaved as people might if they really *had* come to know God. Aimee had heard that some of them said they'd been baptized, not with water, but by the Holy Spirit Himself. Others

10

said God had miraculously cured their diseases, and many claimed to speak a heavenly tongue that only the anointed could decipher. If they were real, such things were certainly the miracles Aimee had been seeking. A wave of excitement rippled through her. She would attend a meeting, and come away either a confirmed scoffer or a believer.

> Would you be free from your burden of sin?
> There's Power in the blood,
> Power in the blood.
> Would you o'er evil a victory win?
> There's wonderful power in the blood.

Only twenty people gathered in the dilapidated storefront on Ingersoll's Main Street that December night of 1907, most of them simple farmers and laborers from the fields and factories surrounding the town. Yet they sang with a gusto that easily outdid the revelers in the beer hall across the tracks. Their singing was ecstatic, with handclapping and foot-stomping, sometimes off-key, punctuated with shouts of Amen and Hallelujah.

Aimee had persuaded James to bring her to Ingersoll half an hour early for rehearsal at the high school, and now she sat in the back row next to her father. She wore only a simple cotton dress, the same one she'd put on for school that day, but the others were clad in overalls and work shirts, or faded housedresses, some frayed and old-fashioned. Aimee wouldn't even have given such garments to the mission—they weren't much good for anything but dust rags. She felt conspicuously overdressed.

But her thoughts were quickly distracted by the sheer energy filling the room. Some people stared at the ceiling, mumbling softly. Others cried "Hallelujah!" their faces radiant. A few danced in the aisle. A man fell to his knees and began babbling words that made no sense. When he stopped, a woman stood and fervently expounded upon the imminent return of Christ.

Full-grown men and women were laughing and crying, waving their hands in the air, intoxicated with joy. Something of enormous significance was happening at that moment, it seemed to Aimee, something transcending ordinary life. People not as intelligent or clean or well dressed as she were experiencing ecstasies she'd never known. Here in this rickety old converted grocery store a miracle was taking place, and in all the world only she and her father and this handful of people knew about it. None of the questions she'd raised in her diatribes against religion were answered, no solutions offered. But she saw God on those people's faces, felt His power in the room, in herself.

11

A white-haired woman with heavy jowls led the singing with sweeping gestures and perpetual smile. Behind her sat a young man with intense blue eyes and thick dark hair. Tall and slender, he seemed awkward in the tiny chair, and when the singing stopped he sprang from it eagerly. Smiling, he seemed to Aimee almost beautiful, with smooth high-boned cheeks and wide, full lips. But it was a thoroughly masculine beauty—jaw firm, facial muscles taut, and eyebrows thick and sweeping.

He spoke without hesitation:

" 'Then Peter said unto them, *Repent,* and be baptized every one of you in the name of Jesus Christ for the remission of sins, and ye shall receive the gift of the Holy Ghost.'

"Repent. Repent!" the preacher cried in a rich, unwavering Scottish accent. "It is the word of *God,* and there *is* no other way. If you love this world, then the love of God is not in you.

"If you would rather spend your time in theaters and dance halls than in Sunday school and church, then you are not of God. You are of the devil.

"If you would rather read novels than the Bible, then you are not of God.

"If you would rather spend your money on fancy clothes than on serving the Lord, then you are lost and without excuse before God."

Aimee moved uncomfortably in her seat. She had no doubt the preacher was speaking to her alone. His piercing eyes seemed permanently affixed to hers. She glanced to the left and right to see if anyone else had noticed, but they all seemed transfixed.

His words cut Aimee like a scalpel. How haughty she had been—and self-satisfied! She'd actually *told* people she was the smartest, most talented, most athletic girl in the school! And when periodically someone would inform her that she was conceited, she'd disdainfully denounce their jealousy.

But that night under the preacher's pounding voice and piercing eyes, those petty games fell apart like paper ashes in a hurricane. She was not merely a little naughty girl, the incessant teller of little white lies and thrower of red-faced temper tantrums. Her sin was more pervasive. She was by *nature* evil before God, and a teary-eyed apology, always effective with Minnie, would account for nothing with God.

She would have to renounce her sins, abandon once and for all the dances and moving pictures, learn to play hymns on the piano and forsake the worldly ragtime. She'd have to abandon hope of being an actress like Sarah Bernhardt, for the theater and the moving pictures were of the devil. If she were to be a child of God, she would have to bear witness to

12

the change in her life, among those whom she'd ignored or insulted, and to whom she'd boasted. She'd have to ask their forgiveness, in fact, and then they'd mock her and she'd be compelled to endure the ridicule humbly and smiling.

The young preacher fell silent. His eyes fluttered and closed, and across his smiling face washed a glow that Aimee believed brightened the room. She gasped, stunned by the awareness of some great energy radiating from the preacher and filling the place. Others felt it, too. Someone whispered, "Praise God! Oh, thank you, Jesus!" Then the whole room became alive with murmuring.

The preacher began to speak, but his voice was softer, musical, and Aimee couldn't understand the words. It was a language she had never heard, and she realized he was speaking the heavenly language of God. She had asked for a miracle, had pleaded with God for just one miracle, and here, right at this moment, her prayer was being answered. She was observing a man who spoke the language of God.

"You stand at the crossroads tonight," the preacher said, and his penetrating blue eyes were fixed on her. "One road leads to heaven, the other to hell. One to life, the other to death." She knew it was true. She stood at the brink of the only decision that would ever matter. Ultimately she would choose God or Satan, righteousness or sin, the way of the saint or that of the world. But she would not decide now, not here in front of those people, her feelings a jumble of confusion and conflict. She turned her eyes from the preacher, and while his voice entreated, she whispered to James:

"Daddy, let's go. I'm gonna be late."

Her mind wasn't on rehearsal that night. She missed cues, forgot lines. It surprised everyone. Some of the girls smirked, and Aimee felt like a fool. When the rehearsal was finally over and she walked slowly down the steps from the stage, James prepared to console her, for he knew how intolerant of herself his daughter could be. Aimee smiled feebly and shrugged.

Without speaking she followed James from the auditorium and climbed with him into the sleigh behind Flossie. Moving at a trot, they skimmed along Thames Street, then along the highway, soon leaving the twinkling lights of the town behind. The only sounds were Flossie's hoofs crunching through the snow, the jingling harness, the swish of the runners. Still, Aimee didn't speak.

She was grateful it was James beside her and not her mother, for Minnie would have gone on incessantly demanding, cajoling, pleading to know what was happening in Aimee's mind. But James, who was himself contemplative, viewed his daughter's silence with the same indulgence as he endured her raging tantrums and rejoicings. Now, in his old age, his daughter had become his only joy, and although she was now seventeen, he still celebrated her every word and action as though she were an infant just learning to walk. James praised her good grades; Minnie scolded for the poor ones. James applauded when she outran the boys; Minnie denounced her for not acting like a young woman.

To James she had always been a perfect little girl, and he had accepted her without criticism, without questions. Had he questioned her that night, she'd have tried to answer, for she loved him deeply. But she'd have had little to say, for Aimee herself wasn't sure what she felt. The stars, astonishingly bright in the cold air, seemed to tug at her. The silhouettes and shadows of the open landscape whispered to her. She knew that somehow a great drama was unfolding, and the stars were the audience, the stars and all the saints in glory and the angels, God Himself. And the stage was not in London or Paris or New York City, no great theatrical stage, but this little country road, a humble farm in a small Canadian village. And a ramshackle storefront church. A handsome young evangelist with a rich, clarion voice played the lead—she didn't even know his name. But when she looked into the sparkling snow, she saw his face, and when she stared at the stars, he was there, his blue eyes deep-set and brilliant, smiling, pleading, entreating. The heroine, the heroine herself was Aimee.

She had never felt the air so crisp. The night glistened brighter than it ever had. It seemed to her that she was stepping forth into life for the first time, as though she had been living all these seventeen years in a gloom she had come to call reality. And now the gloom was falling away and she was seeing life clearly for the first time.

God had granted her the miracle. She had *seen* the power of God working in those people, transforming them into souls possessed by the power of the Holy Spirit. She had *heard* God speaking through the lips of that preacher, and when he pointed his finger at her and gazed into her eyes, she had trembled under God's almighty power. Never in her life had she felt such overwhelming force, and she had fled in fear. But on the road back to Salford that night, she believed the yearning she felt inside was God Himself calling her to salvation.

Three days after Aimee heard the Pentecostal evangelist, she was driving home from school alone when, on impulse, she reined Flossie in. Snow-laden clouds hung low, making the late afternoon gray and depressing. There, desolate and alone, she listened to the preacher's voice echoing through her head as it had for three days: *"You* are a poor, lost, miserable, hell-deserving sinner." In all those years of Salvation Army meetings she'd simply ignored the message of salvation. She'd helped collect the offerings, banged the tambourine on street corners, led the congregation in prayer, delivered the morning Scripture reading—Minnie took great pride in arranging such opportunities for her daughter. Aimee had prayed for sinners, witnessed to sinners, led sinners to the penitent's bench at the altar. Yet not once had anyone told her that she herself was a sinner in need of salvation. Not until the storefront preacher.

"God," Aimee whispered. Then, aloud, *"God, be merciful to me, a sinner!"*

And that was all. But although no one in nearby fields noticed it, the day grew more sunny for Aimee. Every snowflake seemed to sparkle brighter in the knowledge of a miracle whose impact would ring throughout eternity. That moment heaven itself celebrated a poor sinner's return to her Heavenly Father. Tears came to her eyes, but she laughed and brushed them aside, and clucking to Flossie, started off at a precarious canter toward home. She could hardly wait to tell Minnie, to hear her mother's exclamations of approval, to embrace her and sing hymns with her. Oh, the joy of salvation! The excitement of it! It was indeed a great drama, the *true* drama, a reality not found in the science texts, no, not known to Darwin and all those pompous know-it-alls, but nonetheless the most vivid truth of all, not one experienced through the ordinary senses, but *extrasensory,* one whose truth is proclaimed by the spirit. And so, with sure conviction that the saints and angels eagerly followed from the battlements of heaven the progress of her drama, Aimee plunged along the Salford road toward home.

CHAPTER III

At dawn, Aimee slipped out of bed and knelt shivering in the clean sunlight from the frosty window. Her prayer was brief, one of gratitude for the usual things like peace and love and shelter, and also for the smell of bacon sizzling in the kitchen, Minnie's pudgy, comforting face, James's gentleness. She thanked God because she felt strong and healthy, and even pretty—and because of all the people in the world she could have been, she was Aimee Kennedy.

Shrugging away a twinge of guilt at her impatience, she ended her prayer with an abrupt Amen and hastily dressed. A moment later she was in the kitchen demanding breakfast.

The day appeared more sunny than she had ever known. The dishes and silverware seemed to sparkle. James and Minnie were radiant, although neither responded with more than a frown as, in an avalanche of words, she told them of her miraculous salvation.

"Time to go!" she finally concluded. James rose to get his coat. "No, stay here," she said. "I'm gonna ride Flossie. It's such a beautiful day!"

"Better not," said James. "Snow's pretty slippery. You could go down."

"Oh, it'll be all right. God's watching over me now, you know." Aimee tugged on her coat and gloves, plopped her cap on her head, and raced out the door toward the barn.

"Now, you just be careful, or you'll break your fool neck!" Minnie yelled after her. Slamming the door shut, the woman turned to James, her lips pursed. "That girl," she mumbled.

"Sure is acting peculiar."

"So what's new?" said Minnie, rolling her eyes upward and shaking her head.

In the barn Aimee threw her arms around the horse's neck, and the two stood motionless, breathing clouds of steam into the air. The girl dug her fingers under the animal's mane, scratched the hide vigorously.

Moments later, the horse saddled and bridled and Aimee atop her, clinging to her cap and ignoring Minnie's fearful shrieks, the two bolted from the barnyard and off toward Ingersoll. They raced furiously, Flossie's hoofs hurling clumps of snow in their wake, Aimee's hair streaming under her cap, her eyes watering. When Flossie tired, they slowed to a walk. Miles of snow gleamed in the bright sunlight. It seemed to her the world had been dusted with chips of diamonds. The sky was a bolt of flawless satin.

The highway turned right, becoming Thames Street as they entered Ingersoll. Aimee nudged the horse into a canter again. On the left, they passed the Salvation Army barracks, and on the right the huge brick furniture factory. Flashing past the stores and homes, she approached King Street, where one of the town's five automobiles sputtered and stalled, giving Flossie a start. Aimee reined the horse toward an alley beside the Mansion House, one of the town's finest hotels. Approaching the barn behind the hotel, she dismounted.

"See you after school," she said, throwing the reins to a stableboy. "Take good care of her."

She could have walked from there to the school in thirteen minutes, and she had more than half an hour to spare, but still she ran, sliding and stumbling in the snow. When a passerby cautioned her, Aimee laughingly announced, "Don't worry, my Heavenly Father watches over me!"

Dashing north on Thames, she crossed the railroad tracks, passed the depot, and approached the storefront mission on the right. Dilapidated, the faded green paint chipping, it seemed a hallowed shrine to her that morning. If only she could say thank you to someone, perhaps the young preacher himself. She crossed the street and approached the door.

A small sign announced a daily prayer meeting at Sister Barrett's home. Aimee knew the woman, a young mother of six, whose husband worked at the local cheese factory. In fact, Aimee had raced past the Barrett home a few moments earlier. It was right there on Thames Street, a few buildings away from the Mansion House.

She began sauntering toward William Street and the school, but after half a dozen steps she stopped and stared pensively into the snow at her feet. Other students swarmed past her.

17

"Look at Aimee Kennedy," someone cried. "She thinks she's a snowman!"

One of the boys pelted her with a snowball. "She's in a trance."

"She's nuts, that's all."

She ignored them, turned back toward the town, weaving among the approaching students. Breaking into a run, she leaped over a small hedge, dashed across three lawns, and, two blocks farther on, stopped before Mrs. Barrett's door.

The preacher himself answered in rolled-up sleeves, open collar, and faded dungarees, his hair uncombed and falling boyishly over his forehead. She recognized the intense blue eyes.

"Reverend . . . pastor . . ."

"Robert Semple is all. Come in. Come in!" Closing the door behind her, he whisked her coat from her and tossed it in a corner, then led her quickly into the parlor and to the Morris chair near the blazing fireplace. He sat on the hassock facing her, smiling and waiting.

"The other night—" she began.

"You were at the meeting. And praise God, He's spoken to your heart!"

"Yes. Yes!"

"And He's won your precious soul to Himself. So you've come to share your joy, for it's full to overflowing."

"How did you *know*?"

Robert Semple smiled. "Ah, the hunger was in your face that night. And the fullness and peace is there now, as I've seen it in a hundred others. So praise God for you, my new sister in the Lord!" He took her hands between his and shook them robustly.

The doorbell sounded, and Mrs. Barrett rushed from the kitchen with her two babies in her arms. The heavily jowled woman who had led the singing entered, followed by a younger woman. Then two elderly matrons arrived. The Reverend Mr. Semple excused himself briefly, returning dressed in his vested black suit and tie, his hair neatly combed.

"Praise God—seven of us today!" he exclaimed. "Nine counting the infants. We had but five yesterday, with Sister Sadie sick abed. But we prayed for her healing, and here she *stands*—a miracle of health."

Everyone said, "Thank you, Jesus!" and "Hallelujah!"

"There's more, dear saints. We have prayed for souls, and today God has blessed us richly. In our midst today is a new child of God." The elderly women gasped, and all eyes turned eagerly toward Aimee.

Mrs. Barrett introduced her, and then Mr. Semple and the women prevailed upon her to give her testimony. She did so eagerly, with energy and enthusiasm that thrilled her listeners. When she finished, Robert Semple's eyes were moist. He took her hand and that of jowly Sister Sadie, and the tiny group knelt in a circle before the fireplace.

"O Father," he prayed, "we rejoice in this child whose soul is Yours. We rejoice in Your power to change lives. And we thank You, humbly, for letting us see what You have done and letting us help."

Then he sang "Praise God from Whom All Blessings Flow," and all joined.

Just before supper, Aimee galloped into the barnyard. Minnie met her at the door.

"And just where were you all day?" Minnie Kennedy demanded.

Casually slipping out of her coat, and draping it over the chair, Aimee answered:

"Now, where on earth do you *think* I was?"

"I don't know where you *was*, but I know where you *wasn't*. The truant officer rang us up on the telephone. You were playing hooky, Aimee Kennedy, and I'm going to know just what you were up to or else."

Aimee glared at her mother. But she saw in Minnie's face the rare, inflexible anger that would endure no opposition. So she smiled.

"It's no big secret, Mother," she said, slumping into a chair. "The Pentecostal people had a prayer meeting, and that's where I was." Leaping to her feet again, she exclaimed, "Oh, Mother, I just *had* to thank them for showing me the way to God! There were dozens and dozens of them there, and when I told them how the clouds had parted and God's brightness cascaded from the battlements of heaven and flowed all around me, Mother, oh, the tears poured down their faces. But they were tears of *joy*! And they all ran to me and hugged me and said I was a child of God. So maybe it was *naughty* of me to miss school, but I just *had* to share my story. And it made them so happy. And I bet it made *God* happy, too."

"Well, then," Minnie huffed. But her face softened, and she turned to the sink, where she was washing dishes.

"Remember that Easter pageant at the Salvation Army?" she asked in a dreamy voice. "Oh, you was just six or seven. But you knew all the Bible stories, and you used to tell them to your little classmates in the schoolyard when they were having recess. So when all the mothers made the white sashes with the gold letters for their little ones in the pageant— you remember, some said, 'Jesus Saves' and 'Praise God' and 'God is Good'—why, I made yours to say, 'God's Little Child.' "

Aimee wrapped her arms around Minnie's waist and squeezed so tightly the woman grunted.

"Let me go!" she squealed, tossing a handful of soapsuds into

Aimee's face. Then Minnie turned around and hugged her daughter to her.

"Oh, I love you, Aimee Kennedy, even if you are a pest half the time," she said, staring at the ceiling with moist eyes. "There's something in you good and special and not common. And . . . well, enough."

She held Aimee at arm's length. "You get yourself to school tomorrow, and no maybes about it. And now go change your clothes and milk the cow."

After school the next day Aimee sent word to the teacher directing the Christmas play that she would attend no more rehearsals and was dropping out of the production. She explained she was sorry only three weeks of rehearsals remained, but she was sure someone could be found who could learn the part by then. Her life had been totally changed, she said. " 'Old things are passed away; behold, all things are become new,' " she quoted. "I am no longer interested in dancing, ragtime, dating, or even my schoolwork. I am consumed with the desire to learn more about God and to seek His power in my life."

Then she raced all the way to Sister Barrett's home. When the woman opened the door, Aimee was too breathless to speak.

"Come in, child," Sister Barrett said. "Everyone's gone. Reverend Semple's sweeping out the hall for tonight's meetings. But you can sit and have a good warm cup of tea and some sugar cookies if you like."

Aimee shook her head. "I'll be back," she gasped.

Dashing across the lawn, she plunged into the street, dodging two men on horseback from the left and a wagon from the right. Breathless and with a flushed face, she reached the mission and threw open the door.

"Hi," she announced, crumbling into a chair.

"What have we here?" said Mr. Semple, smiling. He dropped the broom against the lectern and sauntered toward Aimee.

"Well, it's Aimee Kennedy, fluster- and blustering through the door, scaring the devil out of me."

"The devil . . . the devil's not in you, Reverend Semple," Aimee gasped. "You're a saint."

"So I am, Aimee. And so are we all who are born again by the blood of Christ, you included. But the devil gets into us just the same."

He straddled the bench before her and, gently amused, studied her face and clear brown eyes.

"It's good to see you again, Aimee Kennedy. We prayed for you this morning. Yes, we asked the Father to give you wisdom and knowledge of Himself."

"That's . . . that's why I came."

"Why?"

"To learn. For you to teach me. I want to learn about . . . the Baptism of the Spirit. The speaking in tongues, everything."

Mr. Semple's face brightened. "Well, then!" he exclaimed. "You have a marvelous hunger for the things of God, Aimee, and I'll be doing my best to see that you are fed. But first"—he retrieved the broom from the lectern and handed it to her—"you sweep. I'll make the fire, and then we'll have a fine service tonight." Walking toward the iron stove against the wall, he declared, "Only a fool would talk about fire in the spirit when the flesh is a-shivering."

Later, as the two huddled near the blazing stove, Mr. Semple opened his large black leather Bible.

"Now, you try to picture this in your head, will you, girl?" he said. "The disciples've just seen Christ. Although He's dead, they've seen Him and talked to Him, and He told them they were to do nothing but wait and they would receive power—the Holy Ghost Himself would come upon them. So now, here 'tis—I'm reading from the second chapter of the Book of Acts:

" 'And when the day of Pentecost was fully come, they were all with one accord in one place. And suddenly there came a sound from heaven as of a rushing mighty wind, and it filled all the house where they were sitting. And there appeared unto them cloven tongues like as of fire, and it sat upon each of them. And they were all filled with the Holy Ghost, and began to speak with other tongues, as the Spirit gave them utterance.

" 'And there were dwelling at Jerusalem Jews, devout men, out of every nation under heaven. Now when this was noised abroad, the multitude came together, and were confounded, because that every man heard them speak in his own language.'

"And then, Aimee Kennedy, Peter stood up and lifted his voice and preached—oh, what a glorious sermon! And he revealed all the Scriptures and showed how this and the other prophets since the days of Moses had foretold the coming of Christ. And then he cried out, 'Therefore let all the house of Israel know assuredly, that God hath made that same Jesus, whom ye have crucified, both Lord and Christ.'

"Then what happened? 'Now when they heard this, they were pricked in their heart, and said unto Peter and to the rest of the apostles, Men and brethren, what shall we do? Then Peter said unto them, Repent, and be baptized every one of you in the name of Jesus Christ for the remission of sins, and ye shall receive the gift of the Holy Ghost.

" 'And with many other words did he testify and exhort, saying, Save yourselves from this untoward generation. Then they that gladly received his word were baptized, and the same day there were added unto them about three thousand souls.' "

Mr. Semple stood and paced as he spoke. "Two gifts, Aimee: first, of tongues—a sign to the unsaved. It was the gift of *tongues* confounded them. Second, the gift of the Holy Ghost—the Baptism of the Spirit. It follows salvation like sunrise the dark of night. A day later, a week, a year, but it always follows. And it shakes you, Aimee Kennedy, from the crown of your head to the corns on your toes. That's what happened on the day of Pentecost, and that's what Pentecostalism is all about."

Then, just before the other worshipers arrived, he led Aimee to the altar. Kneeling, he prayed fervently that God would bestow upon her the Baptism of the Holy Spirit and the gift of tongues.

It was almost midnight when Flossie, her nostrils lined with frost and her head low, plodded into the Kennedy farmyard. Even before Aimee dismounted, the kitchen door flew open and Minnie bustled out in slippers and housecoat.

"Where on *earth* have you been, girl?" she demanded.

"Mother, you're going to catch your death of cold! It's below zero, and you're half naked!"

"Don't you go making believe you care about your poor mother, here all night on the brink of tears with worry. And your father! We rang up the telephone all over Ingersoll and Salford, and not a soul knew where you were!"

Coolly composed, Aimee unsaddled the horse and led her to the stall. She forked a clump of hay and tossed it into the feed bin, filled the water bucket, and placed it inside the stall.

"Drink it quick, before it freezes, Flossie," she whispered.

"Well, what've you got to say for yourself?" Minnie demanded.

"I'm tired."

Aimee brushed past, but Minnie grabbed her by the shoulders. "Now, you tell me what you've been up to, or I'm gonna beat the living dickens out of you!" Minnie screamed.

Aimee slumped back against the stall door.

"Mother, where do you *suppose* I've been? I attended the Pentecostal services. I want to know God. I *hunger* to know Him."

"A girl your age, and you never gave it a thought to ring us on the telephone so we wouldn't worry ourselves to death? Don't you pay no attention to the verse that says honor your father and your mother?"

Ducking past Minnie, Aimee ran toward the house. "I'm tired and I'm going to bed," she yelled.

"You come back here! I've got more to say to you." But when Minnie reached the kitchen, she heard Aimee's door slam closed and the bolt lock slide in place.

"Let her be," said James, who had been sitting silent and motionless in the rocker by the stove.

"I *won't* let her be! All right, Aimee Kennedy, we'll see who's boss around here. Just let me hear you been with them Holy Rollers one more time—I don't care if it's the mission or tarrying meeting or what—and that's going to be the last you set foot off the farm. You won't have to worry about failing all your courses—and that's what you're doing, you know. I'll just take you out of school and be done with it."

"I'm seventeen and I can do as I please!" Aimee shouted from her room.

"Well, we'll see about that," said Minnie. "We'll just see."

That night snow began falling again, and by Friday morning the roads were drifted shut. After breakfast, James drove Aimee in the sleigh to the Salford depot. As the train shuddered forward, she waved to him, a thin, fragile old man with sad eyes, all but his flaming red beard hidden by the blinding snow.

Settling back, Aimee watched the flakes fall like a fine powder over the desolate countryside. Now and again a gust would tear across the crest of distant hills, hurling gleaming sprays over the landscape, piling them against isolated trees and barns.

Across the aisle, one girl said to her companions, "It's gonna be a blizzard sure, my dad says, and he can always tell. What if we got stranded at school, had to sleep there overnight with all them terrible *boys*!"

The others giggled nervously and Aimee smiled to herself. She liked to hear the others on the train. The chatter enhanced the warm, content feeling. So did the steaming windows and the rhythmic sway and clacking. There was a feeling of companionship without having to actually interact with people. She had long ago begun sitting by herself on the train, although some had thought her a snob, or peculiar. Well, let them think what they want to think. She simply couldn't endure to participate in the silly prattle that was the hallmark of those girls—tests, grades, boys, clothes, marriage, and babies. Hardly genuine conversation, mere buzzing to avoid silence, as though it were something evil. Something that might thrust them face to face with the serious questions of their lives—

those about purpose, meaning, greatness—and about the graves that awaited each of them sooner or later.

Even if she hadn't become saved, she'd have been so much different from those girls across the aisle. She'd have become a famous actress like Sarah Bernhardt and performed on the stage in Toronto and New York and London and Paris, the beloved and immortal Aimee Kennedy. But God had opened her eyes, to show her that immortality could not be found in fame, but only through faith in the Saviour. She would know God, she would serve Him. And nothing—no, not Minnie or James or the school truant officer or anything else—would dissuade her.

Even before the train stopped at the Ingersoll depot, she had made up her mind: She would not go to school, regardless of Minnie's threats. She would spend the day praying for the Baptism of the Spirit at Sister Barrett's house.

"The choice is between going to school and seeking God," she told Mrs. Barrett and Mr. Semple emphatically. "I'm choosing God."

She prayed all morning with the others, and when they broke for lunch, she stayed on her knees by the old Morris chair in the living room. Mr. Semple found her there when he returned at one o'clock. He knelt beside her, taking her hand, and they prayed together. At five o'clock she reached for his arm, attempting to stand, but her knees refused to unbend and she fell into the chair. It took several minutes before she was able to straighten her legs. Lifting her skirt, she showed Mr. Semple her bruised knees.

"And it was all a waste, a waste," she murmured, closing her eyes to hold back the tears. "I *felt* God's power, I really did. But now I'll go home and Mom will raise a grand old fuss and who knows if I'll ever get to see you again."

"Well, now, you're mistaken if you think it's been a waste, Aimee Kennedy," said the preacher gently. "You're not to be setting a schedule and telling God He's to follow it. He'll work in His own good time." He knelt at her feet, unlaced her shoes, and began massaging the lower calves of her legs. "This'll get the blood flowing, and then, Aimee girl, you'll be having to dash for the train."

She had never felt such strong and gentle hands as this preacher's. His soft, smiling eyes met hers, and in that moment a flame seemed to ignite in the pit of her stomach and flash over her whole body. It was a feeling much like the Baptism of the Holy Spirit, as others had described it, thrilling her so that she wanted to yield to it in cries and moans, to writhe in its ecstasy. But through her blushing confusion she knew it had not been God but Robert Semple who had touched her, the power of his hands and personality, his lovely face, those eyes, that had moved her to surrender.

Setting out for the depot. Aimee discovered the snow had not let up, but fell now in sheets of large flakes, blasted by gale winds. Huge, wavelike crests leaned against the buildings, blocking the sidewalks, and where the wind howled through the intersections, wind-swept canyons were bordered by snowbanks six feet high, rendering the roads almost useless.

Aimee wound her way around the snowbanks as though in a maze, climbing, plunging. Finally, exhausted and with cheeks stinging, she tumbled into the depot.

"Hope I didn't miss the train," she cried.

"Nope," said the station manager. "Fact is, you could have come tomorrow morning 'n' still not missed it. Ain't gonna be no train tonight. Track's blown shut and ain't nothin' gonna open it, least till morning."

The news startled Aimee. So she'd *have* to stay in Ingersoll—James would never make it through, road conditions being what they were. But she'd still have to ring Minnie on the telephone, and Minnie would insist she stay with the Salvation Army captain.

"A real mess, I'll tell ya," said the station manager, scratching his scrubby gray beard. "And what's a nice girl like you supposed to do for the night? Can't get through with a horse and wagon, and you'll be dead in an hour if you try walking. Can't even ask your Momma for advice, what with the wires down and all. Course, pretty girl like you don't need to worry. Got a nice warm shack and big bed right behind the depot. It ain't no palace, but I got good food 'n' clean sheets with—"

"The telephone lines are down?"

"That's what I said."

"Oh, that's *wonderful!*" Before the old man could respond, Aimee had vanished in a swirl of snow.

The mission services were canceled that night, so after a simple supper of potato soup with the Barretts, Aimee and Robert sat on the floor in front of the fireplace and talked. Reluctantly, in response to Aimee's persistent prodding, Robert told his story. He'd lived all his life in Magherafelt in Northern Ireland, about 30 miles from Belfast. His family were humble grocers, and he'd rather have died than spend his life as they had. So he got a job working on a freighter destined for the United States. When he was only seventeen, he arrived in New York. He washed dishes, swept hallways and streets, sold clothes in a department store, and with the money he saved he set out for Chicago. He was bound to see America, ultimately to find his place in it and to make his fortune.

In Chicago he worked at Marshall Field's Department Store selling Irish linen. One night, sauntering past the open doors of a noisy revival mission, he stopped to watch, and finally walked in and sat down. Robert Semple was no stranger to a sermon—he'd gone to church every Sunday back home, and those Irish preachers had thundered forth with magnificent power. But never until that service in Chicago had he felt the electric Spirit of God Himself. That night his life was changed, he told Aimee, just as hers now was. He determined to set aside all his plans for wealth and success and devote himself instead to preaching the gospel. Last year he'd preached in a few small towns in Canada, then came to Ingersoll. He had returned again this year to help nurture the small group of converts he had made.

"Oh, it's a glorious time to be living, Aimee!" Robert Semple exclaimed. "Never before have the forces of Satan been so powerfully aligned. The children of God are beset on every side. The old-time sins keep on tugging—the lusts of the flesh, pride, greed. But now the Devil's heaped new dung on the old manure—the claims of Godless science, the materialism born of it. Yet, in the midst of all, the true Gospel of Pentecost spreads like wildfire and the revival of faith in Christ is carried as never before throughout the world!"

His fervor stirred Aimee deeply. He spoke of things she'd always felt, of the absurdity of most lives—the tragic cycle of survival: working jobs we can hardly endure to earn the money we need to survive in order to work at those jobs we can hardly endure. "No wonder in such circumstance man becomes an ignoble beast, the spirit that sets him apart shriveled, the soul ignored. The average man is helpless to live a life of divine direction and eternal significance!"

He talked of his plan to be a missionary to China. It would not be an easy life, carrying the gospel to the far corners of the earth. But at the end, he would look back on the harvest of his years and he would know at least that it mattered that he had lived, for the souls he'd led to God would rejoice eternally.

"I know. I know!" said Aimee. "Since I was just a little girl I've felt—I guess you'd say I've felt *destined* for . . . I used to believe, for greatness. But, hearing you talk just now—and no one has ever talked this way to me, you know; I used to think I was really quite peculiar, feeling these things—I know now that what I felt all along was God's assurance that He would call me to *serve* Him and win souls to Him."

That night after Robert Semple went to sleep, Aimee prayed again for the mysterious second blessing, the Baptism of the Holy Spirit. At midnight she fell asleep on the sofa, but the next morning, waking at daybreak alert and excited, she knelt at the big Morris chair in the corner.

"It's time," she said aloud, staring absently out the window at the dawn's pink sky. "You sent the snow so I could stay here and pray. And now the snow has stopped and soon the roads will be clear and I just know it's not all to be a waste. Lord, I won't eat or sleep, not even once more, until you give me the blessing."

"Glory to Jesus," she whispered. "Glory to Jesus." As she repeated the phrase again and again, its hypnotic rhythm stirred her, lifting her to a higher emotional plane. "Glory to Jesus, glory to Jesus!" she cried, the words coming not so much from her own consciousness as an involuntary reflex deep inside her. The feeling of utter contentment flooded her and she yielded to it as though it were the crest of a great wave, and it carried her higher and out of herself.

Only in the periphery of her consciousness was she aware that she was no longer kneeling, but lying on the floor, her body trembling in ecstasy, no longer speaking those words, "Glory to Jesus!" but abandoned to the unintelligible sounds that seemed the product of her passion. As the wolf howls its loneliness and the baby laughs his joy, Aimee babbled her ecstasy.

Robert Semple rushed down the steps buttoning his shirt. "Praise God!" he cried when he saw Aimee. Kneeling beside her, he thanked God for the miracle.

Eventually Aimee fell silent. Then, for the first time, she looked up into Robert Semple's face, a few inches above hers.

"Oh, Robert, it's happened!" she whispered. Her breasts heaved with the effort of her rapid breathing. Robert took one of her hands in his.

"Ah, it had to," he said, and Aimee thought his eyes had never looked so deep and tender. "I was on my knees all night praying for you."

Hesitantly Aimee lifted her hand toward his cheek and touched the skin with her fingers. Her eyes flickered and closed. "I don't know how—thank you. You've changed my life. I just wish . . ." She put her arms around his neck, lifting herself toward him, and before Robert realized what had happened, she had kissed his lips.

Just before 6:00 P.M., Minnie Kennedy pounded with both fists on the Barrett door. When it swung open and Mrs. Barrett offered a smiling hello, Minnie stomped imperiously past her and into the hallway. Her eyes met Aimee's, who had been sitting next to Robert on the sofa.

"Aimee Kennedy, you get out in that sleigh this minute," she said in a low but still trembling voice.

"Well, I guess it's time to go," Aimee announced cheerfully. In a moment she was in the sleigh.

For ten minutes Minnie scolded, beseeched, condemned, and wept. Aimee was an unworthy daughter who wouldn't be satisfied until she had broken her parents' hearts and driven both of them to their graves. She was selfish, egocentric, and immature. Didn't it matter to her in the least that Minnie had thrown away seventeen years of her life to raise Aimee, given her the best of clothes, a high school education, more love and comfort than any other girl in Salford or Ingersoll?

Aimee listened halfheartedly for a while, then let her mind wander. She thought of Robert Semple, the most courageous and magnificent man she had ever known. And then, while her mother wept and railed, Aimee began to sing aloud, "Joys are flowing like a river. . . ."

CHAPTER IV

Everyone, even her most petty and gossipy friends from Ingersoll, agreed on that warm August afternoon of 1908 that Aimee Kennedy made a splendid bride. She had turned her long auburn hair into a thick bun at the back of her head, displaying the summer flush of her cheeks. Now, as she stood in the grass beside the farmhouse, the curve of her bare neck made her seem noble. The high-heeled shoes, hidden by flowing yards of white satin and lace, gave heightened elegance to her posture. Through the flowing veil she smiled, and Robert Semple, towering eleven inches above her, winked back. The exchange was not lost on Julian Fife, white-haired pastor of the large brick Methodist church on the square. He fluttered his eyes, cleared his throat, and commenced to read from the *Minister's Marriage Manual*. Behind him, on wooden chairs borrowed from the church, sat about two dozen neighbors and relatives, and a few of Aimee's closest friends.

"I charge you both, as you stand in the presence of God, to remember that love and loyalty alone will avail as the foundation of a happy home. No other human ties are more tender, no other vows more sacred, than those you now assume."

He lifted heavy, beaglelike eyes to Robert.

"Wilt thou, Robert, have this woman to be thy wedded wife, to live together in the holy estate of matrimony? Wilt thou love her, comfort her, honor and keep her, in sickness and in health; and forsaking all others keep thee only unto her, as long as ye both shall live?"

"I will." He gazed down at her with smiling eyes, and there rushed through Aimee such happiness she felt like crying. Those fine, sensual, smiling lips had whispered love to her each afternoon and preached hellfire each night for months.

The Reverend Mr. Fife turned to her. "Aimee, wilt thou have this man to be thy wedded husband, to live together in the holy estate of matrimony? Wilt thou love, honor, and obey him, and keep him, in sickness and in health; and forsaking all others, keep thee only unto him, as long as ye both shall live?"

"Oh, yes!" Her eyes were damp now.

Robert took her hand in his. She had seen that graceful, calloused hand labor with saw and hammer, had felt its hesitant caress.

"I, Robert Semple, take thee, Aimee Kennedy, to be my wedded wife." His voice carried easily across the lawn, but he spoke to no one but Aimee, and the soft lilt was like the touch of love. His eyes smiled, and she felt both helpless and secure in the glow of his compassion.

"To have and to hold, from this day forward, for better, for worse, for richer, for poorer, in sickness and in health, to love and to cherish, till death us do part, and thereto I pledge thee my faith."

Aimee took Robert's hand in both of hers. She could hardly see his face through her tears when she repeated, "I, Aimee Kennedy, take thee, Robert, to be my wedded husband, to have and to hold, from this day forward, for better, for worse, for richer, for poorer, in sickness and in health, to love and to cherish, till death us do part, and thereto I pledge thee my faith."

For a moment she thought how foolish she must look, not the model of elegance and composure she had set out to be, but a blubbering silly with streaked face and cracking voice. But for once it didn't matter if the whole world laughed at her. In fact, she felt she could laugh heartily along with them, even at herself. Robert loved her. He really loved her.

Although it continued no more than five minutes, the ceremony seemed endless to Aimee. The exchange of rings, Pastor Fife's prayer, kneeling on the satin pillows in the grass, the pastor's benediction, "I pronounce that they are husband and wife together, in the name of the Father and of the Son and of the Holy Spirit. Amen. Those whom God hath joined together, let no man put assunder. Amen."

Robert lifted the veil. With a broad smile, he brushed away her tears, then lowered his head toward her. She felt his lips tighten against hers, and she lifted herself fervently toward him, even as he broke the brief touch.

Most of the small crowd milled around the large terrace at the side of the house, which was separated from the cornfield by a row of dogwood trees and from the barn by the lilac bushes. A few couples had strolled behind the house and into the barnyard to see firsthand Minnie's famous chickens. The boys and young men hovered like flies near the buffet tables covered with pink linen tablecloths and piled high with dishes of potato salad, egg salad, chicken, ham, relishes, beans, bowls of fruit, and lavish bouquets of flowers. Above the center table the dining room window was open, and Byron Jenvey, once Aimee's teacher at the little white Salford schoolhouse, played hymns on the piano. At one end of the table, the tiered wedding cake towered in solitary majesty. At the other, ten-year-old Gladys Wert worked furiously to fill the cups from a large bowl of bright red punch as quickly as they were swept away. Her brother, John, six years older, beat a cloth-covered hammer against the large block of ice that had been brought up from the icehouse. He dropped the shattered pieces into the punch bowl.

Julian Fife sat on a folding chair in the shade of lilac bushes chatting with Captain Harrity of Ingersoll's Salvation Army barracks.

"I'll tell you frankly," he said, "they're a peculiar lot, those Pentecostal folks."

Captain Harrity chuckled. "Well, if you ask me, it was that Semple fellow that's responsible. A good thing he wasn't preaching voodoo, or Minnie'd be roasting one of the neighbors for a wedding feast about now."

"Now, you just bite your tongue, Captain Harrity!" scolded Minnie, startling the preachers. "Here I am throwing the nicest party, burdened with this two-ton tray of goodies, and all you able-bodied men can do is sit on your behinds and gossip like two old hens!"

The ministers rose, protesting, to take the tray from her, but Minnie stepped back.

"Nothing doing," she said. "But I heard you talking about Aimee and them Pentecostal folk, and let me tell you something—I felt just the same as you. And I said to her, I said, 'Aimee Elizabeth, it's of the devil. The Bible says God's not the author of confusion. That jumping around and babbling and all—it's of the devil.'"

Mr. Fife nodded forcefully. "But she's a headstrong child, no doubt about that," he said.

Minnie squinted in indignation. "And I suppose you wouldn't do the same if God Himself was speaking to you—which of course He wouldn't, seeing as how you're a Methodist."

The ministers laughed good-naturedly.

"God had a *purpose* for my daughter. He wanted her for His own work, and today you can see the whole thing unfolding. She's gonna be a minister's wife! My little Aimee. She knew what was best."

Mr. Fife cleared his throat. "Mrs. Kennedy, if I may—if you believe the Pentecostal movement is of God, why do you attend the Salvation Army services?"

Minnie glanced with twinkling eyes at Captain Harrity. "Brother Fife, God works in mysterious ways. He speaks to Aimee through Brother Semple and to me through the captain here." And she was off to the buffet table.

Aimee stood in front of the maple tree, Robert slightly behind her, his hands folded around her waist. Her own hands gracefully cupped his, and she gazed over her shoulder into his eyes, trying to look submissive and passionate.

"Quick, take this one!" she hissed to George Quinn, a tassel-haired boy who, like Aimee, was seventeen. The camera clicked. Aimee struck another pose, staring across the road and up the hill to where the weather vane perched atop the red barn of the Piper farm. Then, imagining herself from the camera's perspective, she tilted her head slightly toward her left shoulder and gazed with large, eager eyes toward the sky.

"Now this one, George," Aimee insisted.

"Just hold your horses," George Quinn grumbled, "I ain't no professional, you know. It takes time to get this thing right. I'm doing the best I can."

While he fumbled with the equipment, Aimee continued looking at the sky. To her right James Kennedy rocked back and forth on his heels. Occasionally he stroked his flaming red beard and pulled his straw hat farther down over his forehead to protect his nose from the sun.

"Tell Mom they can't start eating till I get there!" Aimee instructed her father. "We're almost done." James brushed his hand over his face and limped across the front lawn.

A moment later she was at the buffet table. "Everybody quiet!" she bellowed, clinging to Robert's arm.

"Quiet!"

The crowd grew silent.

"Reverend Julian Fife, would you say grace and then we can all eat."

The pastor prayed in sonorous tones for the sick and afflicted, the lost, the weary, for the food and those partaking thereof. When he finished, Aimee shouted, "Line forms to the left, behind me and Robert."

After filling their plates, she led Robert to the two chairs she had placed in the cluster of dogwood trees at the edge of the lawn. There, in the shade, the train of her gown spread out around her, Aimee gazed into Robert's eyes.

"I love you, Robert," she said softly, and the voice that had firmly trumpeted, "Quiet!" now trembled with feeling. He reached for her hand.

Singly and in couples, the young people wandered from the buffet table, their plates high with food, and sat in a semicircle around the newlyweds. The girls spread out their flowing dresses across the grass making the lawn a mass of pink, white, yellow, and blue swirls. The men loosened their ties and removed their jackets, laughing and flirting with the girls.

"Stop staring," Robert whispered. "Someone's going to think your stomach's upset." He bent over and kissed his bride on the forehead, and a few of the girls sitting at his feet sighed. Aimee beamed.

Throughout the afternoon the festivities continued. With exaggerated seriousness Aimee lifted the dagger above the wedding cake, paused, milking the moment of its drama, then swiftly incised the top tier. When she cut out a small slice and fed it to Robert, the crowd cheered. Then she handed the knife to Minnie and hurried over to the pile of wedding gifts.

She opened them with abandon, throwing the paper in the air and tugging impatiently at the ribbons. She particularly liked a pair of ornate glass candlesticks. "Aren't they just dandy!" she exclaimed.

Shortly after dusk, Robert stood and took a large pocket watch from his vest. He breathed a deep sigh of relief. All afternoon he had maintained a pleased, patient smile, chatted when approached, held his bride's hand. Still, he had crossed and uncrossed his legs a thousand times, scratched his head, picked his fingernails, chewed them.

Immediately Aimee stood beside him. "I'll be just a minute, love," she said. "I've got to change." She ran toward the house. A moment later she returned wearing a handsome navy blue suit.

"My friends," said Robert, shaking the stiffness out of his leg, "Aimee and I thank you from our hearts for sharing our happiness today. Thank you for the gifts, and thank you more for your friendship, and for being here. Praise God for you! And now we must take our leave, or we will miss our train. Stay on and eat—get happy and fat!"

"Where are you headed for?" called Byron Jenvey, who had stopped playing the piano long enough to eat.

"Nowhere that you'll be able to put salt in the sheets or frogs in the closet!" exclaimed Minnie Kennedy. "They're off to Stratford."

"Stratford?" someone exclaimed. "That's a factory town—no place for a honeymoon!"

"It's where God's called us," Aimee declared. "From there we go to Chicago, then to China. We're to be missionaries to the heathen on the other side of the earth." She turned to Robert. "You tell them about it."

While Robert spoke, Aimee rushed to James and said, "Quick, Daddy, get the wagon ready. Robert wants to leave."

"I already got Flossie in harness," said James. "But what's the rush? You ain't even had coffee yet."

"Robert wants to *leave*," Aimee repeated firmly. "He's the boss." James looked quizzically at Minnie, who was standing next to him, and Minnie pursed her lips and stared at the sunset.

Aimee was trembling with impatience when James finally brought the wagon down the driveway. George Quinn and the Pearce boys had decorated it with red and white ribbons and summer roses and bouquets of wild daisies from the fields, and the crowd sighed and cheered at its beauty. Taking Robert's hand, Aimee lifted her skirt and stepped into the wagon, then stood on the back seat, clinging to Robert's arm for balance. Minnie Kennedy stood on her tiptoes and handed her daughter the bridal bouquet.

"Now, girls, come and gather 'round. I'm going to throw the bridal bouquet, and whoever gets it will be the next one that gets married. That's what they say, anyway. But first I want to make a little speech. After all, who ever heard of Aimee Kennedy—I mean, Aimee Semple—being in front of a crowd and not trying to make a speech?"

She waited for the laughter to subside, and then continued. "I just wanted to say this is the happiest day of my life. I know that's corny, but I mean it. I don't know what ever happened to make him propose. It was a miracle, I guess. I didn't even have to use Daddy's shotgun. And, miracle of miracles, he says he *loves* me! Thank you, God. Thank you."

To her own amazement, she found herself weeping again. "What a silly thing I am," she sputtered, "Here, catch!" She spun around, threw the flowers over her head, and fell into Robert's arms. When she faced the girls again, ten-year-old Gladys Wert was holding the bouquet.

"Oh, Gladys caught them!" Aimee announced, disappointed. "What a waste. She won't get married for at least a decade. God help Salford if she's its next bride!"

CHAPTER V

In June the steamer chugged into Kowloon Harbor. Although it was midmorning, the temperature had already soared to 100°, and Aimee, standing on deck beside Robert, had periodically dabbed the sweat from their faces with a soggy handkerchief. Then the boat slipped into the dark water between Hong Kong and the mainland, and Aimee gave no more thought to the heat.

"Oh, look!" she cried over the clanking engine, pointing to an elegant structure perched precariously near a cliff edge on the island. Before Robert could respond, she was pointing again, this time to two junks that seemed on a collision course. Her wide eyes flashed continuously from one point to another, catching every motion with gleeful abandon. Every sight and sound stimulated her—the silvery reflection of clouds in the water, the high-pitched voices crying strange words, the bustling masses along the piers, the thousands of bobbing funnel-shaped hats.

"You're giggling!" Robert exclaimed. "And what is so funny?"

Aimee shrugged. "It's—isn't it so *alive*, so *exciting*!"

Throwing his arms around her, Robert laughed, too.

"Oh, it's alive, all right—you haven't seen the half of it, sweet love," he said. "Smell the perfume of the air? That's the kiss of the jungle flowers. And for that the island's named—Hong Kong: Fragrant Harbor."

He pointed far down the coast to the mud flats of Aberdeen, where thousands of natives lived in hundreds of small sampans, strung together in rows extending far out into the deep blue water.

Scores of junks plied the harbor like legless waterbugs, ferrying people and supplies from the city of Victoria on Hong Kong to the mainland district of Kowloon. Their heavy quilted brown sails flared in the warm breeze. Piers on both shores crawled with activity, and in the deep water an ocean liner unloaded onto junks tied side by side in half a dozen rows six deep, stretching out perpendicular to the ship like an insect's jointed brown legs. Fishing boats, returning with the morning's catch, cut a wide detour around the congestion.

On the island, splendid homes and dilapidated shacks jostled for space at the base of Victoria Peak. From there, the mountain rose eighteen hundred feet into the clouds, its rugged slopes hidden behind savage tropical foliage. Sporadically along the mountainside the jungle gave way to the dramatic lines of white rococo mansions.

"You see there? There!" said Robert, pointing to a humble waterfront building with a wooden cross on the roof. "That'll be the mission —and those on the porch are our brothers and sisters in the Lord. Praise God, they await our coming halfway around the world! Oh, it's a fine day, Aimee. A *fine* day!"

For three weeks the Semples lived at the waterfront mission in Victoria, learning simple phrases, how to count change, the layout of the island. Searching for a place to establish a new mission, they meandered through the slums of the western district, where people slept all night on the sidewalks and prostitutes solicited openly on every street corner. A short distance away, on the island's south side, they rode on horseback through the forests and lush farmland which stretched to the shore of Repulse Bay.

One day they took a jaunt past Aberdeen to where the maggoty waterfront district of Wanchai clung to the foot of Victoria Peak, a heap of jam-packed tenements, flimsy shacks cluttering their roofs. Dilapidated bars and cabarets occupied the ground levels, and drunks and street-walkers milled around like insects. Farther up the slopes, overlooking the squalor, was Happy Valley, a peaceful, spacious community with schools, sports arenas, hospitals, and cemeteries.

Soon after their arrival, Robert, assisted by a veteran missionary, began preaching street corner sermons and reading the Scriptures in the native language. Aimee, accompanied by the missionary's wife, set out to find a home. She trudged up the stone steps of noisy Pottinger Street, through dark, narrow alleys where merchants sold cotton and wool yarn in little stalls with cloth roofs. She found one street occupied entirely by tailors, another by goldsmiths. The cavernous, bleak alley officially called

Wing Sing Street but dubbed by the natives "Rotten Egg Street" was lined on both sides with thousands of crates of eggs and dozens of wholesale and retail egg stands.

In these parts of the city, mongrels ran wild, and Lila, the missionary's wife, insisted many of them ended up in some of the natives' favorite Cantonese dishes. Frequently, rats and deadly centipedes darted across their paths.

"They eat rats, too," Lila said, "Fact is, they sell them at native markets. I shouldn't be telling you such awful things. It's enough to make you sick."

"Oh, it's exciting!" Aimee exclaimed.

That night she told Robert all about it. "They have them right there in the open," she announced. "Rats, greasy geese, dogs, worms—"

"Worms?" he asked.

"Honest-to-goodness worms! Buckets of them. Cost one sen each. Oh, horrible long squiggly things with brown backs and pink bellies and ripply sides! Right there in the middle of the street they buy them and—!" Aimee held her hand high above her head, the imaginary worm dangling from her thumb and forefinger. She threw her head way back and opened her mouth as wide as she could. Then she lowered her hand slowly, slowly, until her fingers were an inch above her lips. Suddenly she opened her fingers, gulped, smacked her lips, and rubbed her hands together.

"Delicious," she muttered, then blanched.

For an entire week Aimee trudged through noisy crowds on steaming back streets, examining dozens of hopelessly shoddy or too expensive houses. When Lila, overcome with fatigue and heat exhaustion, begged a few days' respite, Aimee determined to continue the search herself.

"I know my way around well enough. I'll just make a list of what I find, and then we'll go back and you can do the haggling for me."

"But you're not used to this heat."

"Oh, I'm strong as an ox," Aimee laughed.

In fact, she was glad for the exercise. It seemed to relieve the nausea she'd been feeling. What's more, Robert was out every day doing his part, returning late in the afternoon drained with fatigue, his clothes saturated with sweat, and Aimee had made up her mind to work as hard as he did.

One day she took a rickshaw to the hills above Wanchai and strolled along the wide, modern streets of Happy Valley. She would not have dreamed of searching in such an area, for the houses were all new and expensive, but one of the natives had mentioned to Lila that a whole block of houses adjoining a cemetery was vacant. Late that afternoon, as the temperature reached 115°, Aimee stumbled across the properties. Half an hour later, she located the rental agent. He assured her she could have her choice at a reasonable cost:

"I'll tell you frankly, since you're an American—the natives here are a superstitious lot. That cemetery back there—it frightens them away. Now and then we rent one of them. And if somebody dies—and we all do, you know—why, right away the house is haunted with ghosts from the graveyard. Word spreads like wildfire, and then you're lucky if you can rent any of them. You gotta drop the prices and hope you can get some Europeans interested."

Aimee took the house at the end of the road, across from the entrance to the cemetery. A few days later, she and Robert moved in. Lila insisted they hire a houseboy to do the cleaning, and run errands, and an amah to cook the meals. "It'll cost you two cents a day for each, and it'll ease the burden for Sister Semple, so she can help with the work."

"But I *want* to cook and clean my own house," Aimee insisted.

Lila closed her eyes and shook her head. "It's the natives, Sister. They'll scorn you if you humiliate yourself doing housework. Like the Queen of England driving her own carriage."

So, grudgingly, Aimee hired a houseboy and an amah, though she insisted it was little more than slavery.

The rains came in July and continued three weeks in unrelenting monotony. Nights and days, distinguished only by subtle shades of darkness, became a steaming purgatory. Robert left early each morning, hidden beneath a wide-brimmed rubber hat and coat, to continue canvassing the area. Aimee begged to accompany him, but Robert reminded her that she wasn't feeling well and insisted she stay home and rest.

"I *can't* rest!" she exclaimed. "I'll go nuts, and then where will we be? What shall I do—clean the house? Cook? Sweep? The laundry? They won't *let* me!" She gestured to the kitchen, where the boy and amah were working. "It's *my* house, and I can't even *clean* it!"

Robert instructed the boy to buy a hammock and hang it on the porch facing the cemetery. Thus, even as the rain fell, Aimee gazed upon the solemn funeral processions passing by. The Chinese funerals were the most colorful, with ornate coffins and vermilion banners, long silk dragons slithering in the muggy air. The mourners, all dressed in rubber hats and coats similar to Robert's, shuffled along laden with gifts—food, utensils, clothing—all to be buried with the corpse. The once-colorful paper wrappings drooped soggy and faded.

There were military funerals, too, the coffins carried on rumbling gun carriages draped with flags, accompanied by guards and solitary drummers. The Catholic funerals were more solemn still, the priests in black robes and sandals muttering incantations, their fingers moving rapidly over the rosaries, and behind them four to six pallbearers sloshing through the mud.

But the saddest were the desolate missionary burials. With no banners, no robes, no drums or incantations, a handful of mourners would struggle along with the clumsy coffin. They seemed oblivious to the rain, with drawn faces and expressionless eyes.

One afternoon, when Aimee swung restlessly in the hammock, the houseboy approached her with gestures and animated exclamations she couldn't understand. He seemed to be asking for money to buy mosquitoes.

"I don't understand you," she said impatiently, and when he grew even more animated and incomprehensible, she dismissed him.

A few hours later he returned with arms full of mosquito netting and began tacking it around the porch.

"What are you *doing*?" Aimee demanded. "I can't go anywhere, I can't see anything, and now you're trying to turn even this porch into a prison!" She began tearing down the netting.

"And just where did you get the money to buy this in the first place?" she demanded.

Gazing at the floor, the boy said, "Food money."

"Who told you you could *do* that?" Aimee screamed. "You wicked, wicked boy! You take it down this minute, you return it and get our money back—and don't you ever *dare* do such a thing again!"

Sobbing, the boy set about removing the tacks. He folded the netting carefully into a manageable pile, and without another word left the house.

A few moments later, Robert stepped out onto the porch. In his arms was the netting.

"Where did you get that? I just sent that evil little creature to get our money back. Imagine, spending our *food* money on that and without even *asking* me!"

Robert dropped the netting to the floor and embraced Aimee. But she pulled away.

"I want to know why you brought that back into the house."

"The boy tried to explain this morning, but he doesn't speak English," he said gently. "It's the malaria he's afraid of. The mosquitoes will be carrying it this time of year. He's remembering when eight thousand people died from it here—his sister and father, too, and not more than a few years back. He wants to protect us."

Aimee appeared stunned. Then her face contorted in disbelief. Finally tears welled in her eyes.

"Oh, Robert, I'm just so . . . so tense these days. I don't know what's happening to me."

Robert pulled her close, caressing her hair.

"The boy!" she exclaimed, and rushed toward the kitchen. The youth was there, preparing dinner. Without explanation she threw her arms around him.

"I'm sorry. I'm sorry!" she repeated, hugging and kissing the top of his head.

That night, after Robert fell asleep, she got out of bed and went to the porch, settling into the hammock. The rain had stopped again; a strange and mysterious summer, Lila had said.

She wished she had Robert's patience with such petty frustrations as the weather. Rain or shine, he went door to door inviting people to the Missionary Home for Sunday morning services. Even at midafternoon, when the heat was at its worst and most veteran missionaries stayed indoors to avoid heat stroke, Robert still roamed the streets with his interpreter, preaching on corners and passing out tracts written in Chinese and explaining the way of salvation. Each day he rose at dawn, praying for an hour before breakfast. After dinner, before he and Aimee walked to the top of the cemetery hill to catch the cool breeze and watch the sun set, he studied the Scriptures for two hours. And long after Aimee fell asleep, Robert often prepared sermons at the dining room table.

She looked up to find him standing beside her.

"I can't sleep," she explained.

He knelt next to her, taking her hand and pressing it to his lips.

"Me neither."

"Don't you feel well?"

"Too excited. I've an awesome sense of destiny, Aimee. It's the hand of God touched my life and blessed me, of all men, with the chance to bring to these people the Gospel. Oh, it's not to be an easy lot—it's not easy now and we're just begun. But I know what it is I'm to do, and I can do it if you'll stay by me, sweet love."

"Where God leads you, He leads me," she said, cradling his head in her arms. For a long while she ran her fingers through his hair.

Robert lifted his head so that he could see her face and whispered, "I've been thinking and praying, and talking to the other missionaries, and I think God's been telling me it's time we move on."

"Move?"

"You don't suppose God dragged us across the wide world to be preaching to these who already have the Good News preached to them from half a dozen missions?" he complained. "Oh, it's easy, and it's plush, and girl, that's proof positive it's not for us."

She turned away. "I know," she said. Then she was silent, gazing absently toward the cemetery, where the steamy fog shrouded the tombstones.

"Now, what we'll do, God willing, is pile our little things on a barge and sail up the Pearl River. The missionaries tell of a quaint village by the name of Macoa where the precious story of Christ has never been told and the people are hungry in their souls."

"When do we leave?"

"Before the week's out, if you're willing."

"I wanted this home for us so much," she mumbled. "I worked hard at it."

"And you did wonderfully, Aimee. And God will give you the strength to do it all over again, for He promises He'll not ask us to do what we can't."

Finally she smiled. "Of course I want to go. It will be so exciting! It's just—I've been feeling a little tired lately, that's all. Oh, someday, Robert—someday thousands and thousands of people all over this vast, wild land will come to the Saviour because of your vision."

Her eyes widened, and she rose from the hammock and paced across the porch. "Hordes of the saved," she said with a sweeping gesture. "Armies of them, the whole continent swarming with them, shoulder to shoulder in the service of the King of Kings. And at their head will be my Robert, Saint Semple."

He laughed.

"Oh, yes, Robert—someday on this very spot, perhaps, these people will raise a glorious cathedral. The Cathedral of Saint Robert Semple, and it will be a beacon, like Saint Peter's and Saint Paul's, with people making pilgrimages from all over the world to worship in it."

She swept her arms high above her head to indicate the towering cathedral spires. Then she dropped her head, stumbling toward Robert.

He caught and held her firmly.

"Something *is* wrong," he insisted, leading her back to the hammock.

"No," she said, reclining. "It's just—well, I didn't want to burden you about it yet, but I suppose I should tell you now. We're having a baby."

Robert looked so astonished that Aimee laughed.

41

"You're pregnant?"

"Yup. Three months now."

Hesistantly, Robert rested his fingers, then the palm of his hand, upon her abdomen.

"It's a miracle!" he whispered. He lifted Aimee's blouse and rested his ear on her stomach. "Well, and if he's not already preaching up a storm! You'll get your chance. I just pray you're born with your mom's looks and brains, little Robert."

"Little Robert, is it? That was mighty fast." She laughed again.

He climbed into the hammock next to her and, still caressing her stomach, sang softly:

Oh, sing to me the auld Scotch sangs,
In the braid auld Scottish tongue;
The sangs my father loved to hear,
The sangs my mither sung,
When she sat beside my cradle,
Or lulled me on her knee,
And I wad na sleep,
She sang so sweet
The auld Scotch sangs to me,
And I wad na sleep,
She sang so sweet
The auld Scotch sangs to me.

Sing ony o' the auld Scotch sangs,
The blithesome or the sad;
They mak' me smile when I am wae
And greet when I am glad.
My heart gaes back to Scotland,
The saut tear dims my e'e,
And the Scotch blood leaps in a' my veins
As ye sing the sangs to me,
And the Scotch blood leaps in a' my veins,
As ye sing the sangs to me.

"It's a beautiful song," Aimee said.

"So my mother thought when singing it to me every night."

The air grew cooler, with wisps of fog lingering only in the mountains across the harbor. Aimee's eyes fluttered closed.

"How lucky I am," she whispered, snuggling against Robert.

42

CHAPTER VI

One afternoon a few weeks after they settled in Macoa, in the summer of 1910, Robert stumbled into the cottage, his face ashen, his arms folded tightly across his stomach.

Aimee rushed to him, but he brushed past her and slumped into a chair.

"Robert, what's the matter?"

"Stomach," he muttered. Rising again, he stumbled past the houseboy in the kitchen and lurched out the back door toward the outhouse.

"No worry," the houseboy assured Aimee. "Dysentery. He hurt. But he get better."

Aimee met Robert in the yard and helped him back to the house and up the stairs to the bedroom. "Lean on me," she insisted. "Go on, you're not all that heavy."

She helped him undress and covered him with a light sheet. A moment later, when he tried to rise, she brought him a bedpan.

"No, it's such a mess," he protested.

"Don't be silly. You've never *seen* a mess until you've worked with pigs and cows."

That night she stayed by his side, dozing fitfully in a rocking chair she and the houseboy had carried up from the living room. Robert's slightest moan awakened her, and often as he slept she caressed his long wavy hair and searched his face. During the night Robert frequently awakened with a cry, pulling his knees tight against his chest. Each time,

Aimee dabbed a washcloth in a basin of water and moistened his forehead and cheeks.

After three days, Robert seemed to improve. He still complained of weakness and exhaustion, but for the first time since he became ill, he asked for food. That afternoon Aimee sat beside him on the bed and fed him soup.

"I'm such a nuisance," Robert grumbled. "Oh, and the clock keeps ticking and there's so much to do! It gets me so raving mad I could just . . ."

"Open wide." Grudgingly he obeyed. "It's your fault, you know. You just don't take good care of yourself. You go out in the heat and rain—everybody thinks you're just nuts."

"My body is God's own temple, Aimee Semple. Now, do you think a single hair will fall from me head apart from His will? Besides, this ache in my belly—it's not from the weather, I'll tell you. It's from the food."

"Well, it won't happen again," Aimee said flatly. "I've fired the amah. From now on I'll do the cooking. I won't use vegetables fertilized with human excrement the way she did, and I'll wash the food for a change before it's cooked. And cooked by itself, not along with the laundry! It's a miracle the whole *country* isn't dead of poisoning."

Robert smiled.

"You mustn't worry about the work, Robert. Tomorrow morning I'll do some canvassing, and if you're not up to attending prayer meeting tomorrow night, I can manage it. You just get well."

"But the baby—"

Aimee chuckled. "Not due for almost three months yet. I tell you, I'm *tough*, Robert." She ran her fingers through his hair again. The strands were moist and silky, fine strands that flowed through her fingers. With the back of her hand she brushed his sideburns, caressed his cheek.

The smile on her lips vanished. Her hand moved to his forehead.

"Robert, you're burning up," she said.

"I'm shivering."

Aimee went to the door. "Boy! Come here!"

A moment later the houseboy rushed in, his face eager.

"Mr. Semple's running a high fever. Is it normal?"

The boy's face grew somber. Cautiously he approached the bed, gazed into Robert's face. Then he stepped back, his face going pale. "No," he said, shaking his head. "Fever bad. I get nurse."

In the hour before the nurse arrived, Robert began muttering incoherently through chattering teeth. His body convulsed with brief tremors.

"Cold," he moaned. "Covers."

Aimee had already wrapped him in the only two blankets they had, but she rushed down the stairs to the living room and yanked the drapes from the window. In the kitchen she pulled the tablecloth from the table, took her shawl from the closet, and raced back up the steps.

"All right, honey, everything will be all right," she said, covering him. "The nurse will be here any minute now." Then, saturating the washcloth in water from the basin, she bathed Robert's moist, gray-green face.

Still Robert's shivering continued.

"I'm freezing," he said.

Gently slipping into the bed beside him, Aimee clutched the burning body in her arms, wrapped her legs around him, and rested her cheek next to his. She felt the muscles of his jaw twitch.

"Yes, sweet love, that's better," he rasped. In a moment he was asleep.

When the old nurse arrived, she found Aimee as saturated with sweat as Robert was, for the afternoon heat was stifling. After a brief examination, she said:

"Could be malaria. I'll wire Matilda Hospital and reserve a room. And I'll send some porters with a stretcher. Ought to get him to the river before six so we can get him to Hong Kong by morning."

That night on the boat, Robert's fever broke as the nurse had predicted. He tossed restlessly and repeatedly asked for water. As dawn approached, he grew more calm. "It'll be all right," he whispered. "God is testing us. He'll be building our strength to make us good and faithful servants. It'll be all right, Aimee."

When the boat docked at the foot of Queens Road Central in Victoria, the four porters immediately lifted the stretcher and set off at a jog along the shrub-lined path winding up the mountain to the hospital. Aimee started after them, but the nurse restrained her.

"You take the tram," she insisted.

"I can keep up—I want to be with him."

By cable the Peak Tram almost vertically ascended the base of Victoria Peak. The entire north slope unfolded below it, and with no difficulty Aimee found the porters and the stretcher, Robert lying motionless beneath the white sheet. For a moment she felt overwhelming despair: Behind her stretched the vast harbor of Kowloon and, beyond, China's jagged mountains. The shacks and pointed straw hats were everywhere. The insuppressible swarm of life pulsed and scurried in every corner. And there was Robert, growing farther and farther away, slipping behind this hedge and that roof, lost from sight amid a bustle of passersby. They had come with the reckless vision of transforming a continent for Christ, and had made not a single convert. And now this. How miserable, how petty and feeble their lives seemed.

Her eyes grew wet. "Oh, God," she whispered. "Forgive me—I have such little faith, and I'm scared. You're the Great Physician. I know You can heal him. O God, I'll do anything. I'll never doubt again. I'll go anywhere you say. Just—oh, I need him!"

From the tram terminal, she and the nurse walked the half mile to the hospital, and Aimee entered the women's ward. "You're exhausted," the nurse told her. "And you might be getting malaria yourself. We're going to treat you with quinine as a precaution."

"I want to see Robert."

"You will, in a day or two. For now you stay here. And you rest."

The monsoon came from the south, a flow of warm air that continued uninterrupted for two days. Then, early in the evening, the first large raindrops pelted the windows of Aimee's ward. She had been gazing across the courtyard to the men's wing, where Robert lay. At night, she could see the bare light on the wall, the occasional form of a doctor or nurse bending over the bed. Those were the frail threads that held Robert to her. But then the rain fell in a driving torrent, and it blurred the window so that, even when she rose from her bed and pressed her nose against the glass, the light of the far window shimmered shapelessly in the rivulets and she could perceive nothing. Still, long into the night, she stared at the absurd distortions, her eyes fastened on the glowing.

Nearly a week passed before the doctor permitted her to visit Robert. "He isn't well," he explained. "You mustn't tire him. And you must be as cheerful as possible."

She put on a bright, flowery cotton blouse with puffy shoulders and combed her hair until the long strands gleamed. Standing before the mirror in the bathroom, she slapped her cheeks to give them color.

As she was about to leave the ward, a nurse and doctor rushed past her, stopping at the bed of an old Chinese woman. Aimee had watched her much of the night, the woman's breaths coming in sharp gasps further and further apart, her glazed eyes fastened on a lovely bouquet of flowers the nurse had placed at the bedside earlier in the day. Now the gasps had ceased, the eyes had rolled back into the head, the eyelids still half opened. The doctor checked for a pulse, shook his head. The nurse lifted the sheet over the craggy face. Both hurried from the ward.

Aimee hesitantly moved toward the old woman. Her hand trembling, she lifted the sheet, gazing upon the face for only a moment. A tender smile passed across Aimee's lips, and she nodded before dropping the sheet again. She swept the vase of flowers from the table and hurried from the room.

She ran past the private rooms, slowing as she approached the nursing station. Beyond was the men's wing, and she hurried along the corridor and into the ward, past the double rows of beds. She glanced from one emaciated face to another, unaware of the masks of death staring back at her, searching only for Robert. Finally, in the very last bed, she found him.

He was sallow-faced and gaunt, the skin hanging loose around his skeleton face. For an instant she had an impulse to scream, for she saw in his face that of the old woman. But he had been waiting for her, his glazed eyes turned toward her, a smile on his lips, and so she laughed and said:

"Robert, oh, Robert! You're looking so much better than I expected! And smiling, too!"

"Aimee," he whispered, trying to lift his hand to hers. He breathed in short gasps, sometimes catching his breath for a long while. Then he would exhale with a wheezing sound.

Aimee placed the flowers on the bedside table and took his hand, holding it between both of hers, caressing it. The flesh was damp and sticky, the skin loose.

"Flowers?" Robert whispered.

"Yes. Aren't they beautiful? A very sweet old lady gave them to me just for you." Then she noticed Robert's eyes were covered with a milky mucous.

"You can't see them, can you?" she asked.

"It's cloudy."

She lifted her skirt and, using the corner of it, blotted his eyes gently. "Better?"

He answered with a smile.

"Nothing to it," she said. "We do it all the time with newborn calves. Have to clean their noses, too—ugh."

He tried to smile, to squeeze her hand, but he had no strength.

"It's all right, love," she said. "You rest, and just think about winter in Ingersoll, and that'll make you feel cool. Oh, wasn't it marvelous, Robert, that winter when you led me to the Lord! We were so happy, not a care, and the whole world was ours."

His eyelids fluttered and closed, and she thought he might be dozing. Then tears seeped out with the mucous from his eyes and ran along the sides of his nose and down his cheeks and into the sweat-soaked pillow. Aimee lifted her skirt and dried his face.

"Robert?" Fear gripped her again.

He did not open his eyes as he whispered, "The work. The work will not get done. What a waste. What a waste!"

"Of *course* it will!" said Aimee. Then, with enormous enthusiasm, she spoke rapidly. "Why, Robert, you'll be out of here in two weeks, you'll see. Why on *earth* would God bring us all the way to *China* if He just wanted you to get sick? Why, He could have let you get sick back in *Ingersoll* and saved a lot of money. We're here for a purpose, Robert, and we're going to *fulfill* it. Even your illness is for a purpose. I *know* you'll get well. The work will go on! While you're recuperating, I'll carry it on *myself*. You must have *faith*, my love. Now, get some sleep. I'm going right to the chapel and I'm going to start praying, and I'm not going to stop until the doctors tell me you're *improved*."

"The work!" Robert cried deliriously through his tears. Aimee kissed his hand and left quickly.

That night, over the nurse's objections, Aimee refused supper, explaining that she was devoting herself to prayer and fasting.

"It's no use," the nurse said, her voice reflecting the compassion in her face. "The doctor says there's just not much hope."

"Don't *say* that!" Aimee cried. "I don't believe that. The doctor may be a very fine physician, but he's a human being and no more. He's not the one with the last word—God is. And God, the Great Physician, says, 'Ask and ye shall receive, seek and ye shall find, knock and it shall be opened unto you.' He says He will perform great *miracles* if we ask in faith, move mountains, heal the sick, even raise the dead! So I'm going to spend the night in prayer. I'm going to ask him to make good on his promise. I'll be in the chapel."

Four o'clock in the morning the nurse came for her. It was August 4. Robert was dead. At dawn he was buried in Happy Valley Cemetery in the midst of thundering rain.

PART TWO

CHAPTER VII

Minnie Kennedy received news of Robert's death not at the farm in Ingersoll, but in a dingy tenement in New York City, where she lived alone. Such was her carefully executed plan, set in motion a few days after her daughter's marriage, when Minnie led James to a chair at the kitchen table and poured him a steaming cup of coffee. Then, taking a notebook and pencil from the cupboard, and dragging a chair from the opposite side of the table, she sat next to him, and said:

"Now, James, we've got to be realistic. I should hold my tongue, I know, and God forgive me, but after all you're going on eighty now, James. One of these days, God forbid, I'm going to inherit this farm, and it won't be worth a thing without you, but nonetheless we've got to be practical about such things, don't you think? Well, the day I get the farm, the government's gonna take it away from me for the succession duties, and then where will I be? I'll tell you, James Kennedy—I'll be up the creek, with nowhere to live. And I don't think you'd wish that on me. No, I don't. Not after all I've done for you all these years."

When she was sure he'd grasped her words, she continued. "Now, that's just the half of it. The other half's this—the land taxes are due again. Five hundred dollars. And James, we just ain't got it. That is, *you* ain't. Oh, we could take it out of the savings, sure. But then we'll be at the rock bottom, and I can't believe you'd leave us high and dry like that, with nothing in the world to fall back on.

"So here's my deal, James. You sell me the farm for that five hundred dollars you need for the taxes. Now, of course, it's worth fifty times that, but the farm's as good as mine anyway, as we already agreed. So, instead of losing anything, you're getting the five hundred dollars scot-free. You don't *ever* have to pay it back, and the next time the taxes come due, it ain't your headache anymore. I'm the one's gotta pay the taxes from now on. And being a smart businessman yourself, you'll make me give you a lifetime tenancy, so, no matter what, even if I get run over by a horse and wagon, you can stay here long as you live. It goes right on being your farm, after a fashion. And all I get out of it is, I don't have to pay them succession duties."

James pushed the coffee away untouched. Gazing out the open door, he watched a flock of sparrows flap in the barnyard dust.

"Well, what've you got to say, James Kennedy?" She marched around the table and stood in his line of vision, but he continued to gaze through her.

"I'm speaking to you, James, and you owe me a bit of courtesy after all these years. I never asked much, didn't even know what to ask *for*, just a little girl of fifteen coming to nurse your poor dying wife, and when God called her to glory, I submitted to you body and soul, a man old enough to be my grandpa, just like all the neighbors said. But I stayed, my silly girl's head swayed by your promises. Oh, I'm not complaining. You provided the best you could with the farm and all the road engineering jobs, as you called them. But it's time now, James. It's time to think of me. Sell me the farm."

James stood. He limped past Minnie, pushed open the screen door.

"Make up the papers," he told her, as though that were the end of it.

But Minnie's plan went beyond saving the succession duties.

"Now, James," she explained after the deal was closed. "Since Eve in the Garden there ain't ever been a harder working wife and mother than me. Even the neighbors will tell you. Why, who was it nursed Mother Quinn back to health when she had pneumonia—and cooked all the meals and did the chores? And who is it managed the farm these last ten years, and made the money do? And all without one whimper or complaint.

"But now, James, with our little Aimee gone and all, it's time I do something for myself for a change. I mean, here's Aimee following God's call to the far corners of the earth, and I ain't never even been to the United States, except that time we ran down to Michigan and got married. So I made up my mind, James. I'm going to New York City—yes, I'm gonna do it, and you know why? All these years I've been feeling the call to do something in the Salvation Army, and I put it off for you and little Aimee. But I'm not getting any younger, you know. And their brand-new headquarters for all the continent's there in New York. So that's where I'm going. Oh, I'll be back. But not for a while. I'm gonna go right to the Salvation Army's national headquarters itself and see what I can do."

A few days later James drove her to the depot in Ingersoll, and she boarded the New York City Express. It was there Aimee's telegram reached her.

On a cold, gray morning in April 1911, Minnie gazed from the window to the traffic on Fourteenth Street three floors below and sighed heavily. A cold wind rattled the window and blasted the passersby on the sidewalk, so that they leaned into it with grim faces.

Minnie shivered. "Just like winter again," she mumbled, vigorously rubbing her arms.

Then, as though declaring war on the stark and humorless day, she firmly pulled down the shades and, marching to the gas heater, turned it up full force. She lit the living room's two lamps, then hurried to the kitchen and lit the lights there as well.

"So!" she said in response to the apartment's brightness and gathering warmth.

Before her on the table were the four telegrams, two of them several months old now. The messenger had brought the first in August, while Minnie had been eating lunch in the Salvation Army cafeteria, and she debated whether to finish her lunch first or open it immediately. It would be bad news of course. No one sends telegrams otherwise. James had no doubt died. It was sad, but perhaps just as well. He had written many times pleading with her to come home, but only once—during the summer, when New York had grown intolerably hot—had she returned, and then for no more than a few weeks. She continued writing to him, but not regularly. And the worst of it was (and God rest his soul, if he was dead, he'd never have to know), Minnie had quietly divorced him. It won't make any difference to James, she'd reasoned—what he don't know won't hurt him. And it would set her free to find real love for the first time in her life. Men were already paying her some attention. Perhaps she would marry for love at last. Or if not love, perhaps for money.

But the telegram was from Aimee, and as Minnie read it the strength and color left her face.

"Oh, my Lord," she mumbled.

A month later she got the second telegram: The baby had been born, a girl, Roberta (after her father) Star Semple. Could Minnie send money for passage home? That same day she withdrew most of her savings from

52

the bank and wired the money to Matilda Hospital in Victoria. For three months Minnie heard nothing. Then, in January, Aimee telegraphed that she was in San Francisco, setting out for Chicago and from there to the farm.

The final message, a week old, announced that she was coming to New York.

"Well, now," said Minnie, sweeping the telegrams from the table and stuffing them into a drawer. "It's to be a happy time. Aimee's coming home! And so's little Roberta."

She pulled a huge bag of apples from under the sink and began peeling and slicing them. "Then I gotta put the ham on," she mumbled, reviewing a mental checklist. "And wrap the presents. And the coffee. Oh, we'll have a grand old time."

With drooping head and half-closed eyes, the horse tugged a squeaking hackney along Fourteenth Street until, before a tall bleak tenement, the driver yanked the reins.

"That's it," he said.

Aimee seemed not to hear. Clutching the baby tightly in both arms, she had been staring absently at the horse's twitching ears, her mind drifting through vague recollections of Flossie and the farm and her high school days.

"Here's where you want to go, lady," the driver repeated, hauling the huge steamer trunk from the carriage.

Aimee stood, mechanically handed him a laundry sack, extended her hand, and stepped down to the pavement.

"Well, here we are," she said to the baby. Inhaling deeply, she surveyed the street in both directions, then fastened her eyes on the door in front of her. Finally, hoisting the laundry sack in one arm and clutching the baby in the other, she marched to the door, the hackney driver following.

Minnie was already hurrying down the third-floor steps. "Praise the Lord—you made it!" she cried. "I'm coming fast as I can. Just wait and I'll help you with the baby. This ain't no easy climb, you know, up to the third floor. Now, don't tire yourself."

Aimee and Minnie met at the second-floor landing. After a brief embrace, Minnie exclaimed, "And this is Roberta!" She scooped the infant from Aimee's arms. "Such a pretty girl—and so healthy!" She turned to Aimee, and her eyes grew critical. "But Aimee, my Lord, how pale you are! And so thin! Come. Come on!" Holding the baby in one arm, she wrapped the other around Aimee's waist and led her up the stairs.

At the third-floor landing, she leaned over the rail and shouted to the hackney driver, who was dragging the trunk up the steps one at a time, "Stop all that racket! This is a respectable place. With all that banging I can't even hear myself think!"

The apartment was small, a kitchen on one side of a narrow hall, the living room on the other, a small bedroom and bath at the end. But it was warm and bright, and Minnie had cluttered it with enough second-hand furniture to make it cozy. Beside the sofa was a stack of colorfully wrapped packages, and near the space heater stood an old-fashioned crib, newly painted bright yellow.

"They're for you and the baby," said Minnie, nodding to the packages as she passed them, Roberta in her arms. "One's your birthday present, one's for Christmas, and another for Roberta. And there's one for just welcome home."

Kneeling, Minnie put the baby on the sofa and began undressing her. "My, what a pretty little thing you are!" she purred. Then, to Aimee: "Where's the diapers?"

She had just finished changing the baby when the hackney driver shoved the trunk through the doorway and slumped against the wall.

"It's about time," said Minnie. To Aimee: "There's a dime on the table you can give him."

Aimee reached in the laundry bag and withdrew her purse.

"Here," she said, handing the man a dollar. With widening eyes he stammered several thank-yous.

"Aimee Kennedy!" Minnie exclaimed. "You just give that right back to her, mister. She ain't herself. A dollar!" But Aimee pushed the man out the door, thanking him for his trouble.

"A dollar!" Minnie repeated.

"What do I care?" Aimee said, shrugging. "It was your money—and thanks for sending it, incidentally."

"*My* money?" The color left Minnie's cheeks. She pursed her lips and shook her head in mock frustration. Then, laughing, she hugged her daughter so tightly that Aimee groaned. Taking Aimee's hand and leading her toward the sofa, she said, "Come, take off your coat and shoes and all, and sit down and rest. Or lay down if you want. There's a pillow for your head. You must be dead on your feet and I'll just put the coffee on to warm—it's already perked." Minnie hurried to the kitchen. In a moment Aimee was asleep.

Later, she dutifully opened the gifts Minnie had piled beside the sofa: a long black skirt, a high-collared white blouse with full sleeves, a white sweater for the baby. Unwrapping each new present, Aimee exclaimed her appreciation, but the smiles faded too abruptly, and when Aimee set aside the gifts at last, it was with a faint breath of relief.

"Well!" she said.

"You didn't get the one under the couch!" Minnie exclaimed. She hurriedly withdrew a flat oval package and handed it to her daughter. "No fair opening it until you guess what it is!"

"Oh, Mother," Aimee sighed. "I don't want to guess."

Minnie studied her daughter's face. "You don't feel good, do you?"

Aimee closed her eyes.

Minnie shrugged. "Well, then you don't have to guess. Just open it. Go ahead. Open it."

For a moment Aimee sat motionless, her eyes still closed, pondering halfheartedly whether Minnie would ever permit her a waking moment's peace. But there was nothing for it but to open the package, and so, smiling again, she tore at the paper.

It was a serving tray. No, a painting. An ornate gold-leaf picture frame. Yes. Suddenly Aimee gasped. She held the wedding photograph George Quinn had taken, her head resting against Robert's chest, Robert with lips full and smiling, eyes hypnotic.

"Oh, Mother," Aimee whispered, pulling the photograph tight against her breast.

Minnie saw the tears building. "Oh, Lord, what a dumb thing for me to do!" she exclaimed. "I had it here for a *year*. I just didn't think—and now you're all upset."

"Oh, no, no," said Aimee. Putting the picture aside, she threw her arms around Minnie's neck and kissed her cheek. "It's the dearest, sweetest present. I'll cherish it always, as long as I live."

Minnie embraced her daughter, and for a long while the two clung to each other swaying gently from side to side, Aimee weeping, Minnie staring out the window into the darkening sky. Across the room Roberta murmured in her sleep, and in the street below the rush-hour traffic droned.

Finally, Minnie shook herself from her vacant mood and, holding Aimee at arm's length, said, "Now, you cried enough. It's time you put it out of your mind."

"I tried. Every day. It's no use."

Minnie caressed her daughter's head. "You've gotta think about going on, about your future. What are you going to make of yourself now? What are you going to do?"

"I don't want to do anything, Mom. It's like—like I was in a play and the audience just got up and walked out. I still know all my lines, and all the props are just where they belong. But the theater's empty, and it just doesn't make sense to keep going."

Rising, Minnie thumped her hands on her hips. "I'm ashamed of you, Aimee Kennedy, that's what I am," she scolded. "It's all just so much self-pity. There's no time for such things—life's too short."

Aimee lifted the picture of Robert and herself from the sofa and, searching it with a sad smile, said, "You know, Mom, I was afraid to come and see you."

"Oh, posh."

"I was. And I didn't know why. But now I do."

"Afraid to see your own mother?"

"You were always so good with my little problems. You know—like the time you told me I was a million times better than the other girls, and they were just jealous when they made fun of me."

"You *are* a million times better—better than the whole bunch of them put together!"

Aimee closed her eyes, still smiling. "But, Momma, what if there'd be a problem you *couldn't* help me with? What if all you could say or do wouldn't make any difference, not at all?"

Minnie scowled. "There ain't never been such a problem," she said.

Aimee turned toward the window, and for a while neither spoke.

Finally, with a heavy sigh, Minnie sat next to Aimee, and reaching for her hand said, "Oh, I'm so dumb, making jokes at a time like this. No, there's some problems I don't know what in the world to do about, and there's more of them kind than the other, I'll tell you the truth. They're the ones we take to God, honey. Like the song says, we can 'tell it to Jesus.' He hears us. He—"

"Does He?"

"Why, sure He does, Aimee girl. He hears and answers prayers. 'Whatsoever ye ask in my name, believing—' "

"No. I don't think He does."

"Now, Aimee Kennedy, what's got into you?" Minnie heaved herself from the couch. "Just how *could* you find peace when you go around talking like that? If you ever needed God in your life, child, you need Him now. It's for just such times as these we *need* God."

Aimee rose and walked to the window. A fine rain had begun falling, and in the rivulets streaming down the glass the distorted image of the streetlamps below shimmered.

"Because I need God, does that make Him real?"

"Well, that's a dumb question," said Minnie with a snort. "But why not?" She turned briskly toward the kitchen. "Now, I'm gonna make us a good, hot meal that'll warm your insides and cheer you up!"

Aimee lay awake in bed long after Minnie left for work the next morning, staring at the ceiling cracks, certain she hadn't the strength to move. The leaden feeling that had infused her in past months had dissolved her energy and scattered her thoughts, and now an hour escaped while she pondered a fraying curtain at the bedroom window.

Finally, aroused by the baby's crying and summoning enormous effort, she lifted herself from the bed and, shivering in a thin white slip, stumbled to the bathroom in bare feet, then to the kitchen to heat some coffee, and finally to the crib. She changed the diaper with mechanical disinterest, propped the bottle against a pillow. In the kitchen again, she plunked the coffeepot and an unwashed cup onto the table and slouched into a chair.

With Minnie's constant bustle and chatter absent, the small apartment seemed not cozy but cold and desolate. For the first time, Aimee noticed the table's scars and cigarette burns, the scuffed floor. There were no windows in the kitchen, and now the only brightness came from the living room across the hallway. The once-white walls had yellowed, the paint peeling. Cold, naked, dreary walls.

She would dress and take the baby out to a park, where the sun was shining, and perhaps something of the city streets, the sounds or hubbub or the crispness in the air, would awaken life in her.

Reaching the bedroom, she sat on the bed and searched her trunk for a warm dress. Then she stopped. So many memories there—Robert's Bible, the white jacket he'd worn, the drapes she'd thrown over him that day. . . . She fell back into the bed, the pain creeping up through emotions that were not leaden after all, and suddenly she began crying again.

The spring days seemed to blur indistinguishably, like the clouds that form the blanket of an overcast sky. When Minnie insisted, Aimee would take the baby for long walks, pushing her in a quaint carriage Minnie had discovered at headquarters. Sometimes she wandered along Fourteenth Street to the East River and sat there in the grass for many hours while the squirrels scampered about her. On other days she meandered the few blocks to Union Square, where the pigeons flocked, and threw the birds some stale bread. Still, it was as though she were apart from the world, performing no more than the most meager silent gestures of life. Sometimes the baby's wailing would pull her mind from its rambling. Lifting Roberta from her carriage, Aimee would dab the tiny face dry.

"Poor baby," she would say, clutching the infant and kissing her face. "How long did Roberta cry? Did I ignore you? Did your wicked momma go off and leave you crying? My poor baby." But even while she spoke, her mind drifted.

On New Year's Day, 1912, Minnie patted Aimee on the back and assured her, "Things'll be better this year, you'll see. Good riddance to last year."

"I slept through it," Aimee mumbled. "And I'll sleep through this one, too."

One morning in March, after Minnie left for headquarters, Aimee sat at the kitchen table, a cup of cold coffee in front of her. She had been brooding for half an hour over Minnie's last words: "Might as well start looking for a job, you know. An idle mind's the devil's workshop. And it's no good you just sitting around here all day." Yet how could she find a job when many a day she hadn't the ambition even to climb from bed and dress herself? Only the dread of Minnie's wrath prodded her to action at such times, and then, in the handful of minutes before Minnie's return at night, she would dress herself, change the baby and clothe her, and begin supper. Angrily she told herself that Minnie was so consumed with her own life that she ignored Aimee's sickness of heart. She'd offered hardly a word of comfort, hadn't spoken once of the sadness, the tragedy, only of jobs, money. And always, *always* platitudes.

"I can't stand it!" Aimee snarled. With the back of her hand she swept the coffee cup from the table and it shattered against the wall in a large brown snowflake.

The weather had turned cool again, and from the gray sky a fine drizzle fell. In the street below, people tugged up the collars of their raincoats, huddled beneath umbrellas and pressed grimly along. The new motorcars darted around slow-moving horse-drawn wagons, zipping through gutter puddles and splashing pedestrians.

If it would only stop being cold, she thought, maybe then she could be happy. Perhaps it would never be warm again, and one day the gas heater would fail and the cold would creep through the windows and walls and fill the room like a poison until, curled in a corner, she would freeze to death.

She became aware of the baby's crying, distant at first, then growing shrill and finally exploding into her thoughts.

"Shut up!" she screamed.

Then tears came to her eyes and she ran to the crib. "Oh, baby! Oh, Roberta! I'm sorry." She lifted the infant in her arms, caressed the tiny head. "Momma's going crazy—and I can't help it. I just don't know what to do."

Minnie returned that night to find the kitchen wall splattered with coffee, the cup's fragments scattered across the floor.

"What on earth happened?" she demanded. Aimee, dressed now but lying on the sofa staring at the ceiling, made no reply. Minnie marched to the living room and, standing before her daughter with hands on her hips, erupted in anger. "I'm sick and tired of this!" she roared. "I'm the first to have feelings when feelings're called for. Let the lowliest drunk crawl out of the gutter and come to meeting and say, 'Pray for me, sister,' and I'll bend over backward. But Aimee Kennedy, you're playing me for a fool, and it makes me bristle like a porcupine. Now, what on earth is that mess in the kitchen?"

"I dropped my coffee cup."

"Well, why didn't you pick it up?"

"I forgot."

With a snort, Minnie marched back to the kitchen. "I bet you forgot. No doubt you just laid on that couch all day feeling sorry for yourself. Let Minnie do all the work—that's all right. Well, it's not gonna be that way, and you might as well make your mind up to that now. And I'm not gonna keep paying all the bills, either. You've been here a year and more, and do you have a job? No. You ain't even *looked* for a job. And unless I'm nuts, you have no *mind* to look for one as long as you live—or long as *I* live, anyway."

Minnie flew back into the living room. "Mope, mope, mope," she screamed, her face livid. "That's all you ever do. It must break poor Robert's heart, seated with the angels at the right hand of God this very minute, watching you lay there pining your heart out like a silly goose when there's so much to do in this life. It must make him want to vomit!"

When the anger left her, Minnie clasped her hands and wrung them, then let them drop futilely at her side.

"You just can't go on like this," she said gently.

"I know."

"You got to get out, see people, do things."

"I know."

"Well, then, *do* it. You ain't even been to church since you came here. Now, *there's* your problem. Every Sunday I say let's go to church, and you always have some excuse. If you'd just—"

Rising and brushing past her mother with such briskness that Minnie lost her thought, Aimee walked to the closet, took out her coat, and slipped into it. She took the umbrella from the stand in the hallway.

"Now what're you doing?"

"Going to church." Rushing from the apartment, Aimee slammed the door behind her.

"There ain't no church Friday night," Minnie yelled after her. "And you oughtn't be out on the street after dark." She ran to the door and leaned out over the banister. Aimee was already skipping down the last steps.

"You be careful, Aimee Kennedy, you hear? And you get home early or you'll break your poor mother's heart with worry."

"I'm Aimee Semple, Mother—*Semple*," Aimee yelled back.

Opening her umbrella, she zigzagged through the rush-hour crowd, then dashed across Fourteenth Street, busy with carriages and horses and dozens of popping, squeaking automobiles.

"Watch where you're going, lady!" someone yelled as she drove her umbrella through the crowd. But she kept running, people scattering before her like the Red Sea before Moses.

When she could run no farther, and her round cheeks were flushed, her eyes sparkling, she stopped and leaned against the side of the building. Passersby gazed at her curiously. Crossing her eyes, her tongue lolling out of her open mouth, she gawked back at them.

"Oh, my God!" an old lady exclaimed and hurried past.

She began running again.

"Look out, you big lug!" she told a large man she ran into, and while people stopped to stare, she spun away into the crowd.

A moment later she darted into a bar.

"Hey, c'mere, bud," she yelled. "G'me a rum 'n' gin."

"Sorry, I can't serve you," the bartender explained. "This ain't the ladies' entrance."

"So this ain't no *lady*!" She took a handful of pretzels from the bowl and ran back into the street.

"They're nuts in there," she told a man waiting at the corner for the traffic to break.

"They're nuts out here, too, in case you don't know it," he said in a rather high-pitched voice with a decided Bostonian accent. He'd said, "They'ah nuts out heah." Short but well built, in his early twenties, he stood unflinching, chomping on a huge cigar, as the rain soaked his head and dripped from his earlobes and protruding nose.

"You're going to catch your death of cold," said Aimee.

"Miserable weather."

"Where's your umbrella?"

"Don't have one."

"Well, don't just stand out there getting soaked," she exclaimed. "Here." She handed him the umbrella.

He did not reach for it immediately, and when he did, it was without acknowledgment.

"I suppose you're coming my way, then?" he asked.

"Might as well be, I suppose. I'm not going anywhere special."

They crossed the street, silent for a moment.

"I'm not either, actually," he finally said.

Aimee laughed, shaking her head. He reminded her of a dachshund. "You must be crazy, putting on a suit to go for a stroll in the pouring rain!"

He didn't smile. "I like suits," he said.

They stopped before a small restaurant.

"You hungry? We'll get something to eat," he said.

Aimee's eyes widened and she smiled.

"If this is turning into a date, I ought to at least know your name."

"Name's Mack. Harry McPherson. Everybody calls me Mack. Now, you hungry or not?"

Aimee laughed. "But you don't know who I am, either," she exclaimed.

"What makes you think I *want* to know who you are? I want something to eat, for God sake!"

"You know," said Aimee, her face serious, "I'd sure like to stop for something to eat. How about you?"

But he did want to know about her, and for a long while, as waiters bustled among the crowded tables, he encouraged her to talk about herself. When she told of China and Robert and the baby and explained her despair, she saw her own emotions reflected in his eyes and knew that he was sharing her experience.

Twice he refused the check, sending the waiter to bring additional desserts and coffee.

"It's a factory, for God sake," he growled. "They shove the food in

61

you and send you packing. Well, they're not giving *us* the bum's rush. We'll keep eating and drinking until they close the joint. Now, tell me about your old lady."

About himself he was reluctant to talk, but as midnight approached and the last couples left, he yielded to Aimee's cajoling to explain that he was from Providence in Rhode Island, where his mother owned a boardinghouse and his family for generations had been seamen. He'd come to New York to make a fortune, although he currently ran errands for a wholesale grocer, something of an apprenticeship. He'd learn the trade, and, in a few years, with the money left him by his father, he'd start his own business.

The rain had already stopped when, long after midnight, they left the restaurant and strolled back along Fourteenth Street.

"Oh, no—Mom'll kill me!" Aimee exclaimed when Mack told her the time.

Grasping his hand, Aimee led him at a run along the now-deserted and semidarkened street. Ignoring his grumbling protests, she ran even faster, and in a moment they both stood gasping beneath the streetlight in front of the tenement.

Aimee gazed up into his eyes. "Will I see you again?" she asked. "Or will the exercise kill you?"

He pulled out a cigar, tried to light it, threw the match to the sidewalk, and chomped on it instead.

"Sure," he said. "But I thought maybe—tonight . . ."

Aimee pointed over her head. "Third floor. Just come by." She shook Mack's hand vigorously, then quickly pressed her lips to his cheek and dashed into the hallway.

Minnie was waiting for her in the hallway.

"Where've you been?"

"Shh, you'll wake the baby," Aimee whispered, brushing past her. In the kitchen, she threw her coat and umbrella on a chair and filled the coffeepot with water. Minnie stood behind her, hands on her hips.

"I asked you—"

"Out." Aimee met Minnie's narrowing eyes with a casual smile.

"Why is it you get such pleasure out of torturing me? Didn't I sacrifice enough for you, staying with your daddy when I could've been off having the time of my life? Skimping and going without just so you could have the best. And how do you show your gratitude? By breaking your poor mother's heart with worry."

"Oh, Mother!" Aimee said, throwing up her hands. She sauntered to the living room and stretched out on the sofa, her hands behind her head. "I met a nice man."

"I know," Minnie sneered. "I saw him from the window."

"He's a fine gentleman, really—a Methodist."

"Hmph. That don't say much. So's your father—and Pastor Fife, for that matter."

Aimee giggled. Rising, she went to the window and gazed at the sidewalk below. With disappointment she realized it was empty, for she had hoped that he might stay there for a while, staring up at her window, hoping to catch a glimpse of her. But he had gone. She wondered if she'd see him again.

"I just don't know what to make of you, Aimee Kennedy," Minnie whispered.

"Semple."

"The first time you go out in a year, and you let a total stranger pick you up—and kiss you good night, of all things!"

Aimee closed her eyes and shook her head in mock despair. "He didn't kiss me—I kissed *him!* It was a silly little peck on the cheek, just for fun."

Minnie's eyes grew cold and her face hardened. "No decent girl would go out with strangers. And only a trollop would kiss him."

Her smile vanishing in livid anger, Aimee shouted, "You drive me crazy!"

The baby awoke with a scream.

"First you want me to go out and *do* something, 'stop moping,' you said. So I went out and did something, and now you're not satisfied with that. Nothing I do is *ever* good enough as far as you're concerned."

She stomped into the hallway. "I'm going to sleep," she bellowed, her face still red. "Unless you keep yakking. Then, so help me, I'll pack up the baby and walk right out of this place and sleep in the gutter for the rest of the night—and then you'll be sorry!"

She slammed the bedroom door behind her.

In the room's darkness, Aimee envisioned herself sleeping in the gutter, a fluffy pillow beneath her head, fresh sheets and blankets enveloping her. Burying her face in the mattress, she smothered her giggles.

CHAPTER VIII

"See the color?" Aimee shouted to Mack one Saturday afternoon in the spring of 1912 as, exhausted, they rode the screeching Sixth Avenue elevated back to Fourteenth Street from Central Park. Pointing to a raindrop shimmering in a rainbow of colors on the window ledge, she pressed her nose against the glass and stared at it cross-eyed until it dropped to oblivion.

There were moments, as when the raindrop fell, that would catch her in sudden dread that the gray days would return to leave her cringing and shattered. But such instants passed quickly, as they did that afternoon on the elevated. Smiling, she hooked her arm in Mack's.

She felt enormously grateful that he had come into her life. He'd led her on expeditions to the City Hall area and financial districts where buildings towered eight and even ten stories into the sky, making valleys of the winding streets. And when she'd digested that grandeur, he'd brought her to Bryant Park and showed her the breathtaking new fourteen-story skyscrapers along Forty-second Street.

Some days the two walked hand in hand through the grass of Battery Park and gazed across the bay to Staten Island, or sat at the end of the 130th Street pier, watching the boats sail upriver toward Poughkeepsie and down to the ocean, listening to the laughter and music as it wafted across the Hudson from Palisades Amusement Park on the New Jersey cliffs. Throughout those afternoons, while the pigeons circled the distant ledges, the two would lazily embrace, Aimee planting kisses all over Mack's face.

But those idyllic interludes were rare, for Aimee's hunger for new experiences seemed incapable of satiety; each day she culled the newspapers for new adventure.

That drizzly Saturday afternoon on the elevated had started out just such a day, with the sun shining and Aimee now leading the exploration north along Broadway from Union Square to Central Park. At Thirty-third Street, she took an hour's detour through Gimbel's Department Store, and at Thirty-fourth, did the same through Macy's. When they passed a Victor Talking Machine showroom, Aimee insisted Mack ask for a demonstration. At Forty-sixth Street she cajoled him into buying her lunch at the new Horn & Hardart Automat, where, in a way both marvelous and incomprehensible to her, she could, by dropping nickels into slots, open locked doors and help herself to the food she wished.

"Let me do yours, too!" she begged, taking Mack's nickels from him.

Just south of Central Park were the automobile showrooms, and Aimee dashed through one after another, bouncing on the seats and honking horns until, red-faced, Mack led her away.

"I'm sorry," she said sheepishly when they reached the sidewalk. "Oh, Mack, I'm crazy. I know it!"

Clutching his hand, she led him in a breakneck race along Broadway toward Central Park.

"I want to see the East Side mansions again before it gets dark," she yelled. "Where those disgustingly rich people live. I think I'll make my choice today, Mack—you better start saving your money!"

"You ever think of wearing out—I mean running out of steam like a normal person?" Mack yelled.

Then it began raining, and Mack, with a relieved sigh, insisted they take the west side elevated back.

Even from the train, the city enthralled her. Exclusive brownstones and deluxe shops gave way to parks, vaudeville theaters, and tinselly storefront nickelodeons. Near Longacre Square at Forty-second Street and Broadway, "the Crossroads of the World," as local citizens had begun calling it, she and Mack left the train and walked east past some of the most famous and fabulous restaurants in the world. Crossing Broadway, the Great White Way, so lavish was its lighting after dark, they finally reached Sixth Avenue, and boarded another train. With wheels screeching, it rolled south toward the grimy tenements.

She squeezed Mack's arm and, turning from the rain-streaked window, gazed into his eyes.

"I don't want to go home," she said.

"We can get the subway to Coney Island or go around again on here."

Aimee's eyes softened. She lifted her hand to his cheek. "The subway's too noisy, and I'm bored with this," she whispered. "Can't we go someplace dry and quiet and alone?"

Mack's face, rarely expressive, brightened.

"My room?"

Aimee shrugged and turned to the window. When she faced him again, it was with a smile and a nod. She'd have preferred a more romantic setting in which to confess her passion—the lobby of the glorious Waldorf, a table at Delmonico's. Yet it's here, she thought, in this dingy train full of gawking youngsters and squealing babies and raucous laughter that I'm to be drawn to this cigar-puffing bantam. Yet her face flushed with the hunger she felt. Her eyes glowed with it.

Embracing him, she whispered. "Oh, Mack."

Minnie's haranguing began that Saturday night and continued throughout Sunday, but for a brief respite while she attended worship services at the headquarters. Finally, to diffuse Minnie's tantrum, Aimee agreed to attend the evening service. In fact, she sang the old hymns with fervor, and when the pastor asked for testimonies, she leaped to her feet and, while Minnie grimaced, praised God for her newfound happiness.

That night it appeared Minnie had been appeased, but the next morning while readying for work, she launched another volley of verbosity.

"You must think I'm a real dope, that's what you must think," she complained from the bathroom. "Well, I'm a lot smarter than you figure." Raising her voice, she ordered, "Turn the coffee off—it's perked long enough. And put some eggs on. It won't kill you to help your poor mother—God knows you're not overworked."

Without pausing, she continued: "Them that play with fire get burned, you know. And it's as clear as day, Aimee Semple, you're playing with fire. Not that it's such a bad thing to have a boyfriend, but Aimee— you're a child of God. You should be going with a minister of the Gospel—or at least somebody with a lot of money! New York's full of them—the rich, I mean. Why, look at you. You're pretty as they come. There ain't a reason on earth you can't get yourself a rich man and live easy the rest of your life. If you can't find him in New York, you ain't gonna find him anyplace."

Rushing from the bathroom, she poured herself a cup of coffee. "Ain't them eggs done yet? I tell you, Aimee Semple, you break your poor mother's heart. I had such great plans for you, and here you throw yourself away on a guy who ain't nothing but a nobody."

Rolling her eyes toward the ceiling, Aimee explained, "Will you just *stop*! I'm not getting married, you know—not to Mack, and not to the Vanderbilts. Mack and I have a good time together, that's all."

"That's just what I'm worried about."

"Well, don't worry about it—it's not your business. I'm old enough to decide what I want to do with my life."

"You should be, but that don't mean you are. Ain't the eggs ready yet?"

Sullenly Aimee scraped the eggs from the pan and into a dish, and set them before Minnie.

"Sure it's my business what you do with your life," demanded Minnie between gulps. "I'm your mother, or did you forget it?" Thus she continued until, gulping the last of her coffee, she ran for the door.

"Just don't make any plans for tonight," she scolded. "You gotta stop seeing him every day, and that's that." She started for the door. "Least he's got a job—and thank God for small favors." And with that she left.

Aimee sauntered to the window. In these rare moments with Minnie gone, the baby sleeping, and the room silent, a feeling of desolation sometimes swept over her. It happened when her mind was idle, when she had no plans, nothing at all to look forward to. Gratefully she thought of Mack. The two of them had spun through their few months' acquaintanceship like leaves in an autumn wind, soaring from dance halls to taprooms, from vaudeville theaters to nickelodeons. If Minnie had guessed the half of it, there'd never again be peace on earth!

Yet Aimee hadn't even once asked herself if the fondness she felt for Mack, the hunger for him, the endlessly happy times they shared, might form the embroidery of love. It was a question she knew she'd have to face, perhaps even today, for Mack had told her he'd be coming in the morning, skipping work to see her, for, as he'd explained, he had something very important to talk about. She wondered if he might actually blurt out a marriage proposal. The thought delighted and flattered her so completely that she giggled aloud.

As the morning advanced, the street grew more cluttered with pounding, sputtering automobiles. Hardly a horse-drawn hansom to be seen these days, she thought; everyone buying the new automobiles on time. On the rooftop across the street, she watched two women pinning diapers to a makeshift clothesline. From a window, an old woman hailed a fruit vendor in the street. Four young children ran along the sidewalk, and, to hear their laughter more clearly, Aimee threw open the window. The air was warm already, rich with the city's smells, burdened with its sounds. The cars' horns croaked, trolley bells clanged, and from the distance she could hear the squeaking cable cars. Doors slammed. People yelled above a constant drone of engines and rumble of footsteps. She threw back her head and drew the warm air into her lungs.

If it weren't for the baby, she told herself, she'd be down there, running through the streets again, drinking in the excitement instead of wrestling her rebellious mind into pondering foolish questions about love.

She slumped back into the chair, propping her feet on the window-sill. In truth, she admitted, he was not her ideal, not the kind of fellow a girl could show off, neither tall nor dashing nor sparkling with wit. He was certainly intelligent, but also bullish and sometimes tearfully boring.

Well, there—she'd made herself think about it and she was sorry, for now she felt naughty just as she did when, as a little girl disregarding all of Minnie's sacrifices, she would trample her mother's feelings under foot like a cow in a flower patch. Mack, too, had been selfless and sacrificing, cheerfully taking her to the most outrageously expensive places at her mere suggestion, always paying the entire bill, along with the subway and taxi fares. So generous had he been, in fact, that his paycheck had long ago ceased to cover their weekly entertainments and he had dipped into his savings and finally had begun writing to his mother for loans.

Aimee felt not the least concern about the expenditures—if you're poor, what's the sense of complaining, she thought. But if you've got money, why, money's for spending, isn't it? In fact, it's to Mack's credit that he parts with his money so cheerfully, she concluded.

"But maybe I *do* love him," she insisted, and felt relief at voicing the possibility.

She heard him in the hallway skipping up the stairs two at a time until he reached the second floor and then at a much slower pace climbing the remaining flight. Pressing her hair in place and pushing her blouse more snuggly into her skirt, she rushed to the door to greet him. Draping her arms around his neck, she planted kisses on his flushed cheeks. For several minutes they stood embracing in the hall.

Through the open door came Roberta's waking cries of "Momma!" Rolling her eyes and grimacing, Aimee took Mack's hand and led him inside.

"Heat some coffee," she asked, hurrying to the bedroom. "Make me a cup, too." A moment later she returned with Roberta.

"Now, just be quiet," she demanded. "You'll eat after you're dressed."

"The bottle setting in the icebox—that for her?" called Mack.

"Yes."

"Well, it's warming on the stove—should be ready in a minute."

"Well—thanks!"

"A couple of drops on the wrist, warm but not hot, right?"

Aimee continued dressing the child nonchalantly, but her smile faded and she asked sharply, "Have you ever been married?"

Mack laughed. "Married? Me? Not on your life. No, I just know about babies—a girl I lived with had one."

When he returned with the bottle, Aimee was livid.

"Why didn't you tell me before this?" she demanded. "You just *left* her?"

Mack laughed again, but when Aimee seemed to grow more furious, he just shrugged. "Matter of fact, I think she left me. She just rented a room in Mom's boardinghouse for a while. I wasn't the daddy, if that's what you're thinking—I was about twelve years old."

The flush left her face, but Aimee's eyes still blazed. "Harry McPherson, you're a wretch to pull a dirty trick like that."

Mack dropped his hand to her shoulder, but Aimee pulled away. Then she turned to him and offered a grudging smile.

"So you know all about babies?" She reached for the bottle. Instead, he lifted Roberta in his arms and, moving to the sofa, slipped the bottle between the seeking lips.

"Rather have a steak, wouldn't you, kid?" he said. "She's what—a year and a half?—too old for bottles."

"She eats food, too, of course."

In his rough-skinned, stubbly-whiskered face, bent now and smiling at Roberta, Aimee saw the brazen seaman's heritage but also a surprising gentleness. Roberta felt it, too, relaxed, and long before she finished the bottle fell asleep, the nipple lolling in her mouth. Mack carried her to the bedroom and placed her in the crib, and when he returned to the sofa, Aimee handed him a cup of coffee and a plate of cookies. He nodded in appreciation.

After sipping the coffee briefly, he set it aside and stood again, walking to the window with hands in his trouser pockets. He stood there silhouetted against the sun, the sleeves of his white shirt rolled up. Taking a cigar from his shirt pocket, he popped it between his teeth unlit and chomped on it.

69

The silence grew obvious, and still he didn't speak but gazed out across the rooftops Aimee herself had surveyed during those interminable hours before Mack. She sensed his discomfort and knew that in a moment he would turn to her, perhaps take her hand in his, kissing it, lead her to the sofa. There, on his knees, he'd ask her to be his wife. And what would she say? She had no idea.

Finally he turned.

"I gotta go home—to Providence," he said. "Mom's got her hands full with the house. It needs painting. Says she can't afford to send me any more money." He hesitated, his eyes shifting. "And I got fired, so I won't have to stick around here for my job no more."

"Fired?"

"They said I was taking off too much. It was those times we went places together."

So that's what he wanted to tell her, that he'd been fired and was leaving and wouldn't be seeing her anymore. Oh, he'd write, and whenever he'd get to New York, he'd look her up. She felt suddenly so lonely, and although the room was warm she shuddered and, throwing her arms around herself, hurried to the kitchen. It was as though there had been no spring; the summer had never come; the long rides and picnics in the parks and strolls along the river, shopping sprees, all those many laughs, and all those Nathan's hot dogs shared, the silly races across Union Square, dashing madly for the plunging cable car—they were an instant's dream, with nothing changed. Only emptiness.

"Where you going?" he asked.

"I want some coffee."

She poured it slowly, fighting back the tears and staring absently into the steaming liquid. Finally, with a deep breath, she started back to the living room.

Mack stood leaning against the doorjamb, his arms folded.

"I want you to come with me," he said softly. "You and Roberta."

Aimee's hands trembled and she quickly placed the coffee cup on the table.

"Bring everything you own—your clothes, your shoes, your pet canary if you have one. Everything but your old lady. She stays."

Aimee began to smile, then her face registered confusion. "Are you—are you asking me to marry you?"

"No. Should I? Okay, marry me."

Aimee picked up the coffee cup and brushed past him and into the living room. "Oh, you're so smooth, so absolutely smooth, aren't you? Condescending to marry me, if that's what *I* want! What makes you think

I'd even *agree* to marry you, much less *want* to, a miserable vagabond who can't even hold a job, stubborn as a mule and arrogant as—"

He took the cup from her and placed it on the end table, wrapped a strong arm around her waist, and, tilting her head back, planted soft but firm kisses on her throat, cheeks, and finally her lips. In a moment she was flushed and breathing heavily, surrendering to him.

"You coming with me or not? If you want me to, I'll marry you."

Breathing deeply, Aimee regained her composure and straightened herself. Stepping back, she said, "I've got to think about it. I really do."

"Okay. I'm leaving tomorrow afternoon. Make your mind up by then?" Aimee nodded.

A moment later he was gone.

When Minnie returned from headquarters that evening, the aroma of baking apples and roasting chicken greeted her in the hallway, and she grew immediately suspicious. Inside, the furniture sparkled with new polish. The kitchen floor had been scrubbed, the living room rug swept. Even the windowsills had been dusted.

"I'm in the kitchen, Mom."

Aimee hastily poked a few wisps of hair back into the twist she'd set earlier in the day, and pulling the pot holders from her apron pocket, lifted the roasting pan from the oven. Placing it on the table, she then hurried into the living room, eager to see Minnie's expression of delight. Instead, her mother confronted her with raised eyebrows.

"What's going on?" Minnie demanded.

Her eyes widening in astonishment, Aimee threw open her arms and exclaimed, "What on earth do you *mean*? I wanted to do something *nice* for you—you work so hard. You're just the best mom in the world."

Still, Minnie searched her critically. Aimee stomped her foot, pouting. "You think everyone's always got something up their sleeve."

"I just know my little Aimee, that's all."

"Well, that's what I get for doing something nice—it serves me right."

More hurt than angry, she stomped back into the kitchen. Minnie followed.

"Well, then," she said in apology, hugging her daughter tightly. "Everything smells almost good enough to eat!"

"Almost!" Aimee threw an incredulous grimace over her shoulder and the two laughed and hugged.

71

"I see even the windowsills've been dusted. Aimee Semple, are you sure—"

"Go say hello to Roberta. Out of my kitchen—go." Aimee shooed her mother into the hallway. "How can I set the table with you standing in my way!"

Later in the evening, when dinner was finished and the dishes washed and they sat in the living room, Minnie bouncing Roberta on her knee and making distorted faces to the child's glee, Aimee could contain herself no longer. She had planned to announce it as a big surprise, calling for just such a holiday atmosphere and festive dinner as she had prepared, but Minnie's shrewd insight had intercepted that approach and now, impatient and eager, she abandoned all strategy and blurted, "Well, Mom, you're finally getting me out of your hair again. You'll have your flat to yourself, and it's about time—more than a year. You should've tossed me out long ago, and it's only because you're the greatest mom—"

"What're you talking about? Where are you going?"

But Aimee could see in Minnie's face that her mother already knew. She wished suddenly that she hadn't even told Minnie but had simply gone off in the morning, leaving a note to explain.

In response to Minnie's hostile glare, Aimee bristled. "I'm going to marry Mack, and that's all there is to it. He's got to go to Providence. His uncle died and left him a lot of money and he's to run the company. We're leaving tomorrow." Aimee started from the room.

Minnie leaped up, clutching Roberta to her breast. "You're not doing any such thing!" she screeched. "Running off with that good-for-nothing, and taking this poor little infant with you—whatever put such a crazy thing in your head? You'll run off with that playboy over your poor mother's corpse, Aimee Kennedy. And as for this helpless baby—"

Aimee turned on her, eyes blazing with anger and fists clenched.

"I'll do what I *feel* like doing!" she shouted. "It's not your life. I need someone to love and care for me."

"And your mother's not good enough, I suppose."

"I need a *man*. And Roberta needs a father."

"Say what you mean," Minnie hissed. "It ain't no father for Roberta you're after but a gigolo to keep your bed warm. So the lust of the flesh is to be your downfall, is it, and with such as him. Go ahead, toss aside everything I sacrificed to give you. Trample under foot the memory of your saintly husband. But don't mock the sacredness of marriage—call it what it is: *lust*!"

Aimee's eyes overflowed with tears. Her face was twisted in pain

72

and anger at the unjustness of Minnie's accusation. She began to speak, then, ripping Roberta from Minnie's arms, ran into the bedroom and slammed the door behind her. For a while, Minnie stood at the door demanding admittance, with fists pounding. Then she cajoled and finally pleaded.

Aimee ignored her, dragging the steamer trunk from the closet and in frenzied haste dumping entire dresser drawers of her clothing and the baby's into it. With a sweep she took dresses and coats from the rack and tossed them into the trunk, and from the bureau she gathered her hairbrush, comb, hairpins, and a bottle of cheap perfume. Finally, from the wall above the bed, she lifted the oval portrait of Robert and herself. Gazing at it made her eyes red and tear-filled again, and she quickly pressed it into the trunk and closed the lid.

When she opened the door, Minnie was waiting with a conciliatory smile. "Now, what're you being so silly for?" she purred when she saw Aimee leading Roberta and dragging the trunk. "You're just being foolish and you know it."

But Aimee struggled toward the door.

"You can't be going out so late at night. Somebody'll rob you and who knows what all." Minnie's voice continued to rise. "You got to think of the child. What's to become of her, in the night air like that, not to mention if it rains?"

Aimee dropped the trunk long enough to throw the door open, then tugged it into the hallway and toward the stairs. "You're gonna break your stubborn little neck!" Minnie screeched, lunging for the trunk. "You'll knock yourself down the stairs and crush that poor little girl to death!"

Aimee turned on her with eyes so cold that Minnie released the trunk.

"All right, then," Minnie snarled as the trunk thumped down the steps behind Aimee. "Go off with him if you want to. Throw your life away, but don't say I didn't warn you. And don't come running back to Momma when he tosses you out on your ear for somebody else. I've done all I could for you and I'm through worrying. I got my own life to live. But I'm warning you, Aimee Kennedy, or Aimee Semple, or Aimee Semple McPherson, or whoever you are—don't you *dare* hurt that little one, for she's more precious than gold and deserves far better in this world than—"

Aimee slammed the door behind her and dragged the trunk to the curb, where she hailed a taxi. Ten minutes later she stood at Mack's open door.

"When do we leave?" she whispered.

CHAPTER IX

On a bitterly cold January afternoon in 1913, Aimee huddled near the second-floor bedroom window of the boardinghouse on Claverick Street, Providence, and stared into the almost barren street. From a distance came the clinking of hoofs against the cobblestones, the sound drawing nearer until she saw the animal plodding with lowered head, its rider appearing enormous in multiple layers of sweaters and trousers, a scarf, thick gloves, and hat tugged down over his ears. A moment later horse and rider had vanished and the street was silent again.

Shivering, Aimee pulled her shawl more tightly around her and nestled deep into the crevice of the plush gray chair. But the baby in her womb objected to the curled position, and Aimee, grimacing in pain, sat upright once more.

She was growing fat and ugly, she knew, and she gazed down upon the evidence of her seven months' pregnancy with thorough disgust. Recently she had felt not the slightest pleasure in contemplating the increasing monstrousness of her body, only shame and despair, to which Mack had responded with bullish laughter and a few hollow words of reassurance. She had screamed at him violently, even pounded his chest with her fists, and he had stormed away in anger, neither of them referring to the pregnancy again.

Leaning into the icy wind, two teen-age girls, their faces almost hidden beneath hoods and scarves, hurried along beside the towering walls of St. Francis Xavier Academy. Suddenly, when they were almost beyond sight, they turned and vanished through a small iron gate. From her window, Aimee could see them enter the courtyard, tugging off their hoods and shaking their hair free. She recognized the one girl's long blonde hair and wind-reddened cheeks. In a moment, she anticipated, the young novitiate would turn intense, almost glowing blue eyes toward the window and smile.

She did, and Aimee responded with a faint smile of her own. Then the courtyard was empty.

A handful of fine snowflakes swept past the window.

In the room below, Anna McPherson—Momma Mac, as she insisted Aimee address her—was teaching Roberta a song:

> Apple tree, big apple tree,
> Drop an apple down for me.

The woman sang the words in a voice loud and shrill, pounding the melody in solitary notes on the piano, and Roberta clapped and giggled and tried to sing along. Only when she was with Roberta did Momma Mac allow herself such flights of release, and Aimee was undecided which irritated her more, the woman's rare bombast or her usual grim and proper silence. She was certain Anna McPherson despised her, if for no other reason than that Aimee was the wife of her only son. Aimee had won Mack from her, and although Momma Mac covered it well, Aimee knew the old lady seethed with jealousy and would do all in her power to destroy the marriage.

The front door opened and closed.

"Daddy Mac!" cried Roberta, racing across the room.

The feet of the piano bench scraped against the floor. Mack was no doubt lifting Roberta in his arms. She squealed as he tossed her high into the air. Momma Mac was there, welcoming her precious son home.

"Aimee?" It was Mack's voice.

"She ain't been down all day, not even for lunch," said Momma Mac in hushed tones.

"Aimee?"

She didn't answer. If he really cared about her he'd pull himself away from that doting old woman and come to her side. And if he didn't—she would hate him bitterly.

But when she heard his footsteps, she was sorry he hadn't gone off to the kitchen with his mother to sip coffee and talk incessantly about the mediocre life of a bank messenger. Now he would hug her and kiss her and bore her with his meandering, meaningless accounts, and she with not the slightest interest in such nonsense.

She heard the doorknob turn and then saw Mack's reflection in the window pane, engulfed in cigar smoke and silhouetted against the hallway lights.

"Aimee?"

"How was your day?"

"Why're you sitting in the dark? And it's freezing in here! You're gonna catch pneumonia." He went to the heater in the fireplace and turned up the gas. The flames brightened the room, casting it in a blue-green glow.

"God it's cold in here, and then you sit with just a slip and bare feet and that thing over your shoulders! Why wasn't the gas heater turned up?"

"It smells, Mack. So does your cigar."

"You're crazy," he said, shaking his head. "You're gonna get pneumonia. That's all you need, being pregnant."

It had grown dark. Still, she stared at the window, where a flurry of snowflakes stuck to the glass and glowed blue in the light of the gas heater.

"Put something on, come down and have supper," Mack said.

"I'm not hungry."

"Mom says you ain't been down all day. Come on."

Aimee turned on him. "I said I'm not hungry!"

She saw the swift anger in his eyes, and the pain.

"You know, it's as if you been sitting in this lousy room forever," he mumbled. "I mean, it's been *months* since you ate with the family. I wouldn't be surprised if Roberta don't even know who the funny lady on the second floor is anymore, sitting here shivering in the dark every night." He threw up his hands and chomped hard on his cigar.

"Look, I'm crazy, Mack. All right?"

Occasionally she took Roberta for walks along the cobblestone streets to the river's edge and watched the chunks of ice drift by. Together they would make snowballs and try to hit the ice, but Roberta's fell apart in midair, and so after a while Aimee, gazing absently across the water to where the steamers were loading for the south, manufactured the snowballs, placing them in a neat row, and Roberta hurled them into the water.

Sometimes the two strolled the few blocks to downtown Providence and window-shopped in the shadow of the Industrial Valley Trust skyscraper, where Mack worked. But even on those fresh and sunny days, Roberta's chatter made Aimee irritable and she longed to return alone to the bleak room overlooking the academy walls.

"I'm crumbling apart," she confessed to herself one day, several months after they'd moved to Providence. It seemed her mind had become her mortal enemy, bent on relentless torture, converting even the brightest moments—her daughter's smile, Mack's caresses, the smell of baking ham in the kitchen below—into grotesqueness and despair. The depression seemed to weigh on her in layers, like heavy gray blankets, so that before she could find her way from beneath one, others would tumble down burying her so deep that she felt utterly without hope of escape.

Often she would curl up in the gray chair when Mack left for work in the morning and even then the tears would begin running down her face. Throughout the day she would weep, and Mack would find her still crying there at night. He would say little, except to repeat what he had come to assure himself was the core problem: "You'll be okay after the baby comes. It's the baby. That's what it is."

"God, I hope so," Aimee would whisper, shaking her head.

Shortly after midnight on March 23, 1913, Aimee's moaning awakened Mack. Hastily he dressed himself, then her, called for a taxi, and raced to the nearby Providence Lying-in Hospital.

At the beginning, when the pains were several minutes apart, she made only whimpering moans. But as the severity of the contractions increased, she began a long silent scream, watching it build like a wall of sand to hold back the waves of agony. Later, her eyes wild, her face a sopping mosaic of red blotches, she kicked off the white sheet and clutched the huge mass of her belly.

"I can't. I can't!" she cried.

For hours she punctuated the groaning and weeping with screams, pleading with the doctors, the muscles of her body aching with unrelieved rigidity.

Finally a nurse swathed her face. Another strapped her hands and legs. Hideous agony wracked her, and she thrashed blindly.

"Be strong, Mrs. McPherson," said the doctor. "It won't be long now. The baby's coming."

"No, no!" she screamed. "Help me!"

"Now *push*—push *hard*."

"I'll die!" Even as she summoned the last shreds of strength, she felt her body ripping, a great conflagration devouring her.

"Good, that's good. Keep pressing."

Then it was over. Only the fire kept raging.

"It's a boy, Mrs. McPherson, a virtual giant," said the doctor.

She held the baby for just a moment before calling for Mack. She told him she'd name the baby Rolf because she liked the name and Potter because Dr. Potter had performed the delivery. With the infant nursing at her breast, her hand in Mack's, she fell asleep, and for several days that was her last recollection.

While she slept, the hemorrhaging continued, and Dr. Potter's casual assurance it would cease in due time changed first to concern, then to fear. When the physician finally ordered surgery, Aimee's ashen body lay motionless but for her trembling lips. They repeated almost incoherently the words "Happy Valley."

In her delirium Aimee floated up through the currents of pain, approaching with what seemed eternal slowness the light, the surface. She felt the twitching in her eyelids and realized that she was conscious, the pain greater than it had seemed in the twilight. Minutes passed before she attempted to raise her eyelids.

Minnie sat beside her, gazing at her with lips pressed so tightly together they'd grown almost white. When she saw Aimee's eyes flutter, she responded with a start.

"Aimee, thank God! You scared the daylights out of me! They thought you was going to . . . You don't know how close you came, poor baby."

She took Aimee's hand between hers and massaged it vigorously, as though it would help to restore her daughter's health. "I'd have been here sooner, but I wasn't in New York. I was up to see James. Soon as Mack got through on the telephone, why, I jumped on the next train. My Lord, Aimee, we was all so worried. Mack wouldn't even go to work till the doctor said you'd be all right."

Aimee's eyes faltered. She watched her mother's pudgy little hands massaging hers, felt their warmth and strength, and some fragmented memory, some childhood emotion, recurred to her. She felt not like a mother with children but a child herself. Lifting Minnie's hands to her lips, she kissed them, feeling their roughness.

"Oh, Momma," she sobbed.

"Now, now, it's gonna be all right." Minnie ran her fingers through Aimee's hair, caressed her cheeks.

"Momma, I feel miserable. I hurt so bad inside."

"Well, and what do you expect? You had a hysterectomy, is what they call it."

Aimee was silent for a moment. "I didn't know . . ."

"To save your life. There was nothing else to be done."

"But—no, not that," Aimee sobbed. "I hurt *here*, Momma." She placed Minnie's hand between her breasts. Tears welled in her pleading eyes. "In my soul, and there's nothing I can do."

Minnie pulled her chair closer to the bed. Her eyes fastened on their intertwined hands, and across her face passed a profound sorrow. She seemed suddenly haggard, her energy drained. Finally she shrugged, and lifting heavy eyes to Aimee's, she said:

"My poor baby, when in your whole life did you pay any attention to your old mother, and if you never did it before, why should you now? But Aimee, I'm telling you the truth. You need God. It's your *soul's* sick, and nothing can help a sick soul but God."

Aimee turned her head away. "No, I can't."

"Sure you can, Aimee. 'Whosoever shall call upon the name of the Lord shall be saved!' "

"No." Aimee closed her eyes. "I don't believe anything anymore, Mom. I'd be lying if I pretended anything else. I'd be nothing but a fake, and knowing that would tear me apart."

Minnie took Aimee's chin in her hand and gently turned her head.

"Look at me, Aimee Semple McPherson," she said softly. "Let's bow our heads. Let me pray for you."

"No, Mom," Aimee sobbed. Her eyes closed, she shook her head and turned away again. "I'm going to sleep now," she whispered. Minnie sighed, stood, and went to the door. As she was about to leave, Aimee called in a husky voice, "It was a good sermon, Mom. When do we take the offering?"

The hack pulled away, and Aimee stood on the red brick pavement gazing at the monotonous facade of the white clapboard house on Claverick Street.

"C'mon, you're gonna catch pneumonia and be back in the hospital," bellowed Mack from the doorway, a cloud of cigar smoke encircling his head.

But she continued to survey the house, her eyes lusterless, her face set in stern contemplation. She confronted each board, each pane of glass, and when she was finished, she breathed deeply the crisp air, momentarily resigned. From the window came the sounds of Rolf crying and Momma Mac cooing to him. Suddenly Roberta's head appeared over the windowsill and she waved frantically.

Aimee stared at the child without expression. Then she exhaled, a stream of vapor shooting through the cold air.

"What's keeping you?" Mack demanded.

"I'm coming."

In the following weeks, Aimee found herself sinking again into lethargy and depression, and now the responsibility of the infant seemed more than she could endure. Sometimes Rolf, in the crib only a few feet away, would continue crying until Momma Mac climbed the steps and pounded on the door.

"You want me to help with the baby?" she'd ask gently.

"I was sleeping," Aimee would snap. "I'll manage."

One night, when Mack came home to the baby's frantic screams and learned from Momma Mac that the infant hadn't been fed, he burst into the bedroom with cigar blazing.

"You're either gonna get yourself in shape or I'm gonna cart you off to the nut house!" he bellowed.

Aimee said nothing.

"You *hear* me?" he demanded.

She turned toward him, her eyes bloodshot and swollen, her face wet with tears. It seemed to him not Aimee, but the distorted face of a stranger, dying and resigned to death, the muscles of the face already lifeless, the body sagging. He shook his head.

"It just don't make any sense," he said. "I just can't figure it."

"You remember that night—it seems so long ago, and it wasn't even a year." Her voice was strained, the words deliberate and so soft he almost missed them. "I ran madly through the streets crying a name that only I heard, hoping I guess that in some dark alley or dimly lit hallway or smoke-filled barroom, in a skid-row mission or a foggy waterfront diner, I'd stumble into him and cry, 'Oh, Robert, oh, Robert!' And he'd smile down on me as he once did, and his voice would sing with love and the music of angels and I'd have him again."

She stared at him through glazed, unmoving eyes, until he awkwardly turned away. She reached for his hand.

"But it was you I bumped into, Mack, and you were so good. You tried. It's not your fault, it's mine—but you're not *him*." Her eyes went to the large oval wedding photograph hanging above the bed.

"I've tried with all my heart to forget, Mack. I made love to you. I married you. I had your baby inside me. But I don't *love* you, Mack.

Sometimes I don't think I even like you. And it's so sad, because you're a good man and it's not your fault."

He jerked his hand away, and she saw his face twitch and harden. He moved toward the wall behind the bed.

"So I'm not good enough to take the place of a dead man, am I?" he bellowed, ripping the picture from the wall.

Aimee leaped from the chair. "Don't!" she screamed. "Don't you touch that. Don't you dare!"

"I had to be a stupid fool letting you stick that thing over our bed in the first place!"

Aimee clutched the picture. *"Give it to me!"* she screamed.

He released it and she clutched it to her breast, backing away from him.

"Now, you get out of this room and don't you *ever* come in here again," she snarled.

Mack clenched his fists. "Who do you think you are, trying to kick me out of my own bedroom?"

"Who am I?" shrieked Aimee. "Who am I? I'm Aimee Semple McPherson. Do you know what that means? Do you have the slightest idea? Of course not."

"As far as I'm concerned, it means you're a pain in the neck, that's what it means. And I'm sick of it. I bent over backward to please you, and it's no use, so I give up. You're never gonna be happy, and I'm tired of trying."

"Well, you won't have to try much longer." Her face was so hot it pained her, and she could taste the tears at the corners of her mouth. "Because, I swear to God, Mack, if my life doesn't change somehow soon, I'll kill myself. And if I do, I'll kill you, too, because it's all your *fault*!"

That night Mack took his mother and Roberta out to dinner. Aimee saw the three of them walking away hand in hand, from the small island of light beneath the sputtering gas lamp into the darkness, to appear again under the next lamp, and so on into the distance until she could see them no more.

Now the house was silent. From the courtyard of St. Francis Xavier came the faint sounds of youthful laughter. Beneath the festive yellow and orange brightness of the gas lamps, the young girls raced after each other, their hair whipping the air, while the older ones strolled along the brick walkways in animated chatter. Against one of the lamp posts leaned the girl with the long blonde hair, encircled by several friends. In response to her few words and a casual gesture toward the dormitory, they all laughed, and, throwing her head back, she laughed too, her face radiant in the direct glow of the lamp.

She was Aimee in the Ingersoll schoolyard, and the girls were howling with glee over her imitation of Mrs. Brobst. With one hand securing imaginary spectacles to her nose, the other fluttering out behind her, she marched in a bouncy strut that jiggled buttocks and breasts. Even the boys slapped their thighs and guffawed.

"Oh, you're gonna be a great actress, Aimee!" one of them said, and they all applauded.

Aimee, who'd won the gold medal in the Women's Temperance League's oratorical contest, who'd sold more magazine subscriptions than anyone else in Ingersoll, whose future was rich with the promise of fame and fortune, who'd married the beautiful Robert Semple and learned love in his arms and went all the way to China. She, too, had thrown her head back and laughed with a pure heart into the cold night air. She, too, had known unbridled freedom, unfettered hope.

She could not take her eyes from the blonde girl, but searched with unblinking fascination the vibrant face. In it was something she dimly recognized, an element not physical, yet shaping the features, giving them the glow of the heart's elation. Yes, it was more than mere happiness, Aimee knew, for she felt in herself the long dormant stirrings of such a moment. It was a glow beyond this world's fortunes to give or take, she told herself, a joy not hinging on this earth's frailties. In tribulation it issued peace, in triumph, ecstasy. She had seen it in her own face once, a very long time ago. And in Robert's.

Leaning closer to the window pane, she stared at the blonde girl's face until her breath fogged the glass, then threw open the window exhilarating in the blast of cold air. It seemed to her the children's laughter was as clear as chimes in a cold Canadian night. From somewhere in the distance she thought she heard faintly a great choir, its voice lifted in the old refrain: *Have thine own way, Lord, have thine own way* . . .

"Oh, Robert," she whispered.

Thou art the potter, I am the clay . . .

At that moment her eyes met those of the blonde girl and they smiled and suddenly the two were laughing and waving.

Mold me and make me after thy will . . .

"Oh, God," Aimee whispered. "Oh, God, hold me close."

While I am waiting, yielded and still.

The room was growing cold and the baby whimpered, but Aimee didn't notice. She sank to her knees and folded her hands on the window sill, new tears coming from her eyes.

"I'm so dumb," she said. "I've been so blind, When was I ever happy but with you, Robert, and with the work? Oh, weren't they glorious days, Robert, side by side preaching the gospel and saving souls wherever we went. What dreams we had! And then I just threw them aside—but the Lord didn't. And He'll never give me a moment's peace till I pick up the work we started and carry it on. I know it. Yes, I know that now."

She sat by the open window for a long while that night, feeling the energy seep back into her as though a crucial circuit had at last been restored and great generators were once again churning their power through her. Her mind raced back over the years with Robert and it seemed she recalled their every shared dream, every plan, even the techniques of preaching and soul-winning he had explained.

Finally she whispered, "I'm going to do it, Robert. I'll get the work going again. Please bless me and be at my side. And ask God to bless me, too.

"In fact, now that I think of it, I'll ask Him myself," and she prayed.

CHAPTER X

Aimee was in the kitchen slicing potatoes when she heard Mack, Momma McPherson, and Roberta come home from dinner.

"My, it's way past my bedtime!" Momma Mac exclaimed. "I'm gonna put myself to bed. How about you, Roberta?"

"No." Roberta ran to the kitchen, and a moment later Mack followed.

"Well, look who's here," he remarked, leaning against the doorjamb, his face reflecting pleasure and surprise.

"Oh, I felt like doing something," said Aimee.

Mack came close to her, locking his arms around her waist. She bent her head back, her eyes smiling, and he kissed her lips. Roberta shrieked with glee.

Aimee rushed to the doorway and scooped Roberta into her arms. She kissed the girl's cheeks and forehead and nose and chin, hugging her tightly, "I love you, honey," she said. "Oh, I love you so much. And I'm sorry for being such a bad mother."

"You're my *best* mother!" Roberta declared.

"No, I've been mean and grouchy, and I've ignored you. But I'll be better, you'll see." She put Roberta on the floor and, turning her toward the doorway, patted her buttocks. "Now, it's past your bedtime, so run upstairs and get into your pajamas and I'll be up to tuck you in."

"No."

"Yes!" Mack ordered, and immediately Roberta leaped into his arms and kissed him passionately, then scurried into the hallway and up the steps. Mack took Aimee's hand and pulled her to him. For a long while she relaxed, cheek against cheek, his strong arms around her. Hugging him, she said, "It's been too long, Mack."

"I didn't think you'd ever come to your senses."

She dropped her arms, her eyes flaring, but then, smiling, she hugged him again.

"I suppose so. I've made up my mind—I'm going to be a preacher."

"You're crazy," he laughed.

"I am. I really am."

"Oh, Christ," Mack dropped his arms and turned away, shaking his head. "You can't be a preacher—you're just a woman."

"God's *called* me to preach—it's up to Him to decide, not us. Besides, I can preach as good as any man. And you're gonna help me."

"I will like hell."

"Stop cursing and listen to me." She moved in front of him and took his face in her hands. "Mack, I've been just so miserable."

"I know."

"And all the while the answer was so simple. When was I really happy?"

Mack shook his head. "Don't ask me," he said. "I don't think you was *ever* happy."

"Oh, yes, yes, I was! When I was close to God—I was delirious with happiness then. And tonight at the bedroom window I was watching a young girl in the courtyard across the street, and in her face I saw Robert, and it was as though he was calling me from the ramparts of heaven, from the edge of the universe, down through all the stellar splendor, crying, 'Aimee, Aimee, just preach the Gospel and be happy! Escape your misery. Turn back to God!' "

Mack threw up his hands and strode into the dining room and toward the stairs.

"Where are you going?"

"To bed."

Then he turned and came back into the kitchen. Leaning against the doorjamb, he asked, "I suppose you're gonna get yourself some boards and nails and build a church out in the backyard, put some signs out front, maybe run through the neighborhood screaming to get some attention Sunday mornings like you do the rest of the week."

"Almost—I'm using canvas, not wood, and my tent will be too big for this miserable excuse for a backyard. I won't even set it up in Providence, except to start. I'm going to travel up and down the coast, and maybe someday even across the land, preaching the Gospel."

"Oh, Aimee." Mack stared at the floor and shook his head. "In two weeks you'd be dead of starvation. Me and the kids, too."

"You're the one who said you were a vagabond at heart," Aimee said, raising her voice.

"But not a preacher. The woods are full of them, thousands of them, so-called evangelists—and they're doing it for kicks, not trying to live off it. And there's that guy Billy Sunday. Don't forget him. He can't open his mouth but ten thousand people go hear him. So what's gonna be left for you? Tell me that."

"Well, Minnie says there are six hundred fifty full-time professional evangelists in this country right now, and they're all surviving, so I think one more can live off the crumbs they drop."

"But you're a woman."

"Evangeline Booth's a woman, and she runs the whole Salvation Army in America—and preaches, too."

"But she doesn't go traipsing around the countryside living in tents!" Mack said.

Aimee stepped closer to him, her eyes softening. She took his arm in hers and, turning the gas lamp off, led him to the stairs.

"If Gods called me—us—to preach, let's leave the worrying up to Him. Oh, we won't make a lot of money, Mack. I never in my life wanted money—Minnie and I are as different as night and day on that score. But I *need*"—she looked up into his eyes, searching them in the dim light of the second-floor lamp for a sign that he understood—"I need to be *going* somewhere, and now I know what that means."

The next morning, Aimee was up before Mack, and when he staggered down the steps wiping the sleep from his eyes, she already had eggs sizzling sunny side up and the coffee perking, filling the room with its rich smell. As he came into the room she greeted him with a cheerful "Morning, love," and pressed her body against his. Mack twisted his face in a sleepy smile.

"Looks like I did something right last night," he said, yawning. Aimee laughed.

"You did everything right. Oh, we're going to be so *happy*, Mack! Sit down."

She brought him the eggs and the toast she'd made by stabbing a slice of bread on a fork and holding it over the gas burner. Into a huge cup marked "POPPA" she poured the steaming coffee. While he ate, she stood behind him massaging his shoulders and humming.

After a while Mack shook his head and shrugged. "I don't know what's come over you, but I'll tell you, it's sure a relief," he said.

Aimee smiled. "Oh, I'm *happy*, Mack! I'm going to visit the local churches to see what I can do. Maybe some of them'll let me preach. I'll find out where I can get a tent—we can afford a cheap one, can't we? Something old and torn, and I can fix it myself. And then we'll write letters. We'll sit right here at this kitchen table and write letters to just *everywhere*, and set up an itinerary and—"

Mack pushed his chair away from the table, his breakfast half finished. "So that's what it is," he said, not looking at Aimee.

"What *what* is?"

Mack turned on her. "Last night. And getting up and making breakfast for me like a decent wife for once. And it's all so you can get your own way, ain't it?"

The smile drained from Aimee's face, leaving bewilderment. "*This*"—she gestured to the table—"is because I'm happy. And I'm happy because I'm going to preach again."

Mack sighed. Finally he settled his shifting gaze on Aimee. "You're a pain in the neck," he said. He started toward the stairs, then turned, confronting her again.

"Listen, you're my wife. You're a housewife, understand? And you got two kids, and you got a responsibility to them, too. Now, you want to make a fool of yourself around Providence, go ahead—preach on street corners for all I care, but you ain't getting no tent and I ain't quitting a good job and dragging them poor kids all over kingdom come just because their mother's gone off her rocker and thinks she's gonna save the world or something."

"A good job!" Aimee shrieked. "You're a lousy messenger for a bank!"

"They promise—"

"I don't care if they promise to make you *president* someday—what's to become of *me*? If I was to be nothing but your wife, I'd hate you. I'd *kill* you, Mack!" Her face livid, she screamed the words. "If I had nothing but the kids, I'd *hate* them. That's why I hate everything about this place. It's a tomb, and I'm rotting in it. I hate this!"

She hurled the coffeepot across the room, scalding her arm.

"And this!" She swept the plate of eggs and coffee cup from the table.

"Aimee, stop it! What's the matter with you?"

"And this!" She kicked over a chair.

"And this!" She pounded the cabinets above the sink. Mack came toward her.

"And you!" She turned on him, pounding his chest with both fists. "I'm not going to stand it anymore. No, no more! You can't torture me. I'm done with it. I swear. I'm going to get *out* of here. I'm going to *preach*, and you can't stop me!"

Mack held her arms. "Good Lord, you're crazy," he said. "Nothing ever satisfies you, and nothing ever *will* satisfy you. You're nuts, and you're not going to be satisfied until you make everybody nuts."

"Shut up, shut up!"

"You always get your way, don't you, and you don't care who gets kicked in the teeth. You're going on twenty-five, and you're still just a spoiled little brat."

Suddenly Aimee smashed her knee into his groin, and when he released her arms, she tore her fingernails into his cheeks. He thrust her hands away, but she swung furiously, landing repeated slaps on his bloodied face.

Enraged, Mack swung and Aimee's head snapped back with the violent impact. She staggered away from him, her eyes wet with tears. Then she turned, and with rigid composure climbed the stairs to the bedroom.

For more than a year, Aimee preached at Wednesday night prayer meetings and Sunday night services in the small Pentecostal churches around Providence, not the crusading evangelistic campaigns she envisioned, but prosaic Bible study classes and missionary lectures based on her experiences in China. Finally, Mack was transferred to the four-to-twelve midnight shift at the Industrial Bank and Trust. It was the chance Aimee had waited for.

On a night in the spring of 1915, while Momma Mac slept soundly, Aimee packed the old steamer trunk and most of her clothes and the children's and finally the portrait of Robert and herself. Then she awakened the children, dressed them in warm clothes, and telephoned for a taxi. At the train station they boarded the 11:55 to Toronto. From there they met the connection to Ingersoll.

CHAPTER XI

Lord, it's good to be back, thought Aimee as the train ground to a stop in front of the two-story brick Gothic station house. Minnie Kennedy stood outside the door, a handkerchief clutched in her chubby hand, smiling and waving. Behind her James sat in the wagon holding the reins. The few red whiskers that remained among the invading gray ones in his beard picked up the sunlight so that his face seemed aflame.

Aimee rushed from the train clutching Rolf and holding Roberta's hand, but when the girl recognized Minnie, she leaped into her grandmother's open arms. Aimee kissed her mother quickly, told Rolf to hang on to Minnie's dress, then ran back to take the steamer trunk from the conductor.

"Well, don't just sit there and let her rupture herself, James," cried Minnie. "Give your poor daughter a hand!"

With slow and awkward movements, James climbed from the wagon and limped to the train, where he insisted he could manage the trunk himself. Struggling with it while shooing Aimee away, he finally dragged it to the wagon, permitting the women to help only in hoisting it aboard.

"This is Flossie," Aimee told Roberta, throwing her arms around the horse's neck. "I almost named her Creamie because of her color. Shake hands with Roberta, Flossie. Come on, shake hands."

Aimee reached for the horse's leg and the animal lifted it obediently.

"I taught her that!" Aimee exclaimed. "Years ago, and she still remembers!"

As the old wagon creaked along the gravel road to Thames Street,

Aimee gasped. The street bed was no longer pressed gravel, high in the middle and low at the cobblestone-lined curbs, but was now paved with red bricks, with more motorcars than horses streaming along it.

James Kennedy reined the horse to a stop where the tracks crossed Thames Street, waiting for one of the new Fords to pass.

"Oh, no!" Aimee exclaimed.

"What, honey?" cried Minnie.

"The mission, it's gone."

"Oh, sure. It's tore down. Wasn't safe anymore. They're gonna put a storage shed in there for the lumber company." Minnie pointed straight ahead. "It's *all* gonna be a lumber company. With the tracks going through there, so they can load it right off the trains."

"Progress," James muttered. "Faces change. People change." He spoke so softly it seemed he was talking to himself. "Never has been anything alive that hasn't changed. Nothing wrong with that."

"I know," said Aimee.

So even the mission is gone, she thought. How quickly everything changes and the bottom drops out of your life.

But—oh, God, she could hardly believe it—the marriage had been *seven years ago*. And today, riding through those streets, her girl friends all married no doubt, with their own houses and furniture and children, some of them with cars, too, and Aimee slinking home from a life of backslidden sin, her beautiful husband dead, her testimony for God slandered by her own life and an unholy, shipwrecked marriage. Indeed, she told herself, she had good cause for shame, and for relief, too, at arriving unseen at the farmhouse.

She did not stay there long, only a few weeks, long enough to walk under the apple trees and lilac bushes and back over the dirt road that led to the farthest pasture. She did not even stop to chat with George Quinn, twenty-five years old now, although she'd have liked to discover what kind of a man he'd grown to be. She imagined him handsome and thin. Come to think of it, his body would have been like Robert's, though he'd not have been as good-looking.

Still, she was determined to avoid questions about her life since Robert's death, so she did not see George Quinn. Besides, when she asked her mother about him, Minnie answered, "George Quinn? Why he's married to Gladys Wert. You know her. She's about seventeen now."

Short, chubby Gladys Wert, the ten-year-old who poured the punch at Aimee's wedding.

"What on earth would George Quinn see in her anyhow?" Aimee muttered, pouting.

One balmy afternoon two weeks after she arrived at the farm, Aimee sat on a pillow beneath the lilac bushes and rocked Rolf to sleep in her arms. Far away, along the path leading past the cornfields to the upper pasture, she could see James, slightly stooped, slowly leading Flossie along, Roberta, four years old now, gleefully clinging to the horse's back. Minnie had set up a folding table near the house and was working on a Sunday school lesson. Finally she sat back in the chair, gazed around, and mumbled, "It was right here."

"What?" asked Aimee.

"It was right here. This is the very spot you and Robert stood when you cut the wedding cake. I remember, because the window was right behind you, and Byron Jenvey was in there banging on the piano."

"I guess that's right."

Minnie laid the lesson books on the table, pushed herself up from the chair with a grunt, hobbled to Aimee's side, and sat beside her in the grass.

"Your mind's off somewheres, ain't it?" she said.

Aimee shrugged. "I just want to get going, get moving. I can't stand sitting around."

"It's the mail!" Minnie exclaimed with vehemence. "It's enough to make a saint like me stoop to swearing. I wrote Elizabeth Sharp three weeks ago, while you was still in Providence—it's only up there in Mount Forest, for goodness' sake. You could drive it in a motorcar in half a day! I'm telling you, I know Sister Sharp. Oh, she's got her faults—we all do. But putting things off ain't one of them. She'd've answered that letter the minute she got done reading it. That's her. And there'd've been no beating around the bush—she'd've said yes or no: send Aimee on up with a pocketful of sermons, or, 'Forget it, we got other plans.' It's the mail holding up her letter, I'm telling you."

Roberta came dashing from the barn exclaiming, "Granny, Granny! I rode the horse all by myself. I did—ask Grandpa!"

"That's wonderful—now don't go calling me Granny! I just hate it. Besides, I'm not old enough to be a Granny. Call me . . . call me Bonnie, why don't you? Yes, that's good. I always liked that name. Can you say Bonnie?"

"Bonnie."

Aimee laughed.

"What's so funny? From now on I'm Roberta's Bonnie—and Rolf's, too."

James limped back from the road, some envelopes in his hand, and in an instant Minnie was on her feet and lumbering across the lawn to tear the mail from him.

"Yup, here it is!" she exclaimed, attacking one of the envelopes. "And—praise the Lord, she says—here, listen: 'We have prayed for an evangelist. Perhaps Aimee Kennedy is the one. Will pay expenses plus twenty dollars. Set early date. In Christ, Sister Elizabeth Sharp."

"Hallelujah!" Aimee shouted, waking Rolf. She plopped him in the grass and, running to Minnie, embraced her. "I'll leave today!"

"Don't be so hasty. We'll write and tell her next week, give her time to get some interest going. You don't want to seem too anxious—she'll think you're just starting out."

Aimee cut the laughter short. "I *can't* wait, Mom—I want to get going."

"Now, you just do what your momma tells you, Aimee Kennedy," Minnie scolded, and Aimee tilted her head to indicate grudging agreement.

"But my name isn't Aimee Kennedy," she said firmly, "and when you write to Sister Sharp, you tell her so."

"All right, Aimee Semple."

"Aimee Semple McPherson, Mother."

Minnie shook her head. "Well, Aimee McPherson, then. The other's too long. People can't remember all that."

"Aimee Semple McPherson, Mother."

Minnie threw up her hands and turned to James. "How am I to put up with such a child as that?" she complained. "She's every bit as stubborn and pigheaded as . . . as—"

"As you are," James muttered.

Minnie lifted her eyebrows, pressed her lips tightly together. Then Roberta laughed. "As you are, Granny!" she announced.

"Now, don't go calling me Granny," Minnie fumed.

The train paused at the darkened depot of Mount Forest for a few seconds while Aimee, clutching a small suitcase, skipped down the steps to the platform; then it rumbled off into the forest and Aimee stood alone in the stillness. A moment later, she discerned a horse-drawn wagon moving toward her along the otherwise empty dirt lane that was apparently the town's main street. Finally the vehicle stopped before her, a robust man in his forties at the reins, and beside him a tall, thin, bustless woman the same age.

"Aimee Kennedy?" the woman asked, her voice shrill.

Aimee laughed. "That's what my mother keeps insisting," she said. "Actually, I'm Aimee Semple McPherson. And you're Sister Sharp. It's a *delight* to meet you."

The woman brightened. "My husband, Brother Percy."

Brother Percy took the suitcase and helped Aimee into the wagon.

The brief drive back to the Sharp home was punctuated by Elizabeth's shrill chatter: "Oh, it's not much of a town, I suppose, but we praise the Lord for it, don't we, Percy? To us it's as glorious a mission field as Africa or—well, even China—that's where you were, didn't your mother say? There's the general store, and next to that the barbershop, the—"

"She can see with her own two eyes," Percy mumbled, and Sister Sharp fell instantly silent.

She did not speak again until they reached the unpretentious brick building between the bank and the printshop. The sign above the door announced, "Faith Mission."

"That's it," she exclaimed. "That's the chapel you'll be preaching in tomorrow night."

Aimee felt a surge of excitement. "How many people does it hold?" she asked.

"How many?" Sister Sharp pondered. "How many would you say, Percy?"

"Fifty—seventy-five, maybe."

"Oh, you don't have to worry about that," Sister Sharp comforted. "We never get more than ten or twelve to a meeting."

"Ten or twelve?"

"Nothing to be scared about."

Aimee's face fell. Ten or twelve! Why, there were no doubt *hundreds* of starving souls in Mount Forest! But she said nothing. Only her firmly pressed lips betrayed her resolve.

The next evening at dusk, Aimee sat on the platform beside Elizabeth Sharp. Like lifeless shadows in the drab light of the gas lamps sat nine elderly women. Six or seven more folding chairs had been set up, but were empty. The rest of the room was barren.

"Might as well begin," said Sister Sharp, rising.

"No."

"Hmm?"

"No," Aimee repeated, rising. "Set up a couple dozen more chairs," she ordered, skipping down the steps of the platform and hurrying with long, angry strides toward the door. The nine elderly faithful gazed after her with widening eyes.

Sister Sharp's face turned ashen. "Where are you going?"

"Out into the *highways* and *byways*, Sister Sharp. Tell me—why is it so *dark* in here?"

"Well"—Sister Sharp's face reddened—"we're saving on the gas, you know."

" 'Let your light so *shine* before men that they may *see* your good works,' Sister Sharp, 'and glorify your *Father* which is in *heaven*.' Turn up the lights as bright as they'll *go*, and I'll *pay* you for the gas." Then, grasping one of the folding chairs, Aimee marched out.

The sidewalk was busy with after-dinner strollers. A few families rode by in wagons and carriages. Teen-agers bicycled past. Automobiles chugged along.

Striding to the center of the street, Aimee set the chair down and immediately climbed upon it. With eyes tightly closed, she lifted her face and hands toward heaven. Almost immediately the street grew silent.

She sensed the eyes staring at her. In another moment she heard the footsteps drawing near, rustling clothes as the crowd gathered around her. Someone whispered, "You think she's crazy?"

"Look at her face, how it glows. Maybe she's some kind of saint."

"Or an angel!"

"She's nuts, I'm telling ya!"

For a long while she stood unflinching, until her arms were so heavy she could hold them up no more. Then her eyes snapped open to reflect great excitement. Leaping from the chair she shouted:

"Quick! Follow me!"

Abandoning the chair in the middle of the street, she raced back into the chapel. Sister Sharp had been standing in the doorway, the nine faithful huddling behind her, a look of horror on their gray faces.

"When they get in here," Aimee whispered as she brushed past Sister Sharp, "lock the door and don't let a single one out."

Running to the platform, she assumed the same position she had taken in the street—except that now her eyes were fastened intently upon the ceiling above the door so that she could see when the last of the curious filed in.

Soon they filled every available seat, engulfing and filling with apprehension the nine faithful. Others took the folding chairs stacked against the rear wall and set them up haphazardly around the meeting room. Still others crowded along the walls. Finally, Sister Sharp slammed the door shut and, with a glance of trepidation at Aimee, bolted it.

"Oh, *hallelujah*!" Aimee shouted. The audience fell silent. "I have *prayed* for you," she continued. "Oh, how I have *stormed* the gates of *heaven* beseeching the Lord! 'O Father, give me *souls* for my hire,' I prayed. 'Bring them in from the highways and byways to hear Thy precious *Word*.'

"But you know, I'm just a helpless woman, folks. I ain't got me no bags of tricks. When Jesus wanted a crowd, all He had to do was walk on water. Well, I swim pretty good, but I haven't got that walking on water business yet. Besides, even if I *could* do it, you don't have any water around these parts to walk on."

The audience roared. She could feel them warming to her.

" 'God, we want these seats *filled* tonight,' I said. And what was His *answer*? Oh, God always answers prayer, you know. He said, 'Go outside and *pray* for them and you'll *get* them.' And that's just what I *did*! And here you are! Now, did you think for one minute when you got up this morning you'd be an answer to prayer today?"

There was no preliminary song service that night, no testimony, no offering. Swiftly, smoothly, Aimee maneuvered into her sermon. She walked to the front of the platform, hands folded like a Sunday school teacher, and told in intimate tones the stories from her childhood. Then, back behind the podium, the flow of her words increased in a loose but persistent rhythm; the preaching grew powerful, lavishly energetic, yet profoundly sincere.

Aimee's face took on a new radiance, and although her eyes gazed upward, she spoke to herself, to her own heart. Her tone carried the breath of passion and torment the words could never express. She swept along on a staccato rhythm, interrupting it to purr and whisper, then to resume the upward spiraling:

"Jesus was at the right hand of the Father, and Peter hastened to the Upper Room and tarried until the Holy Ghost was poured out on that great Day of Pentecost. Peter, he that had *denied the Christ*, speaking with other *tongues* as the Spirit gave him utterance, so filled with the Spirit that onlookers thought him *drunk* with *wine*! Hear the *shouts* and *praises* of the hundred and twenty! See the *multitude* come running *together*, *astonished*, *amazed*, in *doubt*, crying, 'What meaneth this?'

"Oh, it meant that the Holy Ghost had come, that the hundred

95

twenty, and Peter—blessed Peter!—had been embrued with *power* from on *high*, and were now able to stand *up* and *witness* with holy *boldness* of Jesus the *crucified*!

"It meant that out of their innermost being now flowed rivers of the *Spirit* that none could *check* nor *gainsay*!

" 'What meaneth this?' cried some. Others mocking said, 'These are filled with new wine.' But Peter, standing up, said, 'These are not drunk with wine, but this is that which was spoken by the prophet Joel.'

"Oh, *hallelujah*! Peter's standing up! Oh, what a change from the *cringing, cowardly, denying* Peter! This *new* Peter had received the *Holy Ghost*, and now, instead of fearing a little maid, he stood boldly before this scoffing, doubting *multitude* and boldly preached in the *Holy Ghost* of *Jesus*, while multitudes turned to the *Lord* and accepted Him as their *Saviour*."

Instantly she became a warrior, the Bible her sword, pointed straight into the faces of the audience. She confronted them unexpectedly and spoke, it seemed, to each individually.

"How are *you* measuring up, brother, sister? Have you received the *Holy Ghost* and spoken in *tongues* as Peter did of old? But don't just *stop* there. After Pentecost, Peter met the *lame* man at the gate and told him, 'Silver and gold have I none; but such as I have *give* I thee . . . *rise up and walk*!' See the *sick* being brought out from all the *villages* and *towns* round about, and when even the *shadow* of Peter fell upon them they were *healed*, *every one*.

"Behold Peter at *Samaria*, and at *Caesarea*, laying *hands* upon the *believers* in the one instance, and, while he was yet *preaching*, in the other, they received the *Holy Ghost* as had the hundred and twenty in the beginning. Follow Peter through his *imprisonments*, his *beatings* and *scourgings*, his *shame* and *reproach*.

"Follow him through his *courage* and *faith*, his *love* and life of *power*. Follow him to his *death* on the *cross*, crucified head *downward* because he felt unworthy to be crucified in the position of his *Lord*.

" *'Follow thou me?'* asks Jesus tonight. Say *yes* to Him, dear children! Follow Him to the *cross*, to the *grave*, to the *resurrection*, to the *upper room*, to the reception of the *Holy Ghost*—on to the gifts and fruits of the *Spirit*, perfect identification with Him in his *death* on the *cross*, and on to *meet* Him in the *air*!

> Following Jesus day by day.
> Nothing can harm while he leads the way.
> Sunshine or darkness, what e'er befall,
> Jesus, my Saviour, is my all in all."

The pianist began playing "Following Jesus." Aimee dropped her head and prayed: "O God, make us like *Peter*. Where we are ashamed, make us bold. Where we are impatient, teach us to tarry." Then, raising her hands high over her head, she shouted, "O *God*! Where we are empty, *fill* us with the Holy Spirit! *Fill us*, O God! We pray for the blessing. We wait on You for the blessing. *Baptize* with the *Spirit* tonight, and fill us with the *joy* of Your *salvation*!"

When she gave the invitation, tears were glistening in her eyes. First a boy of twelve walked solemnly down the aisle and knelt at the altar. Then a man, the boy's father, then two women, then an older lady, one of the nine elderly faithful, and before Aimee was through, eighteen people huddled at the tiny platform, some with heads bowed, but others beaming with overflowing happiness and gratitude. She closed her eyes.

"Oh, Lord, I'm so happy!" she whispered softly so that no one heard. "Thank you, Jesus. Thank you!"

Mrs. Sharp nudged her. "Don't forget the offering," she reminded.

"Tomorrow night, Mrs. Sharp. You needn't make a profit on the first turkey. Close the meeting, will you, please."

Word of the revival at Faith Mission spread quickly, and within a few days the crowd overflowed the small building. "I guess we'll have to buy that new tent," Mrs. Sharp half complained. There had been another tent, the one in which the faithful had first gathered before completing the brick edifice four months earlier. But that tent, said Mrs. Sharp, was old and torn. They'd need a new one.

"How much for the old one?" Aimee asked.

"Oh, it's no good. It's got to be repaired."

"How much?"

Mrs. Sharp pondered. "Well, I guess it's worth eighty dollars. But you should look at it first."

"I'll give you sixty dollars for it, sight unseen—just leave it in the bag," Aimee said.

Thus, Aimee bought a tent.

Sister Sharp's new tent, erected on the lawn beside her home, was thirty by sixty feet, with benches enough for more than one hundred people. Yet, as the meetings entered the final week, many stood in the rear and sat in the grass outside. It was more than Mrs. Sharp could comprehend.

"Why, they're coming from all over, far and wide," she told Aimee one night, just before the service began. "I must say, I never expected this."

"You must learn to expect the *uttermost*," Aimee said. "Christ says, 'Whatsoever ye ask in my name, *believing*—that will I give unto you.' "

The weeks had passed quickly, and the last meeting arrived much too soon for Aimee. That night she stood behind the tent, her stomach knotted, her breath coming rapidly. Brother Percy Sharp was leading the singing, and it sprang from the people, an anthem of victory and celebration.

"O God, O God!" she whispered. "I am swept by Your Spirit, I am Your vessel. *Fill* me, overwhelm me with Your *power*. Give the *blessing* tonight, I beseech you. Your *Spirit* is here, I feel Him! O God!"

"Lord, send the old-time power, the Pentecostal power," the people sang. "The floodgates of blessing on us, throw open wide!

"Lord, send the old-time power, the Pentecostal power—that sinners be converted and Thy Name glorified."

Aimee felt the quivering in her body. Her lips were moving, uttering sounds that weren't words. She felt overwhelmed, lifted somehow out of herself. And in the ecstasy of that moment, she swept into the tent singing:

> All self consume, all sin destroy! With earnest zeal endue
> Each waiting heart to work for Thee; Oh Lord, our faith renew.

Smiling magnificently, she ran up the steps to the platform, caught Brother Sharp's arm, shook his hand, cried, "God *bless* you!" skipped down the steps again, through the audience, continuing to cry, "God bless you!"—sometimes throwing kisses, placing her lips against the cheeks of old ladies, manfully shaking the hands of young men.

Then she turned, running down the aisle, up the steps of the platform just as the song ended.

"Praise God!" she shouted. "Is the Holy Spirit *here* tonight, brothers and sisters?"

"Amen!"

"Hallelujah!"

"Praise the sweet name of Jesus!"

"Precious Saviour!" shouted Sister Sharp, sitting with her mother in the first row.

"I *feel* Him here tonight, brothers and sisters!" sang Aimee, "in greater abundance than *ever before*. His *power* has flooded the whole *town*, dear children of God. People passing on the *street* out there are *stopping* in their *tracks, stunned* by the *power!* Walking over from the parsonage just a few seconds ago and hearing you sing with such *joy* and *rejoicing*, I was literally *swept away* by the *presence* of the *Spirit*. I stopped and prayed right there and thanked *God*—oh, how I *thanked* Him!—for *coming* to us tonight and for the chance to be here in this *meeting*. Now, Brother Sharp, lead us in this last verse—and, dear saints in Christ, let us sing it with *all our souls!*"

After the singing, Sister Sharp collected the offering. A sweet homely lady gave a testimony. Two boys performed a duet. Then the audience stood and sang a final hymn, and even before they were seated, Aimee swept to the pulpit and began preaching in a firm, clear voice.

That night she exhorted, scolded, told jokes and the tragic story of Robert's death, and she saw that every moment she held the audience to her. They laughed and wept at her command, and it seemed she had but to will it and she could evoke shouts of "Amen!" and "Hallelujah!" from every corner.

Finally, as the aura of expectancy grew and Aimee neared the end of her sermon, she lifted her hands high and began slowly, gracefully bending from side to side. "O Jesus! O sweet Jesus!" she said softly, smiling, filling with the same ecstacy she'd felt during the song service.

She heard a man's voice shouting syllables that were not words. Others began crying, praying aloud. When Aimee opened her eyes, the aisles were filled with people, some kneeling in prayer, others trembling, a few lying on the floor.

One woman cried, "God save me!"

Many had gathered around the platform.

"Pray for me, Sister Aimee!" one cried.

Quickly Aimee came down from the platform and clasped the hands of those who knelt at her feet, crying, "God bless you!"

She never officially adjourned the meeting that night. It continued another two hours, the people finally straggling out in twos and threes as the hour grew late. At last, only a handful of worshipers huddled on their knees at the altar, Aimee in the midst of them. And in the back row sat Harry McPherson, his arms folded across his chest.

When Aimee stood and saw the figure there, she guessed it was one of the townspeople who had lingered for counseling. She walked quickly toward him, then stopped, the perpetual smile vanishing. She clutched her throat, said, "Oh," then, "Mack! What on earth are you doing here?"

"Oh, just thought I'd take a little walk. Small world."

She smiled, then laughed. Straddling the bench in front of him, and folding her arms, she asked, "What did you think of the meeting?"

"I got converted."

She took his hand and held it for a moment, her eyes soft and searching. Then she placed his palm against her cheek.

"I missed you, Mack," she whispered, brushing her lips against his hand.

"Why didn't you come home?"

"You know. Can't you understand even now?"

"I said I got converted, didn't I?"

Aimee stared at him. "What do you mean?"

"Not to the religion bit. It's all right, I guess, but it don't do much for me. I decided we'll try it your way. I don't know how I'm gonna be able to look at myself in the mirror. I mean, 'What do you do for a living?' 'Oh, I'm a preacher's husband.' But you got something going for you—God, or guts, or something. Whatever it is, it's real. I'm not gonna try to squash it. I probably couldn't even if I tried. And another thing I know is I'm nuts about you. I love you more than anybody should ever love anybody, because it takes away my self-respect. It don't matter, I guess—it's too late now. I want you to come back home. We'll play it your way."

Her eyes reddened, and suddenly she was weeping. Mack quickly sat next to her and held her securely.

Later, Aimee insisted they walk along the darkened street and plan their future.

"We'll get jobs and work till spring and save every cent, and in the meanwhile we'll hold meetings all around Providence—oh, I bought a tent, by the way. And we can send out tons of letters and set up an itinerary all over the East Coast. Then in the spring we'll pack up and hit the sawdust trail—oh, it'll be so *exciting*, Mack! I'll take care of the planning, preaching, and publicity, you take care of the tent, song leading, and offering. You collect it, I'll spend it!"

"I don't know *how* to lead singing," Mack complained.

"It's easy. I'll teach you."

"You know how?"

Aimee shrugged. "I'll learn. Then I'll teach you." Before he spoke, she kissed him.

CHAPTER XII

The wind raced across Providence Channel north of Narragansett Bay with the low moan of baying hounds. Under the moon's glow it sent silvery gray clouds scudding and hurled foaming waves against rocky bluffs with a boom that seemed to Aimee like a continuing volley of thunder. She sat alone in the wet grass beside a small tent, her gaze turning alternately from the channel to the field where, a hundred feet away, a great tent shuddered in the wind's onslaught. If Mack were only here, she thought bitterly. But he had insisted upon sleeping at home so that he would be fresh for work at the factory. So, without his help, she had set her sleeping tent not far from where New York Avenue ended, and the others had erected theirs nearby, and in just a few hours a miniature city of tents took shape, one for dining, others for latrines, extending like spokes from the towering circus tent where she later preached.

Its center post now listed perilously under the wind's pounding. A few days earlier, dozens of those who had come to the camp meeting for fun and inspiration had helped unpack the sixty-dollar secondhand tent Aimee had bought in Mount Forest only to find it damaged beyond use. For two days they tied and stitched until, with fingers aching and blistered, they erected the forty-by-sixty-foot giant in the center of the field overlooking the channel.

"It's the most beautiful spot in the city!" Aimee had declared upon selecting it as the site for her first city-wide campaign earlier that summer of 1916.

"And the windiest, too," Mack had mumbled.

One by one, the others came out of their tents and watched in silence. Each time the wind swelled into the great tent its canvas panels heaved, then collapsed like the belly of a dinosaur. The center pole began trembling, then suddenly twisted, ripping stakes from the ground. Tied to the guy ropes and driven by the wind, the stakes noisily flagellated the canvas. Then like pistol shots the side poles crashed, and with a loud screech the canvas split from the center pole's peak to the ground. The belly of the shank burst in half. More stakes flew out of the dirt with loud pops. The ropes snapped. Torn remnants of frayed canvas tongues lapped the air.

"My God!" cried a young mother clutching her baby. "The center post's breaking!" She was still speaking when the pole's top half fell through the canvas and crashed onto the benches. Slowly, the remainder pirouetted and, wrapped in canvas, bowed to the ground.

For a moment, no one spoke. Then Aimee announced in a booming and cheerful voice, "Well, brothers and sisters, let's gather around my tent here and pray—thank God for *saving* us. We could all have been crushed like *bugs* if it had collapsed during the meeting! And then we'd all better get some sleep. The Lord's given us a job to do tomorrow."

"It'll take a lot more than work, sister," someone said.

"Yes, indeed, brother. It'll take a miracle. And we'll have one, don't you worry."

The next morning Aimee recruited twelve volunteers to set their tents up one beside the other like boxcars in a freight train. the flaps were overlapped so that, when the rain began that evening, Aimee preached in a leakproof tent 10 feet wide and 120 feet long.

One follower told her after the meeting that night, "Most of us would've just given up, you know. It was pretty discouraging."

"Maybe so," said Aimee, radiating a smile. "But you know, praise God, I only see the *sunshine*!"

So it seemed to those who knew her. From the day she and Mack had returned from Mount Forest, Aimee had hurled herself happily into the ministry. In nearby East Providence, she met Reuben and Christine Gibson, who had begun a small pentecostal mission called the Church of the Firstborn. The doors of the Gibson home, adjoining the church, were always open to travelers needing a place to stay, and eventually the house became known as Faith Home. The Gibsons were older than Aimee— Christine thirty-six and Reuben fifty-one—and more restrained, but they were captivated by her unflagging cheerfulness, and they welcomed her into their home and church with delight.

"People can't be around you long but they just get the fire," Christine said.

The Gibsons gave Aimee opportunities to preach in their little church, and later they took her to skid-row missions and street corner services, and eventually they were the ones who backed her camp meeting. Later that summer they recommended her to friends in Massachusetts, and, while Roberta stayed with Minnie at the farm and Momma Mac cared for Rolf, Aimee preached in Montwait and Onset Bay on Cape Cod.

The Gibsons did not arrange the meeting in Corona, New York, however. During the summer, Aimee received a mysterious letter from a Mrs. Marvel White in that town inviting her to come immediately and "let the revival fires fall." The following day, in a fluster of excitement, Aimee boarded the train for Corona.

"Marvel White?" she asked, standing in the dingy hallway of a Corona tenement, a suitcase in one hand, the letter from Marvel in the other. Before her a large dark-skinned woman in her early sixties rocked back and forth on her heels. Beneath the glaring hallway light bulb, the woman's white and thinning hair seemed almost nonexistent.

"That's me," said Marvel. "And you're Sister McPherson, ain't you?"

Aimee nodded.

"Just call me Mammy White, Sister. Come on in here now and just make yourself homely." The woman took the suitcase from Aimee and led her inside to a large, neatly furnished bedroom. "This here room's for you as long as you like," she said. "Just get yourself comfortable and I'll get some eats ready."

Half an hour later, over tea and homemade bread with blackberry jam, Marvel White said, "If ever there was a town that needed a Holy Ghost revival, this is it. And now, praise the Lord, we're gonna have it!"

"What's the seating capacity?" asked Aimee.

Marvel shrugged.

"Is it a church or what?"

"Honey, I don't know a thing about that. That's all between you and the Lord. You gotta work that out with Him."

Aimee set the teacup on the table. "You mean you don't have an auditorium lined up yet?" she asked.

"No sirree, honey." With an eye-twinkling smile, Marvel continued, "That's up to you and God. Now, what would I know about getting an auditorium?"

Aimee leaned back in the squeaky kitchen chair and pondered.

"Well, Mammy White, God will take care of it," she said finally. "No doubt we'll use one of the sponsoring churches."

Marvel White slapped the table with her thick hand and guffawed. "Oh, dear me, Sister," she said. "You got the wrong idea. There ain't no such a *thing* as a sponsoring church. I'm all there is, honey. If there was a *group*, we wouldn't need a revival, now, would we? Far's I know, I'm the only soul in Corona ever got the Holy Ghost."

"Then no one's made preparations for a meeting?"

"No preparations? Sister McPherson, I been praying for this here revival for two years, every single morning. Got it all prayed through now, and them revival clouds is gonna burst wide open when you start preaching the Gospel. All you gotta do is get the thing going. God'll take care of the rest."

For a long while Aimee sat with both elbows on the table, absently sipping tea and chomping bread, Marvel's big round eyes full of eagerness and apprehension.

Finally Marvel's face sank. "Sister, I know you're gonna say no. I shouldn't a let you think everything was all set up and hunky-dory. But if I'd've told you the truth, why, you'd never've come at all."

Aimee snapped out of her thoughts.

"Why, Mammy, that's not true, not at all! Of course I'd have come. I've been thinking how we could go about getting an auditorium and publicizing the meetings." Standing, she took Marvel's hand and led her to the dilapidated sofa in the corner.

"Here, kneel down—quick. We're gonna pray like we've never prayed before and—praise God—I feel it in the pit of my stomach, the excitement. We're going to claim this town for Christ! Someday, Mammy, when the great Book of Life is thrown open for all the world to read, there'll be an entry dated this very moment—dateline Corona, New York: Mammy White and Aimee Semple McPherson claim this town for Christ. *This* is the moment it began, the Spirit of God hovering *over* us and even now *moving* throughout the city to change eternal *destinies*."

Thus the two fervently prayed, and the next day Aimee made an agreement with the pastor of the Swedish Methodist Church to rent the building for a week of meetings. She mailed letters to the city's pastors and, with Marvel's help, painted posters and placed them in store windows throughout the city. She had fliers printed and the two women passed them out on street corners.

The local ministers promptly condemned her as a fanatic Holy Roller, and that more than Aimee's promotion efforts brought the curious to the small church in throngs every night. She began preaching the Baptism of the Holy Spirit, invited seekers to come to the altar where she placed her hands on them, praying for each so fervently that she trembled as she cried to God for the supreme blessing. Frequently the believer himself began trembling, often dropping to the floor and calling out to God.

One of these was a Sunday school teacher at the city's largest Protestant church. After Aimee touched him, he dropped to the floor trembling and speaking in tongues. His reputation for piety was so widespread that his experience was whispered in religious circles throughout the city. The next day, the wife of a leading citizen had a similar experience, and scores of people came to the altar for counseling. The day after that, "Three were slain under the power and came through speaking in tongues," Aimee said.

By the end of the first week, Aimee's meetings were the talk of the town. The pastors, following their parishioners' lead, came to support the meetings. Rev. W. K. Bouton of the First Baptist Church of Corona invited Aimee to move her meetings there, since crowds now overflowed the Swedish church.

For the first meeting in the new quarters, Mr. Bouton arranged to have on the platform theological dignitaries from throughout the area, including the pastors of Corona's most influential churches. During her sermon that night, Aimee turned to the preachers:

"Salvation is full and free," she said. "But there's a price to pay. We have to take a stand for Jesus. And that can be tough for anybody, but it's tougher still for a preacher. Can you imagine the incredible price a minister of the Gospel would have to pay if he discovered on a night like this that he had *never been saved at all*, never born again, washed in the precious blood of the lamb—if he had to admit to himself and to his congregation that he had never been baptized by the Holy Spirit as the Scriptures teach?"

When she gave the invitation that night, practically the whole congregation responded, including Mr. Bouton himself. People rose from their seats and flocked down the aisles, gathered around the chancel rail, overflowed the chancel, huddled at the pulpit, crowded in the aisles.

A crippled teen-age girl on crutches limped to the front.

"God can heal me," she said.

Aimee rushed to her side. "Praise *God* for you and your faith!" she shouted. "Brothers and sisters in the Lord, can God *heal*?"

"Amen!" came the chorus of shouts.

To the girl: "Do you believe God can heal?"

"Yes," the girl whispered.

"Then *tell* God. *Tell* Him so that we can all hear!"

"I believe!" croaked the girl.

"Can God *heal*?" Aimee shouted to the audience.

"Amen!"

"Can God *heal*?" Aimee aksed the girl.

"Amen!" echoed the girl.

"Will He heal you *tonight*?"

"Yes. Oh, yes!"

"O God! We pray for your *power*! Right this *moment*! *Heal* this girl. *Heal* her! Heal her *now*, O Lord. *Now*!"

Aimee grasped the girl's head in both her hands, abandoning herself to the feeling of power surging through her. The touch ignited in the girl flames of energy, and, with eyes closed and head forced back, she cried out, "I believe! O God, I *believe*!"

"Lift your hands to God and praise His *name*!" shouted Aimee.

The crutches fell. The girl lifted her hands upward, shouted, "Hallelujah!"

"Now turn to the back of the church and praise Him again!"

She did. "And now walk to the piano and praise Him! And now go to the pulpit and tell us your story!"

On the final day of the meetings, Mr. Bouton set up a table in front of the chancel and placed an open Bible on it. Then he told the overflowing crowd that Aimee had been given no honorarium whatever for the weeks she had spent in Corona, but the Lord had called her to Florida and to get there with the large new tent she had ordered would take a great deal of money.

"Let those who give do so as generously as possible," he challenged.

Even Aimee, who was learning to expect miracles, was astonished when she learned that the single offering had produced more than five hundred dollars. "Enough to get to Florida!" she exclaimed.

The campaign's success didn't impress Marvel White. Standing on the deteriorating front steps of her house in a tattered housedress the morning Aimee departed, she said, "You did a real good job, Sister McPherson. Sure did. Just like I expected. It had to work out. It was all prayed through, you know."

When Aimee stepped from the ship's gangplank onto the Jacksonville pier, Rolf in her arms and Mack at her side, she imagined she could hear

106

the trumpets of heaven blaring, as they had, no doubt, on that glorious day when St. Paul entered the gates of Rome to bring the Gospel of Christ to that pagan empire. It was a moment of eternal import, as when Luther tacked his ninety-five theses on the church door, or Joan of Arc rode into battle. For God she was invading a strange city, with no friends, no churches backing her, nowhere to lay her head, and the joy of it drove her to embrace Mack. He raised his eyebrows, examining her quizzically, finally kissing her nose.

While Mack arranged to have the tents temporarily stored, Aimee dashed off a flowery letter to Minnie describing Jacksonville as "a city of sparkling fountains and large hotels, of crimson poinsettias and flaming hibiscus—a city filled with tourists and peopled with throngs who have come to await the time when King Winter looses his icy grasp upon the North and East."

In the weeks before the campaign began, Mack frequently shook his head in wonder at Aimee's perpetual elation. When he smiled at her, his eyes reflected not only love but a touch of incredulity, for she was not only happy, as she had promised to be, but ceaselessly energetic.

Even the fact that their funds were utterly depleted didn't cause her particular concern. The money had been spent preparing for the campaign—renting a piano, lumber for benches, buying two hundred light bulbs and sockets and enough wire to circle the tent and brighten the interior, printing handbills and advertising the meetings.

Their poverty was a secret Aimee kept to herself, however, for she knew Mack would not have tolerated it. He had warned at the outset that he would play the vagabond, the handyman, any role she asked, for he loved her, but he would not permit his family to go hungry—rather he'd quit the sawdust trail in an instant and get a job. But the night before the meetings began, Aimee told Mack:

"We're going to have the best meetings—I just *know* it! But if God's to give us a real blessing, we've got to make some sort of sacrifice."

"You call sleeping in tents a luxury?" Mack grumbled.

"*That's* no sacrifice! Why, soldiers all over France are sleeping in tents this very minute—and in trenches and muddy fields and swamps as well—and getting shot at, too, no doubt, and some killed. And our own boys might end up there soon. If it weren't for the children, Harry McPherson might be drafted and sleeping there himself, and dodging bullets in the bargain."

In a more serious voice, Aimee said, "I know! Tomorrow we're going to make a *real* sacrifice. We're going to spend the whole day in prayer and fasting and passing out handbills."

"Are you kidding? I'm not going without food."

"God *wants* us to fast."

"Don't give me that stuff. I'm eating three good meals a day. You feel like fasting, fast. I don't feel like it."

Aimee said no more. A few minutes later, they slipped into the tent and Mack dozed on the cot while Aimee fanned her sunburned face with an old straw hat. Finally she extinguished the kerosene lamp and lay next to Mack. She nuzzled her cheek against his, then grasped his head with both hands and kissed him deeply.

"There's no food and there's no money, right?" he muttered. She said nothing.

"I guess you're right," said Mack. "God wants us to fast tomorrow. Damn—this is crazy." Then he, too, grew silent and embraced her. But before they slept that night he said:

"I'm getting a job tomorrow, you know."

Aimee kissed his lips. "All right, love," she whispered. "Just—please wait one day. God will take care of us by then. You'll see."

Late the next afternoon a horse-drawn truck creeped across the grass toward the little tent, the driver yelling, "Prepaid package for McPherson." It was a three-foot-square wooden box.

"Open it!" Aimee cried, and Mack ran for the hammer and screwdriver. Inside was a coat and some dresses, beneath them cans of corn, peas, salmon and a box of crackers, rolled oats, sugar, condensed milk, and smoked and salted pork and fish. The note at the bottom declared, "A love offering from your friends at Corona Baptist Church."

"O Lord!" cried Aimee. "It's a miracle. I *told* you! We get to eat after all! I'm so hungry I could eat a horse!"

Mack slammed the lid shut again and began hammering down the nails.

"Nothing doing," he announced. "This food was sent by the *devil* to get us to break our fast. Get thee behind us, Satan. We're taking this junk straight to the river and dumping it in before we yield to temptation."

"No, no—it's from God!" Aimee cried, giggling and wrestling for possession of the hammer while Rolf looked on in confusion. Digging her fingers into Mack's ribs, she made him laugh and release the tool.

"I'm starving!" she exclaimed, pulling the lid off the box again. "Get the can opener."

Aimee made it a point to gather the names and addresses of all those who participated in her meetings, from the tiny mission services in Providence to the campaigns in Massachusetts and Corona, and following the Jacksonville meetings she wrote a form letter to those few hundred friends summarizing the campaign's results:

"The tent meetings opened with a good attendance, and the crowds increased day after day. Practically every state in the Union was represented by the tourists who gathered at this place. The altar was, time after time, filled with seekers for salvation, the baptism and healing, and the Lord did not turn the hungry empty away.

"One brother spoke in Hebrew and a Hebrew scholar who was present heard and understood, Hallelujah! Two young men were healed, one of a broken arm, broken in three places, and dislocated at the wrist; the other a broken hand. Both removed the plaster and the splints before the audience, convincing everyone that they were made every whit whole. One sister was healed instantly of cancer."

The day they took the train from Jacksonville to Tampa, Aimee said, "Mack, it's really going to work. We're building a foundation, people care about us. Why, next year when we hit Jacksonville, just *scores* of people will help us and we won't ever again have to do all the work ourselves. Isn't it just grand?"

"Yeah," Mack said dryly. "We might all starve to death by next year if all we've got to count on is that miserable little box you stick in the back of the tent. At least you might take an offering once in a while."

Aimee frowned. "I don't believe in it," she said. "Robert never took an offering and I won't either. If God wants us on the road, He'll speak to their hearts and they'll drop their money in the box when they leave."

"Sure," Mack muttered.

"Sure!" Aimee exclaimed. Next to her on the seat was a bulging sack. "See this?" She elbowed it. "There's more than a thousand dollars in there."

Mack coughed once before regaining his composure.

"Where'd you get all that?"

"Oh," Aimee shrugged nonchalantly, "it just turned up in that miserable little box."

Tampa simmered with war talk when the McPhersons arrived in the winter of 1917. Aimee immediately prepared a new series of sermons on the "end times," choosing as her text Matthew 24:6–14:

And ye shall hear of wars and rumours of wars. See that ye be not troubled, for all these things must come to pass, but the end is not yet.

For nation shall rise against nation, and kingdom against kingdom, and there shall be famines, and pestilences, and earthquakes, in divers places.

All these are the beginning of sorrows.

Then shall they deliver you up to be afflicted, and shall kill you. And ye shall be hated of all nations for my name's sake.

And then shall many be offended, and shall betray one another, and shall hate one another.

And many false prophets shall rise, and shall deceive many.

And because iniquity shall abound, the love of many shall wax cold.

But he that shall endure unto the end, the same shall be saved.

And this gospel of the kingdom shall be preached in all the world for a witness unto all nations; and then shall the end come.

"We stand now at the *threshold* of the end times, the beginning of the *end*," said Aimee. "We are faced *daily* with *wars* and *rumors* of wars. Nations are rising against *nations*, kingdoms against *kingdoms. False prophets* sway the masses mightily, rallying under the banner of Satan's own archangel, Charles *Darwin*, and through the false religion of *science* deceiving many.

"Yet, according to His own promise in the Scriptures, Christ cannot return to set this sin-swept world free until 'this gospel of the kingdom shall be preached in *all the world* for a witness unto all nations.' Only then, we are told, 'shall the end come.'"

The attendance was not phenomenal, but the income was good, and after three weeks in Tampa, Aimee sent out another batch of letters explaining, "The Lord has given us a Gospel Automobile, with which we are able to hold eight or ten meetings a day, distributing thousands of tracts and handbills, and carrying big display signs of the tent meetings."

From Tampa, they drove in their 1912 Packard to the small town of Durant, then to St. Petersburg. Later, Aimee wrote: "Just a shout of victory from St. Petersburg, Fla., this wicked city where Pentecost has never been preached.

"A great celebration was on when our meetings opened. People played cards and gambled on tables by the sidewalk; the streets beside the park and city hall were roped off at night for dancing, and as the band played the people danced in masks and fancy costumes on the public streets.

"Our snow-white tent, though comfortably situated, and decorated with palms and flowers to make it attractive, was but a poor inducement for such a worldly throng. Standing on the street, giving out hand bills and tracts, I looked at the long line of automobiles and conveyances streaming by in the parades. This week was something in the nature of a Mardi-Gras and the cars were decorated to represent the state or business of the owner.

"Suddenly the Lord spoke to me and said: 'Decorate your car and join the parade.' At first this looked impossible. Surely the decorations must cost an enormous sum of money. But the Lord showed me how it could be done. We built a wooden frame just the shape of a tent; then taking a white sheet (which was one of the luxuries of our camp life) we made of it a miniature tent, stretching it over said frame, using cord for guy ropes, and large nails for stakes. On one side of the miniature tent we painted the words:

"'Jesus is coming soon'; on the other side—

"'I am going to the Pentecostal camp meeting. Are you?'

"Putting down the top of the Gospel Auto, the miniature tent, some seven feet long, five feet wide, was lifted up and set over the car so as just to leave room for the driver. The car was also decorated with palms and wild flowers, which we gathered by the way, tied with tissue streamers.

"Concealing a baby organ under the tent, I sat beneath it out of sight of the crowd, and the Lord shut the policeman's eyes so that we could slip into the grand parade of cars and go the full length of Main Street with our advertisement. We *must* get an audience to our tent meeting, even if we had to sail forth with flying colors into the territory of the enemy to advertise our soul-saving business.

"Early next morning we got in line with the other cars. The brass bands were going by; the liquor man advertised his business, the telephone, the wheat man and the florist; the butcher, the baker, the tourists representing their different states—all were there, having entered and listed their cars. When it came our turn to slip in, the policeman's back was turned, and he was motioning behind his back for us to come on, and holding back traffic from the other direction with his hand, so in we went. We were far enough behind the bands so that our little baby organ and chimes could be heard distinctly, playing 'Just as I am, without one plea, but that Thy blood, was shed for me,' and other familiar hymns such as 'Oh, get ready, oh, get ready, for the judgment day.'

"Thousands of people lined either side of the long street, leaning out of their windows, standing on the roofs—and after the first astonished stare the people began to laugh, and clap their hands and cheer, and that night the tent was packed, and we had no more trouble getting crowds. Sinners were saved, believers baptized. The Salvation Army closed their doors and came in to work with us, bringing their drum and musical instruments."

In March, Aimee, Mack, and Rolf started north to Savannah. The day they reached the city, April 6, the United States declared war on Germany and an instant and cheerful fervor swept the country, with millions volunteering to help in the war effort. Some collected peach pits, used to manufacture gas masks. Others aided in the hospitals, sold Liberty bonds, made bandages, sent sons to fight. From 7 A.M. to 7 P.M. on June 5, 1917, 10 million boys enlisted in the armed forces, and women replaced them in the factories.

Sitting on the front lawn under the maple tree at the farm in Salford, casually knitting a scarf for winter, Minnie Kennedy philosophized in a letter to Aimee, "Some people will kill themselves to keep from being bored." Thus she explained the cause of all wars to her own satisfaction.

Young boys and girls, armed with sticks and toy guns, played Kill the Germans in corner lots. Their parents, who had not gone off to war, played their own games with the 2 million German-Americans living in the United States. Workingmen with German names were fired from their jobs or made to crawl across the floor and kiss the American flag. Others, accused of disloyalty, were publicly flogged or tarred and feathered. In southern Illinois, an angry mob lynched a German-American child.

Books by German authors were removed from library shelves. Orchestra conductors, in fear of reprisal, refused to play works by Beethoven and Mozart. Citizen groups zealously competed in finding Germanic influences in the culture, then exposing them and demanding their removal. German measles became Liberty measles, hamburger became Liberty steak, sauerkraut was changed to Liberty cabbage, dachshunds to Liberty pups. Cincinnati banned pretzels because they had originated in Germany. And in Canada, the town of Berlin, where Aimee and Robert had once preached, officially changed its name to Kitchener.

The government lauded as patriotism even the most excessive zealousness, and contributed generously to the game. Anyone convicted of saying anything "disloyal, profane, scurrilous, or abusive" about the government or the war effort could be fined ten thousand dollars and sent to jail for twenty years. Later, a court decision broadened that law to forbid any historian from disagreeing with the official view that Germany was entirely responsible for causing the war.

About six thousand people were arrested under the new law, and fifteen hundred were convicted and sentenced. Many had merely criticized the Red Cross or the YMCA. Minnie Kennedy considered writing to Washington demanding the Salvation Army be included in the list of nonslanderable institutions.

In Savannah, Aimee purchased four huge American flags and situated them prominently on the platform at all times, two crossed directly behind her and the other two posted like sentinels at the rear corners. "We're not in heaven *yet*," she shouted to the audience, "but we're in *America*—and that's the next best thing!" Such words never failed to produce a standing ovation, and Aimee, catching the fire, would shout, "Praise *God* for this great land of ours! Oh, hallelujah! Are you proud to be an *American*? Let me hear you say *Amen*!"

"Amen! Amen!" the frenzied cry rose throughout the tent.

Before leaving the city, Aimee met F. A. Hess, a Christian printer who agreed to publish her sporadic letters free if she supplied the paper. It would be a newsletter, and Aimee decided to name it "The Bridal Call," after the scriptural metaphor of Christ, the groom, returning on the Last Day for His bride the Church. Of the three thousand she'd have printed, about a third would go to those on her mailing list. The remainder she'd distribute free at meetings, send to pastors who had churches in the backwoods country where an evangelistic team could not possibly go. In that way, she would promote the Pentecostal Gospel in areas no other missionary had ever reached.

"Oh, Mack, isn't it exciting!" she exclaimed, bouncing on her cot with glee their last night in Savannah. "It's really working out. We're *going* somewhere!" A moment later she was soundly asleep.

CHAPTER XIII

That spring of 1917, the trio followed the warm weather north, meandering through the Carolinas, Kentucky, Virginia, Maryland, Delaware. Aimee decided schedules on impulse and altered them as quickly. If attendance at a particular meeting was running high, she'd stay a few days longer; if disappointing—or if she simply grew bored—she'd immediately pull up stakes and move on.

With equal capriciousness she determined the itinerary. A road sign indicating the name of a nearby town might catch her eye and she would exclaim "Mack, turn there—God wants me to preach in that town!" The detour would delay them days, even weeks, but it was just that sense of freedom that made them both eminently happy. She would get there in her own good time, generate the promotion herself, organize church support on the spot or do without. And she would preach until her voice was hoarse—on street corners, in churches and missions, city hall steps, and finally to an ever-increasing crowd under her canvas tent.

Sometimes her reasons for choosing a particular city for a campaign made no sense at all to Mack. In Delaware, pondering her next destination, Aimee read a full-page newspaper advertisement with the headline: "Don't Fail To Go To Long Branch, N.J." Tearing out the page, she enthusiastically held it up to Mack.

"It's a sign from God!" she exclaimed. "Here's where He wants us!"

"You're nuts," he told her. But he shipped the tent, packed the Gospel Auto, and in a few hours they were on their way.

With the car's roof folded down and Aimee's hair whipping in the wind, the car bounced along, its squeaks and pings a staccato counterpoint to the gospel songs Rolf and Aimee perpetually sang. On occasion, even Mack joined in, his voice squeezing from one side of his mouth while he chewed the cigar in the other.

Frequently they spent their last pennies on gasoline; then they would live off the land, Mack catching fish and Aimee helping herself to a few ears of corn from a farmer's field and apples from his orchard. She would explain to Mack, who desired no explanation:

"It's not stealing, you know. God had him plant extra so we'd have something to eat." And when Mack laughed she'd fume, "Don't you think God has the brains to plan ahead?"

They cooked meals by the side of the road on a portable stove, and if there was enough for them, Aimee would insist there was also sufficient for the occasional vagabond who wandered by. At night they'd erect their tiny tent wherever they happened to be when it became too dark to continue—on picturesque mountaintops, windy plains, riverbanks, city lots.

In Framingham, Massachusetts, Aimee contracted with the Christian Workers' Union to print five thousand copies of "The Bridal Call" each month, with responsibility for layout, proofreading, and mailing. To pay the cost, she sold annual subscriptions for twenty-five cents at each meeting. While Mack drove, she wrote the copy for each issue, prepared sermons, designed promotional handbills for future meetings, sketched posters. For the Washburn, Maine, camp meeting she even wrote a skit about the five wise virgins and the five foolish ones.

The Boston campaign that summer started out a raucous celebration, but after the second night teen-age gangs in the area disrupted the meetings with jeers and heckling. Mack called the police, but the chief himself, a proper Bostonian with a distaste for emotional religion, publicly refused to provide police protection. Two days later he dropped dead of a heart attack, and Aimee cheerfully explained to the city's press that God had gotten fed up with the man and had recalled him. As she later explained to her "Bridal Call" readers, "Thereafter we had three men stationed by the tent at every meeting and perfect order."

The Boston campaign was so successful that Mack and Aimee bought a truck to transport the tents and hired a handyman to drive it and assist Mack. When autumn approached and they started south again, the two-vehicle caravan grew to three and four and more as Aimee accumulated temporary disciples who, with nothing better to do, meandered along from meeting to meeting to help witness and pass out tracts.

On one side of the Packard, the Gospel Auto, Aimee painted in large gold letters the words "Jesus Is Coming Soon!" and on the other side, "Where Will You Spend Eternity?" From some of the cars she hung colorful streamers, and on others she tied cloth signs. Thus, with some of her followers standing on the seats playing trumpets and pounding drums and tambourines, others bellowing gospel choruses, the Gospel Caravan puttered south, first through New York City, then Philadelphia, Maryland, Virginia, North and South Carolina, Georgia, and at last to Jacksonville again.

Along the main street of virtually every small town in their path Aimee led the Gospel Caravan, bringing it to a halt at a bustling intersection, where crowds promptly gathered. There, standing on the hood or seat of the Gospel Auto, first one and then another of the travelers gave testimonies while the others passed out tracts by the hundreds. Finally, when the crowd was sufficiently large, Aimee herself would step to the improvised platform with Rolf at her side and preach a brief sermon.

Afterward she would say, "We've learned in these last two years, traveling thousands of miles and, like the Lord Himself, not knowing where we would lay our heads at night, often not knowing where our next meal would come from—we've learned to trust God because He's *promised* in His Word to provide all of our needs abundantly above all that we could ever ask for or think. And He has not *failed* us! No, not once! Rolf, have you ever starved to death?"

The boy smiled broadly as his mother had taught him, only the slight twitching at the corners of his mouth hinting at his embarrassment. He did not like to speak loudly, preferred not to speak at all, even in small groups, but still he opened his mouth wide and shouted, "Praise God! Jesus meets all our needs every day!"

Aimee would smile at him, saying, "Go down where our friends can meet you." As Rolf stood quietly, people would lift him in their arms, kiss him on the forehead, cheeks, lips, squeeze him, bless him, and press money into his hands and pockets.

By five o'clock the sky was overcast, and by six the rain poured down in such great sheets that Mack slowed the Gospel Auto to a crawl. They had stopped to raise the canvas roof and lower the side flaps, but through months of constant use the seams had split, the canvas had cracked, and now water trickled onto the three of them in the front seat and the innumerable packages of literature in the rear. Leaning over the seat, Aimee struggled to cover the boxes of tracts and newsletters and Gospels of St. John with old blankets.

"It's just *awful*," she cried. "Everything's going to be ruined. If you'd have let the others come we could've put it all in their cars and it would be safe now."

"They were eating us into the poorhouse. Why didn't you send that junk on in the truck like I told you?"

"I'm passing it out on the *way*!" Aimee shouted.

Mack shook his head. "At least we should've kept the cots and sleeping tents," he mumbled, his attention riveted to the windshield where, with pathetic irregularity, the flimsy wiper gave him an instant's view of the road ahead.

"I needed every spare inch for the literature."

"Well, that's great. Only where do we sleep?" he asked. "Or are you getting bighearted these days, planning to rent a hotel room?"

"We'll sleep in the car, or by the side of the road. What do we need a tent for? It's warm out."

"Just like a bunch of bums. That's just great. I can't even provide a roof over my kid's head anymore."

"That's exactly what I would *expect* to hear from you," said Aimee, her eyes bright in anger. "That's all anybody ever hears from Harry McPherson lately. 'I need food. I need a house. I need money.' Jesus never complained about material things. Remember, it was He who said, 'The foxes have holes, and the birds of the air have nests; but the Son of Man hath not where to lay His head.' You are drowning in the Sea of the Here and Now."

"Yeah, yeah, yeah," said Mack. "I bet Jesus never tried sleeping in a soaking wet Packard with his knees in his guts and a pile of St. John Gospels jabbing him in the ribs."

For three more hours they crept through the blinding storm, the rain soaking all three of them, Mack periodically exploding in angry outbursts. Finally, pointing to a small railroad station near the roadside, Aimee exclaimed, "Stop there!"

Mack swerved the car off the road and stopped.

"No, right up there on the platform, under the overhang."

"It's against the law to park there."

"I'm not going to have those tracts *ruined*!" Aimee shouted.

"Okay. It's all right with me. You think I care if I get thrown in jail? Not on your life. It's about time I got a good night's sleep anyway. This is so stupid I can't even believe it. One night I'm sleeping in the car, next in a field, on the beach, now in a railroad station. A good night's sleep in a nice warm jail—that's the best thing I heard of in a year. But if we get a ticket, that's your baby. You got all the money and you're gonna pay it."

"Oh, shut up."

It was already growing dark when, their clothes sopping, they scrambled out of the car. While Aimee dried the literature with the remaining blankets, Mack carried the suitcase and Rolf into the empty station house, and dressed the child in warm garments that included a bulky sweater of Aimee's which, even with sleeves rolled up, hid his hands and reached almost to his feet.

"That should keep you pretty snug," said Mack, seating Rolf on the bench while he slipped out of his own sopping trousers.

Later, Mack brought the portable stove from the car trunk and, using rainwater, made some tea. Then, although it was still early, Rolf and Mack huddled together on one of the hard oak benches and, to the hypnotic rhythm of the falling rain, drifted into shivering, sporadic sleep.

Aimee stretched out on another bench, but she slept little that night. Wide awake, she heard the far-off rumble of each approaching freight, felt the building itself begin to vibrate, cringed as the train thundered past.

Long after the sound died away, she stared at the ceiling where the stark streetlamp outside glimmered through the rain and grime on the windows. Her mind leaped speedily from thought to thought; she planned sermons, outlined articles for "The Bridal Call," conceived a skit and a few schemes for generating free publicity at the Miami campaign.

Lately she had thought of little but the ministry. Sleep had become superfluous, eating a necessary nuisance. Even conversations with Mack had centered exclusively on the campaigns.

What a foolish mistake to imagine she could ever have been happy with him, the cigar-chomping little man obsessed with food and sex and money and all the creature comforts, with no real burden for the lost and perishing in sin. What joy it would be to once again share so sacred a calling with a man of Robert's zeal! Mack had become a burden to her. He no longer led the singing, for now Aimee sought handsome and personable young men from local churches to do that. And now that they'd hired a handyman, he was deadweight in that respect, too, frequently spending the day fishing or entertaining himself in the nearest town.

What's more, it seemed to Aimee that, as Mack became less useful, he grew more ill tempered and demanding. When she told him in Tampa, "Don't forget, get a dozen light bulbs," he snapped back, "Get them yourself—who do you think you're ordering around? Maybe you're the big-mouthed preacher, but I'm still the boss in this family, and don't forget it!"

The following night in a field beside a river near Orlando, Mack gathered wood and built a lean-to against two palm trees, making beds of grass and burlap. When it was finished, he strung together palm branches to resemble a Christmas tree, and planted it in the dirt. Later, sitting in front of the lean-to, he watched Aimee and the boy happily scour the roadside for unusual pebbles. Across the highway colored lights sparkled in houses and wreaths decorated the doors. He would be twenty-eight this year. A grown man, lost in the reverie of childhood Christmases, too old for that sort of thing, much too old for the crazy life of a holy hobo.

He watched the boy play, running in circles around his mother, laughing, racing down to the water and splashing in it, scooping it into his hands and running back to splash it on Aimee. It occurred to Mack that Rolf was a happy child. Sleeping in the front seat of the car or under the stars or in a railroad station or a fisherman's hut or on the beach was a continuing adventure, and if he cried because he awoke hungry in the morning, he laughed and was the freest of children all day.

Later, Mack wandered along the road gathering discarded Moxie and Coca-Cola and beer bottles in a burlap sack until finally, after an hour, he had a burgeoning sackful. He took them to a nearby bar, collected the deposits, then went to a five-and-ten-cent store and bought Rolf a balsa wood glider, an inexpensive wooden boat, and some balloons. That night, while Aimee and the boy slept, Mack wrapped the gifts in newspaper and tied them with fiber he had stripped from one of the palm trees supporting the lean-to. He placed them under the tree he'd made.

When he finished, he could not sleep, so he walked in the darkness along the river watching the white water churn over the rocks in the moonlight, staring into the water until the waves made the only sound, until all the traffic on the highway had ceased.

In the morning, when a strip of blue crossed the horizon, he dug some hooks from his travel sack, fashioned a pole from a stick he had found on the beach, dug up some worms, and went fishing. Soon he caught a large freshwater bass. On the way to the campsite he passed a duck's nest and stole the eggs. Aimee and Rolf awakened to the smell of the cooking food.

The morning was pleasant, and after Rolf opened the gifts Aimee gave the boy two packages and Mack one. Rolf was disappointed with the trousers, but liked the coloring book. Mack appreciated the handkerchiefs and socks.

"I feel lousy about not getting you anything," he told Aimee. "There wasn't any money."

"I know," she said. "You got us breakfast and cooked it. That was enough. I appreciate it."

Later in the day the sky darkened and the rain fell again. It beat down on the makeshift roof like relentless thunder, flowed down the lean-to sides and splashed in the open end. The ditch Mack had dug around the lean-to overflowed and the water flooded the grass beds. Aimee and Mack sat facing each other on empty crates while Rolf played in the Gospel Auto.

"For God's sake, Aimee, let's go back home," Mack shouted above the noise of the rain.

"Let's go back! Let's go back!" Aimee screamed savagely. "That's all I ever hear from you!" She jumped up, slipped in the mud but regained her balance. "I'm not *ever* going back. I've told you that a hundred times, and I'm sick of talking about it. *I'm not ever going back!*"

Mack sauntered to the edge of the lean-to and stood so the water cascaded against his forehead and ran down his cheeks. He tilted his head back slightly and puffed out his lower lip. The water flowed into his mouth, gurgling there and gushing out again. He whistled and watched the water squirt out as though from a whale's spout.

"We're broke, Aimee," he said. "There ain't no food, no money to buy food, nobody to borrow any money from. It's time the kid went to school soon. Instead he's living like a gypsy, hand to mouth. What kind of a life is that for any of us?" His voice dropped so that Aimee missed some of his words, but then he exclaimed, "I've had enough, Aimee. I'm just fed up. I think I'd rather die than to go on like this much longer."

Aimee came very close to him, her eyes flashing, "I've made a lot of dumb mistakes in my life," she snarled, "but the dumbest of all was marrying you. If you'd become a Christian and take the blinders off and see things as they really are, then maybe there'd be a chance for us. Then you'd understand. But as it is, you're so wrapped up in the things of this world you can't see beyond the tip of your nose.

"I'm doing what God has *called* me to do and that's all there is to it. You're going to have to *bend*."

"I'm going to have to bend, huh?" Mack dropped into the soggy burlap bed, locked his hands behind his neck, and stared at the canvas roof above his head. "Aimee," he shouted so that she could hear him, "I *have* bent. I bent so far I think I've cracked. In fact, I know I have. I'm broken—right straight down the middle. I'm a mess, and I can't stand to look at myself in the mirror. I wonder sometimes if I'll ever be any different."

"God's going to go right on breaking you until you surrender to Him," said Aimee.

"We're not going to Miami."

"We are so."

"We're going back to Providence."

"I'm going where I *want*. And *my* tents and *my* car and *my* son are going where I want, too."

"Well, then, you pack *your* tents and you drive *your* car and you run your show all by yourself, because Harry McPherson is through."

He slipped into a pair of boots, stepped out of the tent, and went for a walk in the rain.

The next morning, Mack grabbed his fishing pole and shuffled along the river until he came upon an old pier. Lighting his cigar, he dropped his line betwen the rotting slime-covered piles and sat down to wait patiently for the fish to bite. By noon, although he'd caught no fish, he'd relaxed sufficiently to think of Aimee again, and then an ache grew in his stomach. Dropping the pole, he ran across the pier to the grass and then beside the river until he was breathless. Then he walked, then ran again until he reached the lean-to.

The Gospel Auto was gone, along with the stove and blankets.

His belly seemed hollow with loneliness and he felt as though he'd been left to die in this bleak, miserable field. She'd left him without a cent, so that night he slept beside his box of clothes under the lean-to. Early the next morning a taxi stopped on the highway and the driver trudged across the grass to the lean-to. He handed Mack an envelope from Aimee. It contained fifty dollars.

PART III

CHAPTER XIV

During the night, moisture had condensed on the windowpanes of the flat in New York City, freezing into crystal clusters, and now, morning sunlight sparkled through them in multicolored prisms. Roberta stared with large eyes at the patterns and scratched her name in them with the edge of her fingernail.

Minnie buzzed from closets to bedroom, humming hymns while she packed the suitcases. On the kitchen table lay the telegram from Aimee: "Mack and I have separated. Ministry growing and God blessing gloriously. I will never give up. Desperately—desperately—need help. Mother, please come. Please. Please. Your loving little girl, Aimee Elizabeth."

"You're a lucky little girl!" Minnie told Roberta, now seven years old, with long chestnut hair which Minnie brushed a hundred strokes every night. "You and me're gonna see Mommy and little Rolf!"

"And Daddy Mack!" cried Roberta.

"No, not Daddy Mack."

"I *want* to see Daddy Mack," Roberta pouted.

"You *don't* want to see him. But we're gonna go all the way to Florida where there's no snow and everything's just warm and toasty all the time. You'll be happy as a lark."

The train lumbered to a stop at the Miami depot in an ear-splitting blast of steam, and a moment later Aimee saw Roberta leap from the steps and dash across the platform toward her. Sweeping the girl into her arms, she spun her around and around, the two of them exchanging giggly kisses.

"Where's Grandma?"

"Bonnie," Roberta corrected. "She'll get mad as anything if you say Grandma. There she is!"

Setting Roberta down, Aimee ran toward the train.

"Mom! Over here!"

"So how much money's left?" Minnie asked after a brief embrace.

"You're going to be amazed—the meetings are just *marvelous*!"

Taking the travel case from her, Aimee hurried toward the Packard while the others scurried to keep up.

"What about my luggage?"

"We'll get it later—I have a meeting at noon."

A moment later, the Packard whirled away from the station and careened through downtown Miami with horn blaring. An old man in tattered clothes stumbled off the curb and Aimee swerved and screeched to a stop.

"Go ahead, get yourself killed," she bellowed. "But don't complain afterward—it's your own fault!"

An instant later the car leaped forward. Aimee spun the wheel into a left turn, cutting off traffic from three directions.

"Sweet Jesus!" Minnie exclaimed, her pudgy arms embracing Roberta. "For this I came all the way to Miami—to die in a motorcar with a madwoman? *Slow down!*"

Aimee grudgingly obeyed.

"You think if you scare the daylights out of me I'll forget you didn't answer me about the money. Well, I won't—how much is there?"

They had already fled the downtown and were approaching a flat, grassy stretch. Aimee pointed. "See—that's our tent! Oh, Mom, you're in for the greatest blessing of your *life*! The crowds aren't big—just a few hundred—we had five times that many in Boston. But oh, the *spirit!*"

"You're flat busted, right? Why don't you just spit it out and get it over with."

Aimee gave her a sheepish sideward glance and thereafter concentrated rigidly on the road ahead.

When in a swirl of dust the Packard skidded to a halt near the big tent, Minnie gave Roberta an affectionate hug. "Now, run along and find something useful to do—take up an offering or something. Go find Rolf. Your mom and I got some talking to do."

Aimee rose. "Later, Mom," she said. "The meeting's going to start any minute."

125

Minnie grasped her arm. "Sit," she ordered. "They can sing without you being there. Now, what I want to know is, how could you be having meetings in Miami, and all the rich people coming down to keep warm through the winter and some of them showing up at your meetings, no doubt, and still be broke."

Aimee sighed in resignation. She gestured toward the tent.

"They're almost all colored folks. I started out preaching to the whites, and one day I asked one of the pastors why Negroes weren't coming—they're all over the place. Well, that old fellow nearly dropped dead! Down here they don't *allow* Negroes at the white people's meetings—did you ever hear such a thing?

" 'You may not realize it, buster,' I told him, 'but God's color-blind—a soul's a soul, and the colored folks are as hungry for the things of the spirit as the white folks.' He wouldn't listen, so I just closed the white meetings and the next day I put up the tent in the colored section, and I've been having the most *glorious*, spirit-filled meetings ever since—and a few whites have even been coming, too."

"But the Negroes don't have money, and that's why you're broke."

Aimee's face brightened in assent, but Minnie's pursed lips silenced her.

"You go and preach a good sermon, Aimee Elizabeth, for it'll be your last on this spot," said Minnie. "My Lord, girl! It's a *sin* to be wasting yourself like this!" She reached into her travel bag and withdrew a well-worn black leather Bible. In seconds she had it opened to Matthew 25:14.

"Now, listen to this," she ordered: " 'For the kingdom of heaven is as a man traveling into a far country, who called his own servants, and delivered unto them his goods. And unto one he gave five talents, to another two, and to another one; to every man according to his several ability; and straightway took his journey.

" 'Then he that had received the five talents went and traded with the same, and made them another five talents. And likewise he that had received two, he also gained another two. But he that had received one went and digged in the earth, and hid his lord's money.

" 'After a long time the lord of those servants cometh, and reckoneth with them. And so he that had received five talents came and brought another five talents. His lord said unto him, "Well done, thou good and faithful servant: thou hast been faithful over a few things, I will make thee ruler over many things: enter thou into the joy of thy lord." ' "

Lifting her eyes from the page, Minnie glared at her daughter. "And it was the same with the second servant—the Lord just adored him. But then the last servant piped up and said"—she found her place in the Bible—" ' "I was afraid, and went and hid thy talent in the earth: lo, there thou hast what is thine."

" 'His lord answered and said unto him, "Thou wicked and slothful servant, thou knewest that I reap where I sowed not, and gather where I have not strawed. . . . Take therefore the talent from him, and give it unto him which hath ten talents. For unto every one that hath shall be *given*, and he shall have *abundance*; but from him that hath *not* shall be taken away even that which he *hath*. And cast ye the unprofitable servant into outer darkness: there shall be weeping and gnashing of teeth." '

"Now, that's *Jesus* talking!"

Opening the car door, Aimee said, "Mom, I've got to go."

But Minnie gripped her arm. "Ain't you ever read a single word of John Calvin's? Child, it's a *sin* to be poor. Why, if you're broke, you're living in sin this very minute, and there ain't no two ways about it!"

Aimee's eyes flashed anger, but before she could speak Minnie patted her arm, placating.

"Now, don't go worrying about it—God don't hold you responsible for what you don't know. But I'm here to help you now, Aimee Semple McPherson, and we're making an agreement right from the start, right this minute, or you can turn this Tin Lizzy right around and get me back to the train station. And here's what we're gonna agree to: First, you do the preaching and writing your 'Bridal Call' thing and the publicity stunts—that kind of stuff. And I decide where you go, what meetings you take and what meetings you *don't* take. I handle the income and the outgo—all the business. Now, it's yes or no."

While Minnie continued her chatter, Aimee with troubled eyes stared across the field, her lips pressed together. From the tent came the sound of strong, harmonizing voices, the words: "I can hear my Saviour calling . . . Where he leads me, I will follow . . . I'll go with Him, with Him, all the way." Finally she turned to Minnie.

"No," she said, interrupting her mother.

"What?"

Aimee stepped out of the car and started toward the tent.

"Aimee Elizabeth, you come back here!"

"Your train doesn't leave till two," Aimee called. Then, smiling, she turned and walked back to the car. "Mom," she said, "I don't know how I can go on by myself, but I'm gonna try and maybe God will give me the strength. You see, right *here*, right this *minute*, I have something special,

127

something few people ever have—a feeling that *this* is exactly what I should be doing, and it makes me, if not happy, then certainly content. *Yes!* Content with that miserable old tent and going without food now and then and fixing my own flat tires and being heckled and mocked by the nonbelievers and rejected by the bigots and even the pastors. But when I hear those people *sing* like that, and when I feel the *power* flowing through me up there on the platform, oh, Mom, I wouldn't trade it—I sometimes think I wouldn't trade it for heaven itself!"

For a moment Minne was silent. Finally she nodded in agreement.

"Well, then," she said, sliding across the seat and stepping gingerly to the running board and into the dust. She grabbed Aimee's arm and marched her toward the tent.

"The question ain't what *you* happen to be satisfied with—it's what *God* wants that counts," she said. "Now, why would God want you wasting your time reaching a *hundred* souls when you could be reaching a *thousand*—or five thousand, or God knows how many.

"Look, do your poor mother a little favor—let me say hello to the folks. I'll show you what I mean. Maybe you could tell them I was your sister."

Aimee rolled her eyes. "Mother!"

"All right, say I'm your mother—but don't blame me if they call you a liar."

When Aimee introduced her, Minnie came to the podium in short, hurried strides and boomed, "Now, Sister Aimee's got a problem, but she's too good-natured to even mention it, so it's a good thing God brought me here just in time. See that little box back there, the one where the offering's supposed to go? Well, it ain't been *going* there, at least not much, and now Sister Aimee's been called by the Lord God Himself to preach the Gospel in the North—now that the warm weather's coming back— and there just ain't no money for her to get up there. So God's led me to tell you about it, and what's more, to take an offering right here and now.

"Sisters and brothers in Jesus, we gotta give like we're giving to *God* and not just to Sister Aimee, for *He's* the one's gonna hold us responsible if this poor little woman and her babies starve to death on the road instead of getting where they belong and preaching the glorious Gospel of Christ. Now, Sister didn't have no *idea* I was gonna do this, and that's why we don't have no offering plates to use. So . . ."

Instantly she removed her bonnet and tossed it to a man in the front row.

"Mister, you start the hat around on this side, and"—she pointed to a man in the third row—"you with the hat on your head, pass it around on

128

that side. Folks, let's give till it hurts—and then a little bit more. And you at the piano, play something."

She turned to Aimee. "Now," she whispered, "you just watch and see what God can do when you give Him a little help."

That afternoon, while Rolf and Roberta chased each other through the aisles and between the benches, Aimee sat on the platform beside Minnie and counted the money. When she glanced up, her eyes were wide with astonishment.

"It's ten *times* the usual!" she exclaimed.

Minnie primped. "Told you so."

Folding her arms, Aimee meandered in the sawdust in front of the platform, her eyes sweeping the tent's interior. "Yes, we could do it," she mumbled. "With ten times the money we could run newspaper ads and print some more 'Bridal Calls' and—"

"There's just no telling how far you could go, and that's my point."

"The children need new clothes."

"Sure they do."

"And I could certainly use another dress—this one's so worn even the patches need patches."

"That's what I'm saying."

Aimee spun to face Minnie, her eyes bright with zeal. "Oh, Mom, do you think I could be a really *big-time* preacher—I mean, right up there at the top?"

Minnie breathed deeply. "From the day you was born, I never thought otherwise," she said firmly. "You're a child of *God*, consecrated to Him at six weeks of age, and He alone knows the heights you'll reach for His glory."

"Oh, hallelujah!" she cried, pirouetting. Then, racing down the aisle toward the children, she cried, "I'm *it*, and here I come, so run for your lives!"

When Aimee took the tents down in Miami, she shipped them to Mack, who was working at the shipyards in Jacksonville, with a note that Minnie, who had come to help, considered them an unnecessary expense. He had helped pay for them, she said, so he could have them to sell for whatever he could get.

"They're worth a thousand dollars or more!" Minnie protested, but halfheartedly, for Aimee was adamant and Minnie was satisfied to get the tents off her hands. Besides, in just the first few months of spring 1918, she had already made Aimee and herself a good deal of money simply by replacing the box at the rear of the tent with an elaborately talked-up offering. By eliminating the tents she'd save repair, labor, and shipping costs; sponsors now provided the meeting place—an auditorium, church, tent, or whatever—along with pleasant accommodations—"No more sleeping in tents!" Minnie declared.

Yet, as she insisted, she asked no more than did every other established evangelist of the day. "And them others are a dime a dozen," she fumed. "They get up and bray for an hour and give their invitations and the people come forward and that's that. First off, you're a *woman*, and that by itself's a drawing card. And you don't just preach—you speak in tongues and call down the Holy Spirit and you even do healing! Now, where else are they gonna get such a bargain, I'd like to know?"

Thus she explained her reasoning to the pastors who, reading of Aimee's glorious campaigns in complimentary issues of "The Bridal Call," wrote for details. And thus the pastors agreed.

In June, while traveling north to the Great Philadelphia National Camp Meeting, where Aimee was scheduled to replace a well-known preacher who had taken ill, they held a short campaign in the Holiness Church of Roanoke. After a faith healing service there one night, two young men approached the platform.

"Mrs. McPherson, I'm sorry—" the more youthful-looking one stammered. "My wife—she ain't well, and . . ." he shrugged, turning awkwardly to his companion.

"She's my sister. She's dying," said the other. "She's been reading that paper you put out, and she begs you to come and pray for her."

Aimee glanced toward the front row, where Minnie was watching her intently.

"We can pay you," said the younger man.

"I don't want you to pay me. It's just that I don't—all right, I'll get my car and follow you." Without hesitation she hurried to the door and ran across the grass toward her car. Wide-eyed, Minnie bustled after her exclaiming, "Where on earth are you off to this time of night? Here's your wrap—you'll catch your death of cold!" But Aimee ignored her. With wheels squealing, the Packard plunged forward and followed a small truck down the winding dirt road.

Giddy with fatigue, ready to laugh or cry, she opened the window and breathed deeply the rich, sweet smells of spring, and for a while that relaxed her. Then the road veered and she almost plunged into a clump of trees. A moment later the trees at the roadside played a trick on her imagination, transformed by her headlights into a leaping monster, and she swerved across the road, gaining control of the car again at the last instant. She cursed herself furiously and punched the steering wheel.

The truck darted to the right, stopping at a house a hundred feet from the road, and Aimee drove in behind it. Without speaking, the two men led her inside and directly to the bedroom.

When she saw the girl, shivering under a pile of white wool blankets, the glazed eyes unblinking, Aimee's knees grew weak. But she swept past the men, moved quickly around the old man and woman huddling at the far side of the bed, and, lifting the pallid young hand between both of hers, whispered, "What's your name?"

"Heather," the girl rasped.

The brother brought Aimee a chair and she sat, still holding the limp hand. She caressed the moist forehead and brushed the hair back across the pillow.

"Why not close your eyes and rest awhile? I'll stay."

The girl's lips moved in an attempted smile. Then she turned away, her eyes moistening. "I'll rest soon enough," she whispered. She turned to Aimee again. "What'll heaven be like?"

"Oh, dear Heather," Aimee said, her voice soft and her eyes growing distant. "If the choice were mine, I'd have gone to heaven long ago. Saint John had a vision when he was on the Isle of Patmos, and God showed him heaven, its streets of pure gold, clear as glass, gates of solid pearl, a crystal sea." As her eyes searched the room, her face reflected such joy that she seemed to gaze upon the celestial paradise. She created a chorus of angels against one emerald-encrusted wall, the throne of God Himself against another, and in the center the Tree of Life.

"Oh, hallelujah!" she cried softly, "There's no pain there, Heather, no sorrow. We're in *heaven* at last, and no one will suffer and die, and we will not lose those we love."

For a moment she could not go on. Then she began singing softly,

> There's a land that is fairer than day;
> And by faith we can see it afar.
> For the Father waits over the way
> To prepare us a dwelling place there.
> In the sweet by and by—
> We shall meet in the sweet by and by.

The girl had fallen asleep. In less than an hour the rapid, shallow breathing ceased and she was dead.

"Let's pray," Aimee said wearily, because she knew it was expected.

She prayed fervently that God would be with the girl's parents and brother and husband and make her life and her passing a testimony. She prayed for faith in God's wisdom at times when it is so hard to understand His ways. She thanked Him for making the girl's promotion to glory as swift and painless as it had been, and ended by saying, "The Lord giveth and the Lord taketh away. Blessed be the name of the Lord! In Jesus' name, amen!"

One of the men helped her off her knees at the side of the bed. She looked up smiling, her eyes red and wet with tears. "Thank you," she said. She patted everyone's hand and held each one firmly and reassuringly for a second. She hugged the old lady, and kissed her on the forehead.

"I'll be happy to stay an extra day and preside over the funeral if you'd like."

"That would be awful kind, Mrs. McPherson," the husband said. "Heather would like that. Come on, I'll lead you back to the campgrounds."

"No, I'll find it. Good night."

Again, she smiled tenderly, then turned and left. Long before she reached the campgrounds she began crying. An hour later Minnie found her in the parking lot, lying across the seat weeping in agonizing sobs.

"It's the influenza," said Minnie, gently petting Aimee's head. "It's killin' 'em off all over the place—a pandemic, they call it. Killin' more people than the war, they say."

Aimee sat up, wiping her face.

"You look just terrible, your face all streaked like that, and red and blotchy. And just look at your eyes!"

"I don't care about my eyes." Her voice was dull. "I want to get away from here."

"We're leaving tomorrow."

"No—I said I'd stay for the funeral." Minnie began to object, then refrained. "But that's not what I mean," Aimee said. "I want to go from here, from the East. I'm tired of it—I'm bored, and—oh, God, I just want to get away."

She began crying again, and Minnie wrapped her arms around her and held her tightly. "Well, I been doing some thinking, you know," she said. "We got an invitation from Tulsa, and they're willing to guarantee expenses and a basic net. No doubt we could line meetings up here and there all across the country."

"Let's go all the way—out of California!" Aimee exclaimed, wiping her face dry.

"And why not!" Minnie exclaimed. "Now, I got me to New York City and Miami, it's high time I take a look at Los Angeles. Sure, we'll do it—get ourselves a new car and off we'll go. But I'll line up the meetings and some free room and board first—no sense being foolish."

Aimee laughed. Throwing her arms around her mother, she squeezed her so tightly Minnie groaned.

"I love you, Mom," she said.

"Well, we ain't going anywhere if you crack my ribs, you know. Come on now. You're gonna get some sleep. Or you ain't gonna be in any condition to drive clear across the country."

CHAPTER XV

On October 23, 1918, the new seven-seater Oldsmobile raced out of New Rochelle, New York, and headed west. Six-inch-high gold letters on the doors announced, "Jesus Is Coming Soon—Get Ready," and asked, "Where Will You Spend Eternity?" In the front seat beside Aimee sat a middle-aged, matronly stenographer, Sister Louise Baer, whose responsibility it was to transcribe all of Aimee's dictation during the day and type it at night, for Aimee had determined that, rather than waste time simply driving, she might also write her autobiography and sell it at her meetings—along with photographs of herself, perhaps.

In the rear seat, Minnie sat between Rolf and Roberta, the three of them cramped together to make room for the cases of tracts and "Bridal Call" newsletters. Beneath their feet were piles of blankets, the portable stove, cooking utensils, and some of the suitcases. The others had been strapped to custom-made brackets on the trunk lid.

Additional brackets had been welded to the fenders to support cots and a pup tent for the children, and four poles designed to slip into channels in the front and rear of both running boards. With a canvas blanket draped over the poles and the front seat folded back, the car became comfortable as a sleeping tent for the three women on the many nights Minnie had been unable to arrange finer accommodations.

They had been on the road for more than a week before Minnie confessed to her illness. Aimee had been too engrossed in dictating to Sister Baer and following maps to notice, but one morning Roberta brushed her hand against Minnie's cheek and exclaimed, "Boy, are you

Crowds ten thousand strong and extending
several blocks wait to view the body of Aimee
Semple McPherson. October 7, 1944.
Los Angeles Times photo

A week after her return from the desert,
Aimee still appears somber and wan.
Los Angeles Times photo

Aimee tells her kidnapping story to hundreds of Foursquare children. To her left is her son, Rolf, now president of the International Church of the Foursquare Gospel. To her right, daughter Roberta. June 28, 1926. *Los Angeles Times photo*

On June 27, 1926, Aimee returns to Los Angeles to an unprecedented reception—orchestras, city officials, and thousands of cheering fans. *Los Angeles Times photo*

Aimee Semple McPherson the lecturer/actress, leaving on her vindication tour
in January 1927. *Los Angeles Times photo*

Aimee, with her grammar school classmates, Ethel Page recalls, holds the sign, still frowning; she had had a spat with the teacher before winning the honor of holding that sign. *Author's collection*

The Salford, Ontario, schoolhouse Aimee attended from 1900 to 1902. Byron Jenvy taught there. *Author's collection*

The grave marker Aimee had erected in the Harrison Street Cemetery in place of the obelisk, which for generations paid tribute to the Kennedys buried there. *Author's collection*

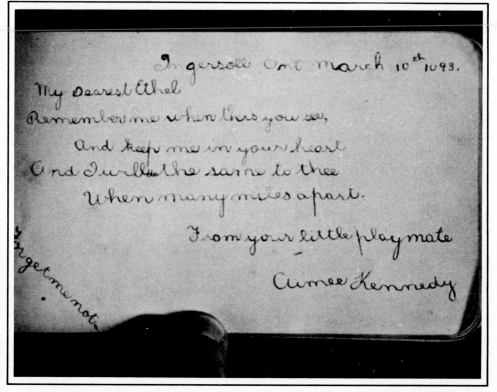

At thirteen years of age—and throughout her life—Aimee preferred to think of herself as "little." Here is her entry in Ethel Page's autograph book from grammar school. *Author's collection*

The Ingersoll Railroad Station, to which Aimee returned in 1915 after leaving Mack.
Author's collection

Aimee's Salford farmhouse as it stands today. The barn, Minnie's lilacs, and dogwood are gone; only the vast, fertile fields James Kennedy tilled remain. *Author's collection*

Aimee leads her followers in receiving the Baptism of the Holy Spirit. Such experiences, common in the early days of her ministry, were revived in the late 1930s and continued by her until her death. *Courtesy, Bancroft Library, University of California, Berkeley*

A year and a half before her disappearance, a warm, matronly woman built Angelus Temple, the radio station, and Bible school while building a reputation as one of the nation's leading spiritual figures. February 20, 1925. *Los Angeles Times photo*

Minnie Kennedy and granddaughter, Roberta, are grief-stricken at Aimee's apparent death. Roberta has just preached at Angelus Temple, and Minnie has announced that the sixteen-year-old daughter of Robert Semple would assume the leadership held by her mother. May 24, 1926. *Los Angeles Times photo*

Aimee in temple regalia, December 1935. *Los Angeles Times photo*

The final scene. As a last concession to the press, Roberta (right), about to weep, poses with Rolf and Aimee, who clutches her son's hand. Moments later, Roberta won her suit against Willedd Andrews, Aimee's attorney. October 27, 1937. *Los Angeles Times photo*

Deputy District Attorney Murray (left) interviews Kenneth Ormiston in December 1926. To the displeasure of both Murray and the press, Ormiston proved affably uninformative. *Los Angeles Times photo*

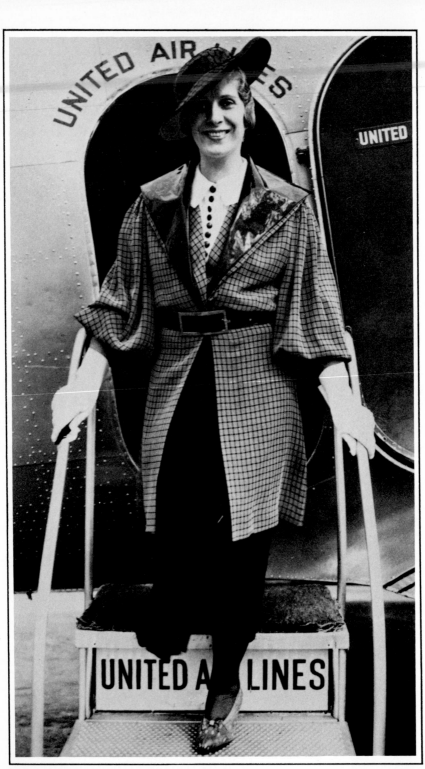

Aimee boards a plane for Portland to attend a Foursquare Gospel convention, dressed as always in the finest and most expensive clothes. July 2, 1935. *Los Angeles Times photo*

A gala celebration at the temple greets Aimee after her return from the desert. Behind her, at the extreme right, is Minnie. *Los Angeles Times photo*

L.I.F.E. Bible College. *Author's collection*

Angelus Temple interior. *Author's collection*

The temple parsonage when Aimee lived there. *Author's collection*

In October 1927, Aimee held a short campaign in San Diego. Here she stands beside her Studebaker near the Hotel del Coronado, striking a pose for photographers. Witnesses who identified her during her disappearance made much of the large ankles.
Historical Collection, Title Insurance and Trust

A thoughtful Aimee is photographed in her San Diego hotel room preparing a sermon, 1927.
Historical Collection, Title Insurance and Trust

hot!" Sister Baer confirmed it in a tone that permitted no denial: "You're burning up with fever—*that's* why the aspirin's disappearing and you're bundled three-deep in sweaters. You've got the influenza, no doubt."

Since she knew they were too far along to turn back, Minnie made no effort to deny the diagnosis. She'd labored many hours to set up an itinerary, writing letters to scores of "Bridal Call" subscribers all across the country, sometimes even ringing them up on the telephone, and when finally all plans were made, nothing short of death could have induced her to change them. She had suffered in silence all along, endured the fever and cramps and intestinal upset stoically. But now that it didn't matter, Minnie gave free vent to her discomfort.

"That's right, I've got the influenza, and I'm sick as a dog. I need at least two blankets before we go a step farther—it's a miracle from heaven I'm still alive, I'll tell you that. Hospital wards full of the sick, morgues loaded with corpses. Thank God for His mercy."

But by then Minnie was already improving. And the stronger she felt, the more intolerable she became. "Why don't you stop driving like a maniac?" she screeched when the car thumped over a pothole in the road. "Can't a body be sick in peace?"

"This tea's terrible," she grumbled during lunch. "If I don't die from the influenza, they're gonna poison me. Either way you'll be sorry, you'll never find anybody that'll work hard as I do. Roberta will miss me, anyway, won't you, Roberta?"

As they passed through Illinois, Minnie's fever broke and she began feeling almost well again, so that her heart was not in her complaints. Finally she abandoned trying to keep the eagerness from her voice when she spoke of the trip.

"You know," she told Aimee one morning, "if we ever make it over these godforsaken cow paths and get out there to California—which I ain't betting on —you'll be the first woman that ever did such a thing, Aimee Semple McPherson—driving from New York to California!"

Louise Baer shook her head. "Emily Post did it in 1915. It was right there in *Collier's*."

"She *did not*," fumed Minnie. "She *rode* in the car—her son did most of the driving. Aimee's the first woman to *drive*!"

"Mommy's the first!" cried Roberta, and Rolf applauded.

Aimee laughed freely. She'd been at the wheel daily for two weeks and a half, except for a day when a Kansas rain squall washed out the road. Often she began driving before sunrise and continued late into the night, following the Lincoln Highway from New York to Philadelphia, the National to Indianapolis, the Pike's Peak, Ocean to Ocean, and now the

Big Four Highway to Kansas City, Missouri. In spite of their impressive labels, the roads west of Illinois often deteriorated to untraveled dirt lanes, cluttered with branches and boulders that required removal before the car could pass. On occasion the roads came to an abrupt end, and even using the *Automobile Blue Book*, Aimee could not find her way and wandered across dust-clouded prairies and cowpaths for hours before stumbling upon another road.

Early in November the temperature dropped in the midwest, and at night their breath condensed as frost on the tent's canvas ceiling. But the rain was the greater enemy, transforming even the better roads into slithery swamps through which passage was impossible. One rainy night, Aimee looked in on the children to find a stream of water pouring on Roberta through a hole in the tent. She propped an umbrella over the girl's chest.

When the road was dry, Aimee raced along at twenty-five miles an hour, five miles above the speed limit in most states, hitting bumps and ruts with such violence that Minnie exclaimed more than once, "Well, this trip'll be the death of me, sure. Was I born, have I endured for this—to die in the middle of nowhere with a crazy lady at the wheel?"

Immediately upon arriving in Tulsa, Aimee set about organizing volunteers into a promotional blitz. Her favorite strategy was to pack an army of helpers into the Gospel Auto and hold short street meetings at all the major downtown intersections.

At one, a passing driver blared his horn, drowning her words and distracting the listeners.

Immediately she shouted, "Hallelujah—the trumpet of Michael the Archangel! Look, look!" Pointing to the sky, she exclaimed, "Christ returns!"

Every eye turned heavenward.

"No, it wasn't the trumpet of the archangel, just an old motorcar horn," she admitted, "But listen! What if it *had* been the Christ—He *will* return, you know—in a moment, in the twinkling of an eye, when we expect Him not. Will you be ready? Or will you say, 'Just a minute there, Lord, I've got to get saved first. There was that lady preaching there on the street corner, and she told me all about You, but I was too busy heckling and having fun. There was too much to give up. I put it off, and now—' "

She clapped her hands together, the sounds cracking like gun shots. "The Bible says, 'Choose you *this day* whom ye will serve!' "

She brought bands of musicians to the street corner meetings, then charts and large illustrations. Sometimes she acted out a parable from the

Scriptures. The crowds grew so large in certain areas that the streets had to be closed to traffic. Every few minutes she would announce the evening services, urging the people to come, and the attendance increased steadily at the formal meetings each night.

Because many continued ill with influenza, Aimee decided to conduct healing services. Concerning them, she later dictated to Sister Baer, "We stood for hours at a time praying for the sick, and Jesus helped those who came to Him. A man with severe stomach trouble and a sister with running sores, internal troubles, were healed, also influenza, heart trouble, etc. We were called into houses where poor people were lying so low their eyes seemed glassy, and the rattle in their throats, but the Lord marvelously raised them up. Bless His name!"

They left Tulsa late in November, the glorious celebration of the armistice ringing in their heads, racing west on roads so smooth and dry that Aimee pushed the car to forty miles per hour. Coming upon an occasional irregularity in the road, she would stop dictating midsentence, spin the wheel, and send the car careening around a pothole or some such obstacle, boxes tumbling, suitcases skidding, the five-gallon cans of surplus gasoline clanging together. A moment later she would finish the sentence.

Late one afternoon the clouds turned gray and a fine rain fell, so Aimee stopped to raise the car's canvas roof and eat a quick lunch. Fifteen minutes later, she started the car again and drove along the slick road for more than an hour. Then the car slid to a stop.

"The road's gone!" Aimee cried.

Six inches of water buried it, washing over the shoulders and onto the prairie like a vast, motionless river.

Turning to the map of New Mexico and checking her pocket watch, odometer, and compass, she finally mumbled, "We can't be more than fifteen or twenty miles from Santa Rosa."

To the north, she could see the mountains, deadly at this time of year with their treacherous passes sealed by swirling snowdrifts. Natives at the gasoline stations and restaurants had warned she could be lost in those mountains until spring. Peering to the left, she saw a sea of mud flats and gulches.

"We'll have to keep to the road," she said uneasily, starting the car forward again.

Through the rain-streaked windshield, she saw sections of the road stretch before her like islands of mud. When the submerged expanse grew particularly long, she grew anxious that she had driven off into the prairie and would become utterly lost and they would all perish from hunger;

only the jolt of the tires sliding into the road's deep ruts reassured her.

The mud grew thicker, reaching the axles. It held the car back and impaired traction so that, even with the engine racing, the car progressed inch by inch.

"Move—*move!*" Aimee pleaded, clutching the steering wheel so tightly her fingers grew white.

Finally the tires slipped into a particularly deep rut and the car settled to the running boards in mud. Aimee shifted into reverse and raced the engine, then into forward again and did the same, splattering half an inch of mud across the windshield. Still, the car made no progress.

"Well, don't just sit there—get out and push!" Aimee demanded of Sister Baer. With a lingering glare, the stenographer threw open the car door and stepped into the oozing mud. Grumbling, Minnie followed her. A moment later, while Aimee pressed the accelerator, the two women pushed with all their strength, and the car inched forward. Then it slipped into ruts even deeper than the first, the spinning wheels showering the women with mud. Minnie threw up her hands.

"It ain't gonna do no good," she shouted over the roaring engine and the rain. "We're stuck, and that's that."

Aimee turned off the headlights and the engine and, leaping from the car, pounded on the hood with both fists.

"I can't *stand* it!" she screamed. "We can't be more than ten miles from the city!"

"Well, having a nervous breakdown ain't gonna do no good," said Minnie.

Wiping the rain from her face, Aimee sloshed her way to the trunk and set about unpacking it. First she unstrapped the suitcases and tossed them in the car. Then she removed the food cartons, water containers, books.

"Here, you hold this," she ordered Sister Baer. "You take that one," she told Minnie.

"What on earth are you doing?"

"Looking for the skid chains."

A moment later she found them, along with the jack.

"Give me the lantern, Roberta—who's got the matches?"

Feverishly Aimee scooped the mud from a foot-square space under the rear bumper, using the jack base as a shovel. After digging almost a foot, she reached solid ground and set the jack base there, then quickly assembled the jack and cranked.

Dragging the cumbersome chains nearer the tire, she hoisted them over it, ran her fingers along the inner links, searching for the fasteners.

"I can't find the hooks!" she screamed, raising her fist to pound the car. Then, with a glance at the perilously unstable jack, she dropped her aching arm.

"Bring the lantern over here!" she ordered Minnie, angrily throwing herself onto her back and slithering beneath the car.

"Hold the light underneath here. That's it. Now—*there!*"

Half an hour later, with the chain secured around the second rear tire, Aimee started the motor and the Oldsmobile lumbered forward—a foot, a yard, a hundred yards. Now the road was entirely submerged, and through the long hours of rain it had become a quagmire, a mass of brown grease into which the car settled deeper and deeper. Finally the Gospel Auto labored to a shuddering standstill.

Aimee slammed the transmission into reverse, raced the engine and popped the clutch, jabbed it into first, back into reverse. The tires whined, the engine roared, but the car moved not an inch.

Aimee threw open the door.

"Louise, put it in forward and give it some gas!" she ordered, leaping from the car. Minnie followed, and together, digging their heels into the mud and leaning their shoulders against the trunk they pushed.

The spinning tires blasted Aimee's face with mud, blinding her. She reached for her skirt, but that, too, was soiled. Stumbling toward Minnie, Aimee lost her footing and fell sprawling.

"Good Lord!" cried Minnie.

"I'm all right. Let me be."

She lay there motionless for a long while, the rain washing her face, fighting the urge to cry or explode in rage and rip the tire iron from the trunk and bash the Gospel Auto into a hundred thousand pieces.

Finally, with complete self-possession, she stood and made her way to the driver's door, and tapped Sister Baer on the shoulder.

"You can stop racing the engine now, Louise," she said sarcastically.

"Mom, you stay here with the kids. Louise and I'll take the lantern and go for help. We'll go all the way to Santa Rosa if we have to—don't expect us back before morning."

Stumbling into gulleys, tripping over boulders, they'd hiked about two miles when, approaching a slight rise in the road, they saw a flickering light in the distance.

"There!" Aimee exclaimed, and tugging at Sister Baer's arm, she hurried forward.

It was much farther than it seemed, and they made slow progress, for the mud in this area was sometimes a foot deep. Suddenly, with renewed frustration and anger, Aimee plunged ahead with the lantern, leaving Sister Baer straggling behind.

Now she could see the glow was a lamp in the window of a small adobe set back a few hundred feet from the road. Behind it was a huge structure, many times the size of a house—a barn, no doubt. And in the front yard were some bulky objects, appearing in the dim light to be wagons.

"Hello? *Hello!*" shouted Aimee over the wire fence. Behind her at some distance Sister Baer complained that she was unable to see the road.

The adobe door opened and a short figure, a man, stood silhouetted against the brightness of the room, a lantern in one hand, a shotgun in the other.

"*Qué quiere usted?* What do you want?"

"My car's stuck," Aimee gasped.

"I do not—*no trabajo en los coches*—I do not work the coaches," the man answered, stepping back into the adobe.

"You *listen* to me!" Aimee screamed, rushing through the gate. The light fell on her face, the shotgun pointed at her chest.

"I'm a preacher of the Gospel of Jesus Christ, and I won't *allow* you to turn your back on me like this! We are *stranded* out there"—she pointed down the road,—"three poor, helpless women and two tiny children, and no men to help us. You just *must* do something!"

Lowering the gun, the man burst into laughter. "*Ay*, Señora, you are covered with thee mud!"

Aimee's eyes blazed with anger. "How can you—" she brushed her fingers across her forehead, felt the mud. Her dress was unrecognizable; her feet seemed made of clay. She burst into laughter. Sister Baer, by her side now, gazed at the two laughing figures in fear and bewilderment.

At midnight, the horse-drawn buggy halted beside the Oldsmobile. Taking the man's arm, Aimee led him to the car where the children, huddled against Minnie, slept soundly.

"This is Manuel," said Aimee. "God's sent him to help us."

"Well, let him get to it," Minnie grumbled. "I'm a cake of ice as it is."

But even Manuel's horse was of no use, and at two o'clock in the morning he threw up his hands.

"It's no hope!" he exclaimed. "You get on the wagon, sleep at my house. We fix mañana."

Sister Baer's eyes widened in fear. "What if he rapes us?" she exclaimed.

"You'd rather freeze to death?" asked Minnie, hoisting herself from the car on wobbly legs.

"Don't wake the kids," said Aimee. "They're bundled warm and sound asleep. I'll just snuggle up with them till morning."

"Nonsense," said Minnie. "You'll freeze to death."

"I won't freeze to death—besides, it'll be light in a few hours. Go on, don't keep Manuel waiting."

By seven-thirty the Mexican was back, this time with four horses, six burly friends, and a wagonload of timber. In minutes the car was chugging along toward the adobe, where Manuel's wife had prepared a hearty breakfast.

Later that day, as the Gospel Auto continued toward Santa Rosa, Aimee dictated another "Bridal Call" entry to Sister Baer:

"We had not gone more than a mile when we saw God's reason for holding us back; deep washouts and gulches had to be crossed, and only good light and careful driving could have saved the car and its passengers. But the Lord was with us, and the guard of angels was never more real to us, and although water came over the fenders at times, we never had to stop again."

Late that afternoon, the Gospel Auto sputtered along the main street of Santa Rosa, a spectacle so shabby and forlorn that all eyes turned to it in whispers and laughter. Then, from a small crowd that had formed, a young man and woman emerged and ran hand in hand toward the car.

"Praise God for your sign!" the man exclaimed, pointing to the mud-smudged gold letters on the Gospel Auto. "We know where we will spend eternity!"

Aimee clasped the hand he'd placed on the windowsill. "Praise the Lord for you, brother!" she exclaimed. "We've come all the way from New York and —"

Before she finished, he opened the door and motioned her to slide over. "Get in, Edith," he told his wife. "The Lord has led you to our home for the night—oh, we're so grateful for you! We haven't seen a single born-again Christian in a year!"

That afternoon, while the travelers bathed, their hosts and children washed the Gospel Auto, loaned them dry clothes and soaked their soiled ones, then fed them a hearty meal. After supper, everyone gathered in the living room near a blazing fireplace to sing and pray and give testimony. Finally, Aimee, her voice rich with music, read from the Scriptures and told the grand story of her life.

The next day Aimee and her team moved on through New Mexico, then north toward the Datil Mountains, then, finding the passes blocked by snow, turned south again to Deming, New Mexico. At a restaurant there, they met a caravan of three cars headed toward Phoenix, and Aimee joined the group. One of the men even volunteered to drive the car for her, so for two days Aimee relaxed in the back seat with Minnie and the children.

When the caravan reached Phoenix, Aimee struck out alone again, heading north to Needles, California, to avoid the deep sand of Yuma. Often, while crossing the desert, she would come upon stretches where no roads existed, and she would navigate through swirling sand and sagebrush relying entirely on her small compass and the sun and stars. She searched the glaring sand till her eyes burned for sight of the road or a gap between the mountains, any sign that she was moving in the right direction. One night she saw a glow in the sky and knew she was approaching Needles.

From there, a modern boulevard stretched through the desert to San Bernardino, and a fine highway took them to Los Angeles.

CHAPTER XVI

Pastor Jacobs, a burly and balding man in his fifties, held the door open with one hand and searched the wall for the light switch with the other. After an inordinate delay, punctuated with his mutterings, he found it and half a dozen bulbs cast their dim glow along the walls to reveal the thousand seats and stage of Victoria Hall.

"Can't we get something on the first floor?" Minnie whispered to Aimee, clutching her throat. "Them stairs is enough to kill a person."

"There isn't any space on the first floor," said Sister Evelyn Blake, a slim, expensively dressed woman in her late thirties. "The dormitory and cafeteria are down there."

"Oh, this is fine!" exclaimed Aimee, squeezing Mrs. Blake's arm. Then, taking Mr. Jacobs' hand between both of hers, she exclaimed, "How can I *thank* you? People won't mind climbing a few steps."

"They won't, huh?" Minnie turned to the pastor. "How many people climb them on a Sunday?"

Mr. Jacobs removed his glasses and dropped his eyes. "These are trying and difficult times," he said. "The end times, the last days."

"Amen," said Sister Blake, nodding vigorously.

"Lately the city's overrun with fakes," Pastor Jacobs continued. "Satan's own false prophets are converging upon Los Angeles by the dozens. Cultists in this town preach salvation through everything from weight lifting to orgies of the flesh—it's unthinkable, abysmal. One impostor teaches mind reading as the road to God. We've got the temperance crowd, the brain-breathing cult, the evangelical atheists. Why, they've even invaded our own true faith, the false prophets. In the last three or four years, I wouldn't be surprised if a hundred different evangelists have hit Los Angeles—sponsored, you know, by every two-bit congregation that wanted to rob members from the other churches."

He turned to Sister Blake for confirmation. "Indeed, there must have been a hundred—five of them called themselves 'The Singing Evangelist,' three 'The Boy Evangelist,' five more 'The Gypsy Evangelist.' There was one billed himself 'The Railroad Evangelist,' another 'The Businessman's Evangelist.' The church down the street had 'The Cowboy Evangelist,' another a few blocks away 'The Labor Evangelist.'"

He looked to Mrs. Blake, who nodded in agreement.

"Oh, we could have done the same, I suppose—I get their advertisements in the mail every day: 'We'll thrill your congregation to their toes.' 'I'll convert thirty-four percent of the population of any town I visit.' 'With Jesus as my witness, I'll give twenty-five percent of the offering to any pastor who invites me to conduct evangelistic services at his church,' Well, to my way of thinking that kind of thing isn't of God, and I would rather have a small congregation built on the rock that is Jesus than have every one of these seats filled every Sunday and know that it was not Christ but a flimflam artist that brought them in."

His face brightened into a smile, and he said, "Which is, by the way, precisely why we've invited you here, Mrs. McPherson. We've followed your meetings and seen how God has used you to bring salvation and Holy Spirit baptism, and that's proof enough your work is of God."

"Why, thank you," Aimee beamed.

"So how many come to your meetings, Pastor Jacobs," Minnie repeated dryly.

The pastor replaced his glasses and glared at Minnie with a dour expression. "Twelve," he said.

Grasping the pastor's arm, Aimee led him along the aisle toward the stage. "Sister Blake, Mother, come quickly," she said. "We're going to wrestle with God until He promises the blessing—and Pastor Jacobs, we're going to ask in faith, *believing*, not that twelve seats be filled, or ten times twelve, but that *every* seat in this hallowed hall be filled!"

Her stomach knotting in excitement, Aimee rushed to the lectern and, lifting her hands as in benediction, slowly surveyed the auditorium.

"O *Lord!*" she cried. "We *know* it will take a miracle, and we rejoice and praise Your name even now, for we know it will happen. The seats will be *filled!* The Spirit will *descend!* Souls will be *saved* and *baptized*, the crippled will be *healed!* And this day and the days to come will be recorded with joy eternal in the Book of Life!"

Later, the four walked to a luncheonette not far from the mission to plan strategy. It was Minnie, clearing her throat, which had grown hoarse from overzealousness during the prayer session, who spoke first:

"Well, what's been done?"

Lowering his head, Mr. Jacobs gazed over the top of his glasses, his eyes questioning. "About what?" he asked.

"About all the letters I wrote you, God bless me—all hours of the night, and it made no difference whether in the freezing mountains or the roasting desert, I just went about my Father's business."

"Oh, yes! Well, Sister Blake," to whom he expressed an appreciative smile, "has advanced us the money for the newspaper ads, and the whole congregation joined in making up posters and putting them in store windows—we must have two hundred around the city by now."

"The American flags and flowers?" asked Aimee.

"We borrowed the flags from the mission," said the pastor.

"I'm donating the flowers from our greenhouses," added Sister Blake, "and I have some extra drapes—they're a lovely powder blue—for the backdrop, as you refer to it, Mrs. Kennedy."

"What about the other churches?" asked Minnie.

The pastor, avoiding Minnie's stern gaze, removed his glasses and rubbed his eyes. "A couple of smaller ones are cooperating," he said, "but as I explained, the competition is a major factor. The larger churches won't help—if Christ Himself were to preach at Victoria Hall, they'd not participate."

Aimee's face reddened. "How *dare* they turn their backs on me," she demanded, pounding the table, "a poor, helpless little woman with two shabby nurses' uniforms to her name, with nothing more to ask of the world than a chance to preach the Gospel?"

"This town's full of shysters, Mrs. McPherson," said the pastor. "Some, respected preachers of the Gospel, would slit your throat if by so doing they could add your congregation to their own. It's money in their pockets, and that's the beginning and the end of it."

The waiter brought their food, and Aimee, who poised her knife and fork over the enormous bowl of meatballs and spaghetti even before the waiter took his hand away, speared one of the meatballs and raised it in its entirety to her mouth, blinking her eyes closed long enough to say an instant's "Thank you for this food, amen," before clamping her mouth shut around it. For a few minutes, while the others chattered, Aimee devoted her entire concentration to wrapping great mounds of spaghetti around her fork and gulping it down. Finally, the edge of her hunger sated, she primly dabbed her sauce-stained lips and said:

"Two more things, Brother Jacobs. First—of course, it's a *lovely* auditorium, glory to God, and we'll be seeing great miracles there, I know. But it's *torturously* dingy. Now, the Scriptures tell us it's the *devil* who loves darkness, for he's the prince of darkness, but praise God, we're the children of *light*! So, brother, I'd like to see bright lights all *over* the place tomorrow night—I mean, *hundreds*, Pastor Jacobs. I want it bright as a sunrise, bright as our faith in the Lord. Let the devil *keep* his dingy rooms and alleys—ours is a faith bright as the firmament!"

Over the top of his glasses the pastor squinted skeptically.

"Why, of course, she's *right*," said Sister Blake. "It's gloomy as a graveyard up there."

"Of course," the pastor nodded immediately, smiling at Sister Blake. "We'll have those lights up by this evening."

"Oh, that's *marvelous*! And the drapes, and the flags, and flowers—it'll be just *grand*."

Then, lowering her voice, she confronted Mr. Jacobs directly: "And what about the orchestra."

At first the pastor averted her gaze. Then, facing her squarely, he said, "I'm afraid that's out of the question. We believe musical instruments have no place in the church."

"Oh they don't, don't they?" exclaimed Minnie. "I suppose the Salvation Army's of the devil!"

Aimee had lifted her knife and fork and was about to attack the spaghetti again, but she set the utensils aside and, gently grasping Sister Blake's arm, asked her earnestly, "You mean you don't even have a piano?"

"Well, yes, we do."

"No one ever performs a violin solo or even a trumpet solo?"

"Certainly, every Sunday—but an orchestra—that seems so worldly."

"Oh, I *know*—I know how you feel. But the fact is, if God can use the talent of *one* of his children and bless us through that testimony of song, why can't he use *ten* of his children and give us a tenfold blessing? Oh, He can. *He can*!"

She turned to Pastor Jacobs. "Brother, today the devil has got the greatest bag of tricks the world's ever known—the automobile, the movies, novels of immorality and decadence. Godless science texts, false prophets. Drinking, dancing, and debauchery among our youth as never before in the history of the *world*. Atheism rampant. Jazz and jitterbug, bobbed hair and painted lips. Oh, the devil's got himself a mighty army!

"But Pastor, the Lord God is on our side—and He's given us the resources to take a *stand* against this encroaching worldliness! Who *says* the Gospel of salvation has to be dull? Why, it's the most stunning, dramatic story ever *told*!" She turned to Minnie. "Yet, we tell it like old Miss Hartwell taught seventh-grade history—yawn, snore. An orchestra isn't *sinful*—it's what we *do* with the orchestra that makes it a weapon in the devil's army—or the *Lord's*! I say, let's throw Christian musicians into the front lines of battle!"

Pastor Jacobs lifted his eyes questioningly to Sister Blake, who shrugged and finally nodded her approval.

In the six weeks following that spaghetti lunch, Aimee became famous in the City of Angels. Some people flocked to the meetings at Victoria Hall to hear the much-advertised Christian orchestra; others were curious to see the woman preacher. Sensation seekers came to view the Miracle Lady heal the crippled and dying, a promise made by the promotional material Minnie had forwarded. Still others had heard of the baptism and speaking tongues, and a few, distraught with the era's materialism, sensationalism, and unbelief, yet lacking a faith strong enough to hold them, came to be persuaded.

In less than a week crowds filled the one thousand seats of Victoria Hall each night. At the popular Sunday afternoon service, the auditorium and prayer room behind the stage overflowed with people. Others sat on the rostrum, stood in the aisles and on the stairs, and when the ushers finally closed the doors, scores congregated on the sidewalk.

The following week, Minnie rented the Los Angeles Philharmonic Auditorium, the city's largest facility, with a seating capacity of 3,500, and she personally guaranteed the fee of one hundred dollars for three hours. Aimee would fill it, she knew, and a single offering would bring in ten times that.

Outside the building, Aimee suspended a banner eight feet high and fifty feet long declaring in bold letters, "Aimee Semple McPherson— Lady Evangelist—Nightly 7:30 P.M. Full orchestra, choir, Holy Ghost revival."

Every day Aimee arose before dawn to write for "The Bridal Call" and prepare a sermon. Immediately after breakfast, she set out on the daily round of street corner gatherings, luncheon prayer meetings, afternoon services, conferences, and preparation for the ever more popular evening crusade. Late each night, while Minnie and the children slept, Aimee huddled over a small table in the Blake library sipping tea, munching cookies, and writing the final chapters of her autobiography. Minnie, sometimes rising in the early morning hours to find Aimee still working in the study, vigorously scolded her for abusing her health. "Even a plow horse needs his sleep," she warned. "One of these days you're just gonna collapse, and then where will you be?" But invariably, with a smile and a pat on Minnie's buttocks, Aimee sent her mother back to bed and continued her work.

Far from weakening, she seemed to grow stronger each day. Never had she been so energetic, never so driven, for she saw now a reality she'd never imagined, a vision Robert alone had conceived—the preaching of God's Word to literally thousands.

Late in the afternoon on the first Sunday in February 1919, more than four thousand people jammed Philharmonic Hall for the concluding service. A two-hundred-voice choir shared the stage with the orchestra and to the left, near the front, sat Aimee and Pastor Jacobs and Minnie, flanked on each side by a committee of local pastors who had belatedly offered to support the crusade in hopes of adding a few converts to their own congregations.

That day, Aimee preached with such power that even her mother was astonished. She measured every pause, every gesture and inflection against another self in the audience, the doubter, the dreamer, the desperate seeker of thrills and escaper of boredom, and thus she chose the precise phrase, toss of the head, sweep of the arm, whisper, or shout to elicit hypnotic response in her audience self.

"Oh, what a *blessing* we've had here. And it's not my doing—oh, no! I'm just a little woman, God's handmaiden, the least of all saints. And no pastor has done it, grateful as we are for their help. And the glory goes not even to our marvelous Christian *orchestra* and this awesome two-hundred-voice *choir*, but praise God for the blessing they've brought and let's give them a hand, folks!" To the bewilderment and indignation of the pastors, Aimee led the congregation in an uproarious ovation.

"The glory goes to *Him*!" she shouted, clapping hands and pointing with extended arms to the ceiling. "I *rejoice* and am *humbled* and *grateful* that my mother—they call her Ma Kennedy now, you know—" Minnie nodded to the audience with a shrug and smile of resignation "—that Mom and dear little Rolf and Roberta and I have been able to help in the Lord's work here in the City of Angels in some small way. Oh, God has laid this city on our hearts and we so desire to stay among you."

She walked slowly to the front of the stage, stretched her arms out toward the audience pleadingly. Her voice now imploring, she said, "I want to take just a moment to ask you to *pray* for us with all your *hearts*. I don't want to burden you with our problems—God knows you have your own. But our little troop faces some grave difficulties right now. We've come to Los Angeles at the Lord's *leading*, and we feel now that He would have us find a permanent *home*. The children need schooling and friends, a normal life like other boys and girls, and yet the calls keep coming from all over the United *States* for me to go and preach. My dear mother has promised to stay and take care of the children if we can but find a *home*, but we seem destined to continue on from city to city with no place to lay our *heads*."

She gazed up into the crowded balconies. "Beloved, *pray* that God will prepare a *place* for us so that I can go about my Father's business untroubled about the children's welfare."

She felt the hand of Pastor Jacobs on her shoulder. He was smiling paternally.

"Children of God," he intoned, his arm hovering over the vast audience, "I think the Lord is speaking to us right now, leading us to do something for this dear saint who has labored for these past six weeks to bring hundreds of souls into the kingdom of God. How many of you feel we should take a special offering which Sister McPherson can use as a down payment on a home?"

Thousands of hands waved in the air.

Suddenly Mrs. Blake stood to her feet in the third row. "I have a piece of land I would like to give to Sister McPherson," she shouted. "She can build her house on it."

Gasps of surprise swept the audience.

"Praise the Lord!" someone shouted. Minnie smiled her approval.

"Well, hallelujah!" shouted Mr. Jacobs.

Aimee buried her face in her hands and brushed her eyes, although there were no tears. Then, throwing open her arms, she shouted, "Oh, *thank* you, Jesus!"

A suntanned, muscular youth in the balcony leaped to his feet and bellowed, "I can help dig a cellar!"

Another man volunteered to lay the foundation, another to do the lathing, the plastering, the carpentry, the wiring. A contractor volunteered to design and supervise the project.

From all over shouts of praise arose until the audience was swept with fervor. Minnie Kennedy, trying to appear inconspicuous, motioned to Pastor Jacobs.

"It's just a *miracle*, ain't it?" she exclaimed. "But, you know, just to be on the safe side—maybe you should take that offering anyway."

CHAPTER XVII

While volunteers hurriedly erected the two-story bungalow on Orange Grove Drive near West Adams Boulevard on the western fringe of the city, Aimee drove to San Francisco for another campaign, the first leg of a rigid preaching schedule Minnie had set up. From there she traveled by Pullman to New York City for a city-wide "Holy Ghost Revival," which won her nationwide press coverage, describing her efforts to "drive the Devil from New York." One syndicate published with illustrations seven of her sermons offering teen-age girls advice on how to avoid "the Pitfalls of a Great City." For added attention, Aimee had workmen erect over the main tent an enormous sign announcing the meetings.

In Baltimore, sponsors rented the city's largest theater, the Lyric, for three hundred dollars a day. Since Minnie's new promotional material heralded Aimee as a healer and miracle woman, local newspapers head-lined the claim and a multitude of sick and curious filled the auditorium nightly. And indeed arthritics discarded their crutches, victims of stomach cancer felt miraculously improved, others were able to hear and see better.

When the meetings were temporarily suspended for the Christmas holidays in 1919, Aimee ignored Minnie's fearful protestations and, using the tight schedule as an excuse, flew all the way to Los Angeles. She inundated Minnie for hours with every aspect of that rare adventure.

From Baltimore she rushed to Winnipeg, Manitoba, for a city-wide revival at Old Wesley Church. On the first night, Aimee told a half-full auditorium of middle-aged and elderly churchgoers, "I am not here for a *vacation*! I'm a Canadian by birth, and I tell you, I am not so fond of winter in Canada. I'm here to 'work the works of Him that *sent* me while it is *day*.' I am here to win souls to *Christ*! There is not much *time*. Prophecy is being *fulfilled*. The end is drawing *near*, and *none* of us can afford the luxury of sitting here in church while people are out *perishing* in *dance* halls and *bawdy houses* all over this city!"

The next morning Aimee went to the police station, held a service for the prisoners there, and won the police chief's respect, then hurried to the Winnipeg *Tribune* and stirred the editor's interest. That night, accompanied by reporters and two police officers, she visited the city's dance halls, whorehouses, and gin mills. The following day *Tribune* reporter Carolyn Cornell described in a feature article the previous night's escapades, and thereafter Old Wesley Church could not contain the crowds.

From Winnipeg, Aimee preached in Washington, D.C.; Dayton, Ohio; Alton, Illinois; some mining towns in West Virginia; Philadelphia; Montreal. At each meeting she made scores of converts and collected offerings amounting sometimes to thousands of dollars—Aimee was never quite sure how much, for she relegated to an assistant the responsibility of counting it and sending it to Minnie by wire.

When she learned that one campaign had netted almost two thousand dollars in a week, Aimee clapped her hands in glee.

"Two thousand!" she exclaimed.

But it was the accomplishment itself, not the money, that elated her, and after that initial outburst, she never gave it another thought. She had no need for money and cared not the slightest what Minnie did with it. For herself, the campaign sponsors provided all her needs, and Minnie forwarded to her once a month a small allowance, sufficient for clothing and travel expenses.

Only once that year did she break her promise to send Minnie all the offerings. It was spring, and she was preaching in Lethbridge, a small town in the Albertan Plains of Canada. At four o'clock on a frigid and blustery morning she'd stepped to the deserted platform and, suitcase in hand and head bent into the wind, skipped along the empty street dodging mud puddles until she found a hotel. It was a sleazy relic, but she was cold and weary, and lonely, too, and so she checked in and slept a few hours, not even minding that the bed had not been changed between occupants.

That afternoon, after changing hotels, she inquired from a bellboy the location of the church where the meeting would be held, and learned it had burned to the ground. The sponsors apologetically explained Aimee would preach in the only available arena—an ice-skating rink. They built a deck over the muddy earth, were constructing a platform of scrap lumber, and even agreed to decorate the overhead beams with flags and banners if that would be acceptable. But the building had no heat, and would remain damp and cold.

"You've every right to cancel," said one of the deacons. "We don't have much money, but we'll try to pay your travel expenses."

"I believe we can heat up that old rink just fine!" she replied. "Certainly we'll have the meetings."

"It's a rickety old wooden structure," the deacon cautioned. "It'll burn like kindling if a spark gets to it."

"Praise God, I hope so! We're going to pray down the fire of the Holy Ghost, and I believe He'll set such a blaze in that arena the whole *town*'ll be warmed by it!"

That first night, she preached with a tambourine at her side, and when, after fifteen minutes, she noticed a few people shivering, she announced: "Oh, yes, dear God—we're on our way to glory. Marching to heaven this very minute. Marching. *Marching*! Oh, praise His name— everyone on your feet. Marching to Zion—let's all sing it, and you at the piano, play it with all your *soul*! And while we sing—oh, I can feel the Spirit of God here with us tonight—while we sing let's make a big *circle* all around this great auditorium. There must be a thousand people here tonight, and we can make a complete circle all around, and I'll get right down there and *lead* us in a march that'll get our blood *stirring* and our souls *soaring*. Praise God, let's march to *Zion*!"

When the parade ended, she looked out upon an audience of perspiring faces, and preached a sermon vividly depicting the flames of hell.

When the campaign ended, Aimee gave the entire offering to the deacons. "You can't go on meeting in that lousy rink," she said. "This should be enough to get you started rebuilding the church."

Minnie's reaction, although volatile, was short-lived, and by the time Aimee returned to Los Angeles in the fall of 1920, the matter was forgotten.

Aimee had been traveling nonstop for more than six months, often preaching to thousands without electronic amplification, sometimes conducting two or three meetings a day, continually developing fresh publicity pegs, and although she enjoyed every minute and felt she could have gone on like that forever, Minnie insisted she come home for a rest.

"You can bring your book up to date," she told her daughter on the telephone. "They're just about all sold—made a pile on 'em. It's time we come out with an updated edition, and maybe we can sell it to the same people. Besides"—Minnie's voice took on a sense of significance—"I got a proposition to make you." She would say nothing more on the phone.

Aimee's curiosity was piqued, as Minnie had intended, but another factor played an even more crucial part in Aimee's decision to return to Los Angeles for a few months. Surrounded by thousands, basking in the adulation of hundreds and idolized by a few, she had grown more and more lonely.

It struck her first in the third-rate hotel in Lethbridge, but more poignantly in Philadelphia one night when the last amen echoed through the great halls, the last seeker confessed in repentance and Aimee walked alone to the car where a young chauffeur held open the door. The meeting's euphoria slowly dissolved, and a feeling of emptiness swelled inside her. For all its expense, the hotel room would seem a prison, and she desperately wanted to see people, relax and share a laugh or two with them.

Perhaps she would go for a long walk along a bright and busy street, or have another dinner in a crowded restaurant—a committee of pastors had dragged her through a dismally boring one earlier, throughout which she had displayed the necessary airs of piety demanded on those occasions. But at such an hour the restaurants would be closed, the streets deserted.

"Are you married?" she asked the young driver casually.

"Yes, ma'am."

"Are you a Christian?"

"Yes, ma'am, certainly am."

Aimee sighed. "Well, praise the Lord," she muttered.

In her hotel room that night she wrote to Minnie agreeing to come home when the campaign ended.

Aimee had just collapsed on the sofa, her suitcases still unpacked, when Minnie, bustling into the parlor with a cup of coffee and a plate of cookies, announced, "We've gotta start investing some of that money—it's crazy letting it sit around the house and over there in the bank. You can't trust them banks, anyway."

Aimee declared her disinterest with a long sigh. She sipped the coffee, munched a cookie. Finally, in response to Minnie's impatient glare, she said, "That's your department. What do I know about investing money?"

"Nothing. Which is why I came up with this bright idea, and it's the best thing no matter how you look at it. Come here." Minnie hurried to the window.

"Come on, come on."

Groaning, Aimee set the coffee and cookies down and heaved herself from the sofa.

"See that?" Minnie pointed across the road. "It was nothing but an empty field last year, and now—houses going up all over the place! This city's getting built like crazy. We put money in real estate and we'll end up *millionaires*, I'm telling you."

Rolling her eyes and throwing her hands toward the ceiling in desperation, Aimee turned back to the sofa. "So invest in real estate. Who cares?"

"Not just *any* real estate," Minnie demanded. "A church. A tabernacle!"

Aimee hesitated. Continuing to the sofa, she sat again, and thoughtfully lifted the coffee cup to her lips. Minnie rushed quickly to her side.

"They're *all* doing it! Why, there's the Churchill Evangelistic Tabernacle up there in Buffalo, and Paul Rader's got one going in Chicago, Elsner's got plans in Philadelphia, and Andy deWitt Johnson there in Fort Wayne. All the big names're building their own church, and you know why? I'll tell you why—'cause it kills two birds with one stone. It's the Lord's money given by the Lord's *people*, and it should be used for winning souls and not making big profits in the stock markets to stick away in the preacher's pocket. And the second reason's that preachers need looking out for, too—why should the butcher and the baker and the politicians and everybody else get looked after in their old age, but the preachers go hungry? Nothing doing! You build yourself a *church*, Aimee, and you can go on preaching just like you do—all over the country, all over the *world*, if you want. But then you got yourself a base, a place where you know if you can't go barnstorming anymore, God forbid, you got a congregation that'll take care of you and at least put food on the table and a roof over your head. It's—"

"Hush, Mother," Aimee said softly. With eyes wide, her lips curling in a smile, she placed the coffee cup down.

"It's marvelous!" she exclaimed, leaping up. "It'll be like I'm in two places at once; saving souls through the campaigns and the church, *too*!"

She began pacing rapidly from the parlor to the dining room and kitchen, then back again. Minnie followed, getting in the way. "Oh, we're going to make an *impact* in this city!" Aimee declared, her eyes narrowing. "The devil's had his day, splintering the denominations, scattering false doctrines like sand in a windstorm. Now it's the *Lord's* turn. Yes, yes, Mom—it's a *marvelous* idea!"

Minnie beamed. "Well, that's what I *said*, didn't I?"

Aimee had stopped at the kitchen window and now gazed upon several huge wooden crates in the yard.

"What on earth are those?" she asked.

"Oh, they been there for months."

"What *are* they?"

"Remember them tents you gave Harry?" Minnie smirked. "Well, I guess he don't want them. He mailed them all the way from Jacksonville—C. O. D., wouldn't you know!"

When the children came home from school, Aimee, her eyes moist, smothered them in kisses and silently embraced them for so long that Rolf finally broke away and ran to the toilet. A moment later Aimee exclaimed, "Rolf, Roberta! Let's go for a ride!"

"Where to?" asked Roberta.

"All over. We're going to find a place where God wants us to build a church!"

With the children chattering in the back seat and Minnie hushing them, Aimee drove to the dead end at Century Boulevard, left to Figueroa Street, then right toward downtown Los Angeles, past Exposition Park, across Olympic Boulevard. When she reached Glendale Boulevard, she ignored Minnie's order to turn right into the heart of the city and swerved left toward the suburbs and Hollywood, where the new, scandalous moving picture studios conducted their evil business. One day, she thought, she might preach in the midst of them, a Daniel before the murderous lions, a Paul before the heathen rulers of Rome.

After driving a few blocks along Glendale, she approached Echo Park, a quiet grove surrounding a sleepy lake. Children splashed in the shallow water at the shore's edge while mothers pushed carriages along the shaded paths lined with fern and colorfully flowering plants. Old people gathered to play checkers and talk beneath tall palms and eucalyptus.

Where the park ended, Glendale Boulevard swerved to the right, making a fork with Park Avenue. Aimee steered to the curb. Between the two roads was a wedge-shaped expanse of several acres, barren except for a large wooden sign announcing it for sale.

"This is it!" Aimee whispered immediately. "We'll build a tabernacle here overlooking the park, and the intersections leading right to the door—oh, it'll be grand!"

"Well, it's a good neighborhood, as far as that goes," said Minnie. "Drive over by the sign, so I can take down the address. Might as well go have a talk with the owner right now, see how much he wants for it before it gets gobbled up."

A few days later, Minnie bought the land for cash, which left her with no more than a few thousand dollars in savings. Thus, she determined to launch Aimee on campaigns of greater splendor and proportion than they had ever considered.

"And I know just the place!" Minnie exclaimed. "San Diego! Here, look at this." From between the pages of her Bible she extracted a newspaper clipping. "Listen," she demanded. "'San Diego . . . a haven for invalids . . . twenty-four percent of the population plagued with illness, as compared to a national average of six percent . . . three hundred suicides in ten years, attributed to despondency and depression over ill health.'"

Minnie held her daughter with stern eyes. "If ever there was a city that needed God, Aimee Elizabeth, San Diego's the one," she said.

Aimee turned away. "I don't like doing the healing, you know that."

"You just can't turn your back on all them people!" Minnie shouted. "They ain't got a thing in the world to live for unless you give them some hope. Just stop thinking about *you* for once and give a little thought for them poor souls who'll die in misery and despair if the Miracle Lady don't come to preach in San Diego!"

Aimee confronted Minnie with angry eyes. "I'm *not* a Miracle Lady—what's the *matter* with you! I've made up my mind I'm not going around saying I'm a healer anymore, and that's that. If it happens in a meeting—if God leads someone to come to the altar and ask me to pray, then who am I to refuse? And I'll be happy as anyone, for it'll be a real miracle. But that's the only way."

"There's something you gotta realize, Aimee—without the miracles, there ain't gonna be no crowds. Sick people have souls, too, you know, and if they come to get healed and they get saved in the bargain, who cares *why* they came? They got saved, and that's what counts. So I say praise God!"

"I don't want to talk about it," Aimee shouted, and ran up the stairs to her room.

Minnie said nothing more. The next day she hired an experienced advance man who, armed with promotional literature and money sufficient to fulfill his instructions, departed for San Diego to organize the Christian churches in a solid union behind the campaign and saturate the city with publicity for it. When Aimee casually questioned Minnie's enormous investment in new promotion, Minnie smiled knowingly.

"Just priming the pump," she said. "Just priming the pump."

Giving little thought to the approaching campaign, Aimee spent many hours cheerfully concocting plans for her church. She'd already decided to call it the Echo Park Revival Tabernacle, envisioning it not as a typical house of worship but a theater where skits and pantomimes and tableaux could be presented to illustrate her sermons.

"See, Mom," she announced one afternoon, waving rough sketches

156

in front of Minnie's face. "We can build the tabernacle like this, like a megaphone. Here's the platform, at the point, with the choir along this wall and the orchestra over there. These are the aisles."

"That's nice," said Minnie. "What do you think it'll cost?"

Aimee supposed ten to twenty thousand, much of which would be raised at the San Diego meetings. What's more, she'd already written an article for "The Bridal Call" describing her plans for the 3,500-seat wooden arena and asking readers to send contributions.

Minnie said nothing until the following day. Then she explained cheerfully that the city's building codes prohibited a structure of wood with a seating capacity of 3,500. "It'll have to be concrete," she announced.

So Aimee contacted Brooke Hawkins, builder and contractor with the Winter Construction Company, and authorized him to prepare drawings according to her plan for a cement and steel class A auditorium.

"And you might as well put in a balcony—it should seat maybe four thousand," she added. "And give it a big dome, like the Capitol." It would be the largest unsupported concrete dome on the American continent, Aimee began telling people. She envisioned bells chiming out over the city from the belfry. Bells and angels would dominate the decor: frieze work with bells on the front of each balcony, angels painted at the top of the walls, standing wing to wing. There would be brightness and pageantry and joy everywhere—and lest anyone think the stage and spotlights and curtains and orchestra pit worldly, Aimee personally designed huge stained-glass windows to flank the walls of the auditorium.

Standing on the barren pie-shaped chunk of land across from Echo Park with Brooke Hawkins one afternoon, she explained all her plans in detail and advised him to rework his drawings to conform.

"It will be a lovely building indeed, young lady," said Hawkins. "And it will cost you about a quarter of a million dollars. How much do you have to put down on it?"

"About five thousand."

"That ought to be enough to dig a hole for the foundation."

"Well, you just get your steam shovels to work," Aimee replied curtly. "I'll worry about the money!"

Pressing the automobile to its utmost, dashing across busy boulevards and squealing around sharp turns, she raced back to the house and burst in on Minnie, who was sequestered in the study praying. Throwing open the door, Aimee bellowed:

"We need money!"

Minnie's head jerked up, her eyes snapped open, and, clasping her chest, she exclaimed, "You scared me half to *death*!" Grasping the chair, she labored to her feet.

"It'll take a quarter of a million dollars—that's what Hawkins just said," Aimee continued. "And that's just the shell!"

"A quarter of a *million*?" Minnie shook her head. "Aimee Elizabeth, you're nuts. Even with the concrete it can't be nowhere near that much."

"I changed the design a little, added more seats."

"Changed it a *little*!" cried Minnie. "For a quarter of a million dollars you no doubt added the pearly gates and hired a flock of angels for the choir!"

Aimee began to speak, but Minnie cut her short. "Now—you're gonna have to cut back, and that's that. Where on earth's the money supposed to come from? No bank's gonna give a preacher a mortgage in the first place—much less a *woman* preacher without a working husband and with two kids to support in the bargain. There just ain't no way we can get that kind of money."

"Yes, there is"

Aimee sauntered to the window. Below her on the front lawn Rolf and Roberta were busily enlarging a hole they'd begun digging a few days earlier when Minnie told them of oil strikes in the surrounding hills.

"My mind's made up," she said thoughtfully. "I want to build this place so solid it'll stand and stand, and be a monument long after . . . after we've all gone to glory."

She turned to Minnie, her eyes growing bright. "And that's how *God* wants it, too. *I* was going to be satisfied with wood, but God said no. It's to be cement and steel. Every day the Lord gives me a new vision of its grandeur!"

"Well, He better be giving you the money, too," said Minnie dryly.

"Oh, He will—He will! It'll come from the meetings. I'll ask for special donations. We just need more people out, that's all."

Minnie collapsed into the chair and with tightly pursed lips stared at Aimee. Finally she said, "I'm doing the best I can. I can't do miracles, you know."

For a moment Aimee was silent. Then she said so softly it seemed to Minnie she was talking to herself, "I can. I can do miracles. Or God can, and He uses me." She turned to Minnie. "I'm just afraid, Mom—I guess I don't have enough faith. What if someone comes to *me* instead of the doctor, and then he dies? What if he dies right there in front of me. . .?"

"Well, if that's what was bothering you, you should've said so! I'll just go and screen everybody first—find the ones with the greatest faith, for it's only by faith can they be healed anyway. And if they're in need of the doctor or the hospital, we'll see they go there—maybe after you heal them, maybe before."

The two embraced for a long while.

"I want a glorious temple, Mom," Aimee said softly. "And I want it to last forever."

Minnie searched her daughter's eyes. Finally she said with a seriousness that matched Aimee's, "Well, I'll do what I can. At least I'll give you a campaign down there in San Diego that'll keep them talking for years to come, and after that—who knows?"

CHAPTER XVIII

"They think it's just a big joke!" Minnie bellowed, fanning the air with a copy of the January 6, 1921, San Diego *Union*. "A lousy paragraph on the *sports* page—and not even by itself, just stuck onto that *boxing* story. I'm so mad I could spit!"

Aimee laughed. "And did you notice this?" she asked, taking the newspaper and holding it up to Minnie. "It's sandwiched between two Tijuana Race Track ads!"

"They make a mockery of us, and you laugh!"

"It's funny! Listen."

"I don't want to listen—I already saw it."

" 'Just how wicked we are will be spread to all who care to listen from the Dreamland Ring tonight and for several nights thereafter by Mrs. Aimee Semple McPherson, woman evangelist, who was introduced from the ring last night,' " Aimee read. " 'When the evangelist declared that San Diego needs a revival, Dreamland resented the statement with a round of boos and hoots. Here Mrs. McPherson pulled up a bit, sparred for time and countered somewhat diplomatically. When she said she wanted to meet the worst sinner in San Diego, it was noted that many of our prominent citizens ducked their heads.' "

"Go on, make a joke of it," Minnie fumed. "The whole city'll be laughing before long and then where will we be? We'll be lucky to have enough money to pay for the hotel room."

A week later, with the campaign half over, it seemed Minnie's prediction might approach fulfillment. Aimee ran newspaper ads on the theater page urging readers to "Hear the Miracle Woman Evangelist—Mrs. Aimee Semple McPherson," she had the ring decorated with palms and banners, and in place of the traditional church organ she used an ultramodern grand piano. To launch the song service in spirited fashion she acquired a handsome and dynamic young leader. Yet, each night about half the arena's three thousand seats remained empty.

"I don't know what you're waiting for, Aimee Elizabeth," Minnie complained after the service one night. "We got a week left, and the place's half empty."

"All right, Mom, all right," Aimee responded irritably. That night she announced her first healing service.

On Saturday, January 15, the arena could hardly hold the crowd, and thereafter every meeting included healing. The San Diego *Union* headlined an article the following Friday, "Canes, Crutches Discarded Upon Prayers of Woman Preacher."

"Jamming the seats of Dreamland Arena," the report said, "filling the aisles and overflowing the sidewalks into the streets, more than three thousand people came to hear Mrs. Aimee Semple McPherson, evangelist, pray for the sick and to see with their own eyes just what miracles were performed in the ring last night. After the altar call, the afflicted crowded to the ring by the score and sought the aid of Mrs. McPherson. The woman evangelist prayed for them, anointing them with oil.

"Although she expended every effort possible, Mrs. McPherson was unable to pray for all the afflicted present. All around the ring they flocked, eager to ask the woman evangelist's aid. Personal testimony by the *afflicted* after they had been prayed for provided an unique feature. Without exception, this testimony was given spontaneously, and appeared to come from the heart of the speaker. Many of them were deeply moved."

The campaign became the talk of the city and was extended two more weeks. Aimee began holding three services a day, the evening meeting often lasting three or four hours. Newspaper ads were changed to read simply, "Sister McPherson," the hours she would speak, and her sermon topics.

Before sunrise Tuesday morning, while Aimee slept, Minnie washed and dressed and took the car to Balboa Park, where, later in the day, Aimee would hold the last meeting of the campaign, a climactic open-air healing marathon. As she approached the parking lots near the new Organ

Pavilion, she was surprised to find a few hundred people already gathered in the first rows, although the meeting wasn't scheduled until 10:30. Behind the occupied benches were others, providing seats for perhaps five thousand, flanked by a columned promenade curving gracefully from each side of the pavilion.

Minnie recognized the ushers, thirty young men with crimson sashes, white slacks and jackets. Bustling past the interminable aisles of benches, she waved her handkerchief for their attention.

"Who's in charge?" she demanded, and when one of them raised his hand, she said, "All right, scatter the nurses along the front here, and the first five rows keep for the sick—make them people move back. Tie some cords and close them benches off. Before anybody gets into the sick area, they gotta get a white card from me. Set the screens up way over there in the parking lot, and if anybody comes for healing, that's where you send them. Anybody got any questions? No? Good—let's get to work."

At 9:45, Aimee, dressed in a plain white nurse's uniform and flowing navy blue cape, hurried to the waiting car. A moment later the chauffeur nudged the limousine into the traffic, and they hummed toward the park.

She had preached so often the past six years that she'd come to rather ignore the nervousness, but today it intruded with a stubbornness that sent her heart racing and dampened her hands. Peering over the driver's shoulder, she could see the great arch spanning the park's entrance, the palm and eucalyptus climbing the hill behind it. Directed by uniformed Marines, cars moved into the park double file in a steady stream. People surged by the hundreds around the automobiles, up the hillside, and toward the Organ Pavilion. Aimee strained to see the streetcars unloading hundreds more.

Deftly the driver steered around the incomprehensible traffic tie-up and nosed toward the arch. He tapped the horn briefly, and immediately all traffic was halted while the limousine breezed past.

Snapping her head from side to side, her eyes wide and alert, Aimee saw cars everywhere—on the street, tennis courts, grass. It seemed the limousine would never get through the crowds. Then the driver turned into a narrow road winding up behind the Organ Pavilion and halted before a guard whose hands were raised. With a smile of recognition, the officer promptly waved them on, while another leaped to the running board, shouting, "Make way! Out of the road. Let us by!"

As the limousine approached the pavilion, photographers and reporters ran toward it. Motion picture cameras clacked, flash guns popped. The police commissioner himself opened the car door, taking Aimee's arm and shouldering a path through the crowd.

"About ten thousand people out there, you know," he told her.

"Oh, praise the Lord! Isn't it just *grand!*"

"Every available police officer in the city's on duty—and about a hundred Marines helping with the traffic."

From where Aimee stood on the platform, the multitude spread fanlike before her, beyond the benches to the right and left and so far back the faces blurred together into a gray cloud. In wheelchairs, lying on stretchers, crowding the benches, a montage of ages and colors, their hands and faces now uplifted toward her.

The great organ boomed and the two-hundred-voice choir in white robes, seated in the pavilion's shell, burst into song. An instant later trombones, saxophones and violins caught up, and finally the Salvation Army band, each member dressed in a red and blue uniform.

Her body tingling with the mass of energy sweeping the crowd, Aimee walked to her chair in the center of the stage and, kneeling, prayed. Then she stood and moved quickly to the lectern, where the frenzied applause and deafening roar of ten thousand voices greeted her.

The first to pass before her was an old man on a stretcher, suffering from what Minnie had diagnosed as tuberculosis of the spine. "Brother, have you *faith* that Jesus Christ will heal you *now?*" Aimee asked him.

"I have, Sister!"

"Then, in the name of Jesus *Christ* of Nazareth, take up your *healing*—rise up and *walk!*"

Immediately the old man scrambled from the cot and walked, then ran across the platform, then down into the audience, clapping his hands and shouting Hallelujah! until his joy spread through the audience and thousands of voices cried, "Praise God!" "Hallelujah!"

A woman came to the microphone to explain that three months earlier she had been struck by an automobile. Her leg had been fractured in four places and the bone refused to knit. Examining the injured leg, Aimee described it to the audience as a terrible sight, a gaping, angry hole running through the center of the limb, discolored and perfectly black. Yet, when she finished praying, she announced with a gasp that the blackness had that very moment disappeared and the natural color returned.

"Oh! The pain is all gone!" the woman exclaimed.

A very old lady suffering from stomach cancer and rheumatism crept toward Aimee, crying in pain. "I ain't had a minute's relief in a year," she croaked. "Oh, Sister, heal me. I can't stand the suffering no more."

"O God *bless* you! I can't heal a single person. I can't do a single miracle. But *Jesus* can. The God who made our bodies can heal them and

He *will* heal them. He *will*. He *will*! In the name of Jesus Christ, we *rebuke* this cancer and command it to melt away like the snow before the *sun*! Rheumatism, we rebuke you in the name of Jesus and command you to *loose* this body! Sister, in the name of *Jesus*, be thou made *whole*! Go in peace and serve the Lord in a *well*, *sound body*, from this *hour*!"

And the pain vanished, and the hoary skin twisted into a joyous smile. Weeping with abandon, she seemed unable to say thank you enough, finally declared to the cloud of faces—more people than she had ever met in her life and themselves an extraordinary miracle—that she had indeed been instantly healed by God and Sister McPherson.

All day long the procession never faltered. At 1:00, Minnie ordered the Salvation Army band to play and tugged Aimee through a door in the pavilion shell.

"Now, you eat this," Minnie demanded, handing her a sandwich.

"I'm not *hungry*. Jesus fasted forty days and forty nights. Oh, Mother, it's a time of great and marvelous *miracles*! They're being healed *instantly*! The power is so *strong* here today! Perhaps not since the days of Christ Himself has there been such an outpouring of the Spirit. And it's me, Mom—not Moody or Aquinas or Saint Augustine or Luther or Billy Sunday, but Aimee from little old Salford—that God's using for one of the great miracles of the ages!"

Fifteen minutes later she was back on the platform to thunderous cheers. All afternoon the ailing filed by, and Aimee prayed for each with unflagging fervor. An organ recital scheduled for 3:00 P.M. at the pavilion was canceled. At 4:30 Minnie announced that, according to the numbered registration cards, Aimee has already prayed for and laid hands on 380 sufferers. Yet, many hundreds still waited in line and in the audience for the touch of the Miracle Woman's healing hands.

An hour before sunset, Aimee left the platform and walked through the audience. "I am going to walk through the rows one by one, seat by seat, and grasp your hand and pray for you!" she cried. "There is no other way I can reach you in the remaining hour."

Suddenly the masses on the fringe pressed toward her, jostling, crushing. Some screamed, others fell, and Aimee stumbled back to the steps. Fingers clawed at her uniform, fists smashed into flesh. A few, touching her dress, cried, "I'm *healed*! I touched her and was *healed*!"

On the platform, while the guards kept the crowd from the steps, Aimee cried, "Chaos is of the *devil*, not the Lord. The Lord gives the blessing to the *meek* and the *patient*."

Finally the crowd quieted.

It was not the fatigue of seven hours that brought tears to her eyes, not the sweat pouring down her face and clothes, the hoarseness that made even swallowing difficult, nor even the emotional strain of maintaining so high and uncompromising a zeal. All over the audience the sick, perhaps thousands of them, still clamored for her, still lifted withered arms, with no hope but her, and now utterly desolate.

Summoning all her energy, she cried with a voice full of feeling, "You don't *need* me to touch you and pray for you each and every one! It's *God*, working through your *faith*, Who heals. Bow your heads *now* and pray this very moment with me, *believing*, and God will do miracles all *over* this great audience. It's His *promise*! He'll *heal* you!"

She beseeched God for His name's sake to open the floodgates of heaven and pour forth miracles as never before since the days of Christ. All over the audience exclamations of joy mingled with cries of astonishment.

With her "Amen," the choir and orchestra burst into the triumphant cords of "Power in the Blood," and Minnie whisked her off to the waiting limousine.

Back at the hotel she cried briefly, unsure why, then took a long bath and a short nap. Later, after combing her hair and putting on a clean dress, she and Minnie went to a restaurant for dinner, and from there to the White Temple Baptist Church, where she addressed the youthful members of the city's United Christian Endeavor.

In Los Angeles a registered letter from Leonard W. Horton, Esq., of Providence, Rhode Island, informed her that Mack had filed for divorce. But for fleeting fantasies on those lonely cross-country campaigns, she hadn't given him a serious thought in more than two years, hadn't wondered for a moment what had become of him, whether he'd found someone else. Yet now, with the letter crumbling in her hand, she struggled against a wave of intense loneliness. She responded in anger.

"I don't *believe* it," she insisted to herself, storming through the house. "You want to hear something funny?" she yelled up the stairs to Minnie. "Mack's filing for divorce. It's a bluff—he can't be that stupid."

Pacing with rapid, aimless steps, she bellowed, "*He's* divorcing *me*—and on grounds of extreme cruelty and desertion, of all the crazy things I ever heard! Well, let him *go*. He'll see. He'll never find anyone like me if he lives to be a hundred. He *won't*, you know."

Leaning over the railing, she shouted to the second floor, "It's the stupidest thing I ever *heard* of! I make more money in a week than he makes in a year! He could've been rich! Are you *listening* to me?"

The bathroom door opened. "What on earth are you *screaming* about?" Minnie demanded. "Can't a body take a bath in peace?"

Aimee draped herself disconsolately across the banister. "Oh, Momma, Mack's going to divorce me," she said, her voice trembling.

"My God!" Minnie exclaimed. A moment later she bustled down the steps in a bath towel. "And right now of all times, when I've got you booked in St. Louis and San Jose and Denver. You just *can't* be divorced."

Her head still buried in her arms, Aimee held up the letter and Minnie quickly skimmed it. Finally, she said softly, "Well, then, he's gonna do it."

Aimee lifted wet, pleading eyes to Minnie's.

"Now, don't you worry," Minnie consoled, patting her daughter's head. "It won't be so bad. You'll file a countersuit tomorrow. He'll win, but at least it'll be a smoke screen. And if word gets out, so what? There's nothing in the Bible saying you can't get divorced—just you can't get *married* again as long as he's alive. Still, we don't have to go advertising it. What people don't know won't hurt 'em."

Minnie stared at Aimee sternly. "Now, there's nothing to worry about, Aimee Elizabeth—so why are you crying?"

"I just feel so lonely, Momma."

"Well if that's not the dumbest," Minnie fumed, stomping back up the stairs toward the bathroom. "You ain't seen the man in two and a half years, didn't even mention his name in all that time, and now all of a sudden you're lonely for him."

On April 12 the Providence County Court granted Harold McPherson the divorce and custody of his son, Rolf, although he made no effort to exercise it. His mother and another tenant at the boardinghouse, Miss Elizabeth Reid, had served as witnesses, testifying that Aimee had threatened to kill herself and Mack; a great actress, she would throw herself into hysterics at will in order to have her way.

By then, Aimee had put the whole matter out of her head, for the St. Louis campaign absorbed her day and night. In June, Denver newspapers announced the meetings there with banner front-page headlines: "The Deaf Hear, the Blind See, and the Lame Walk." Aimee preached to as many as fifteen thousand nightly, and one evening, according to an official police report, about eight thousand more were turned away. In the three weeks of that campaign, Aimee reached almost half a million people.

Describing those meetings to her "Bridal Call" subscribers, Aimee cheerfully quoted a letter from Presbyterian minister E. L. Krumreig: "I have had the pleasure of being present during a whole campaign—or

166

nearly so—with all of the leading evangelists of our day and time. I only had to hear Mrs. McPherson preach a few times and to note the result of her ministrations in order to determine myself that she is undoubtedly the greatest preacher-evangelist in the world today. . . . I am most assuredly convinced she is the world's greatest evangelist!"

During the first six months of 1921, Aimee earned more than $100,000—she was never quite sure how much, but she knew that in addition to the regular offerings, the St. Louis people donated $16,000 specifically for the tabernacle, and in Denver the building fund contribution was even larger. When she offered "Bridal Call' subscribers the chance to be "chairholders" in the tabernacle—a $25 contribution would purchase one chair—thousands responded.

In the fall, during a campaign in Rochester, she telephoned Brooke Hawkins, the contractor. "It's not going to be *big* enough," she told him. "I'm drawing immense crowds all over the nation and I *know* we're going to need at least a thousand more seats. I want you to add another balcony."

In January 1922 she held a short campaign in Fresno, then moved to Wichita for three weeks in May and on June 9 opened for another two weeks in Denver. By then the tabernacle's outer structure was almost complete and the workmen were constructing the dome.

In the fall, just before leaving for Australia and New Zealand, where Minnie had arranged brief campaigns to offset the expense of much-needed vacations, Aimee preached in Oakland, California. There, she finally addressed herself to her growing number of critics—the old-line Pentecostals who denounced her for quietly eliminating the tongues-speaking and Holy Ghost baptism from her services in exchange for city-wide support from the big denominations, and representatives of these very denominations, who grumbled against the campaigns' emotionalism in general and the healing services in particular.

A year earlier, Aimee read an article by a widely respected religious educator, B. J. Morris, Ph.D., who investigated the long-term effect of her divine healings in Denver and found them generally unsubstantiated. Writing in the *Pacific Christian Advocate*, Morris quoted a C. S. Bluemal, M.D., who had conducted similar research in Denver: "There are beyond question a few positive cures, for there are many cases of hysterical lameness, deafness, blindness, aphonia, etc., which yield to the stimulus of intense emotion. These various hysterical manifestations are often brought on by shock or emotional stress, and they disappear under like conditions. During the war, hysterias frequently occurred as a result of shell shock, and they were often "miraculously" cured by the administration of ether to the stage of excitement. Such cures are the only positive cures that an evangelist can make. They are not miracles, but they are extraordinarily spectacular."

Other Christian journals—*The Congregationalist* and the well-known *Moody Institute Monthly*—said the same and their skepticism left Aimee with a sense of fear and guilt she could neither fathom nor shirk.

In San Francisco, at a precampaign press conference, a reporter asked whether she planned any all-day faith healing services. While Minnie sat across the room with mouth gaping in astonishment, Aimee made an instant decision.

"I say very definitely, right now, that I do not wish the lame, the halt, the blind, and the crippled to crowd my meetings. That is the portion of my work to which I am least attracted."

It was *her* ministry and no one else's, she stormed later in the day, easily drowning Minnie's frantic screeches. She'd preach what God *told* her to preach, not what pleased the ministers or public or President of the United States even! Then she stormed to the desk and, pen in hand, wrote for "The Bridal Call": "You may say that I am in the middle of the road. On one side stands the cold, frozen, worldly church. On the other, is the frenzied fanaticism and boasting manifestations which brings discredit to the precious Holy Spirit. I stand in the middle, however, for a sane, wholesome power of the Holy Spirit which brings honor and souls to the Lord Jesus Christ. I have maintained this position without catering or compromising to the favor of either extreme. I seek to give no offense to either side but to keep life and doctrine straight to the Word. I take the hand of the one who is burning with fire and zeal and put it in the hand of those who are cold and dead, thereby lifting both to the Word and Spirit and a sane, sweet, powerful, humble, balanced, soul-winning position."

That night, still aroused, she told her audience, "I'm not Baptist or Methodist or Pentecostal or anything but *Christian*. I believe in the infallible inspiration of the Scriptures. And I believe in the *Foursquare Gospel*—Jesus Christ as Saviour, Baptizer, Healer, and Coming King!"

She liked that term—the Foursquare Gospel—so much that she used it several times in every sermon thereafter, and eventually changed the name of "The Bridal Call" to "The Bridal Call Foursquare." Her tabernacle would be interdenominational, simply the Church of the Foursquare Gospel.

At her last meeting in San Francisco, she made another major announcement. "How *mightily* God has moved!" she exulted. "*We* set out to build a little old wooden revival tabernacle, but God said, 'Build a house unto the *Lord*, a glorious temple of God in the City of Angels. And *we* planned to call it the Echo Park Revival Tabernacle—but God has laid a new name on our hearts. It shall be called *Angelus Temple!*"

She began applauding the name herself, and instantly thousands joined her. "*Angelus Temple!*" she shouted again, beaming.

"Angelus Temple!" the audience echoed.

At two o'clock in the afternoon on New Year's Day, 1923, Aimee climbed a precarious flag-draped scaffold above the temple's main doors and faced a crowd of two thousand in the street below. She wore not the traditional nurse's uniform but a flowing white silk gown, and in her hair she had pinned a large red rose to match the color of her lips.

She spoke briefly, telling the story of her life with tear-brightened eyes and enthusiasm that denied its innumerable repetitions, then made the formal dedication. Descending the scaffold again, she personally led the crowd through the huge glass doors—crystal doors, she had insisted—and into the 5,300-seat auditorium. Like a Broadway theater, the rows of seats dropped in tiers to the orchestra pit and stage, framed with elaborate latticework and a great-carved plaque overhead declaring: "Jesus Christ, the Same Yesterday, and Today, and Forever."

At the rear of the stage, huge curtains flanked a large baptismal pool, and behind it a painting of the River Jordan covered the entire wall. Above the stage the thirty-foot-high gold facade of the organ spanned the entire wall, divided by a mural of Christ with hands outstretched, one toward heaven, the other toward Aimee.

CHAPTER XIX

On a hot morning in July, the front door chimes rang at the new parsonage beside the temple and overlooking Echo Park, and Emma Schaffer, Aimee's new secretary, hurried to answer. Opening the door a width sufficient to permit extension of her plain and somber face, she gazed directly into a man's neatly vested and jacketed chest. Her eyes quickly darted up the dark tie and neatly tailored white shirt collar to confront a handsome, smiling face.

"Yes?" Emma barked.

"I'm Kenneth Gladstone Ormiston," the man said, sweeping the hat from his head. "Mrs. McPherson is expecting me."

Emma flung the door wide.

"Wait here," she snapped, and vanished through huge doors to the left.

Kenneth Ormiston tugged a white handkerchief from his jacket pocket and dabbed his brow. His eyes swept the foyer—the colorful ceramic tiles of the floor, the red wrought-iron spiral staircase and stained-glass window behind it. Beneath the steps a luxuriant patch of tropical plants flourished, and behind it glass doors opened upon an atrium with a small pool and marble sculpture of a nude male.

Emma Schaffer projected her head between the great wooden doors. "Come," she said, gesturing.

Peering through the open doorway, Aimee saw him limping toward her, tall, lean, and slightly balding, yet young, no more than thirty. She rose from the desk and, brushing past Minnie, who sat on the sofa opening envelopes and dumping contributions into a large bucket, hurried to the door.

"Praise the Lord, it's good to meet you, Mr. Ormiston. I'm Aimee Semple McPherson. Come in and sit down." Leading him to a chair opposite the sofa, she gestured to Minnie. "This is Ma Kennedy, my mother and the power behind the throne—the one who writes the checks, so be nice to her."

Ormiston smiled pleasantly. Glancing around the room, his gaze lingering on the photograph of Aimee and Robert hanging above the piano, he said, "It's a lovely home."

"Isn't it?" Aimee exclaimed. "I designed it myself, you know. This is supposed to be the living room, but it's so bright and pleasant we moved a few desks in and made it an office, too. The dining room's across the hallway and the kitchen right behind it. There are four bedrooms upstairs, and yet Mom and I have to sleep together, and Roberta and Rolf, too—we've got four unwed mothers staying with us right now. The place is becoming a *home* for unwed mothers. Their families have kicked them out, and they've come to us for help, and we just *can't* put them out in the street . . ."

"Let's get on with the business," interrupted Minnie. "I got work to do."

Aimee cast her a furious glance, but when she turned to Ormiston she was smiling again.

"I want a radio station," she said. "The studio will be on the third floor of the temple and we'll put the antenna on the dome. I'd like to be on the air by January first—we'll kick off 1924 with a bang. And I want the best—money's no object."

"It most certainly *is* an object," interrupted Minnie. "What do you think this is, a backwoods camp meeting? It costs a *fortune* to run this place."

"Stop interrupting me, Mother," Aimee scolded, staring Minnie into silence. She turned to Ormiston with a helpless sigh, rolling her eyes. "What I mean is, we have the money to build the station, to build it right, and that's the way I want it. In fact, that's the way I *insist* upon it." She glanced quickly at her mother, and Minnie turned away and kept silent.

"I want this station to reach all over the West. I want it to reach the Canadian border, and to carry the message of salvation throughout northern Mexico. I'll need facilities to play records, and also to make them, because I'm going to be traveling from time to time and I want to leave recorded messages behind so my people won't have to be without me for even a single day. Some of them practically worship me, you know!" She

171

laughed, passing it off with a wave of her hand, but the thought gave her great satisfaction.

"Just what's your background, Mr. Ormiston?" asked Minnie.

"I built the Los Angeles *Times* station. I'm the manager there right now. My degree in electrical—"

"No, no, no," interrupted Minnie. "You sent us them qualifications in the mail. What's your *religious* background?"

Ormiston's eyes met Aimee's and he said as though only to her, "Perfect attendance at the First Presbyterian Church of Santa Monica from five to ten years of age. Not much after that, I'm afraid."

Aimee laughed with uncommon charm.

"Then you are an atheist," Minnie declared.

"An agnostic."

Minnie turned a stern face toward her daughter. "I still say we should find a Christian for this job. We shouldn't be giving the Lord's money to the devil."

"Mother, how can you be so *rude*! Mr. Ormiston's not the devil, and you owe him an apology for even *suggesting* such a thing! Besides, we've advertised for a Christian engineer and there just aren't any. I think we're very fortunate to have Kenneth Ormiston apply for the job and,"—she turned and smiled at him,—"I intend to hire him. Sooner or later he'll get saved, won't you, Mr. Ormiston?"

"Anything's possible, Mrs. McPherson."

"Well, how much do you want?" asked Minnie curtly.

"Three thousand dollars a year."

"Three thousand—that's robbery! Nobody gets that much, not even me! This is the *Lord's* work, remember. I'll give you two thousand and no more."

Ormiston stood to his feet, still smiling pleasantly. "That won't be sufficient," he said. "Please don't get up. I can find my way out."

"Well, how much *is* sufficient?" Minnie demanded.

"Three thousand dollars."

"All right!" said Aimee, leaping to her feet. "You're hired! Congratulations. Mother, put him on the payroll as of today. Let me walk you to the door, Mr. Ormiston—I'll call you Ken, if you don't mind, and you may call me Mrs. McPherson. Meet me here a week from today at 6:45 A.M. sharp with all this business about what we have to get and why and where we should put it—you know, how much space it will take up—the whole works. And I'm not sure I'll agree with everything you want to do, so be prepared for disappointment."

172

Returning to the office, she found Minnie standing in front of the sofa, clenched fists resting on her hips. "How *dare* you hire anybody without my approval?" she demanded. "How *dare* you offer to pay anybody one red cent without my say-so!"

"I'll hire who I like and I'll pay him what I feel like paying him," Aimee responded cheerfully.

"Oh, no you *won't*! You got the business sense of a canary. If it wasn't for me, you'd still be preaching to a hundred black folk somewhere in a Florida swamp, catching your death in the rain and snow, you and your poor kiddies starving. It was me told the freeloaders to get lost and kept you from running hither and yon all over the place for peanuts. I'm the one made 'The Bridal Call' pay, and put fifteen thousand people in front of you in Denver—and you *know* it. It was money spent in the right places—and *not* spent in the wrong places."

Aimee took Minnie's clenched fists and, patiently opening them, held the chubby hands between hers. "All right, Mom, I apologize as usual. I appreciate you, much more than you can imagine. I'd just fall to pieces if I couldn't depend on you." Aimee kissed the tip of Minnie's nose.

Then she quickly turned away, walking across the room to the windows and standing with her arms folded, her face petulant. "But sometimes I want my own way, and I have every intention of getting it. After all, I'm as important as you are in this partnership, and I can't see why, if I like somebody and I want him on my staff, I can't have him there."

"Oh, now it comes out. Now you admit it!" exclaimed Minnie, her eyes wide with the sense of conquest. "It's not the radio station you're so concerned about. This fellow Ormiston just strikes your fancy. Well, let me tell you something, Aimee Elizabeth—three thousand dollars a year is just too much to pay for a boyfriend!"

Aimee's face grew red with anger. Her eyes flashing, she screamed, "Oh, I should slap your face for that! What a dirty mind you have! Of course I'm hiring him for the radio station. There just *isn't* anybody else. Even if I didn't *want* to hire him, we don't have a choice. And in case you don't know it, you miser, three thousand dollars is a perfectly reasonable salary for a trained radio engineer these days!"

Minnie had long ago learned she couldn't reason with Aimee when she was in a furor, so she merely sauntered out of the room and climbed the winding stairway to the second floor. But when she reached the second-floor landing, she leaned over the railing and called down, "All right, hire this high-priced Ormiston fellow. But I'm warning you, Aimee

Elizabeth—be careful. You're a silly child sometimes for all your years, giving in to every whim that flitters through that head of yours. You'll do yourself more harm than you can guess if you're not careful."

Aimee gave Ken Ormiston and the radio station little thought that fall, for, while maintaining an exhaustive schedule at the temple, she was also distracted by a minor revolt when some members formed a committee and drew up a formal three-page complaint, handing it directly to her. Angelus Temple had become too commercialized, they insisted, and Minnie Kennedy too dictatorial. She refused to give any account of the money received and paid out, held all the property in her own name personally without a board of trustees or other responsible group to supervise temple affairs. When members criticized her, she excommunicated them immediately in the most casual manner—she removed their membership cards from the files and tore them up.

Minnie was "pernicious, hurtful, antagonistic, unchristian, unjust, and nagging," her method of discipline unnecessarily severe. Moreover, they complained, Minnie relied on a "corps of helpers who are of her same temperament. . . ill-bred, uncivil, snappy, overbearing, and unchristian in their attitude toward the public, the members, and those trying to be of service to the church."

Aimee had proved herself "kind, loving, and Christ-like, beyond reproof or comparison in these days," but she was urged to take control of the temple herself, transfer property titles to a board of trustees, and get rid of Minnie. In view of Minnie's "splendid handling of the financial affairs thus far of the temple," the committee suggested that, if she resigned voluntarily, she be given a cash payment of $25,000. And if Aimee failed to dismiss her, the complaint hinted, "facts and witnesses are being gathered for the preparation of the action to be filed" with the district attorney, which would result in "much notorious publicity and a great hindrance to our work."

The first thing Minnie did when she finished reading the complaint was to march to the church office, withdraw the membership cards of those who, according to her spies, had been on the committee, and tear them to shreds.

"Why can't you be nice to people?" Aimee demanded when her mother stomped back into the parsonage. "They only want what's best for the temple."

"You just worry about the preaching—I'll worry about the business. I know what I'm doing."

Thereafter, the committee dissolved, never acting on the threat to expose the temple's financial secrecy for fear the truth would in the eyes of the world slander the Lord's work everywhere.

The matter proved far less troublesome than Aimee had anticipated—a few confrontations with the dismissed members, questions from the curious. And to each query she responded identically:

"Praise the Lord, I work eighteen hours a day, seven days a week, and if our Heavenly Father in His mercy hadn't sent Ma Kennedy to carry so much of the burden, I'd just collapse in a day. I don't even *think* about her end of the work. I just can't. I must *trust* her under God's leading to make the right decisions."

She hadn't exaggerated the demands on her time. Since the temple's opening, she'd preached as much as twenty-one times a week, lectured at civic clubs, conducted fund-raising campaigns, taught at the Evangelistic and Missionary Training Institute, the Bible school she'd organized with a handful of students who met in the temple and parsonage for classes. Every Thursday night she held baptismal services, by the end of September submerging some two thousand people and adding them to the temple's membership roster. And in February with the opening of station KFSG—Kalling Foursquare Gospel—she took on the additional responsibilities of a daily early morning broadcast, *The Sunshine Hour*.

She reached the third floor still wiping the sleep from her eyes, responding to Ormiston's cheerful good morning with an irrepressible yawn. He laughed.

"Come, sit here," he said, wheeling a chair beside his at the control panel. "Nervous?"

She slumped into the chair. "I'm too sleepy to be nervous," she answered petulantly. "I don't usually get up at 5:20 you know—I must look just *terrible*."

Taking a thermos from the console, Ormiston filled a cup with steaming black coffee and placed it in front of her.

"You do," he said.

"Thank you," Aimee mumbled. Then her eyes widened and she glared at him while, ignoring her, he threw switches and adjusted pots.

"Don't worry, this isn't the moving pictures," he said casually. "Nobody important will see you." When he finally turned to her, his eyes were gentle and smiling. Blushing, she turned away, sipped the coffee.

"You have your sermon?" he asked, "We're on in a minute and a half."

175

"Oh, goodness!" she exclaimed, quickly setting the coffee aside and rooting through her purse. "I *am* nervous. How many people'll be listening?"

Ormiston pondered. "It's pretty early," he said. "I don't think you'll reach more than a million."

"A *million*!"

"Well, Phoenix, Seattle, Reno, San Diego, L.A.—give or take a couple hundred thousand." He glanced casually at the clock on the wall above him. "Here we go," he said, throwing two switches, dropping the needle to the spinning record, turning up the pot.

Quite to her surprise, Aimee found herself looking forward to the early morning broadcasts. Ken always had coffee ready, and after a time she began bringing fruit or doughnuts, and in the remote and sleepy atmosphere of the studio they shared many a laugh and grievance. Often she stayed long after *The Sunshine Hour* had concluded, and while Ken played recorded music, they talked.

"I see the Ministerial Association's on your back again," Ken said one morning before the broadcast.

"Oh, those pests!" Aimee bellowed. "I'm too showy, too sensational, you know. We have bands and orchestras and little plays and colored lights and flowers—what a fuss they made just because I sprinkled rose petals in the baptismal pool. They were *beautiful*! And they *smelled* nice, too. But they said it was too theatrical, so we stopped the rose petals. And were they satisfied? I should say not. I'm just too *worldly*, they say. Well, you know what *I* say? The devil with them! And don't think I don't *mean* it, because I do. Where is God giving the blessing? Tell me that. In *their* churches, half empty every Sunday morning, and the ones who *are* there snoring in the back rows? They might as well drape the black crepe over the doors right now and forget it."

"Apparently you're putting the small churches out of business."

"That's what *they* say—they're driving the members away themselves. Take that Reverend Jacobs—he's as dull as death! So his little church at Victoria Mission folded—if he wants to blame somebody, let him blame God. *He* anointed me and gave me the gift of evangelism."

"And let him blame himself. He's the one who bores his audience—I should say congregation, I guess."

Ken chuckled, and finally the flush left Aimee's cheeks and she, too, smiled.

"So you're going to ignore it?" Ken asked.

"I'm resigning from the association." Rising, she folded her hands beneath her chin and batted her eyes. "Minnie says I'm the symbol of purity and innocence, so I can't do what I was going to—which is to call a press conference and tell them just what I think of those phony preachers! I'm just going to quit." Lowering her voice, she added as though in confidence, "But I'm staying in the Chamber of Commerce. They won't chase me out of that—I'm too rich."

The sound of their mingling laughter warmed and cheered Aimee and she blurted, "I'm glad for these few minutes every morning, Ken—it's the only relaxation I get all day. If I'm not bickering with Minnie or smiling for the photographers, I'm praying for an old biddy's ingrown toenail or hobnobbing with a politician—or preaching, of course. And it's wearisome, I promise you."

He said nothing, but gazed at her with eyes that seemed strong and patient, fatherly eyes that held no judgment. After a moment she felt her cheeks flushing. Still, she didn't turn away.

"You're fascinating," he said.

Perhaps he would reach for her hand, she thought, or kneel beside her and, taking her head in his hands, pull her to his lips. It would be beautiful and innocent, and she would not resist that good friend who brought the sunshine to her life.

Ken glanced at the clock on the wall. "Fifteen seconds to air time," he said casually.

"What? To what? Fifteen seconds!" She ran her fingers through her hair, struggling to concentrate. "My notes—where are my notes?"

Ken reached into her purse and handed her the handwritten papers, cued a record, adjusted some control switches.

"Stand by," he said. With eyes closed, Aimee took a deep breath, then nodded to him.

"God bless you and good morning from KFSG, the Angelus Temple radio station of sacred word and song in Los Angeles, California," Ken announced. "And now, the founder of Angelus Temple, Aimee Semple McPherson and *The Sunshine Hour*."

To those close to life at Angelus Temple, the widely publicized fact that Aimee received only twenty-five dollars a week in salary produced sly chuckles; the Echo Park Evangelistic Association provided her with an all-expense-paid home, auto, and, through charge accounts at every major department store in the city, even her wardrobe. But there was another irony of which Aimee alone seemed aware: her schedule was so demanding even the twenty-five dollars was superfluous—she couldn't find time to spend it. She'd already graduated the first-year class of Bible students and sent many of them out with temple support to start branch churches or Lighthouses, as she called them, throughout the country. Coinciding with the dedication of each new Lighthouse, she usually planned a spectacular campaign, channeling converts into the new mission.

In the summer she discussed plans to raise a five-story building for the Bible school, which would henceforth be called the Lighthouse of International Foursquare Evangelism, or L.I.F.E. Bible College. To everyone who would contribute a dollar, she announced, she would send a miniature sack of cement as a symbol of her gratitude. Many thousands sent the money.

Another matter occupied a great deal of her time in the fall—so much so, in fact, that Minnie thought it utterly ridiculous and didn't mind saying so. The year before, Aimee had taken it into her head to enter a float in the Tournament of Roses Parade in Pasadena, thereby proving to the world that the things of the Lord can be every bit as colorful and impressive as those of the devil. But the whim had occurred too late for the temple's volunteer craftsmen to execute her design successfully and the float took no honors. Next year, Aimee assured the disheartened workers, they would indeed win.

Thus, early in the fall of 1924, she called together a score of the temple's most talented artists and craftsmen, filling them with the vision of how souls could be won to Christ if they could only create a prize-winning float. And on January 1, 1925, the Tournament of Roses' first prize was awarded to Angelus Temple.

Aimee spent little time with Ken Ormiston that year, except for those brief interludes each morning, and even they were often crowded out of schedule, replaced by marathon sessions in which she recorded a week or two of sermons at one sitting. But although she didn't see him for days, and then for only an hour, she often discovered him in her thoughts. She admitted to herself with no shame that he stirred her with desire, his tall, lean body resurrecting the flaming memories of her youthful passion for Robert. But apart from that she felt fondness and gratitude, for he was what she needed most—a friend. Neither critical like Minnie nor groveling like the thousands who clawed at her every day, he remained compassionate, yet proud and strong. Fleetingly she fantasized his arms around her, forcing her to him, lifting her to his lips. But she caught herself abruptly, frustrated and angry and guilt-stricken, too, for he was a married man and she a preacher of the Gospel of Christ, and according to the Word of God the very thought at that moment had been equivalent to adultery. Thereafter, she guarded against such daydreamings, and even treated Ormiston with curtness the following day.

Still, she was grateful for him.

That spring of 1925 James Kennedy died. He was ninety-three then and he sometimes felt he'd outlived the whole world, except for George and Gladys Quinn, who stayed alone on the Quinn farm down the road since George's folks died, and the Pearce family right across the road. A few years after Minnie left, James Kennedy's youngest son by his first marriage, Larry, came to live with him and helped around the farm and cooked the meals. But then Larry had a heart attack and died. "My boy, my boy," James had muttered at the grave, forgetting that Larry had been sixty-three years old.

From then on, James paid the Pearces ten dollars a week to take his meals with them. Each morning and evening, rain or shine, summer and winter, he shuffled across the dirt road and up the long drive to the Pearce farmhouse. It was certainly an easy, relaxed life. In the winter he shoveled the coal himself—he was not too old to do a little work around the place. In the afternoons he whittled, and sometimes, if he was in an especially good mood, he would repair a chair or table for a neighbor. Sometimes he made his own lunch. Whatever he prepared for himself he shared with his German shepherd, Smokie. If he felt like eating in the kitchen, he put the dog's plate there, too. And if he ate in the dining room, Smokie ate in the dining room. The dog was good company.

On Sundays he went to the Methodist Church just as he always had. The Quinns took him. After church, some people usually insisted he come to their house for dinner and he would protest just enough to have them insist, but not enough to discourage them. Late in the afternoon his hosts would drive him to the old farmhouse again. And that is when he felt most lonely, thought about his first wife, when they were both young and when the house and the farm was full of laughing children and bawling calves and chickens and horses and the smell of lilacs and roses, and his body stirred with desire and energy. He thought of Minnie and Aimee and was very proud of both of them, doing the Lord's work as they were. Aimee had sent him clippings of the great crowds that were coming to her meetings all over the United States, and James carried them to the church and showed them to all the people.

"We'll be there to see you one of these days," she always wrote when she sent the clippings. But she had not been there in five years, and James Kennedy quietly assumed she would never come back. "She's just so busy with her business," he explained to neighbors. "Doing a man's work, you know. It's a wonder she doesn't wear herself out."

Toward the end, his eyes began failing him so he couldn't read at all. Instead, he listened to his new radio each night, and then, with his cane, he went for long, limping walks with Smokie at his side. Finally he went to bed and slept very soundly. Sleeping had become his favorite pastime.

He wrote to Aimee perhaps once every six months, dictating the letters to Mrs. Pearce. She wrote back as frequently, and every month James received a copy of "The Bridal Call Foursquare." Mrs. Pearce was delighted to read it to him.

When he died, Aimee sent flowers and Minnie took a train to Ingersoll, arriving just in time for the funeral. It was held at the Methodist Church in Salford, and the place was crowded. After the service, a short, stooped old man came up to Minnie and said, "I worked for Jim Kennedy when he built that bridge over the swamp down the road. Everybody said it was a damned fool idea. But Jim said if we could build a floating bridge across that swamp it would save us a mile and a half of road. So he thought the thing through and he built it. And by God they were using it for fifty years until they came along with these automobiles and concrete highways and all."

Immediately after the burial, Minnie listed the farm with a real estate broker in Ingersoll and hired two laborers to help pack in large wooden crates everything she thought usable.

James was buried in the Harrison Street Cemetery, about twenty feet to the right of the main entrance on the Ingersoll-Salford Highway and only a few hundred yards from where Aimee had been converted seventeen years earlier. His body was laid to rest beneath the Kennedy family monument, his name carved in the stone next to that of his first wife and Larry and a sister and his parents.

CHAPTER XX

Sunday evening, while the organist played "All to Jesus I Surrender" in sweet, stringlike tones, Aimee earnestly pleaded with the audience for a quiet offering: "You know—not the tinkling kind, just some soft rustling. Let's make this a *paper* offering." She motioned the ushers forward, then stepped back to the hand-carved red velvet chair referred to by one reporter as the throne of Angelus Temple from which Sister Aimee reigned as queen. While the ushers moved swiftly up the aisles, Aimee lifted the receiver of the telephone beneath the chair.

"How's it coming through, Ken?" she whispered.

"Good. The levels are fine. You sound worn-out."

"I'm all right." Then she added, "Did I tell you my father died?"

She thought perhaps he'd hung up, but finally he asked somberly, "You want to talk to me?"

The concern in his voice ripped across her frayed emotion and her lavish smile dissolved into a sob. Quickly she checked herself, forcing the smile back.

"Let's talk about it," said Ken.

"I'll be up for coffee after the service," she answered and hung up.

Two hours later she sat across from him in the control room.

"You were superb, of course—as usual," he told her. "You have a great facility for renewing yourself when you step before an audience."

"It's not me. It's the Holy Spirit. He renews me and speaks through me." Then her eyes twinkled. "But why am I wasting my time preaching to you? I promised myself I wouldn't do that anymore, and I may even stop praying for you. Go to the devil if you like. It's your life. I've got too many *important* things to worry about."

She meant to laugh, but the somber concern in his eyes stopped her. She stared at him silently for a long while, the compassion she saw in his face stirring in her an inexplicable pain.

"Oh, Ken," she said, turning away, "I'm going to cry." Burying her face in her arms, she sobbed quietly. When she felt Ken's hands on her shoulders, his strong fingers kneading the tense muscles, she abandoned herself to long, hard crying. A moment later, with a few sniffles, she grew silent. Ken pressed a handkerchief into her hand.

"I just *love* to cry," she said, her voice trembling. "I haven't done it in years! It's such fun—I should've been a professional mourner at Jewish funerals."

She felt his fingers brushing her ears and playing gently along her neck, and an involuntary sigh of pleasure escaped her.

"You need a vacation."

"What a joke!" Aimee exclaimed, dropping her head to her arms again. "Take Aimee Semple McPherson away from Angelus Temple and it would close up overnight."

"No, it wouldn't."

"Yes, it would."

"No, it *wouldn't*" Ken said firmly. "Get some big-name preachers and evangelists to fill in and your precious flock will be royally entertained in your absence." He paused. "Perhaps that's what troubles you—they'll get along just fine while you're gone."

Aimee turned on him with anger in her voice. "Shall I tell you something, know-it-all? I'd trade this whole place—temple, parsonage, Bible school, and radio station, too—for a decent canvas tent and an open field. I'd do it tomorrow if I could."

Ken smiled.

"You don't *believe* me."

"You love the splendor and glamour too much."

"Oh, Ken," she exclaimed, rising, pacing the tiny studio, "it's a *bore*! You don't know! Everything's got to *conform*. My whole life's scheduled and rehearsed. We can't even get the Holy Spirit anymore unless it's the right day of the week. The newspapers tell me how I should dress, the ministerial association how I should baptize, Minnie how I should take an offering—and you how I should preach for the *airwaves*. I can't even stub a toe without somebody's permission! I wish I could do something on impulse just *once*."

Before she realized what was happening, Ken bent over and touched her lips with his.

"Like that?" he said seriously.

She gasped, her pulse quickening, her mouth open in astonishment. In silence she stared at his lips only inches from her own, taking long, deep breaths. Her eyes riveted to his mouth, she lifted her arms to his neck and pulled him to her.

As soon as their lips touched, she broke away, stood to her feet, and walked quickly to the door, brushing from her dress imaginary wrinkles.

"You shouldn't have done that," she said, shaking her head in confusion. "I must be very tired. Good night."

As she opened the door, she felt Ken's hand on her arm. "Let's go for a cup of coffee," he said.

She reached for his hand to push it away, but when her fingers touched his she held them, studied their slender gracefulness. When she looked up into his face, her eyes were moist again.

"Oh, Ken," she said. She felt his arms encircle her, pulling her gently against him, his hand caressing the back of her neck until, surrendering, she rested her head against his chest. Hesitantly she lifted her arms to return the embrace.

They took Ken's car to a small all-night soda fountain in Hollywood patronized by weathered prostitutes and young, toughened hustlers and the sad, eccentric people of the night. Around one table huddled half a dozen bohemians, dull-eyed and sullen, their muttering lost in the bawdy laughter and bantering of the crowd.

How strong the tug of the world and its ways, she thought. How evil entices us. And yet she felt no tinge of guilt, only excitement rushing through her, making her body tingle. She had renounced the world, turned her back on it, preached against it, against riotous living, naked debauchery, the lusts of the flesh. But for all that, the world was still in her, as vital as her breath, and she did not deny her hunger for it.

They stayed for a long while, Aimee astonishing Ken with her animation, frequently interrupting herself exclaiming the marvel of a new sight or overheard conversation.

Finally Ken rose and went to the counter to pay the bill.

"I don't want to go home yet," Aimee pouted when he returned.

"Come," he said, taking her hand. "We'll go for a drive. There's a place on a hill not far from here—it overlooks the whole city. Very romantic, you know. But I'll warn you—it's a steep drive, and the car usually overheats. It'll take about two hours for the thing to start working again. I wouldn't want you to get bored."

Aimee laughed nervously.

When Ken left her in front of the parsonage at 3:00 A.M., Minnie was standing at the living room window and rushed to the foyer.

"Where have you *been*?" she demanded the instant Aimee opened the door. "I was all set to call the cops I was so worried."

"I went for a ride," Aimee said dreamily.

"With Kenneth Ormiston! I'm right, ain't I?"

"Uh-huh," Aimee agreed.

"I *knew* it! The pastor of Angelus Temple setting a fine example for her ten thousand members. Well, this's gone far enough, Aimee Elizabeth, and we're gonna put a stop to it right now, before it turns into a first-class scandal."

Aimee slumped on the wrought-iron stairs, her elbows resting on her thighs, her chin in her hands. "Can't we talk about it tomorrow, Mom? I'm tired. It *is* three o'clock in the morning, you know."

"Do *I* know? I been sitting here all night worrying my poor heart sick over you. I been looking at nothing but that clock for five *hours*!"

Minnie threw up her hands in despair. "I just pray to God nobody seen you get out of his car. There's talk enough already about them telephone conversations you and Ormiston carry on all during the service. It won't take long before they're whispering about a lot more."

Aimee giggled. "I fail to see what's so unusual about a broadcaster chatting with her engineer," she said.

"This thing has gone way beyond a business relationship, and you know it," Minnie growled. "They ain't all a bunch of fools, you know. They can put two and two together. They know what they see and hear."

Aimee's eyes flashed sudden anger. "There *is* nothing to put together," she shouted. "If anyone, including you, sees evil in my relationship, it's conjured up from the evil of their own souls and filth of their own depraved minds!"

Minnie opened her mouth to speak, then changed her mind. She pondered Aimee's words thoughtfully. Finally she said, "Well, maybe I was wrong to . . ." Then her yes widened and punching her fists onto her hips she scowled, "Here I am—I must be going nuts, doubting my own eyes and ears. Oh, you're an actress, Aimee, you're the best—lying to your own mother so sincere like that, so even I, who knows what a fake you can be, believe you. But not for long."

Glowering, Minnie approached her daughter. "Look at me," she demanded. Aimee raised weary eyes to confront her mother's awesome anger. "I'm not going to have you tear this temple down around us— you're gonna fire Ken Ormiston."

Minnie's face tightened, her body grew rigid in anticipation of Aimee's imminent outburst. Instead, Aimee closed her eyes and smiled with weary contentment.

"All right," she said. "I'll fire him tomorrow." Then her eyes flashed open and she added sternly, "He gets two months' notice and two thousand dollars severance, and I don't want the slightest chirp out of you or I'll get on the phone this minute and tell the newspapers I'm twelve months' pregnant and we don't even know who the father is!"

Minnie's expression flashed from shock to frown to humor. She ran to Aimee, pulling her off the steps and throwing her arms around her.

"Some days you tire me out," she said, "and others you make me so mad I could spit. But Aimee Elizabeth, there's never a day goes by I don't love you with all my heart."

Aimee kissed her mother's forehead and slowly led her up the stairs.

"I'm tired of being without money all the time, Mom," Aimee said. "While we're making changes, let's change that, too. I want the first offering of the month—it doesn't even have to be counted."

Minnie looked at her daughter with new consternation. "What on earth would you do with all that money? Why, some weeks it's five thousand dollars and more!"

"I'd invest it—or just save it. Or spend it on pretty clothes. I love pretty satin things with lace and all. It doesn't *matter* what I do with it—I earn it and I deserve it."

Shaking her head and shrugging, Minnie agreed.

A week later, complaining about the constant noise of constructing the Bible College, Aimee told Minnie she'd be spending two or three days a week at the exclusive Ambassador Hotel, checking in after the evening services so she could get a good night's sleep and awaken to a quiet morning's work. Minnie responded with knowing and haughty disgust, but she kept silent, preferring the few weeks of farewell liaisons be expressed in the Ambassador's discreet privacy, rather than flaunted before the flock of Angelus Temple.

Sometimes Ken and Aimee spent whole days together in the room, the warm sunlight falling across them, Aimee's head snuggling against his shoulder, her fingers twisting the hair on his chest into curlicues. Lazily he would kiss her forehead, her eyelids, her cheeks, her lips, until passion flamed in both of them again.

One afternoon while Ken was thus arousing her, she asked somberly, "Am I a hypocrite? I am, aren't I—preaching and running a church, and then behaving like this?"

Tousling her hair, he whispered, "Preachers need some loving, too, don't they? You know, it's the damnedest thing—"

"Don't curse." She pressed a finger gently against his lips.

"They'll tell you out of one side of their mouth that God can do no evil. He's the author of all that's good. If you corner them, they'll even admit the naked body's good, made in the image of God, we're told. And if you pin them against the wall, they'll have to say even sex is good—God made it, didn't He? But saying it will leave a dirty taste in their mouth and they'll hate you for bringing such a filthy question up in the first place." He pulled Aimee's cheek against his chest.

"No, baby, you're no hypocrite," he whispered in her ear, sending shivers along her neck. "You're just normal."

"I agree!" she said cheerfully, and buried her face in his chest.

At year's end, Kenneth Ormiston left the temple. "All things work together for good," Minnie sighed with relief. Aimee seemed perfectly content, had given up the room at the Ambassador, and had even initiated several new programs at the temple: The Foursquare City Sisters provided nurses, food, clothing, and furniture for the needy, helped the sick with their housework, and cared for their children. Operators on duty around the clock arranged to meet urgent problems immediately, whether or not the caller was a temple member, whether the need was for money or spiritual counseling. Aimee increased the temple's departments to twenty-four, and boosted the Bible College's enrollment to almost a thousand.

She started a Children's Church to keep youngsters entertained while their parents were at the main service, and began a night school for laborers who couldn't attend day classes at the Bible College. She organized a training program for radio announcers, kept an eye on a music department that included three bands, three choirs, two orchestras, six quartets, a glee club, and two dozen soloists.

Long after Minnie and the children went to sleep each night, Aimee remained at her desk sketching plans for another spectacular sermon dramatization with props and stunning costumes and staging, which she'd made an integral and much-heralded part of the temple program. On occasion a simple melody would occur to her and she would plunk it out on the piano and write lyrics to match, leaving the arrangement to the music department the next morning.

Even before Ken departed, Aimee began complaining that she'd maintained an exhaustive pace ever since the temple opened two years earlier, and when she suggested a vacation, Minnie was quick to agree—a leisurely and spiritually enriching tour of the Holy Land, to be chaperoned by Minnie herself. After all, she reasoned, the offerings amounted to as much as ten thousand dollars a week, the operating expenses little more than half that, and there was no reason some of the difference shouldn't be spent revitalizing the two of them for the good of the work. But Aimee objected.

"I won't go," she said. "We can't both leave the temple at the same time. Somebody has to be here to make decisions—although God knows I need a vacation."

Half fearing an uprising that would somehow see the temple sold out from under her in her absence, Minnie reluctantly agreed to stay at home, but insisted Aimee take fourteen-year-old Roberta along as a traveling companion.

January 11, 1926, thousands of well-wishers from the temple gathered at the railroad station to wish Aimee farewell. With Roberta at her side, she stood on the open deck of the observation car dressed in a sleek blue suit, a bundle of American beauty roses cradled in her arm. The nationally known young evangelist Paul Rader had agreed to fill the Angelus Temple pulpit in her absence and stood behind her until, with a wave of her hand, she summoned him to give the benediction. Then the train creaked and shuddered and began moving slowly along the track, Aimee waving and shouting benedictions. The crowd began singing, "God Be with You 'Til We Meet Again," and Minnie, surrounded by reporters, wept.

"I just can't help it," she said. "There goes the greatest living evangelist, maybe the greatest evangelist of all time. It's the best thing for her, I guess, but I hate to see her go."

She hated it more than the reporters imagined, for watching Aimee's fervent farewell, the radiant joy in her face, Minnie suddenly realized how complete a fool she had been. Aimee was the one who had casually suggested the two of them take a vacation—and Aimee had subtly manipulated Minnie out of it. Once Minnie reached the car, she made no effort at amiability but curtly ordered the driver to the parsonage and instructed Emma Schaffer not to disturb her for the rest of the day. But by dinner her anger subsided and she admitted that some good might come of it after all. Aimee couldn't be with any man for three months and still stay interested in him, she told herself. Maybe she'd get this silliness out of her system, thousands of miles away from the temple and reporters, and if that's how it worked out, Minnie would be just as happy.

From New York, Aimee and Roberta sailed to Ireland, traveling by train from the coast to the quaint town of Magherafelt in the rich, fertile hills of the north. The Semple general store and attached stone house were precisely the same as Aimee remembered them when, on their way to China fifteen years earlier, she and Robert had detoured briefly to visit his parents. But the old man and woman were older still, Mrs. Semple more frail, the two brothers gone off to Belfast, the two daughters married.

A great fuss was made over Roberta, the living image of her father, everyone agreed, and that first night in the quaint town Papa Semple set the fireplace to blazing and called upon his two daughters and neighbors to visit, then trudged through the snow and fetched his finest ham from the smokehouse. Mamma Semple baked a pie and cake, and that evening, with the smells of gingered apples and perking coffee, the sounds of crackling logs and laughter, the party in Roberta's honor was a festive time.

Aimee stayed in Magherafelt a week, she and her hosts lost in animated reminiscences, each of them now laughing, now in tears. "I was sitting right in that chair, and he came through the door with his arms full of wild heather," Aimee recalled. "He knelt right there and held out to me the first bouquet I'd ever been given."

Momma Semple pointed through another door. "It was in that very bed he was born," she mumbled.

When the week ended, she left without Roberta, for the Semples at her prodding had asked to keep their granddaughter with them. Before boarding the train for the coast she took Momma Semple's face in her hands. Her eyes moist, she said, "Momma, it's been so long, and yet I love him as much today as the day we were married."

The old woman put her frail arms around Aimee's waist, then held her away. "And maybe it's been long enough," she said in a quivering voice. "Maybe it's time to find love again. He would want happiness for you."

Aimee kissed the old woman's forehead. "God bless you, Momma!" she said, and ran weeping to the train.

She met Ken in London, as they'd planned, and together they flew to Rome, checking into an expensive hotel in the new Ludovisi Quarter near the Piazza di Spagna as Mr. and Mrs. George McIntire, although Aimee provided great amusement for the bellboys and hotel clerks by spelling it "MacIntyre."

The days unfolded mellow and aimless, and seemed to Aimee the richest of luxuries. She thought she must be getting irredeemably lazy, lying in bed simply to absorb the sensuous pleasure of cool sheets and Ken's warm hands against her body. No Minnie screeching her awake, no sermons demanding to be preached, conferences to be held, or the multitudes pressing all feeling from her with the weight of their inexhaustible adulation and demands. Some mornings, relaxing there past noon with the sun caressing her skin, she imagined herself a sleek silver fish basking in a lazy current.

Finally she would awaken Ken and ask him to make love to her, and then they would shower together and walk to the Caffè Nationale, a popular restaurant for tourists on Corso Umberto I, where cars were bumper to bumper, all honking and zooming through alleys and across boulevards at homicidal speeds, although the only automobile traffic law in the whole city forbade cars to move faster than pedestrians walk. Terrified, foreigners scattered from the path of these cars, the taxies, horse-drawn carriages and the screaming, clattering trams. Only the natives walked on without fluttering an eyelash, oblivious to the chaos.

After breakfast they would stroll through a part of the city they hadn't seen. Days washed together into montages of wine carts and yapping dogs, fruit shops, horses dressed in bright red pompons and tassels drawing wagonloads of vegetables. In the afternoons the wagon drivers took naps in their now empty wagons, leaving it to the horses to cautiously wend their way through heavy traffic and narrow alleys back to the stables.

Stalls overflowing with bright flowers crowded every corner, the petals damp with the spray from a nearby fountain. The boulevards were redundant with palaces, many converted to stores, offices, apartments, or restaurants. Seminarists by the hundreds cluttered the streets, those from Germany clad in cardinal red robes, the Irish in black ones edged with red and without a sash, the Scottish purple cassocks with crimson sash, the Americans black with blue edging and red sash. Still others displayed flowing blue robes with red sash, and a few had purple gowns.

They spent many afternoons meandering through galleries and museums and the great cathedrals that filled Aimee with wide-eyed speechless awe. When they rested, it was at Ken's insistence, for the war wound that had shattered his hip made walking sometimes painful and always fatiguing. They would stop at a sidewalk café, Ken ordering beer and Aimee espresso.

In the evenings, they sometimes sat for a couple of hours near a fountain in any of the several piazzas they happened to be near, and watched the orange sun wash the city with its color and bathe in brightness the tired faces of the people hurrying home from work. When twilight settled over the city and they could see the stars appearing, they'd stroll through nearby alleys in an unhurried search for a restaurant. Sometimes it was late in the evening before, fatigued and smiling, they slumped into the chairs of a small pub.

Late one afternoon they strolled through the Pincio Gardens, where great trees shaded sculptured bushes and green-black boscage, and exquisite marble statues raised out of the embrace of dark fern. Aimee took Ken's hand, pressing it to her lips. The smile she lifted to him was full of contentment, and she offered it indiscriminately to all the lovers she passed as well, those embracing on the benches, kissing behind trees, arms intertwined as they strolled along the wide paths; gathering at the steps of the Villa Medici, and beside the shallow fountain where the thick, neatly trimmed ilexes grew.

She enjoyed watching the young Latin boys walk; they moved with such sensual, effortless grace.

At sunset, they wandered past the Church of the Trinità dei Monti to the parapet where a view unfurled that brought a gasp from Aimee. Before her, the grand flower-decked, sprawling Spanish Steps unfurled, 137 great slabs of marble descending to the fountains of the Piazza di Spagna.

It was a moment of incomparable magic—the retreating sun igniting the marble obelisks and gold cathedral domes, the ancient grandeur, the languorous beauty of young lovers. In the piazza below, old ladies in shirts and work pants, their hair gathered in colorful bandanas, displayed brilliant bouquets to passing throngs while beautiful youths in tight garments lounged impatiently along the steps, their bushy curls dusted with the sun's gold.

Beyond the piazza, two domes dominated the skyline.

"St. Carlos," said Ken, pointing to the one on the left. "The other's St. Peter's. That's the biggest church in the world—St. Peter's. How's this for a bit of perspective—you could stack three Angelus Temples one on top of the other and they'd still fit beneath that dome."

Later, in the purple glow of dusk, they walked through a nearby park, past art studios where young men modeled nude, single-story buildings with plastered walls of soft yellow and beige, with tiny lawns sprouting cacti, colorful plants, and lavish foliage. From the streets came the sound of laughing children and from nearby outdoor cafés the throaty quarrels of men arguing sports or politics over drinks.

They came to a parapet from which the lights of the whole northern part of the city and much of the western glittered below them.

"The Pantheon's out there—you can't see it now, but it's there, all right," Ken said. "Agrippa built it thirty years before Christ was born. Two thousand years old, and it's still in pretty good shape."

Aimee gazed across the rooftops into the darkness, then turned back into the park to see the endless procession of lovers, their faces almost ecstatic. She felt her throat tighten, happiness and sadness welling in her. Finally she turned to Ken, burying her face in his chest.

"I don't want to go back," she mumbled. "Oh, Ken, I'm so happy!"

For a long while he held her tightly and said nothing.

A week later, while Aimee was having breakfast alone and Ken slept, a bellboy handed her a telegram forwarded from the Semples, who were the only ones aware of her address in Rome. As she read the message, her face grew ashen. Leaving the food unfinished, she hurried through the lobby to the elevator and a moment later ran along the corridor to her room. Frantically she searched her purse for the key, then, muttering under her breath, pounded the door with both fists until, naked and wiping the sleep from his eyes, Ken opened the door.

"What took you so long?" she demanded, slamming the door behind her and locking it. "A terrible thing has happened!"

Rushing past him, she threw herself into a chair near the window.

"Whatever it is, it can't be the end of the world," Ken said sarcastically.

"It just may be," Aimee answered. "Read it for yourself." She handed him the cablegram.

Ken skimmed the page. Finally he muttered, "How the hell do you think they got the story?"

Aimee stood, her face stony, and folding her arms across her chest, paced the room. "Your wife," she said coldly. "They haven't a single shred of evidence we're together, and they can't write a story on guesswork."

"Can't they?"

The color left Aimee's face again and she shouted, "No—I won't let them do that to the temple! It would *destroy* those people—they *believe* in me." She rushed to Ken, grasping his hands. "You must leave today for Seattle by the fastest route possible. Call Minnie from there. Tell her the radio station's coming in loud and clear. A casual call, you know. Oh, it'll be so funny—Minnie *hates* you, but she'll be so happy to hear your voice she'll *beg* you to return to the temple—and when you show up there she'll give you the biggest kiss of your *life!*"

"Well, then," said Ken, grimacing, "you can forget the whole idea."

Aimee laughed. "Then I'll go back to Belfast, pick up Roberta, and maybe preach in England. They begged me to, you know. We'll show the world we have nothing to hide. While the scandal mongers do their dirt, I'll humbly win souls—even on my vacation."

She turned to the window. Across the alley in the window of a crumbling brown and yellow house, a young mother sat nursing a naked baby boy from her full breast. She was perhaps eighteen, her long black hair tossed back over her shoulder, her eyes wide, yet serene as she watched the people passing on the cobblestones below.

Aimee turned back into the room. "What's to become of us?" she asked softly, her eyes reddening.

"No, don't cry," Ken said, pressing her head against his chest and with his fingers brushing her hair back from her forehead.

With tears filling her eyes, Aimee lifted her face to him, "Would you marry me?" she whispered.

He kissed her forehead. "I *am* married, Aimee—and if I got divorced and you married me, the church would call you an adulteress. There's just no way, short of wrecking the temple."

"I'll *find* a way!" she exclaimed.

Taking her head in his hands, Ken kissed her deeply. "I've got to get packed and moving," he said.

"Oh, I'll think of a way, Kenny. Don't worry. I'm not going to lose you."

In less than a week Kenneth Ormiston made his phone call from Seattle and a few days later he appeared in Los Angeles to squelch any rumors that he was traveling with Aimee Semple McPherson. On almost the same day, the wire services carried a story that Mrs. McPherson had arrived in London with her daughter, and was planning a series of meetings in the Royal Albert Hall. Thereafter, the American press carried frequent stories of Aimee's trip. She and Roberta traveled through France to Marseilles, took a ship to Port Said in Egypt, crossed the Suez Canal, and finally reached Jerusalem. From there, they continued to Nazareth, Jericho, Hebron, Galilee, and then on to Cairo. As a precaution, should word leak out that Aimee had been in Italy, she returned there with Roberta. The two of them visited Venice, Rome, Naples, and Pompeii. Then they returned to London for a series of meetings, and on Easter Sunday Aimee filled the Royal Albert Hall, the largest auditorium in the British Isles, making front-page headlines in London and throughout the world.

On Saturday, April 24, Aimee returned home from her vacation, Roberta at her side. Twelve thousand admirers met her with screams and applause at the Los Angeles railroad station. Another five thousand crowded the streets surrounding Angelus Temple and blocked traffic for half a mile in every direction. The city's acting mayor presided over an official welcome home ceremony.

PART FOUR

CHAPTER XXI

At 6:00 P.M. on Tuesday, May 18, 1926, newsboys cried the headlines of their extras all over the city: "Evangelist McPherson Believed Drowned!" Phones clanged in every police station and newspaper office in the city and the Angelus Temple switchboard buzzed ceaselessly as multitudes demanded to know whether the story was true. Outside the temple, two hundred people had already gathered in the streets, the crowd growing every moment.

At seven o'clock, a somber-voiced KFSG announcer told listeners, "We have very sad news. We believe Sister McPherson has been drowned. Tonight we feel she is asleep in the ocean. We ask prayers for Mother Kennedy, Mrs. McPherson's mother."

Jay W. Arthur, chairman of the temple Board of Elders, had brought Minnie the news earlier in the day, after Emma Schaffer, Aimee's secretary and devoted companion, phoned him from the Ocean Park Beach and blubbered a few words into the receiver, before dissolving into hysterics. Finally, Frank Langan, who managed the Ocean View Hotel from which Emma was phoning, took the receiver and conveyed to Brother Arthur that Aimee had been swimming far out in the ocean and had disappeared, virtually before her secretary's eyes.

Arthur found Minnie engrossed in tabulating temple accounts. With white face and trembling voice, he blurted, "God bless you, Mother Kennedy. I don't know how to tell you—Sister went swimming this afternoon at twenty minutes to three and she hasn't come back yet."

Annoyed by the interruption, Minnie gave him a stern glance.

"They've looked everywhere," he said. "Sister just can't be found."

Finally, Minnie understood. The color draining from her face, she slowly placed the pencil in the ledger and closed the book. Her eyes fluttered and closed, and she held her forehead in her hands.

"Drowned," she said with crushing finality.

Others rushed in from temple offices to comfort her, and Minnie, with eyes red and watery, face drawn, repeated, "I think our little Sister is gone."

The phone rang. Someone answered it and said it was Frank Langan from the Ocean View Hotel with the message that Aimee still had not been found.

"She's drowned," said Minnie.

"No, Mother Kennedy," insisted Langan, "not far as we know. We just haven't been able to find her. You'd better come down."

"You do all you can," Minnie mumbled. "I don't think it would do me any good to come down. Where's her car?" It was an expensive new Kissel.

"Right here in front of the hotel."

"Put all her belongings in it and bring it to the temple. I'll send somebody down for Sister Schaffer." Then Minnie hung up. "Go get Emma," she told Brother Arthur. "And tell them reporters I can't talk yet—I'm a nervous wreck. And I don't want Emma talking to 'em either!"

When the secretary arrived hollow-cheeked and weeping, carrying Aimee's yellow and white sports dress, shoes and stockings, her Bible, and her purse containing two hundred dollars and some change, Minnie whisked her up the steps to her bedroom and locked the door behind them. She took her daughter's belongings from the secretary.

"Here, sit down," she said, thrusting the fragile woman into a chair. "And for goodness sake, stop crying."

"Oh, I can't. I just can't!" Emma sobbed. "She's dead. I know it. If I had only been there, I might've saved her!"

"How could you save her?" Minnie scolded. "You can't even swim. Besides, what's the Scriptures say? 'All things work together for good to them that love God, to them that're called according to His purpose.' Now, before you go yakking to the reporters, I want to know exactly what happened, step by step."

Early that afternoon, Aimee had driven to the Ocean View Hotel, where she'd kept a room since her return from the Holy Land three weeks earlier when she'd suddenly taken a great fancy to swimming. She had gone to the beach almost every day, using the hotel room to change into her flowery green bathing suit and later to rest and dress.

While Emma watched from the shade of a beach umbrella, Aimee went for a brief swim. Then, slipping into a beach robe, she set to work on her Sunday sermon.

A while later, she sent Emma to make a phone call canceling a 4:30 appointment and also to get her some orange juice at a restaurant on a nearby pier. When Emma returned, Aimee was in the water again, diving and surfacing like a porpoise. Emma closed her eyes and rested. When she looked up again, Aimee had vanished.

Minnie nodded her approval, and with Emma at her side, confronted the press, saying only, "There's no doubt my little daughter, our dear Sister, is drowned and gone to be with the Lord." At those words, Emma Schaffer broke into uncontrollable tears.

That night, fifteen thousand followers knelt and prayed for Aimee's soul in the Bible School auditorium, and hundreds more gathered on the sidewalks and lawns around the temple. At the beach, additional hundreds huddled in the sand singing hymns. A few attempted to run through the breakers in search of Aimee's body, and were restrained by the police. Others knelt alone in the sand and prayed. Many stood gazing into the ocean until the first glimmer of dawn.

Minnie Kennedy's great secret pressed inside her like a tumor, cutting off her breath, swelling at the base of her throat, and forming a tight little knot there. She would swallow continually, but the lump would not disappear. At times she felt almost overwhelmed with fear that her secret would suddenly rage out of control, bringing her imminent destruction. On those occasions, many times a day, she walked around the parsonage and the temple ashen and drawn, her eyes wide. She heard the reporters and the temple workers whisper among themselves that she was obviously overcome with grief, and indeed she was, of a sort.

She had realized within seconds of Brother Arthur's announcement exactly what Aimee had done, and from that moment Minnie's peace had been shattered. When she trembled, it was not with grief as the others thought, but with anger. She fully anticipated Aimee's reckless scheme would bring the temple crushing to dust like the walls of Jericho and heap upon the two of them, and Rolf and Roberta as well, the scorn and slander of those who had long denounced them, and of those she had loved and trusted. It would be only a matter of time.

In her heart, Minnie prayed she was wrong, that God would somehow deliver her from the shame that seemed inevitable and bring her blessed news that Aimee's corpse had been discovered.

All afternoon and late into the night the blue Chrysler sped north along the Coastal Highway toward Monterey with Ken Ormiston at the wheel and Aimee beside him.

"Won't Minnie be in a tizzy by now!" she exclaimed. "Well, she should be happy—now she can do just as she pleases for the rest of her life. And I'll do the same."

It was almost 4:00 A.M. when the blue Chrysler veered left onto a narrow, winding road leading toward the ocean. Moments later they drove through the village of Carmel, where neat little homes and shops nestled along shrub-lined brick sidewalks. Slowly the car moved along the darkened main street, the sound of breaking waves growing louder until in the gleam of the headlights Ken read the street marker: Scenic Drive. He turned left.

The Benedict cottage Ken had rented was the last on the right. Fronting on the beach with sand dunes rolling south to the horizon, it offered almost total privacy. On the north side, a neighboring cottage stood not ten feet away, yet blocked from view by a stucco wall surrounding the Benedict place.

Ken parked the car in the garage.

"Tired?"

Ken groaned.

"I drove that far every day for *weeks* when we crossed the country," she said brightly, hastily adding in response to his pointed scowl, "I *know* how exhausted you must be."

Aimee would have stood long with her arms around Ken in the privacy of the cottage patio, gazing up at the stars, but the salty breeze from the ocean had turned cold, sending shivers through both of them. After a brief kiss they hurried inside. It was small, a living room featuring a large stone fireplace, a kitchen, and upstairs a bedroom, all attractively furnished. After a cursory survey which concluded in the kitchen, Aimee exclaimed, "It's wonderful! And it's just ours, all our own." She lifted her lips to Ken's.

A sudden glare of light from outside startled her. Ten feet away, in the second-floor window of the neighboring cottage, a woman held a nursing baby in her arms. She waved pleasantly. Aimee pulled the drapes shut and switched off the light.

"Let's go to bed," she said.

To Ken's amusement and Aimee's delight, news of her disappearance filled the front page of both the Los Angeles *Times* and the San Francisco *Examiner* the next day. Photos of Minnie, Angelus Temple, Aimee, and the ocean into which she had vanished illustrated sensational stories of the more than five thousand people crowding the beach at Ocean Park in search of her body. Minnie Kennedy had sent the Reverend Mr. D. V. Alderman, pastor of the Pasadena Lighthouse, to supervise the effort. A dozen rowboats had scoured the area where Aimee had been last seen; divers searched the seabed at every suspicious shadow. Farther out, motor-driven boats swept the ocean floor with grappling hooks while, half a mile from shore, two airplanes continuously circled a few feet above the ocean surface. One short item quoted an expert on international ocean currents from UCLA who suggested the evangelist's body could have been swept northward under Lick Pier and become entangled in a roller coaster scaffold that had collapsed and tumbled into the sea a few years earlier. Authorities said they would check that possibility using deep-sea divers.

While Aimee read the stories in Carmel, millions of others did so in their homes throughout the country, courtesy of the wire services. Reporters from leading newspapers descended on Ocean Park by the score, each in a frenzy to get the definitive scoop.

According to the press, hundreds of McPhersonites spent Wednesday night and Thursday morning on the beach, pleading with Sister McPherson herself to return from the dead, thus giving birth to a rumor that at precisely 2:30 P.M. Thursday she would rise from the water and hover in the air as Christ did before His ascension. Unlike Christ, Aimee would preach a glorious message.

One old man tore away from the chanters and plunged into the ocean declaring that Aimee, standing on the waves in robes of spotless white, had beckoned him to save her. Police rescued him.

When bystanders suggested she could not have drowned or her body would have been washed ashore by the tide, Aimee's followers kicked, shoved and punched the blasphemers. One woman who audibly doubted the drowning theory had to be rescued by police.

But, said the press, despite the determination among Mrs. McPherson's followers to have her dead, a view pronounced with profound finality and frequency by the temple's co-owner and manager, Minnie Kennedy, rumors persisted that the evangelist was alive and well. The newspapers printed every one of them, regardless of how far-fetched or irresponsible, along with others that she'd been slain by bootleggers, politicians, gamblers, and the Mafia, kidnapped for a huge ransom, crossed the border into Mexico; someone heard her screaming in the water, another chatting on the beach with a pretty blond girl, and in dozens of places in downtown Los Angeles. Against Minnie's protests, J. W. Buchanan, manager of the Los Angeles Bureau of the Burns Detective

Agency, hired by a wealthy member of Angelus Temple, tracked down every rumor, even the most implausible: Aimee'd died in an underwater struggle with a sea monster; a whale had devoured her; a sinister man who'd been standing on the sidewalk across from Angelus Temple for several nights had murdered her and eaten her body to hide the evidence. Mr. Buchanan said he'd never encountered a case where so many rumors grew so fast, but he was satisfied that Aimee had drowned, and at Minnie's request dropped the investigation.

By Sunday, the scene at Ocean Park reached epic proportion, with cots, camp stools, blankets, lunch baskets, and tents scattered over the beach near the road. A temple patrol formed a human chain along the entire fourteen miles of ocean front and another five thousand people swarmed along the beach. A Coast Guard cutter joined the search, sailors in small boats dropped grappling irons, and the newspapers hired another two airplanes to hunt for the body far out at sea. Ships five hundred miles away were instructed by radio to be on the lookout for Aimee's remains.

Minnie Kennedy, between three jam-packed services at the temple that day, rushed to the beach to pose grief-stricken for photographers and insist to reporters that her daughter's body had been washed under Lick Pier and would never be found. "Oh, what shall I do? What shall I do? Tell me!" she cried, shedding genuine tears.

That afternoon the police department took on additional temporary recruits to help control predicted riots—men armed with clubs had been reported running across the beach. What's more, it was said a temple patrol intended to use violence, if necessary, to capture and hide Aimee's body, thus preventing it from being desecrated by souvenir seekers who might rip off the fingers, toes, ears, and such.

At nearby Venice, business flourished. The dance halls opened at dawn, blasting the beach with jazz, to which the members of Angelus Temple responded with boisterous hymns. Other Aimee supporters harassed concessionaires selling posters of Aimee rising from the sea, and attempted to tear to shreds another peddler who briefly displayed an unflattering life-size model of Aimee. Police rescued him, but not the model.

Well-known daredevil Al Jennings crouched on the wing of an airplane that skimmed the ocean. Had he spotted the body, his plan was to parachute into the water, dive-bombing the corpse so that his parachute would mark its exact location.

Some distance away at the Manhattan Beach, a man in his early twenties named Bob Browning had come to spend a relaxed day in the sun. Although he shared no interest in the search for Aimee's body, he had been in the water only a short time when he thought he saw an object floating. Immediately he swam through the choppy surf for almost a mile, then sank. An hour later his body was found near two dead seals.

In Ingersoll, Ontario, Canada, taxi driver George Mitchell, hearing of the presumed drowning on the radio, drove out to the old Kennedy farm in Salford and cut several bushels of new leaves from the maple tree in front of the house, then brought them to Los Angeles, where Minnie, standing at the edge of Lick Pier, scattered them across the water. She muttered something about the alpha and the omega, the beginning and the end, and offered $25,000 reward to the person who produced Aimee's body.

An astonished reporter for *The New Republic*, assigned to cover the McPherson drowning, wrote: "On the street car the conductor asked you for news or told the latest rumor as he took your nickel, and the other passengers freely joined in with their own views at the greatest length. (A notion seriously advanced was that jealous confreres in the Ministerial Union had done away with her.) At twenty-minute intervals newsboys ran through the streets bearing fresh extras with false news: her body had been found, she had been seen in Winnipeg, the kidnappers had made their demand for ransom, she was in a Los Angeles hotel, her body had been washed out to sea. Some of the newspapers—not all—behaved pretty badly, making up their fakes for one edition in order to deny them an hour later. And meanwhile, Aimee's radio was pumping away all day and far into the night while hundreds of thousands listened in. Aimee's mother, Aimee's adolescent daughter, Aimee's assistants, offered radio prayers, sermons, hymns sandwiched in among the news reports which said, 'No news.' "

The *New Republic* reporter described an unexpected result of the supposed drowning: "Los Angeles gets much of its supply of [prohibited] alcoholic liquor from ships which lie offshore in the Pacific Ocean and put cargoes on the beach from small boats. During the first fortnight that Aimee was gone, hundreds of devoted disciples tramped the strand day and night waiting for her body to wash ashore. Naturally the followers are all militant dries, who would simply love to snitch on a rum runner. The men with the wet goods were forced to move up to San Francisco and dispose of their cargoes there. This brought about a bad oversupply, even for that thirsty community; prices broke, and many a hard-working dealer went quietly, anonymously bankrupt. All because of Sister."

On Tuesday, May 25, a week after the disappearance, the press—

dropping the clumsy Mrs. McPherson and routinely headlining the evangelist as Aimee—uncovered two new leads. One was a report from Mrs. Sylvia Oberman, a middle-aged housewife who lived at 67½ Rose Avenue, near the Ocean View Hotel. She told reporters she was sunning her baby on the beach at about two o'clock on the afternoon of May 18, when she saw Mrs. McPherson chatting with a man about thirty years old, tall, neatly dressed in a gray suit and Panama hat. She had seen Mrs. McPherson before and was sure she was the woman in the green bathing suit with the embroidered flowers across the breast.

As the man limped away, said Mrs. Oberman, the evangelist called, "Good-bye, Denny," or "Benny."

The second finding was that Aimee had been to the Clark Hotel in downtown Los Angeles the morning of the eighteenth. Thomas S. Melville, the hotel's doorman, said he saw her enter the lobby, take an elevator upstairs, and emerge about fifteen minutes later. He described the yellow dress she was wearing and said she carried a briefcase on which was stamped in gilt letters the name Aimee Semple McPherson. Another witness said she observed Aimee talking with a well-dressed middle-aged man fitting the description of Kenneth Ormiston, who had been staying at the Clark Hotel.

"Fiddlesticks!" Minnie told reporters when confronted with the published story. "Aimee owned no briefcase."

"They're just so clever," Aimee fumed, tossing the newspaper onto the sofa beside Ken. "Oh, if I really *were* a miracle lady for just a *day*, I'd rise up out of that water in front of all those five thousand people flinging seaweed from my brow and point a soggy finger at every miserable reporter and crooked politician in *sight*—and I'd tell them just where their infidel doubts and slander will damn them to on Judgment Day!"

"Why not?" said Ken. "It should fit just right—this whole thing's a little unbelievable!"

Raising her eyebrows, Aimee stepped back. "So you're a skeptic, too, are you? Well it'll work—you'll see. Oh, I'm smart, Ken, smarter than the whole pack of them. That's why I'm sending you to Los Angeles, even tonight if you can make it. District Attorney Asa Keyes is looking for you, and since you have nothing to hide, you're glad to stop by his office. Say you got tired of L.A., so you went looking for work elsewhere. Make up anything—just make sure the press sees you."

Leading him toward the stairs to the bedroom, Aimee paused before the kitchen entrance. Even through the closed window drapes the bright sun illuminated the neighbor's second-floor bedroom and Aimee could see the woman sitting near the window. She squeezed Ken's hand tightly.

"I don't feel safe here," she said. "Everyone's reading my story. Even *she* knows Aimee McPherson's vanished, and—Henry Benedict has seen me. I just don't want to stay here. We need someplace more private, and I think I know where."

Before Ken left for Los Angeles, Aimee gave him the Arizona address of Donald Yoder, whom she had met when she built the Bible School building. Although neither Yoder nor his wife was involved in the temple, they'd become intimate friends of Aimee's and Minnie's. Aimee told Ken to call Yoder, explain the whole story, and ask for his protection.

That afternoon, with the sky growing overcast and a cold wind blowing in from the ocean, Aimee shrugged off a wave of loneliness and sat beside the window with an open Bible. She read hardly a paragraph when her attention wavered. Rising, she emphatically lowered the shade and closed the drapes, shutting out the bleak day. She did the same at every window, then brightened the cottage by lighting every lamp. Finally she rolled the clutter of newspapers into balls, stacked them in the fireplace, and laid on top the few logs remaining in the garage woodpile. In moments a roaring blaze drove out the chill.

But it would be a cold night, no doubt, and she'd need more wood, so she telephoned the Leidig Wood Company, according to Mr. Benedict's instructions. Soon the delivery man arrived, a quiet, simple fellow in his mid-thirties, so unassuming that Aimee chatted with him at length, grateful for the company. Over coffee, the man explained in broken and ungrammatical English that he was a French Canadian, and for a long while they reminisced about their homeland. Finally when Ernest Renkert tipped his hat and awkwardly backed out the door, Aimee pressed a five-dollar tip into his hand.

The cottage seemed particularly quiet after the lumber wagon chugged away, with no sound but the waves rushing along the shore, the occasional cry of a bird. For a while Aimee sat near the window again, the Bible resting in her lap, her eyes darting about the room with increasing restlessness. Sighing, she stood again and paced the room, then stopped at the window, raising the shade to absently examine the monotonous expanse of ocean. A few rays of sun had found their way through the clouds, casting islands of brightness across the water.

"I can't *stand* it!" she cried. Kicking her slippers across the room, she raced up the stairs to the bedroom. She'd take just a brief walk, perfectly discreet—no one could possibly recognize her. A casual stroll along the side streets, past the quaint shops and artists' studios that had made Carmel so well liked among the wealthy vacationers like the Rockefellers and the famous movie stars. She would *not* sit here bored and lonely when so much life taunted her so close-by. Dressing quickly, she pulled her enormous, floppy hat down over her ears, carefully tucking every strand of hair beneath it. She slipped on the sunglasses.

Gazing into the mirror, she smiled broadly at her reflection. But that smile itself gave her a jolt of fear, so familiar had it become, and she quickly erased it. She would remain somber, speak to no one.

Skipping down the stairs, she ran through the patio and eagerly pulled open the gate.

A few children playing a block away were the only people in sight, and Aimee sauntered toward them confidently. As she approached, they stopped and stared at her curiously. Startled, she crossed to the other side of the street.

While she stood there pondering which direction to take, a car approached from the opposite direction, an old man at the wheel and a woman of the same age beside him. The car slowed to fifteen miles per hour, the driver scrutinizing Aimee intently. Aimee saw him point in her direction and pull the car to the curb. The woman gestured, and the car picked up speed, then again slowed.

Aimee turned and ran crying all the way back to the cottage.

She spent the rest of the day alone and unhappy, reading briefly, deciding to prepare a delicious meal for herself but discarding the idea for lack of patience. Finally, wearing Ken's heavy coat over her own, she strolled along the beach for a while.

Shortly after dark she climbed the steps to the bedroom, and, sliding beneath the sheets, read lengthy passages from the Book of Proverbs in the new Bible Ken had bought her. The verses reminded her of the days when, as a child, she'd sat with Minnie beneath the maple tree at the farm reading those very words in unison. She shut off the light and snuggled into the pillow.

"Good night, Lord," she said to herself. "Good night, Kenny. Good night, Aimee."

At eleven o'clock that night she was startled awake by the bell at the gate. "Western Union telegram for Mrs. McIntire," a man's voice called.

The message said simply, "Lease expires tonight."

Yoder's going to take us in, she thought jubilantly. Immediately she dressed and packed the suitcases.

Three hours later, the sound of an automobile engine approaching the cottage awoke her from a shallow sleep on the sofa. In the glow of smoldering embers in the fireplace, she hurried out to admit Ken. Together they carried the suitcases to the car.

The blue Chrysler raced south until sunrise, when Ken turned into the parking lot of the Andrews Hotel in San Luis Obispo. It was a quiet, unpretentious place that seemed to Aimee considerably safer than the highway in bright daylight. At 6:15 Ken scribbled the name Gibson on the dozing desk clerk's registration card, and the bellboy took them to their room.

Late that afternoon, they dined in a dark corner of the hotel restaurant. "I can't *stand* being caged in," Aimee had stormed when Ken suggested room service. "We'll eat in the dining room where I can see *people* and hear *voices*—or I'll go *insane!*"

When darkness fell, Ken checked out and drove the car to a side door where Aimee waited. Moments later they turned south again on the Coastal Highway.

Just before midnight, on the outskirts of Santa Barbara, Ken said, "I think someone's following us."

"Don't speed," Aimee replied, her voice calm. "If the police stop us, everything's over."

As they drove into the city limits, the other car raced past them with horn blasting, the driver motioning Ken off the road. Immediately a well-dressed young man leaped from the car and ran toward Ken's closed window demanding:

"Who are you?"

"Who are *you*?" Ken replied.

"I . . . my name is Wallace Moore. I'm a reporter for the Santa Barbara *Morning Press*. Now, will you tell me who you are?"

"Frank Gibson—why?" Ken's expression was casual, even pleasant.

"Where are you from?"

"I'm a hardware man from Sacramento. Why?"

"Where are you going?" The young reporter made an effort to sound authoritative.

"Los Angeles. We'll be at the Alexandria Hotel there. Reach us at any time after nine o'clock in the morning if you want to ask any more questions." Ken started the engine again.

Moore bent down for a better view of Aimee, but the lights along the road reflected on the window and the car's interior was dark. Aimee huddled against the far door, a large red hat pulled down till it touched the high collar of her cape, virtually smothering her in disguise.

"How do you do?" said Moore, but Aimee haughtily ignored him.

Wallace Moore sighed. "We got a phone call a couple hours ago from a desk clerk in San Luis Obispo. Aimee Semple McPherson and her boyfriend are supposed to be heading south. You're driving a car fitting the description of the machine Kenneth Ormiston and Mrs. McPherson are supposedly riding in."

Ken's face took on a look of astonishment. "My God!" he exclaimed, "We'd hate to be mistaken for *those* two people!"

Moore wasn't put off. "Is this companion—this woman your wife?"

Suddenly angry, Ken snapped, "Of course!"

"Oh, well—I didn't mean . . ."

His anger apparently growing, Ken slammed the car in gear. "I guess this isn't Mrs. McPherson then," said the reporter. "I'm sorry to bother you." He hurried back to his own car.

"Turn around, go north again," Aimee said.

"Why?"

"Just do as I say. He's fooled now, but he won't be long. When he makes up his mind it was us, he'll have every policeman and reporter from here to San Francisco looking for us, but we'll be on our way south again."

Ken popped the clutch and spun the blue Chrysler into a U-turn, speeding out of the reporter's view. Then he turned right, snaking through the city and back to the Coastal Highway.

CHAPTER XXII

Thirty miles northeast of Yuma, in the pine-dabbled foothills of the Castle Dome Mountains, the Yoder ranch lay secluded. Behind it were the impenetrable mountains, before it the desert, punctuated with a smattering of cacti and sage and flowing in lazy undulations to the horizon. For a quarter mile through that sand, the private road to the ranch stretched in a straight line before dividing, the left fork sweeping to a half circle of wooden shacks, storage sheds, a barn and silo. To the right, the road stopped at a spacious parking area before the elegant new Yoder home. Several hundred yards behind it, virtually hidden by a wall of cacti and eucalyptus, was the adobelike guest cottage where Ken and Aimee stayed.

After a few hours' sleep that first night, Ken drove the car back to San Francisco and checked it into a garage there, then wrote and mailed a short letter to Herman Kline, chief of detectives for the Los Angeles Police Department. It was in response to young Wallace Moore's story, which had made the front pages of all the newspapers. "It is utterly absurd the way the newspapers continue to use my name, and the mass of lies they print concerning me and my movements," wrote Ken. "Apparently they have absolutely no regard for the truth. I think yellow journalism is committing one of the greatest crimes of all time." Ken claimed he'd loaned his car to his good friend Frank Gibson, who'd used it to take his wife and himself to Los Angeles. Most painful was the brutal way in which they were slandering the name and memory of Sister McPherson. "I do hope her body is recovered quickly," Ken concluded.

By the following day, he was at the ranch again, holding Aimee securely in his arms.

Thus they meandered through days of predictable pleasures, hiking together through the scrubby foothills, or wandering to a nearby hilltop to watch long black shadows of cacti streak the sweeping glow of sand. Back at the cottage, Ken built a fire each night to drive out the inevitable chill, and Aimee heated coffee and filled a plate with cookies, setting it all on a small table between their two rocking chairs. There, facing the fireplace, they read and talked each night away.

One evening a couple of weeks after they came to the cottage, Aimee startled Ken with her laughter. He glanced at her quizzically.

"What's so funny?"

"How's your rheumatism, Pappy?" she asked in a crackling voice. Her smile grew a touch melancholy. "We're like the hoary aged, aren't we?" But before Ken could reply, her mood changed. She waved the newspaper at him.

"Have you seen this?"

"Not yet—you've been reading it."

"Momma's being *superb*! That Herman Kline told her, with all the reporters around, of course—everyone's got to get his name in the paper, you know—he told her he was doing a final investigation to set things to rest and declare me dead. And Minnie burst into *tears*, poor thing! I wonder if she believes it all. She says—listen: 'I hope you will look into everything. You'll find we are not people who owe money, that we pay our bills and conduct our business affairs along business lines. Our finances are all right. We are not broke.' I tell you, if Christ came down from heaven surrounded by a thousand archangels, while the rest of us fell prostrate in awe, Minnie would be out selling it to the moving pictures!"

Feeding on each other's amusement, they both doubled over in laughter.

"What's so funny?" Aimee finally gasped.

"I don't know!" And they again burst into loud guffaws.

"We must be going stir crazy," Ken said.

"Listen to this," Aimee said, still laughing. "Minnie's going to be another Aimee Semple McPherson. They say she staged my entry—you know, dim lights, spotlight focused on the door, roll of drums, crash of cymbal. Who throws open the door, practically knocking an usher over the balcony, and stands there clad in a dazzling white silky robe but Ma Kennedy!

" 'She hurried down the ramp, her right hand held high in the temple salute, a Bible clenched under her left arm, a cheerful smile on her face. The drooping sleeves and train of her robe billowed out behind her, but she was a poor substitute for the glamorous Sister McPherson. Ma Kennedy marches with the precision of a Salvation Army lassie, a jaunty, pudgy little angel, headstrong in her determination to beat the Devil into the ground. The crowd applauded wildly.' "

By now Aimee was laughing so raucously that tears streamed from her eyes. Clutching her stomach, she dropped to her knees on the rug.

"A pudgy little angel!" she repeated, rolling onto her back.

When the laughter subsided, she gazed for a long while at the ceiling, her eyes unblinking, her face growing sober. She turned back to Ken, found his eyes on her, a soft smile on his lips.

"What were you thinking?" he asked.

"I wasn't thinking at all," she said seriously. "I was feeling—I don't know what, not sadness, really." Shrugging, she said, "I don't *want* to understand it. Besides, nothing important, anyway. The paper says District Attorney Keyes and detective Kline are closing the investigation. Looks like I'm dead and gone at last."

They were silent for a while.

"Bored?" Ken asked. Aimee said nothing.

"I knew you would be."

"I'm not bored with *you*—it's this desolate purgatory," she exclaimed, gesturing. "I can't *stand* it."

Another two weeks passed, each day a replica of the one before, its pace prescribed by the dawdling blaze of sun, its perimeter by their need for privacy. Across the unwavering uniformity of sand and heat fell the occasional relief of passion and laughter, but less frequently as the days trudged on, and at last rarely.

One evening just before dusk, Aimee took Ken's hand and silently led him to the hill where they'd often watched the sunset. For a long while they sat in the sand, their arms around each other, while the whole sky glowed pink with a brillance reflected across the vast sweep of the desert. When, much later, the western clouds became crimson and purple, neither had yet spoken.

Finally no more than a slender strip of color shimmered where the desert met the sky. Aimee took Ken's hand and pressed it to her lips.

"I'm going back," she said simply.

"I know."

"I can't help it."

"I know."

She turned to him with eyes glowing. "I didn't think you'd understand." Throwing her arms around his neck, she cried, "Oh, Ken, I love you so! We'll still be together, I swear it. It's just—"

He silenced her with his fingers on her lips, then with a kiss.

That night, planning the strategy of her return, Aimee longed for Minnie's sound judgment to guide her. Several alternatives had occurred to her.

Finally, recalling a newspaper report of a ransom note that had demanded half a million dollars for Aimee, she determined to use the ruse to pave the way for her return. On a typewriter Ken had brought with him, she quickly wrote to Minnie:

"Exactly a month has elapsed since we grabbed Aimee McPherson and now is the time for action. We nearly bungled it once, but we've moved her to a safe place now and have doped out a plan of ransom payment that is absolutely safe to us. Do what you like with this letter (we realize you got to use it to raise the dough) but the next one must be kept absolutely to yourself and its instructions followed exactly or there will be grave consequence to your daughter.

"First, in order that you may know without a doubt that Aimee is alive and in our hands, we are enclosing a lock of her hair. Her middle right hand finger has a scar on it you ought to recognize, suppose we chop it off and send it along to kill your doubts? Though we've treated her respectfully in fairness to her position and value to us, what the future holds for her is entirely up to you. Our alternative is to sell her to old Felipe of Mexico City. We are sick and tired of her infernal preaching, she spouts scripture in answer to everything.

"We took her for two reasons—First, to wreck that damned temple, and second, to collect a tidy half million. We have held her for a month during which time her name and standing have been just about ruined. We had to fight hard to kill that "drowning" idea of yours but a little palm oil brought forth plenty reports of her being seen all over the place and the newspaper hounds were only too anxious to play it up. They seem to have an ax to grind too and sure helped us grand. You've taken some of our girls, damn you, and given us many a jolt, but guess we are square now, eh?

"Now get busy. Have the $500,000 ready in big bills. Watch for the final letter of instructions which will reach you next Friday. That letter you must keep absolutely confidential but you will alright when you read it. Follow the instructions exactly and on that same night you will have your little Aimee back and we'll have the dough. If anything slips, Felipe gets her."

Till Friday,
The Avengers

The newspapers on the nineteenth made no mention of the ransom note. On the twentieth they described three gala Aimee Semple McPherson Memorial Services at the temple, with a combined attendance of some seventeen thousand and an offering rumored at forty thousand dollars, for which Minnie urgently pleaded in order that the Bible School building and other projects Aimee had undertaken could be completed.

Thus the papers had described the memorial service, making no mention of the ransom note. On the twenty-first the silence continued. By then Aimee was furious.

"Why doesn't she give it to the *press*?" she screamed. "It explains everything. They would've been *prepared*!"

The next morning, after skimming the newspapers and still finding no mention of the letter, Aimee walked alone far up the scrubby foothills behind the cottage, leaping from one jagged rock to another until she reached a small plateau. Turning, she discovered she'd gone much farther than she'd anticipated, for the cottage where Ken still slept was no bigger than her fist. She could see a very great distance now, to California, no doubt, the desert stretching to the horizon.

The time is at hand, she thought, here in this parched Gethsemane, her one beloved disciple in blissful sleep below. A peculiar dread had coiled inside her since her decision to return, a feeling that, suggesting weakness, frustrated and angered her. Yet, she could neither assuage nor ignore it. She'd have preferred a less complex resurrection, but could think of no plan that pleased her, for the one inflexible standard was that her return be every whit as dramatic as her disappearance. She would return, not cringing and pathetic, claiming some farcical bout of amnesia or emotional collapse, no weak, pitiable slinking back, but the glorious triumphal entry of a world-renowned warrior of the cross, full of power, a queen returning in victory to her throne.

Her eyes bright with eagerness, Aimee lifted her head proudly over the desert.

"Nevertheless, not my will but thine be done, O Lord," she whispered.

Shortly before eleven o'clock that night, a car slipped across the border between Douglas, Arizona, and Agua Prieta, Mexico, swept through the raucous town and into the still, dark plains to the south. At the Gallardo Road, the car turned east toward Niggerhead Mountain, proceeding along the dirt road for two miles. Finally it stopped.

Ken turned off the headlights and silenced the engine. The night was so dark that for a moment Aimee couldn't see his face.

"Afraid?" he asked.

"Terrified. What if I run into a band of *murderers*? It's not impossible, you know. Or the *real* Felipe. Or step on a rattlesnake or fall in a hole and break my leg. I could *rot* out there before they'd find me."

Ken's hand trembled as he reached for her cheek. He laughed nervously. "You're the one who wrote the script, love," he said. "You're the director, producer, and star. You can still cancel if you want to."

"No."

Ken pulled his hand away. "Then let's not sit here talking," he said abruptly. "I can't stand drawn-out good-byes."

Aimee ran the back of her fingers across his cheek. He pushed her hand away.

"Are you angry?"

"Of course not." In a husky voice he added, "I already miss you!"

"Oh, Kenny, don't *talk* like that!" Aimee cried. "You'll break my *heart*! We'll be together again, as soon as everything quiets down. I *know* we will! And I'll always love you!"

Shaking his head, Ken chuckled bitterly. "Kiss me good-bye and get out of here, damn it," he said.

"But just for a while," Aimee answered. She kissed him deeply.

"Anything you say." He started the engine. Aimee stepped out into the desert and slammed the door.

The car spun in a U-turn, scattering sand into Aimee's face and hair, and plunged careening along the road toward Agua Prieta, the taillights growing smaller and smaller until they became one tiny red speck and then vanished.

Aimee stood alone in the darkness.

CHAPTER XXIII

Through scudding clouds the thin edge of the moon struck shadows across the terrain. In the sporadic light, jagged rocks and desert plants seemed to stir in some eerie rhythm with the far-off moan of wind. Yet, the air around Aimee was still and silent.

Turning from the direction Ken had driven, she walked quickly along the road toward a small shack, not more than a mile away, according to a map she'd studied earlier in the day. Still, the time seemed endless until she discerned at the horizon the structure's black hulk against the sky.

Stopping, she peered intently. No illumination issued from the building. A thrill of fear swept through her with the thought: supposing they're dead, or murdered, or if outlaws live there—the desert's full of them.

She approached steathily, saw that the door was open, weeds overgrowing the steps. No horses or automobiles were in sight, no fresh tire tracks. The shack had been abandoned.

She sighed in disgust, realizing she'd have to go to Agua Prieta, four miles back through the desert. Blisters had already developed on her small toes—had she given it a thought, she'd have worn more comfortable shoes. And she'd have brought a flashlight—in the darkness, she could stumble upon a rattlesnake or poisonous lizard and die on the desert like the most lowly insect.

Behind her a night animal skittered across the cabin floor and Aimee plunged forward, consumed with terror, running until, with burning lungs and pounding heart, she felt herself swooning. Mocking her childish fears, she slowed to a walk, focusing her mind on those happy days with Ken in Rome, when they'd sat at the fountains and watched the young Italian boys moving by. Thus she escaped for a while the hell of endless sand, darkness, and whisperings.

An hour past midnight, still a mile from Agua Prieta, she approached a large building surrounded by a fence against which a savagely barking dog repeatedly hurled itself. Aimee stood motionless for a long while, until a light in a nearby doorway illuminated the porch of a shack and a short, unshaven man in undershorts.

"*Halt's Maul, du Gottverdamter Hund*!" he bellowed, squinting into the darkness: "*Quien es? Who iss dare?*"

"Do you have a telephone?" Aimee moaned. "I've . . . I've been kidnapped!"

The man reached inside, produced a flashlight which he directed on Aimee.

"No telephone we have—who are you?"

"I need the police. Where is a telephone?"

The man studied her. "Police? What is it you have done?"

"I haven't done *anything*!" Aimee cried. "I want help!"

"Who are you?"

"Who are you? Who are you?" Aimee mocked. "Who do you *think* I am? The whole *world* knows who I am!"

The man grunted. "You are betrunken, nein? Come inside, sleep. I get dressed."

But Aimee had already begun stumbling along the road toward the lights of town. Twenty minutes later she came upon a large, pillared home, a chandelier brightening the hallway and porch. Pushing open the gate and grasping her forehead, she stumbled to the door.

"Hello! Hello!" she cried.

"Hello!" a masculine voice replied. "I am coming."

A moment later a man and woman appeared at the door to find Aimee lying motionless near the gate. The man felt for a pulse.

"I think she is dead!" he said.

Wednesday morning, June 23, the small town of Douglas, Arizona, throbbed with activity. Many of the town's thirteen thousand citizens milled in the streets and bars and on the sidewalks questioning each other and making sonorous pronouncements. Mayor Kenton had declared a holiday, and William McCafferty, editor of the Douglas *Daily Dispatch*, hurriedly prepared an extra on what he headlined the biggest news story in the town's history.

The feverishness emanated from the local hospital, where, authorities had finally confirmed, the nation's most widely publicized preacher recuperated from experiences more startling than any novelist would dare invent. For six weeks, investigators by the thousands had searched land and sea for Aimee Semple McPherson, and she had returned, not to some high and mighty place, but to the humble town of Douglas, thus bestowing upon the town worldwide fame and a most festive spirit.

The hospital itself was a riot of confusion, the halls crowded with reporters, officials, and police officers charged with ejecting scores of well-wishers and the curious. Amid the disorder, doctors and nurses elbowed their way to their patients.

Before Room 105 stood a battery of uniformed officers past whom proceeded only a select crew of medical personnel and a few high-ranking law officers. Inside, surrounded by dozens of bouquets from her public, Aimee, clad in a plain white hospital gown, relaxed with a glass of lemonade. A few cactus thorns had already been pulled from her ankle, the two blisters on her toes treated. Nurse Meriba Shinn had even completed her report—the patient was in good condition, suffering no serious sunburn, no cracked or parched lips, no swollen tongue, emaciation, or dehydration. Her temperature, pulse, and respiration were normal, and she had not been drinking alcohol.

When the nurse asked her if she wouldn't like a few hours of privacy so she could sleep, Aimee smiled wanly. "No," she said. "No, let's get on with it."

By 6:00 A.M. Douglas authorities had telephoned the Los Angeles police, and an hour and a half later, Aimee spoke to Minnie by telephone from her hospital bed, the call monitored by detectives at both ends of the line.

"Mother?" she said, her voice trembling.

"Don't say anything!" Minnie hissed.

Aimee broke into sobs. "Mother—it's me—it's really me! The police say you don't believe it, you think I'm dead. Oh, Momma!" Aimee's words became incoherent with her weeping.

After a long pause, Minnie said, "I'll get there as soon as I can. You just get your rest."

Blotting the tears away, Aimee ordered a breakfast of poached eggs, oatmeal, and an orange, which she finished quickly while answering questions from the police and waving her hair with a curling iron she'd borrowed from a nurse. At her request, a volunteer brought her a pink silk dressing gown and white negligee.

Shortly after 8:00 A.M., satisfied with her appearance, she told a nurse who insisted she rest, "I don't *want* to rest. It's time I see the reporters. I just can't refuse them my story—they'll take it to hundreds of thousands!"

Throughout the day, journalists and photographers streamed through the room to hear Aimee tell with ever-increasing enthusiasm of how a woman named Rose had led her from the beach to a waiting car under the pretext that a dying infant in the back seat needed her prayers. There, a man named Steve held a drug-saturated cloth against Aimee's face until she fell unconscious.

"That was the last thing I remembered until I came to, desperately ill, perhaps hours and hours later," she explained. She found herself in a small room of a two-story house, the only light a kerosene lamp.

Eventually, Steve ordered her to write a letter to Minnie demanding a $500,000 ransom. Aimee said it couldn't be raised.

"'Why, you've got a *million* dollars,' Steve told me. I said the money was tied up in Angelus Temple and all I had was a deed of trust. 'I'll make you write that letter!' Steve told me. One of them grabbed my arm and Steve burned my fingers with a lighted cigar. I told him to go ahead and burn me, and never moved my hand." She showed reporters two scarred fingers.

Eventually she was blindfolded and moved to another location, a shack in what she assumed was the Imperial Valley of California but proved to be Mexico's Sonora Desert. When Steve again demanded she write the letter to her mother and Aimee again refused, he cut two locks of hair from her head and stuffed them in an envelope with a letter of his own, addressed to Minnie.

"Then on Tuesday, Rose said she was going to town for supplies. She bound me with straps and rope and left me on a cot. While I lay there, I noticed a jagged tin can on the floor. It was square like the cans we use for maple sugar in Canada. I rolled off the cot to the floor and managed to squirm to the can. By rubbing the straps and ropes against the jagged edge and pulling and tugging, I managed to cut them."

Climbing through an open window, she ran aimlessly. "I imagine, from the position of the sun, it was about eleven o'clock in the morning. It was hot. I stumbled many times as I ran. Finally I sighted a mountain, which people around here tell me was Niggerhead. I ran on for hours. Finally I came to a fence. My hope went up when I finally came to a road."

The rest of the story is history. Frederick Conrad Schansel, the slaughterhouse watchman, greeted her in his underwear. She ran from him, collapsing on the lawn of Ramón Gonzáles' home. Johnny Anderson took her in his cab to policeman George W. Cook, who admitted her to the hospital. These gentlemen could fill in the details.

The evening editions of some papers artfully embellished Aimee's testimony: "Her feet were blistered from the hot sands during her fourteen-hour flight across the searing desert floor. Her ankles were bruised and torn by ropes. Her shoes were virtually cut to shreds."

"Woman Evangelist Escapes Abductors," headlined *The New York Times*. "Aimee Tortured for Huge Ransom," declared the Los Angeles *Examiner*.

But a few more enterprising reporters filed quite different stories, revealing that her clothes were not at *all* torn—not even dusty—and had survived a day's hike in 120° temperatures without a single perspiration stain. Even her shoes were unmarked. Jerry McDonald, the Cochise County sheriff who spent much of the day scouring the desert for the kidnappers, described for reporters the county's terrain: hilly, with out-juttings of shale, overrun with mesquite, cactus, and catclaw. He and his deputies had returned to Douglas—in broad daylight—covered with burrs and dust, their boots scratched and pants torn by the catclaw.

Sheriff McDonald also explained that, according to Aimee's account of the escape, the shack in which she'd been imprisoned had to exist within a radius of just a few miles.

"Three roads make a triangle out there," he said, "and it can't be more than ten or fifteen miles across the longest way. You've got the Gallardo Road running east to west, Agua Prieta to Niggerhead Mountain. She couldn't have crossed it unaware, and she said she crossed no roads. But if she did, there's the seven-foot-high international boundary fence parallel to it, and she'd certainly remember that. From Niggerhead Mountain due south is the old road to Cenesas—the Gallardo Ranch fence runs beside it all the way, four strands of barbed wire. She couldn't have gone through *there* without knowing it, either.

"Then there's the brand-new highway from Agua Prieta to Cenesas, northwest to southeast. We're mighty proud of that road. It's traveled pretty heavy, and if Mrs. McPherson had gotten that far south, she could have hailed help with no trouble. But she wasn't down that far. She says she walked toward the mountain and then came in along Gallardo Road. And that's what the footprints tell us, too. Point is, we probably don't have more than a dozen square miles to search for that shack.

"Now, there ain't only three shacks in the whole damn triangle, two of them lived in by old natives of the area. The third one's abandoned, but it don't fit the lady's description. Besides, you can tell by the dust on the floor nobody's been in there lately."

When Aimee read those comments the next morning, her eyes blazed. "Did it ever occur to Sheriff McDonald," she demanded of the reporters gathered at her bedside, "that the shack could have been *portable!*" She promised to search for the shack herself the following day, the reporters accompanying her if they wished.

She also telephoned the editor of the local Bisbee *Review*, which she'd read that morning. "You referred to my disappearance as a mystery," she scolded. "Nothing is at all mysterious about it—I was *kidnapped.* Now please, *please* help me put to rest all those terrible rumors the devil's people have been spreading. God *bless* you!"

But the rumors flourished. That afternoon, Minnie escorted her daughter from the hospital to a suite at the nearby Gadsden Hotel. She held her silence until she locked the hotel room door behind them. Then, leaning back against the door with narrowing eyes and pursed lips, she stared in bitter accusation at her daughter.

Aimee exclaimed, "What a relief to be out of that hospital! It was like being on *trial!*"

"You *are* on trial—and me and the temple with you." Minnie spoke in a low voice that quivered with finality. "So you went and did it, just like I knew you would. And now you've destroyed everything."

"What are you *talking* about?" Aimee demanded. "You think I *wanted* to be kidnapped?"

"So you'd even lie to your own mother, would you? No, I don't believe you, and the police don't believe you, and half the reporters don't, either. In a month or a year or however long it takes, nobody—*nobody*—is gonna believe Aimee Semple McPherson."

Taking a newspaper from the stack on the dresser, Minnie read, " 'C. E. Cross, a cowboy who has ridden this country for twenty-six years and knows the area well, says of the shack in which Mrs. McPherson claims to have been a prisoner, "I do not know of an adobe house such as the one described by Mrs. McPherson within a hundred and fifty miles of Agua Prieta and I know every house in this vast area." The chief of the Mexican Border Patrol, Pedro Demandivo, says his men know every foot of ground within fifty miles and none of them knows of such a cabin. Every inch of that territory is covered once every two days, and so even a new cabin could not have been built.' "

Minnie tossed the paper aside and lifted another. " 'Antonio Gabiondo, chief of the Mexican customs guard, says, "I have three sons, and they all own large tracts of land around Agua Prieta. Almost all the land over which the search has been conducted is owned by my family. Do you think that if such a shack existed we would not know of it, we who have lived here all our lives? It is a preposterous assumption!' "

Contemptuously, Minnie threw that paper, too, aside and lifted a third. " 'It was Ramón Gonzáles, the man who found Mrs. McPherson on his lawn, put his opinion most bluntly,' " she read. " 'He said, "I do not wish to say anything against the lady, but I think the lady's a liar.' "

"*The lady is a liar!*" Minnie screeched. "Oh, Aimee, what a terrible thing you did! The people ain't dumb. Half of them didn't even believe it when you fainted in front of the newsreel cameras, and the nurse told the reporters she didn't believe it either. And I didn't believe it, Aimee Elizabeth, not for a minute—not the fainting, or that crazy kidnapping story or even the drowning. And before it's over the whole world's gonna know the pastor of Angelus Temple, a preacher of God's glorious Word, is a *liar* and a *cheat* and an *adulterer!*"

Aimee's face grew ashen. Laying her hand against her cheek, her eyelids fluttering, she looked away, then back to Minnie. Tears overflowed her eyes and ran down her face and her shoulders trembled, but when she confronted Minnie it was with unblinking eyes and unwavering voice.

"It's regrettable, isn't it—that I didn't really drown? But I'm alive, and we'll just have to endure that, I suppose. Mother—" her eyes grew fiercely intense. "My story is *true*, every word of it. You can believe it or not, that's your business. But I'll stick by it, and so will those who believe in me, for, Mother, if an angel should come down from heaven and tell my people that Sister is not a child of God, *they wouldn't believe it!*"

Her composure shattering, Aimee broke into uncontrollable weeping.

After a moment, Minnie came to her side. Holding her daughter's head against her breast, she said, "Well, then, if you say it's true, I'll believe you. If a mother's place ain't at her daughter's side at a time like this, then what is? I'm the only one you got, Aimee Elizabeth, the only one you ever had, in fact, except yourself. You can count on me."

"Oh, Mom, God bless you!" Aimee cried, hugging her desperately.

The next morning, as Aimee had promised, she led reporters and authorities on a search for the shack. It was futile. Returning to the hotel, she told Minnie to start packing. "I'm not staying around here another minute," she fumed.

That night, bidding the press farewell at the depot, she referred briefly to critics of her story. Her voice trembling, she cried, "Before the

God in whom I have every faith and belief, every word I have uttered about my kidnapping and escape is *true*! If I have been unable to answer any questions propounded by a score of newspapermen, detectives, attorneys, friends, even my own mother, I have told them, 'I do not know' or 'I do not remember.' My story is *true*!"

Offering a five-hundred-dollar reward to the individual who located the shack in which she was kept prisoner, she bid farewell to the reporters and citizens of Douglas and boarded the train.

At every stop along the route of the Golden State Limited, crowds pressed around the train and cried for her. At 3:24 A.M., fans gathered at Maricopa Junction depot, but Aimee was asleep. At Yuma, though, she stepped out on the platform of the observation car and cried, "Praise the Lord! The hour of resurrection has come!"

At Colton, California, five thousand persons gave her a wild ovation, a few admirers wrestling through a police barricade to shake her hand and touch her clothes.

"Praise God!" one of them shouted. "She was dead, and now she lives!" Hundreds wept, while others mumbled prayers of thanksgiving. One radio network transmitted from a remote studio at the depot to every station in Los Angeles and a dozen more throughout California. Asked to identify herself for the listeners, Aimee laughed and, as she had done perhaps a thousand times in the past two years, stepped to the microphone to declare, "This is Aimee Semple McPherson of Angelus Temple, Los Angeles, California."

The crowd cheered frantically and Aimee knew that 100,000 people sitting by their radios all over the state were rejoicing with her. "Praise the Lord!" she cried. "God bless you all! I'm just bubbling over with *joy*!"

Someone handed her a slip of paper. She read it, then shouted, "Praise the Lord! I have here in my hand a telegram from Douglas, Arizona. It says the shack where the kidnappers kept me prisoner has been *found*! Oh, isn't that glorious news? Dear friends, it was bad enough to go through the *ordeal*, but to have your word doubted is *worse*! There couldn't be any thinking person who would imagine for a minute that these stories doubting the report of my kidnapping are true. How many in this crowd *believe* my story? Those who do, raise your *hands*!"

Thousands of hands flailed the air.

"O dear *God*!" Aimee cried, her voice cracking with emotion. "Pour out your blessing abundantly on all those police officers who have stood by me so loyally and helped to make my burden lighter. O God, we pray for Rose and Steve, who plucked your servant from the vineyard where she labored day and night for you. Dear Lord, ever bless these wicked people who have caused these things to happen and bring them to *repentance*. Oh, this is a *glorious* day!"

For miles through the suburbs of Los Angeles, the train flashed past throngs lining the tracks. Multitudes gaped from windows and rooftops, hills and bridges, waving, cheering, blowing horns, exploding firecrackers. When the train rolled into Los Angeles depot, a concert of clanging bells, blaring horns, wailing sirens, and 50,000 screaming voices greeted it. The Angelus Temple band played. At last Aimee stepped to the observation car deck and shouted, "God bless you! God bless you!"

The Los Angeles Fire Department band struck up "Praise God from Whom All Blessings Flow." Overhead, an airplane pilot showered the crowd with roses.

Emma Schaffer, carried through the crowd by a cordon of temple workers, ran up the train steps and greeted Aimee with tears and kisses. The captain of the fire department pinned a gold badge on the lapel of the gray suit Aimee wore and declared her an honorary fire chief. Someone handed her a great sheaf of American beauty roses.

Behind her, Minnie Kennedy cried, overcome with relief. She listened as her daughter's efforts to address the crowd were repeatedly overwhelmed by shouts of "God bless you, Aimee!" "Welcome back, Sister!" "We love you, Aimee!" Minnie turned to detective Herman Kline, who stood beside her.

"Oh, they love her so!" she sobbed.

Aimee was smiling, her face radiant, her large eyes and mouth recognizable far back in the crowd. *Fifty thousand people*! she thought. They believe me. *They* know every word is true!

She turned to the reporters crowding behind her. "What a glorious entry to the City of Angels!" she exclaimed. "Like Christ's triumphal entry into Jerusalem!"

"That was on Palm Sunday, wasn't it," asked one journalist, "the same week Jesus was crucified?"

In the clamor, no one paid much heed to official reports that no shack had been discovered after all.

The death and resurrection of Aimee Semple McPherson promised to become the biggest newspaper story in the city's history. It made headlines daily, often photo-illustrated, for publishers found circulation figures soaring in direct proportion to their McPherson coverage. It was, as one wag declared, a story even the overactive imaginations of some journalists could not much improve upon, abundant as it was in all the right ingredients—sex, mystery, underworld characters, spooks, kidnappers, the ocean, hot desert sands, an escape and a thrilling finale—and, of course, religion. It is, said Carey McWilliams, "a kind of compendium of all the pervading nonsense, cynicism, credulity, speakeasy wit, passion for debunkery, sex-craziness and music-hall pornography of the times."

Thus, millions avidly followed the unfolding saga, each day's news leading to further quarrels between those supporting Aimee and those denouncing her. The citizens of Hoboken were as fervent in their opinions as were those of Los Angeles, and as divergent. But those who defended her found their task growing progressively more difficult.

The week after Aimee returned to Los Angeles, Cochise County Sheriff Jerry McDonald wrote to Los Angeles District Attorney Asa Keyes: "I have helped revive people who have been exhausted on the desert and have been near the point of exhaustion myself. One symptom is always present—*insane craving for water*. In no part of her story does water play an important part. In my opinion, the first request from Schansel at the slaughterhouse would have been for water. I have no desire to cast any reflections on anyone, but my conclusions are that Mrs. McPherson's story is not borne out by the facts."

The press also paid much attention to the corset Aimee had been wearing when carried into the Douglas Hospital. According to a saleswoman at a Los Angeles department store where Aimee shopped regularly, that corset was the exact size, style, and brand Aimee preferred—a strikingly thoughtful provision for a couple of brutal thugs to have made, commented the press, since Aimee had been kidnapped wearing a bathing suit.

Such observations and discoveries seemed to explode like land mines with every step Aimee took. A photograph of her in the Douglas Hospital room, taken early on the morning of her return, showed her wearing a wristwatch she had owned for several years. How did she get it, the newspapers demanded.

Yet, Aimee, promptly resuming the furious schedule she'd maintained before her disappearance, gave not the slightest hint that such revelations troubled her. Photographers complained about the impossibility of catching her without her brilliant smile, and even in the privacy of the parsonage, Minnie never saw her daughter frown.

Minnie herself responded to the avalanche of bad news in gray-faced silence. "I won't have to give account for words I don't say," she told Aimee one afternoon. "As far as that goes, neither will you."

"You worry too much," Aimee answered. "You *always* worry."

Minnie threw up her arms in bewilderment. "Well, one of us has got to, and it's for sure you don't—though I can't for the life of me figure out why."

Aimee laughed. "This silly little fuss isn't doing us any *harm*! The *world* knows who I am today. We're packing the temple like never before. The offerings are enormous. Hundreds are getting saved, scores baptized."

"Oh, Aimee," Minnie wailed, "don't you see where it's all headed? Don't you—"

"Of *course* I see—and that's the best part! Oh, what *rejoicing* when we finally prove the *truth* and every newspaper in the land carries the message of my glorious *vindication*!" Her face flushing, she exclaimed, "Christians all over the world will drop to their knees in prayers of *thanksgiving*! My dear people at the temple will fall prostrate with joy. And even Minnie Kennedy will smile! Yes, it will happen—I pray to God every night He'll make the truth known to the whole world, and I know He'll answer in His own good time."

Minnie studied her daughter in silence, her mind jumbled with questions. "I hope so," she finally mumbled. "I sure hope so."

With Aimee's assurances ringing in her ears, Minnie felt renewed confidence, but a few days later she again viewed her daughter's downfall as inevitable, to be brought about not by the press or law officers or politicians, but a preacher like Aimee herself, the Reverend Mr. Robert Shuler of the twin-spired brick Trinity Methodist Church, a few miles south of the temple in downtown Los Angeles.

Forty-six-year-old "Fighting Bob" Shuler, although boasting no national fame, had a reputation in Los Angeles second only to Aimee's. Driven from the pastorate at the University of Texas in Austin after making unsubstantiated attacks against local politicians, he assumed the Los Angeles pastorate in the fall of 1920. He immediately set about not only condemning sin but utilizing it as a major attraction. Said one contemporary, "In common with all other intelligent pulpit psychologists, he realized that interest in depravity filled more pews than the love of virtue. But he went several steps farther. It was not interest in their own sins, he recognized, which lured the saints to worship, but fascination with the sins of others."

Consequently, he made his first headlines by alleging that a group of high school girls had posed naked for photographs. Next, he attended a Shriners' festival, won a ham on a wheel of fortune, and immediately had the donor of the ham and the operator of the wheel hauled off to jail on charges of operating a gambling device.

A few months later, an anonymous supporter came to Shuler's study one night urging him to stand near the door of the city's most notorious night club if he wanted a really big story. Accepting the suggestion, Shuler stood for hours in the rain, and reaped a rich reward. Eventually the middle-aged, married chief of the Los Angeles Police Department stumbled from the club clutching to his side a provocative young woman whose brother and husband were both much-sought-after criminals. Shuler followed them to a hotel, then gave the story to the press. When it hit the front pages and the police chief was fired, Bob Shuler was entrenched as a Los Angeles institution. Only Aimee Semple McPherson wielded more influence.

Thus, Bob Shuler set aside the Scriptures and began preaching regularly on the Aimee Semple McPherson case, thereby boosting Sunday morning attendance at Trinity to several thousand, surpassed in the city of Los Angeles only by Aimee herself. Shuler uncovered no new information, but with a gift for oratory, he condensed and clarified the facts already reported. Inevitably, the Monday morning papers quoted Shuler's suspicious questions:

Why had Minnie, who directed the kidnappers to the beach where Aimee was swimming, so Aimee said, never bothered to tell authorities about that fact, although her daughter disappeared immediately thereafter? Why, if Aimee had indeed been kidnapped, hadn't the district attorney indicted the mysterious Steve and Rose? "Is it customary for a district attorney to remain passive and inactive when it is charged that three kidnappers lured a woman into an automobile, demanded ransom of five hundred thousand dollars for her release, and defied the laws of the state of California and the county of Los Angeles? When our district attorney states that he has received no evidence of a kidnapping, is the public to take that statement as meaning *he does not accept Mrs. McPherson's story as evidence?*"

Minnie explained Bob Shuler's motives with scorn: "It's clear as day—he's out to destroy the temple and steal the congregation for himself," she told reporters. But secretly she harbored a particular dread of this combative preacher, for she understood his motives as clearly as her own.

Aimee responded to Shuler's continuing attacks in a tone far different from Minnie's. In answer to reporters' queries, she smiled with disarming good nature. "A dog may bark at a queen, but the queen doesn't necessarily have to bark back," she said cheerfully.

Finally Shuler, who headed the Church Federation of Los Angeles from which Aimee had resigned two years earlier, drew up a resolution and had the executive committee release it. The newspapers published it in full:

> Whereas, it is apparent to all that either a crime of the most terrible nature has been perpetrated against Mrs. Aimee Semple McPherson, or else a fraud and hoax that is a shame throughout Christianity have been attempted and the Christian religion is being criticized and even condemned as a result of conflicting stories that are being circulated to right and left;
>
> Now, therefore, be it resolved: First, that the executive committee of the Church Federation of Los Angeles declare itself absolutely neutral as regards the supposed and reported differences of opinion that may exist between Mrs. McPherson and those whom she terms her "enemies"; second, that we solemnly confirm that the district attorney, the sheriff, the police department and the grand jury as impaneled in Los Angeles County should make an honest, sincere and thoroughly adequate investigation of this whole matter, without fear or favor, and report to the people their findings . . . we go on record as demanding to the offices of the law that they do their duty in this matter irrespective of consequences.

No one, not even Minnie, was less pleased to see the resolution in print than District Attorney Asa Keyes. He was a politician of skill and shrewdness born of many years in the arena, and he recognized at the first word of Aimee's reemergence in Douglas a conflict so potentially volatile that many a career including his own could perish, should the conflagration erupt. It was therefore no ineptness on his part, but rather a long-pondered decision that inspired Keyes for several weeks to take no action whatever. It was his earnest though little anticipated hope that the remarkable Mrs. McPherson, who had campaigned for every charity, helped win pay raises for city employees, distributed countless thousands of dollars to the poor and needy, and no doubt had more influence in the city than Keyes himself, would quietly slip back into her previous life and let the matter rest. He hoped, also, that by some miracle the newspapers would abandon what had proved the best-selling saga in the city's history and that Bob Shuler would do the same with a gimmick that had already doubled the attendance at his church and incalculably increased his notoriety.

Yet, even with such strokes of impossible luck, Keyes realized the pastor of Angelus Temple had numerous additional enemies who could not be expected to permit so marvelous a weapon for her destruction to go unwielded—not only the dance hall managers, theater operators, and vice interests, all of which she'd ceaselessly castigated, but also the ever-chafing pastors whose congregations had flowed into Angelus Temple.

With Shuler's resolution, Keyes realized he could procrastinate no longer. He went before the grand jury with a request for kidnapping indictments against Rose and Steve, harboring the fervent hope that, far from escalating the case, such a step would lead to its prompt dissolution. Aimee McPherson, after all, was the only witness who could testify against the kidnappers, and when she refused to appear—as she certainly would—the case would be closed.

"I knew it—Lord, I just *knew* it!" Minnie ranted when word reached her of the subpoenas issued for Aimee and herself, along with Emma Schaffer, Brother Arthur, Roberta, Rolf, and several citizens of Douglas and Agua Prieta. "When will it end—*when*?"

They were in the living room of the parsonage, Aimee at her desk preparing a "Bridal Call" article and Minnie pacing nervously between the door and window. Laying down her pen, Aimee leaned back in the chair and observed her mother coolly.

"Why should you *want* it to end? You couldn't buy this publicity for a million dollars."

"And what if you go to jail? What good's the publicity then, when the last filthy slander's been flung and you're rotting away in some prison?"

With a hearty laugh, Aimee put down her pen and stood. "How on earth could I be *arrested*, Mother?" she asked jovially. "I was the victim, not the kidnappers."

"Well, that may be—"

"It *is*—my story's *true*!"

"So you say. But true or not, if that grand jury decides you lied, they'll slap you with perjury and obstructing justice and maybe even mail fraud if they get it in their heads you had anything to do with that kidnap letter. Oh, Aimee, you're just a silly little girl in your head, with not a bit of the real world getting through to you. Can't you see how *awful* this whole thing is?"

Her eyes reddening, Minnie turned in shame from her daughter's now somber gaze. "I've been telling you for a month to just keep your mouth shut, and the whole thing will die down. But you don't pay me no mind. You just go on and on, getting in deeper and deeper."

She turned to her daughter again. "I called a meeting this afternoon with that young lawyer, Roland Woolley, and our friend Judge Carlos

Hardy. He's on our side, and God knows it's time we got some professional advice." Breaking into sobs, she pleaded, "These are smart men, and you just gotta listen to them, Aimee, and do what they say."

Aimee pondered thoughtfully. Finally she shrugged. "All right," she said. "I'll listen."

That afternoon, Attorney Woolley sided with Minnie, adamantly opposing Aimee's appearance before the grand jury. But silver-haired Judge Hardy, a devoutly religious man, although not a temple member, had every faith in Aimee's story and every confidence the investigation would prove it true. On the other hand, if she declined to testify, he said, the world would deem her guilty of the thousand rumors and blasphemies circulating against her, and the work would suffer.

"Those who believe in her will go on believing," Woolley countered. "If Mrs. McPherson withdraws into silence, the press will soon drop the story for lack of material and public interest will wane."

In the end, even Minnie grew undecided which path to take, for she held the learned Judge Hardy in enormous respect. The decision was Aimee's, and Minnie was not in the least surprised to hear her daughter conclude, "My character has always been spotless, my life has always been the church. I won't rest till I convince even the *doubters* of the truth of my story in its every detail!"

CHAPTER XXIV

The crowd began gathering soon after dawn at the massive Hall of Justice in downtown Los Angeles. At 9:30 on that July 8, Bible-carrying temple workers cordoned a path from the street to the building, and precisely on the hour, while hundreds leaned from office windows and peered from nearby rooftops, a convoy of limousines escorted by police motorcycles drove to the curb. Three armed sheriff's deputies hurried to open the door of the lead car, and a moment later, to riotous cheers, Aimee stepped out. She was dressed not in some smart or stylish fashion the public had come to expect of her, but in the simple white crepe dress with flowing sleeves and starched collar accented by the long blue cape she donned exclusively for temple services. Immediately seven other women wearing identical uniforms stepped from the crowd, forming a wedge with Aimee in the center. In height, hairstyle, and facial features the eight markedly resembled each other.

"Which one's Aimee?" a photographer shouted.

The crowd fell silent.

"You're not *sure*, are you?" Aimee's trained voice rang clearly through the crowd. "Yet anyone who wants to get his *name* in the paper can claim to have seen me anywhere on *earth*, and it's good for four columns. Thank the Good Lord people aren't as stupid as the newspapers *think* they are!"

Quickly she skipped up the steps, turning before the massive doors of the Hall of Justice to face the crowd. Camera shutters clicked.

"God bless you, Sister!" someone shouted.

227

"Hallelujah."

Aimee raised her right hand in the temple salute. Thousands mimicked the gesture.

"My dear ones," Aimee shouted, "I am led like a lamb to the *slaughter*!" Suddenly she laughed. "But I will make you this *promise*, beloved—unlike the lamb, Aimee Semple McPherson will open her mouth and bleat for all she's *worth*!" The crowd roared in approval.

Hurrying into the building, she paused for a moment before the courtroom door. "Now, you must go and pray for me," she told the seven uniformed women. "It's a closed hearing. Not even the reporters can follow me—for once!"

The setting was precisely as she had imagined. An absurdly large chamber, nineteen jurors sitting in a semicircle before the gray-haired judge, the tall, rotund Asa Keyes himself confronting her from the end of a long table. A deputy sat as his side.

She began repeating in minute detail the story of her kidnapping, her face and voice conveying such sincerity that for a moment even the district attorney appeared to wonder if the preposterous story might not be true.

When Aimee finished and he began questioning, his doubts vanished. He asked how she obtained the wristwatch she wore at the Douglas hospital.

"Miss Schaffer gave it to me, or Mother did," she answered. "I don't remember." Then she changed her mind. "I believe I got it when I returned home. I think it was on the dresser." She emphatically denied having the watch when she was in Douglas, and when presented with a photograph showing it on her wrist when she was in the Douglas hospital she exclaimed with equal assurance, "Then Mother must have brought it!"

"You are positive of that?"

"Oh, I am positive of it. I don't remember—it's not important."

All day the questioning continued—concerning the shack, the foods she ate while kidnapped, the length of her hair, rumors of continuing quarrels with Mrs. Kennedy prior to her disappearance. Keyes raised questions concerning Kenneth Ormiston, Donald Yoder, and his blue Hupmobile—a witness had reported seeing Aimee and both men in such a car the day before her return from the desert.

Hour upon hour the district attorney thrust hardly disguised accusations and Aimee parried sometimes with finesse, occasionally with hauteur. Finally, fatigued, Keyes asked his assistant to take over. An hour later, he resumed the questioning himself, bombarding Aimee with an array of paradoxes and contradictions she'd proposed. Still, with unflagging cheerfulness she defended her story.

Late that afternoon she stood before the seventeen men and two women of the jury, her hands folded circumspectly before her.

"I want to say that if character counts a little—I want you to look back," she began. "I was converted at seventeen, married an evangelist, preached the Gospel in my humble way at home and then sailed for China, never expecting to come back to this land but willing to give my life for Jesus. I buried my precious husband there. I came back with my little baby in my arms, born a month after her father died. I took up the Lord's work as soon as I was able to go on.

"I had no great denominations in back of me, but I began very humbly. Until this crushing thing that none of us can explain why God would even permit, although we cannot question that—it would be wrong to do that—I was on the pinnacle of success so far as my work for God was concerned. But I have not always been there. I began preaching under the trees to farmers in their blue overalls sitting on the grass and using the piazza as a mourner's bench. But from there, with the sixty dollars that came in the collection, I bought a little tent, a poor little tent very full of holes, and from that I saved my money and bought a bigger one, and that has been the story. I drove my own stakes, patched the tent, and tied the guy ropes almost like a man. And then came the times when we began to get bigger buildings and theaters costing sometimes as much as one hundred dollars a day, where I have preached to as many as sixteen thousand a day."

Her voice was heavy. She looked back like a laborer across the ages of her life and gazed with weary rejoicing on what she had accomplished. "Then came the building of Angelus Temple. I came here and got a vacant piece of land and hired horses and scrapers and bossed the men myself and went out to build a foundation with my little capital. I told people my dream to preach the gospel as God had given it to me, and they came to help me, not here, but from other cities, through "The Bridal Call," my little magazine. I have never put my money in oil wells or ranches or even clothes or luxuries. My great thought has always been—and this can be absolutely proved—for the service of the Lord and my dear people.

"*Naturally*, I have preached a gospel which made some enmity. I have gone unmercifully at the dope ring, gambling, liquor, tobacco, dancing, and made the statement that I would rather see my children *dead* than in a public dance hall. I have perhaps made enemies with such talk, but in everything I have tried to live as a *lady* and a *Christian*.

229

"Perhaps you are skeptical. I don't blame anyone who should doubt my story, because it *does* sound absurd. But it *did* happen, ladies and gentlemen. I would not work seventeen years, and just as I saw my dearest dream coming true, sweep it all over!"

She argued against contentions that she had suffered amnesia, sought publicity, had fallen in love, had undergone an abortion. Her voice ringing through the courtroom, she cried, "I would rather never have been *born* than to have caused this blow to God's *Word* and His *work*! I had rather I had never seen the light of day when the name of Jesus Christ, whom I love, should be *crucified* and people say, 'There is Sister. She has been preaching, and if her story is wrong—!'"

Her voice trailed almost to a whisper. "That's the sad part to me—not only that my children should go through life and have people say, 'See what her mother did,' but the blow to my work is the greatest thing."

Asa Keyes was no sentimentalist, but the expression on his face reflected profound regret. One of the two women on the jury began weeping. Even jury foreman William Carter allowed his gaze to falter. He finally stared at the floor.

"I pray," Aimee said softly, "—I don't need to ask that you will give this your most earnest consideration, and that you will pray about it on your knees, because it concerns the church and it concerns Christ, and the eyes of the world are on a religious leader and upon this case. And people may come and say, 'I saw Sister McPherson here,' 'I saw her in a dance hall,' 'I saw her in a saloon there.' Just look at me. Look at my children and my family."

When she sat down, there was silence. Then one of the jurors asked her in a gentle, respectful tone, "Mrs. McPherson, are you aware that two young men died in the search for your body in the ocean?"

Aimee's face grew ashen. Staring at the floor, she answered, "If it is true, I am very, very sorry."

Later that week, document analyst Milton Carlson told the grand jury the "avengers' " letter was positively not a bonafide ransom note. "It's too long for kidnappers who mean business, and it's preoccupied with ridiculously detailed and unnecessary descriptions of how the crime was perpetrated. What's more," said Carlson, "it was the work of an educated person who spelled well and put words together in a grammatically correct fashion, yet who made some effort to interject movie-type underworld slang."

In mid-July a new witness appeared before the grand jury, automobile dealer Charles Pape from Tucson. Identifying Aimee first from photos and then in person, he swore he saw her with Donald Yoder and another couple standing before the Club International in Agua Prieta three days before she stumbled out of the desert.

"Of that I'm certain," he insisted. "I particularly noticed her lovely auburn hair and piercing eyes."

"He's a *liar!*" Aimee thundered to Minnie in the parsonage. "How stupid do they think I am? If I *had* been there—which I wasn't—I'd've worn the darkest sunglasses and biggest hat I could find!"

Her bitterness found further expression at the evening service. "There was no lack of witnesses to give false testimony when the *inquisition* dragged helpless women from their homes and condemned loved ones to the racks," she cried. "And likewise today, there has been no lack of witnesses that saw me here, there, *everywhere*, now that my story has been told. But we are all *for* this investigation. At last we shall be vindicated."

On July 20, 1926, the grand jury filed its report: "The county grand jury had presented to it for consideration the evidence in the alleged kidnapping of Aimee Semple McPherson and finds there is insufficient evidence to date to warrant an indictment against alleged kidnappers."

And Aimee released a formal statement: "The official investigation not only bears Sister McPherson's story out, and proves it true, but reveals her to the world as a truthful, upright woman who has withstood the attack in a religious, God-fearing manner. Today she stands vindicated and unafraid."

Three days after the grand jury's verdict, Los Angeles Chief of Detectives Herman Kline boarded an early morning train north to Carmel. The day before, Monterey police chief William A. Gabrielson had called Asa Keyes with a tip: He was convinced Aimee McPherson and Kenneth Ormiston had stayed in Carmel from May 19 to 29. The Los Angeles County district attorney groaned miserably, cursed the fate that had thrown the McPherson fiasco in his lap, and finally ordered Kline to Carmel.

From photographs, Mrs. Daisy Bostick, a real estate agent, identified Ken Ormiston as the George McIntire who'd rented the cottage. Mrs. Jeannette Parkes, who lived in the neighboring cottage, identified Mrs. McIntire, whom she'd seen at 4:00 A.M. on May 19, as Aimee.

Henry Benedict gave Kline a box of items the McIntires, as he still called them, left behind: a battery-powered radio, a can of ground allspice, a bottle of rubbing alcohol, newspapers from Los Angeles and San Francisco, a Bible, five books, and a handwritten list of groceries.

All day, with a growing contingent of reporters trailing behind, Kline and Chief Gabrielson interviewed witnesses in Carmel and Salinas.

That night, Kline called Keyes: "I've got fourteen witnesses here who've positively identified Ormiston beyond the slightest doubt," he said. "I've also got a grocery slip here in McPherson's handwriting. It's the same style as the sermon notes she left at the beach the day she disappeared."

"Oh, *Christ!*" Asa Keyes whined into the receiver. "Why the hell is this happening to *me*? We're all gonna drown in this goddamn thing before it's over. God *damn it!*"

Bob Shuler packed an overflow crowd into Trinity Church Sunday afternoon for a widely publicized Truth Rally. "If Mrs. McPherson's story is true," he roared, "then an infamous injustice has been done to her. But if her story is false, and if she fabricated the whole affair for purposes of her own, then an outrage has been committed against true Christianity!"

Aimee countered by presenting a gala dramatization on the temple stage, to an audience that jammed the auditorium and Bible School, and overflowed five thousand strong into the streets and Echo Park, where the service was boomed over the public address system. The play, *Satan's Convention*, took place in hell, where the devils agreed Aimee was their most crippling foe in Los Angeles, probably the United States, possibly the whole world. They schemed to destroy her, Satan himself finally choosing the method: They'd slander her reputation. Aimee, who did the narration, interjected, "You know, sometimes I think it was made easy for me to escape my captors so that all this slander about me being seen here, there, everywhere, could be *circulated!*"

At the conclusion, two angels descended from the dome of Angelus Temple to exonerate her. "In the three and a half years that the doors of Angelus Temple have been flung wide open to the world, forty-six thousand men and women have answered the call to the altar here!" Aimee cried. "Oh, praise the *Lord*! Forty-six *thousand* new jewels in God's crown. Forty-six *thousand* sinners saved from the clutches of the devil! And oh, dear people, nine thousand eight hundred and nine *baptized* right here on this *platform*! Praise *God!*"

Her last words were drowned in cheers.

Minnie grew ever more grim and silent. Each day the newspapers castigated her daughter anew. One physician wrote suggesting Steve and Rose be granted immunity and even given a reward if they would only reveal the technique whereby they kept a woman unconscious for fourteen hours, clad all the while in a dripping wet bathing suit, without permanent ill effects.

Only rarely did an item bring a smile to Minnie's lips. One was a letter from an attorney: "I am satisfied," he wrote, "that I can prove from the oral testimony of the past few weeks that the city editors of the leading dailies combined and kidnapped Mrs. McPherson and staged her comeback so as to make copy."

Another writer told the Federation of Churches of Los Angeles to go to hell, and a respondent replied that sending those ministers to hell would be unconstitutional—cruel and unusual punishment from the devil's point of view.

While Minnie bustled around the temple and parsonage in stony gloom, Aimee continued to radiate confidence—not the lightheartedness of earlier months, Minnie noticed, but a sterner determination.

"It's *my* fault if people don't believe me," she'd said once. "Let everyone say what they will—I don't want anyone's pity. I've spent my *life* persuading people of the truth and I can certainly do it again now."

But there had also been a night when Minnie came into Aimee's bedroom to find her lying across the bed in tears. Hurrying to her, Minnie took the trembling shoulders in her pudgy hands.

"Momma," Aimee wept, "I'm so . . . so confused sometimes. Everything's changing inside me."

Minnie lifted her daughter and held her tightly. "Well, it's no wonder you're mixed up," she said gently. "You been dragged through hell—I pray to God every night for them to just leave you alone, it makes me so mad."

Lowering Aimee to the pillow, she caressed her forehead.

"Now, I'm gonna get you some warm milk and a pill to make you sleep good," she whispered. "In the morning you'll be like new. And don't worry. God'll make it okay—I know He will."

On a pleasant morning early in August, Emma Schaffer answered the parsonage door to find young Blanche Rice flushed with excitement. She'd been manning the temple information booth, she said, and a lady—she gestured to the middle-aged woman with auburn hair standing behind her—had walked in off the street with the most startling news.

"Please, she must talk to Sister McPherson immediately!"

"I just can't keep quiet any longer!" the woman exclaimed, stepping forward. "It wasn't poor Mrs. McPherson up there with that Ormiston fellow. *I'm* the one they're looking for!"

Emma gasped.

Minnie Kennedy threw the door wide open.

"Who is this?" she demanded.

"I'm Mrs. Lorraine Wiseman, but my husband was killed—"

"And you say you were the one in Carmel?"

"Yes—yes!"

"Well . . ." Minnie scrutinized the woman's face. "She does look like Sister, don't she?" she muttered. Emma somberly agreed. "Maybe you're an answer to prayer," Minnie said. "And maybe you're not. Come on in and tell me your story."

On May 17, said Mrs. Wiseman, her sister had telephoned to say she was ill and planning to stay with a friend at the Benedict cottage in Carmel for a few weeks. The following day, Mrs. Wiseman traveled south from San Francisco, where she lived, to assist in her sister's convalescence. She remained at the cottage almost every day until the twenty-ninth, when her sister and the man—Ken Ormiston—left.

"*I'm* the one everybody mistook for Mrs. McPherson!" Mrs. Wiseman announced. "It so happens I'm a dead ringer for her, which is why everybody—the grocery boy, that Benedict fellow, the neighbors—they all got it in their mind it was *her* up there."

Minnie pondered. Finally she called Aimee.

"Why, I'm certain of it!" Aimee exclaimed. "Doesn't it make perfect sense?"

Minnie was still skeptical. "We've got crooks and four-flushers coming out of the walls," she said. "Everybody's out to make money on us."

"Let me talk with her alone," said Aimee. "I'll find out whether she's telling the truth—you'll just frighten her away."

When they were alone, Aimee smiled radiantly. "I'm sure you can help me," she said. "But there's so much for us to talk about. You must tell me just *everything*—for example, why on earth you wore black satin slippers to a place like Carmel. Didn't Mr. Benedict remark about that— how rough the terrain would be on them?"

"He sure did—yes, he did!" remarked Mrs. Wiseman.

"You know, you ought to stay right here at the parsonage, so we'll have time to be together in private. Even Mother Kennedy mustn't hear us talking this way. She'll misunderstand. She's a very distrustful person, unfortunately."

She agreed to pay Mrs. Wiseman's expenses without question and in cash up to five thousand dollars, again without Minnie's knowledge. Then, calling Minnie back into the room and assuring her she believed Mrs. Wiseman, she asked how to proceed.

"Get your sister—bring her here," Minnie said.

"It's Mrs. X," Aimee retorted. "She's married and has three children, isn't that right, Lorraine? She won't come forward or give her name."

Minnie pursed her lips. "Well, we gotta have some proof. Maybe if she signs an affidavit. Then this here woman can take it to Keyes and tell her story, and maybe he'll believe her."

That afternoon, while Minnie dictated, Aimee wrote the affidavit for Mrs. X to sign. The next morning, Lorraine Wiseman left with the document to be signed by her sister with an X in the presence of a judge. A few days later, Mrs. Wiseman presented the paper and her story to Asa Keyes.

But the district attorney evinced a thorough lack of interest in Lorraine Wiseman, her affidavit, and her tale, urging her to return to San Francisco and honest employment. The next day, Aimee, through her attorney, presented Lorraine Wiseman to the press.

The story broke in Los Angeles on Sunday, August 22. "I have been to the district attorney's office several times and told and retold my story," whined Mrs. Wiseman, "but they don't seem to care to make it public. That's why I'm telling it to the press. Mrs. McPherson must be vindicated, and knowing what I do, she will be, if it takes my lifeblood!"

People began to wonder whether Sister Aimee had indeed been kidnapped and railroaded just as she'd claimed all along. Fighting Bob Shuler temporarily harnessed his pugilative tongue, and the district attorney refused to comment. Even Aimee said little except to explain to her congregation the evening the story broke, "This woman got in touch with *me*, saying she must make this public. I tried to dissuade her; I didn't want to see anyone suffer as I have suffered. Nevertheless, she went to the district attorney and gave him her information."

Only Mrs. Wiseman herself, exulting in the publicity, continued talking, virtually taking up residence in the city's newspaper offices. Her babblings, sometimes irrational, usually disjointed, were extensively quoted: "I have done nothing criminal. The fact that efforts were made to hound me has caused me to act with the least possible publicity. Also, you can realize the undertaking that I have faced, and see that it is one that sears the very soul; so why should I blaze it to a morbid world?"

Even Minnie came to believe Mrs. Wiseman's story. On September 10 she told reporters, "You can depend on her—she's a very high-class woman. Anybody who's talked with her and been with her would know that."

That same night, a reporter for the *Times* telephoned Lorraine Wiseman. "I admit we've acted as if we didn't quite believe your story," he said. "But we've made up our mind to back you to the limit. Why don't you come on down to the office and we'll talk about paying you for a series of articles."

Mrs. Wiseman hurried to the office and was presented not with a contract but an array of information regarding her that left her momentarily speechless: During the last two weeks of May, she was not in Carmel, but worked as a seamstress in Los Angeles, according to her landlady, employer, and a host of witnesses; she was wanted in several California cities for cashing bad checks; the sheriff of one county had issued a warrant for her arrest for nonpayment of a one-thousand-dollar loan. What's more, her name was not Lorraine Wiseman but Villa May McDonald Wiseman Sielaff.

"I am not Villa May McDonald!" Mrs. Wiseman declared. "She's my twin sister!"

But her landlady and two of the people who had accepted bad checks entered the room and made positive identifications.

Two detectives searching her purse in the newspaper office discovered a packet of photographs of Mrs. Wiseman and Aimee posed identically. A notebook contained a list of the items appearing on the Carmel grocery slip and an itemized expense account totaling more than two thousand dollars.

At one o'clock in the morning Lorraine Wiseman was jailed on the phony check charges. When Aimee heard the story, she told reporters, "I was never so surprised in my *life*! I must admit I believed her and sympathized with her in what seemed to be her deep trouble. She was so *convincing*."

Two days later the *Times* rival, the *Examiner*, paid Mrs. Wiseman's bail and whisked her off for an exclusive interview. Still she refused to cooperate until she first talked with Mrs. McPherson. A reporter pretended to place the call and returned with the message that Mrs. McPherson had washed her hands of Lorraine and refused to talk to her. Then Mrs. Wiseman told her story.

A total stranger had approached her in a downtown San Francisco hotel on July 30, she claimed, urging her to go to Los Angeles to help in the Aimee Semple McPherson case, for which she would be well paid. The next day she met with Ma Kennedy, who told her that, if she could produce "Miss X," the woman who was in Carmel with Ken Ormiston, she would be paid five thousand dollars plus expenses.

She agreed, persuading a friend to come from Philadelphia to sign an affidavit. The friend had since vanished and couldn't be located.

Mrs. Wiseman explained that Ma Kennedy had dictated the Miss X affidavit and Aimee had written it in longhand. Then she produced the document in Aimee's writing.

Three days later, Aimee told her radio and temple audience, "I have been informed from reliable sources that I may be arrested tonight. So stick around and you may see something!"

"God bless you, Sister!" someone in the audience shouted. Suddenly five thousand voices cheered her.

"I have been a little simpleton," Aimee exclaimed. "Everyone has said I've talked too much, but I couldn't see why I shouldn't talk when I knew everything I said was the *truth!*"

Waving to Minnie in the second balcony, she cried, "Am I talking too much now, Mother?"

"I don't blame you!" Minnie shouted back.

"Yes, we listened to this woman's story and told her to go ahead and do what she could," Aimee pleaded. "We insisted that her story should not go public until it had been thoroughly *substantiated.* We gave this woman money as we did detectives and others who had come to us with claims they could help us clear up and substantiate my story. With her arrest we were *dumbfounded!*

"Here's a woman arrested as a passer of bad checks. Yet, despite those charges, her story was given credence over *mine*—I, who for seventeen *years* in the work of the Lord have borne a stainless reputation—against whom *nothing* can be found in the whole seventeen *years!* Sometimes I *pinch* myself to see whether this is all *true* and I, a pastor of the Lord, an American citizen, and the mother of two children, am being so persistently *persecuted*—and it *is* persecution! *Never* has anyone been so persecuted as I have been!"

Dropping to her knees, Aimee cried in a quivering voice that stunned even the most hardened listener, "One day I will meet my God in heaven, along with my friends and all my loyal followers and my beloved husband, Robert Semple. And"—her voice rang thrillingly through the temple and over the airwaves—"as I expect to meet my God, *my story is as true today as it was the first time I told it!*"

The next morning, Asa Keyes issued felony complaints against Aimee, Minnie, Ormiston, and Lorraine Wiseman. Said Keyes, "From the time the story that Mrs. McPherson had been drowned was broadcast throughout the country, there has been the tainted atmosphere of a gigantic hoax surrounding it. As time has progressed, this increased with the exposé of the unbelievable story of the kidnapping and the brazen activities of Mrs. McPherson and her friends to build up a false alibi for her.

"It is my duty and I can do no less than exert the full power of my office to bring this woman to the bar of justice in order that she may have a fair and public hearing. It is with regret that I take action against a person so high in the religious esteem of many persons, but the community and upright members of all religions must welcome a fair and open hearing of the situation, which has become a nationwide scandal."

Specifically, Aimee and Minnie were charged with perjury and manufacturing false evidence, carrying maximum penalties, as the press cheerfully pointed out, of forty-two years.

With far less enthusiasm, the press also pointed out some weeks later that Lorraine or Villa May Wiseman's estranged husband was making every effort to have her recommitted to an insane asylum in Salt Lake City, Utah, where, ten years earlier, she had been treated for ungovernable lying.

CHAPTER XXV

That autumn, nationwide fascination with the wayward Sister Aimee reached an unparalleled level. Every nightclub comedian was said to include an off-color Aimee routine in his repertoire. Bars blatantly advertised "Aimee cocktails," and traveling circuses flaunted a new sideshow attraction, "The True Story of Aimee McPherson's Disappearance in Photographs."

Charles Magee wrote a lengthy set of verses called *Antics of Aimee*, which, the newspapers said, were selling all over the country at twenty-five cents per copy. Two stanzas were widely quoted:

> Day and night she'd proclaim to the halt, sick and lame
> Salvation through Christ to be free—
> But the glittering gold that streamed from the fold
> Stamped her system as straight COD!
>
> Some said she would hie straight to heaven to lie;
> Mother said she'd lie under the pier—
> It seemed from the lying ascribed to her dying
> She was in for a lying career!

Such booklets, a smattering of newspaper material laced with the sin-and-scandal scenes for which the public craved, became best sellers all over the country. Equally successful were the serious and semiserious pamphlets. One, "The Story of Aimee Semple McPherson—Was She Kidnapped?" by Charles and Ben Williams, described the evangelist:

"Look at her deep set eyes, rather round, medium large, burning with a strange fanatical light, but nicely under control. In the depth of those eyes you read great intelligence, cunning and possibility for unlimited hate if you cross her, but not sensual love. The love you read in those eyes is love of cause, love of power, plaudit and acclaim.

"Her mouth is remarkable. Look at it closely, it is what built Angelus Temple, her powerful broadcasting station, her palatial home and the living Church of which she is the head. It is a large mouth, but it does not impress you that way, because it is really in exact conformity with the rest of her face.

"It took a million years to make that mouth, and it is solely and entirely the mouth of an Evangelist. It is the most powerful broadcasting station of a clever, very active and intensely ambitious brain, and together with her big physical broadcasting station, there is no telling what it may do.

"Padlock it and throw the key away is perhaps what her lawyers would like to do. But while her mouth has perhaps got her into much of her present trouble, it will no doubt be a great aid to her lawyers in getting her out of trouble.

"A remarkable face. A remarkable woman, perhaps the most remarkable woman in America today."

Confronting the trial issue, the Williams team concluded, "The evidence is strong enough to convict any ordinary person, but Aimee is no ordinary person, and so you cannot tell just what may happen; perhaps Aimee is justified in not pleading guilty until she hears the evidence." If convicted, "she will reform the whole prison and possibly induce the officials to turn their graft money into building a temple in the backyard."

"In most districts in the United states she has far outdistanced even Queen Marie, Peaches Browning, and the Old Faithful Word Geyser, the Hall-Mills case," wrote Bruce Bliven in the November 3, 1926, *New Republic*. "This, as every editor knows, is as it should be. Of the unfailing heart-string pluckers, the Peaches Browning case has money and sex; Queen Marie, sex and snobbery; the Hall-Mills case, sex, crime and mystery; but Aimee's affair has sex, money, mystery, crime and the invaluable unique aspect, which these can only envy: religion."

Even H. L. Mencken, writing for the Baltimore *Sun*, had a good deal to say about the evangelist and her case: "What she is charged with, in essence, is perjury, and the chief specification is that, when asked if she had been guilty of unchastity, she said no. I submit that no self-respecting judge in the Maryland Free State, drunk or sober, would entertain such a charge against a woman, and that no Maryland grand jury would indict her. It is unheard of, indeed, in any civilized community for a woman to be tried for perjury uttered in defense of her honor. But in California, as everyone knows, the process of justice is full of unpleasant novelties, and so poor Aimee, after a long and obscene hearing, has been held for trial.

"The local district attorney has the newspapers on his side, and during the progress of Aimee's hearing he filled one of them, in the chivalrous Southern California manner, with denunciations of her. But Aimee herself has the radio, and I believe that the radio will count most in the long run. Twice a day, week in and week out, she caresses the anthropoids of all that dusty, forbidding region with her lubricious coos. And twice a day she meets her lieges of Los Angeles face to face and has at them with her shiny eyes, her mahogany hair, her eloquent hips, and her lascivious voice. It will be a hard job, indeed, to find twelve men and true to send her to the hoosegow. Unless I err grievously, our Heavenly Father is with her."

While newsboys screamed the headlines of their extras, "Aimee Near Arrest!" Aimee herself lay ill with a nasal cyst her doctor had lanced a few hours earlier. Pain and a high fever had kept her awake most of the night, and when she did finally doze, the nurse Minnie had hired awakened her for medication. Now, gazing apathetically through the French doors to the darkening sky above Echo Park, she ignored the hubbub surrounding her: messengers continually bringing baskets of flowers, Emma reading get-well telegrams, the bedside phone jangling, Minnie offering consolation.

The nurse withdrew the thermometer from between Aimee's lips and studied it. "One hundred and two," she told Minnie. "Your temperature's going down, Mrs. McPherson. You'll be fine in a few days."

"Thank you," Aimee muttered, still staring out the window.

Roberta came in with an ice pack, handing it to the nurse, who agilely placed it on the swollen area of Aimee's nose and cheek. Wincing, Aimee expelled a long sigh.

"I'll see the reporters now."

"You really should rest," said the nurse.

"Emma, hand me my hairbrush, will you, and the mirror and makeup." Removing the ice pack, Aimee sat up while the nurse rearranged the pillows. "Put some flowers over here beside the bed, will you. It'll look nice for the photographers. And Mom, tell the switchboard to put through a few calls from my people—let the world see how I'm loved!"

Taking the brush from Emma, she stroked her hair vigorously. "Roberta, bring in some chairs—if they have to stand, they'll *certainly* give us a bad press. Nurse, tell the reporters just what the doctor said."

Peering into the hand mirror, Aimee's mouth fell open, "My Lord," she mumbled. "What a poor, puffy face you have, little Aimee!" Emma offered her the cosmetics.

"No!" Let them *see* my pain. Let them *know* what torture they inflict by their lies! Bring them in—now!"

The reporters found her weeping. Querying the nurse, they learned her temperature had dropped, the infection was not spreading, but the doctor was concerned because the cyst had been perilously close to the brain. The phone rang, a member of the congregation wishing Aimee a quick recovery, and Aimee profusely sobbed her gratitude. Glancing at her watch, she told reporters she could give them only a few minutes, for it was time she prepared for the baptismal service.

"Are you crazy?" Minnie blurted. "You're in no condition for that."

"I must," Aimee demanded weakly.

"Call the doctor," Minnie ordered the nurse. "See what he's got to say."

A moment later the nurse hung up the phone. Turning to Minnie, she explained, "He says it could kill her."

Aimee burst into tears. "I hope they're satisfied now! They've *crucified* me and reviled me unmercifully! I hope they see their work is nearly completed! I'm going to *prison*—I know it! I've been hounded like a wild animal. It's been a *hunt*. I tell you, no woman of the streets, no common prostitute, was ever given less consideration than I've been given!"

Minnie quickly whisked the reporters and nurse from the room, stepped into the hall with them, and closed the door, leaving Aimee alone.

It had been a mistake to go, Aimee thought. It had been a mistake to come back, to yield to every flitting current of her feelings like a child. But it was done, and she would not waste time with regrets. Instead, she'd fight—not the sniveling defense of the past, but a vicious, singleminded attack. If only she could confide in Minnie—what an invincible team they'd make!

Kicking her legs over the side of the bed, she stood swaying, but with eyes gleaming. "I'm going to fight like I've never fought in my life—and when those big shots go down, great will be the fall thereof."

The next evening, to the cheers of six thousand people, Aimee skipped down the temple ramp in a satiny white gown, a spray of roses pinned at her breast, Roberta clutching one arm, Rolf the other. Sweeping to the microphones with energy that startled her listeners, she attacked District Attorney Asa Keyes, who, a few days earlier, turned loose a young couple who'd claimed Aimee had hired them to manufacture evidence. One said he was the man who contacted Lorraine Wiseman, and the other said she was "Miss X." A six-hour drilling proved them impostors.

"The district attorney *released* these two people after they *confessed* they'd been hired to manufacture evidence!" Aimee cried. "Why were they released when they are admittedly guilty of what we are merely *charged* with? Oh, that Mr. Keyes, he means to do plenty to me! He has already blasted my name with trumpets across the world—settling it before everybody that I am the worst ever! Upon what meat does this Caesar feast himself that he should demand the virtue and blood of a woman evangelist, rather than that of self-confessed liars and extortionists with records in penitentiaries and asylums fastened to them? Jesus trod the way before, and we are going *through* with Him! Pontius Pilate, even Calvary, has no terror for us! Father, *forgive* them, for they know not what they *do*!"

She begged her followers to rain down upon newspaper editors a thunderstorm of protest against their viciously prejudiced reporting. She pleaded with those who loved her and believed in her to read not another word of the vile filth the Los Angeles papers were publishing. Such a boycott, she explained, could do more to inspire fairness in the case than anything else.

Next, she determined to remove Chief of Detectives Herman Kline from the case.

Of all those investigating Aimee's story, Kline had been the most relentless. A gruff and shrewd veteran, now in his early sixties, he had arranged and monitored the first telephone exchange between Aimee and Minnie. He had interviewed her in the Douglas hospital bed, had accompanied her back to Los Angeles on the train. Kline himself had checked out the most farfetched leads and it was he who had interviewed the Carmel witnesses. Realizing that without his tenacity the case would lose momentum, Aimee hired two detectives and gave them a single assignment: "I want Herman Kline off my case."

On a Sunday evening a few weeks later, Kline stopped for dinner at a fancy restaurant in the Los Angeles suburb of Azusa. Another solitary diner soon struck up a conversation, later offering Kline a drink, which the detective accepted. Half an hour later, Kline climbed into his car and started back to Los Angeles.

He had driven no more than a few blocks when the vehicle he was following came to an abrupt halt and Kline's car hit it. Instantly a man leaped from the car behind Kline's and shouted, "Stop that driver!"

Later, that same man told police Kline had zigzagged across the road, driven at excessive speeds, tailgated the car in front of him, and was certainly intoxicated. Smelling liquor on the detective's breath, the police certified him as drunk and arrested him.

The detective who had been following Kline immediately telephoned the temple parsonage with the news. Minnie hastened to Azusa, gathered facts and photographs, hurried back home, and telephoned all the local newspapers. That night she broadcast the story in detail over the temple radio station, and although the Los Angeles dailies played the story down, the suburban papers gave it sensational coverage. One headlined it, "Taxpayers Up in Arms over Kline's Asserted Debauch!"

Kline was suspended and held for departmental trial. Found innocent because the detectives refused to testify against him, he was nonetheless permanently removed from the Aimee Semple McPherson case, and retired a few months later.

Next, Aimee held a tea party for the city's most influential women, many of whom were outspoken crusaders for sexual equality.

"I tell you, ladies," Aimee said after everyone had grown relaxed and comfortable, "I have never yielded one *inch* to a man—and you can ask my dear *mother* here if that's not so. I have *beaten* the men at their own *game*. Who ever heard of a woman preacher—and a *successful* one at that? How *foolish* I was to think they would suffer such humiliation without a fight! I want you women to know the depths to which these men will stoop—inventing stories, hiring witnesses, slandering, dragging a woman's name and reputation into the slime of the gutter, just to 'keep a woman in her place,' as they say. And this Robert Shuler—so called *Reverend!*—is the greatest offender of them *all!*"

Immediately the women drafted a formal declaration of support for Aimee. The most outspoken gave interviews, and within a few days thousands of women in Los Angeles militantly supported Aimee against the district attorney, the press, and sometimes their husbands.

Shuler himself, who still preached regularly on the McPherson case, received hundreds of condemning letters. Said one, "Bob: You are a dirty dog and ought to be killed piece by piece. If she wants a friend Mr. Ormiston, that's her affair. Can't a Christian have a friend? More than that, if there wasn't a cabin in the desert, couldn't God build one and then take it away? Answer me that one, you dirty dog." It was signed, "A White Man."

Another exclaimed: "I will not call you Brother any more than a skunk is a brother. You are a disgrace to the animal family. You raise Old

Ned because a woman becomes so tired with the religious cranks and religious nuts that surround her that she once in awhile wants to get away from them to where she can be natural. Shame on you! Mrs. McPherson is a human being, isn't she? Perhaps she has repented of any little things she may have done wrong. Mrs. McPherson has healed me of seventeen diseases already and I am going back to the Temple to be healed again next month."

From the pulpit and over the radio, Aimee openly declared war. "The time at last has come for a showdown," she cried. "Another drastic attempt to assassinate the character and chastity of a defenseless woman has fallen of its own wickedness. And now comes the showdown. It *is* a showdown. Not before officials and officialdom, not before judges and grand juries, but before the great American public! If the *chivalry* of American manhood, the wonderful *sympathy* of American womanhood will sanction the *suffering*, the mental and physical *anguish* which I have withstood, then I am content. But I have held my peace *long enough*!

"Now I will reveal a sequence of sinister events, a chain of evidence that will make the motive of the whole damnable conspiracy apparent to every man, woman and child in the civilized *world*. Then, perhaps, if no effort still be made to find my abductors, at least no further efforts will be made to find me where I never was."

She demanded to know why suddenly the little town of Carmel was filled with witnesses, when, months before, when any one of these witnesses could have collected twenty-five thousand dollars in reward for producing her, no one moved. "Wherefore do their memories run so suddenly and so positively at the instigation of a Los Angeles district attorney who purports to be investigating not the perpetrators of a crime, but their victim?

"Of *course* they can identify my pictures!" she shouted, her voice snapping like a whip through the large auditorium. "Who is there in California, throughout the whole of *America*, after my photograph has been broadcast for all these weeks in every newspaper of the land, who could *not* identify me? I marvel they did not produce seven *thousand* witnesses! But why didn't they come forward *before*?"

She had one more powerful enemy, she knew—District Attorney Asa Keyes himself, who prosecuted the case—and she singlemindedly set about destroying him. First, she assigned her detectives to scour every detail of his past. "Nobody's perfect, so I'm told," she snapped. "Get something on him that'll stick." Then she arranged to write for the Editors' Feature Story syndicate a serial, "Saint or Sinner? Did I Go from Pulpit to Paramour?" Carried in newspapers throughout the country, it vigorously denounced her accusers, particularly Keyes. "What brought about District Attorney Keyes's change of belief? (Originally he had not wanted to prosecute the case.) Did the overlords of the underworld who are fighting me, and who are heavily interested in Los Angeles, have anything to do with it? 'Scheme, scheme, scheme' cry the pack, snarling at my heels, biting at God's cloak."

On September 27, the first day of the grand jury's pretrial hearings against Aimee and Minnie, only a small crowd milled near the courtroom door in the Hall of Justice. Few of Aimee's supporters were among them, for she had asked them the night before to stay away. "We won't go on playing into their hands!" she'd exclaimed. "They want a circus for their front pages, but we won't give it to them—and we won't read their newspapers either!" Now she approached the massive doors with slow, somber steps, her face colorless and unsmiling. As she passed through the crowd, several people hissed at her.

"Whore!" a voice whispered.

Aimee stopped, her eyes wide with incredulity. Regaining her composure, she smiled defiance into every face, meeting each set of eyes one by one. In silence, she proceeded to the courtroom.

That day, three witnesses denied Aimee Semple McPherson was the woman they'd seen in the Carmel cottage. Jesse Lynch Williams, the Western Union messenger who delivered the telegram was the first, followed by William H. McMichael, a carpenter who'd worked next door to the Benedict cottage almost every day. He said he'd seen the McIntires many times, and insisted when asked to identify Aimee, "Never saw her before in my life." Finally, August C. England, town marshal of Carmel, testified he'd ridden on horseback past the cottage daily and had seen the man and woman living there many times. He'd observed her with and without her hat and with and without her sunglasses at a distance of only a few feet.

"Will you tell the court whether or not Mrs. McPherson was the woman at the cottage?" asked Aimee's attorney.

"She is positively *not* the woman," answered the marshal.

The mystery of the wristwatch was also solved that day—at least to the believing public's satisfaction. Emma Schaffer was called to the platform by the prosecution and answered all questions with rigid composure. Her answers were brief, but loud and to the point. When Keyes questioned her about the jewelry Aimee wore that day she disappeared, Emma answered emphatically. "She had no jewelry."

"Was the watch in her purse?"

"No."

"But Mrs. McPherson said she always had her watch with her. She believed she left it in her purse at the beach."

"Sister McPherson is a busy woman," Emma snipped. "She has to keep thousands of important things in her mind, and can't be expected to keep track of her watch all the time. As a matter of fact she could not have had her watch that day, because I had taken it to a jeweler some days before to have it repaired. It was there all the time Sister was missing. I picked it up myself and gave it to her after she returned from Douglas."

Emma said she knew nothing about a wristwatch on Mrs. McPherson's arm when she was photographed in the Douglas hospital.

When Emma was dismissed, Aimee pulled the secretary to her side and kissed her. The grim, tight-lipped Emma wept with gratitude.

That night from the temple platform Aimee again attacked Asa Keyes. "The vile insinuations which fell from the lips of Mr. Keyes during his examination today could not, in my opinion, exist in the mind of any *pure* man! He has subjected me today to the most exquisite cruelty and suffering that the human mind can conjure up. Asa Keyes—if you are listening in, you are a dirty, lecherous *libertine!* I urge every single taxpayer listening to my voice to contact your office and demand immediately an accounting of the money—thousands upon *thousands* of *dollars*—that you have been squandering—you and your wife and your assistants and their wives—on trips to *vacation* resorts in Carmel, Douglas, Arizona, and Mexico for what we are supposed to *believe* are investigations into *my* integrity."

She followed the verbal attack with a release revealing that Keyes, who had been voted an annual secret fund for putting thieves, murderers, and other criminals in prison, had been improperly diverting the money to the McPherson case, and possibly to personal accounts, and had already requested another five thousand dollars for the same purpose. Chairman McClellan of the Los Angeles County Board of Supervisors promptly issued a criminal complaint against Keyes. According to an assistant, the district attorney began drinking heavily about that time.

Aimee's ceaseless efforts to persuade the public of her story's veracity began to reap results. A reporter quoted several typical citizens: "Maybe she was in a trance." "I say, let the poor woman alone. I ain't got nothing against her but the way she gases about it." "It's dirty politics. She's a saint. I never did see a nicer bunch of boys and girls than she has got down to her temple."

A wealthy matron exclaimed, "I think she's perfectly marvelous. Such poise! Is it true she took drama under Bernhardt?"

A young woman with a short skirt and bright yellow hair gasped,

"All the men are in love with her—the lawyers on both sides and all the reporters!"

A banker grunted, "Utter foolishness. It will cost the county one hundred fifty thousand dollars before they're through. Why don't they just drop the case?"

Still, the trial dragged on. Several witnesses came up from Douglas again, and all testified in Aimee's favor. But Milton Carlson, the handwriting expert, identified photographs of the grocery lists as Aimee's handwriting beyond question. He particularly stressed that she had an unusual characteristic of switching from longhand to print and back again as a child might.

"You see," Aimee whispered to a reporter sitting nearby, a melancholy smile on her lips. "See how childish my handwriting is? I've just never grown up."

After five weeks the defense closed and the hearing ended, one of the longest in California legal history, with 3,600 pages of transcript. Aimee's lawyers called for dismissal on the technicality that if no kidnapping had taken place, as the state contended, then Aimee had committed no crime in seeking indictments against criminals who did not exist. Six days later, the judge ruled, "After full examination of the entire evidence, there is sufficient cause to believe the defendants guilty." Aimee and Minnie Kennedy were ordered held for trial on three counts, carrying a total maximum prison sentence of forty-two years. The trial was scheduled for January 10, 1927.

Hearing the news, Minnie became so agitated she required sedation, so certain was she that she would spend the remaining years of her life in prison. Aimee, however, was almost serene, sweeping from one temple department to another consoling her flock with assurances that the case would be dropped. "God has given me a sign," she said. "You mustn't worry."

In fact, she had secretly added two more men to her private staff, two reporters who had been active in investigating the scandal against her. They were Ralph Jordan of the *Examiner* and James Kendrick of the *Times*. One would ghostwrite a book for Aimee explaining her version of the kidnapping. Another would act as her personal manager on a "vindication tour" to begin as soon as the trial closed. It would cost Aimee incalculable thousands of dollars, but it would work.

The grand jury had handed down its verdict on November 3. On the twentieth, Mr. Benedict of Carmel died. At about that time, Aimee stopped speaking of the disappearance. The newspapers stopped referring to it. Bob Shuler, noting a decrease in attendance and concluding that six months of the McPherson case had bored his congregation, found other people to condemn.

Kenneth Ormiston arrived from Chicago one morning at the Los Angeles district attorney's office, to everyone's astonishment. He was arrested and released on bail, and addressed reporters in the corridor of the Hall of Justice.

"I'm very happy to be here in Los Angeles," he said, "and face the charges brought against me in a square and dignified manner. Intrigue and hokum are as thick as a San Francisco fog, and it most certainly is not my intention further to complicate the situation. Nor is it in my mind to enter the spotlight as a figure of public interest. Let me make it clear that my movements were entirely voluntary throughout, and I was not captured and dragged to the city."

The weather turned sour. Aimee told reporters, "I am sorry Mr. Ormiston came all the way back from Chicago to find it raining here."

Thus the matter rested through December. During the holidays, Aimee cheerfully led the temple through Christmas and New Year celebrations.

Asa Keyes waited until January 10, the deadline, before indicating his decision. That day he called a press conference. "The fact that this defendant fabricated a kidnapping story or that she spent time at Carmel are not, in themselves, offenses of which this court can entertain jurisdiction," he said. "Reputable witnesses have testified sufficiently concerning both the Carmel incident and the return of Mrs. McPherson from her so-called kidnapping adventure to enable her to be judged in the only court of her jurisdiction—the court of public opinion." At Keyes's request, the grand jury dismissed the case.

At the temple, Aimee received the news with exultation. "Praise God—He's given us the *victory!*" she exclaimed.

Rumors spread that Asa Keyes had been paid thirty thousand dollars to drop the case. The Los Angeles County Supervisors started a thorough investigation, and, although acquitted of those charges, Keyes was found to have accepted bribes on another occasion. He spent nineteen months in San Quentin.

CHAPTER XXVI

Minnie paced the floor of Aimee's bedroom like a caged lion, stopping only to cast fierce glances at her daughter, who, with apparent nonchalance, tossed clothes into the suitcases on the bed.

"You ain't even been listening to me!" Minnie bellowed.

"Of course I have—how could I help it with you screaming in my ear?"

"And?"

"And I'm going. I said I was going a month ago, and a day ago, and an hour ago—and I'm going." Outwardly, Aimee maintained her casual composure, but silently she determined that if her mother repeated just one more time her list of objections to the vindication tour, she'd scream herself into a faint.

But Minnie didn't pursue her haranguing. Instead minutes before Aimee's departure, the bitter glare in her eyes dissolved. Throwing up her hands in despair, she sank into a chair and stared at the floor.

"If I could just understand you, Aimee," Minnie said. "Maybe you know what you're doing, leaving the temple just when it needs you most. Oh, Aimee, you should be devoting yourself to the flock, setting an example. Let the whole world look at you, and let them see a perfect child of God, a dedicated minister of the Gospel. Then, no matter what they said about you in the past, they'll every last one of them live to hang their heads in shame for their lies and slander against your good name!"

Bouncing to her feet again, Minnie hurried across the room to

Aimee. "You must let the past be *forgotten*," she cried, "not preach about it in every city in the land, for the love of God!" Minnie grasped Aimee's arm. "Why are you doing this crazy thing, Aimee—*why?*"

Aimee's eyes flashed anger, but, pulling her arm free, she turned away without speaking. Why *was* she leaving now, to preach her own innocence rather than the Gospel of salvation? These were feelings she could not explain. She knew only that she had served the temple for what seemed like eons, had found a barren lot at the dawn of eternity, and had built upon it the temple, the Church of the Foursquare Gospel, the Bible college and radio station and on and on, had brought them into existence and had led them to maturity. And now that it was all complete, Minnie would have her be buried under that azure dome, as absurd a living death as any she had ever known in Providence or anywhere.

But she'd been born for a life far beyond the clockwork mechanizations of a single edifice or commitment, or even a single love. How could she tell Minnie, who had always believed everything with such literal simplicity, that in some obscure way the accusations of the last few months—the damning denunciations of the Robert Shulers, the charges of hypocrite and whore and fraud and gold digger—had released her to a life of incomprehensible magnitude? She would not merely lift the ignorant elect rejoicing to the gates of heaven, but would reach the greater masses who floundered as she had in the cold and empty abyss of hell.

"Mom," Aimee said, a new softness in her voice, "if God's led me to take this tour, who are you—who is *anyone*—to stop me? I'm to be 'all things to all men, that I might by all means save some,' just as Paul was. Hundreds and *hundreds* who would never set foot inside a church will come to know the Saviour. The form's different, yes. But I'll be as much about my Father's business, doing the work of an evangelist, as ever."

Closing the suitcases, she whisked them from the bed and rushed into the hall with Minnie hurrying after her.

"I just *know* it's the right thing," Aimee called over her shoulder, skipping down the spiral stairway to the foyer. "You'll be proud as can be when you read about the meetings in the papers."

"And what about Ralph Jordan?" Minnie demanded. "Will I be proud of that, too?"

He was standing at the foot of the stairs, the former *Examiner* reporter, tall and ruggedly handsome with curly blond hair. Minnie gasped, as much taken aback by the cigarette smoke curling from his nostrils as by his presence. Aimee greeted him with a warm smile and handed him the suitcases.

"Now, Mother, I don't want you coming to the station. No need to waste your time. Pray, won't you, that the Lord will bless, and say good-bye to the children for me."

She nodded to Jordan, and he threw open the door for her.

The tour started with a couple of lackluster one-night stands, January 23 in Kansas City, the 25th in Omaha, then a week in Des Moines, three days in Indianapolis, two in Chicago. The Boston Ministerial Association voted not to support Aimee's lecture on her disappearance, so she canceled plans to visit that city.

On February 18 she arrived in New York City, wearing a yellow suit with white fur collar and buttons, so fashionable and expensive it received special attention on the society pages. She answered with fresh vitality the inevitable questions about her kidnapping, then told a New York *Times* reporter, "The *world* is wearing seven-league boots today, but the *Church* goes right on tripping along in slippers. No wonder our young people are carried along in the ever-churning whirlpool of this world's tawdry pleasures.

"Young people are told in schools that God didn't create them. They hear from *pulpits* things that Darwin never would have said in his palmiest days. They're told there's no future life. *Naturally* they set the pace as rapidly and as worldly as they can—there's nothing to look *forward* to! The fault's not with the youth—it's with the churches and the homes."

The Roosevelt Hotel's station WRNY, which had previously agreed to broadcast three of Aimee's sermons, rescinded the invitation with the simple official statement that permitting the controversial evangelist to use their facilities "seemed bad policy." Three more local stations also refused before WODA of Paterson, New Jersey, agreed to permit the broadcasts.

That night, wearing a tasteful but obviously expensive gown, and accompanied by a retinue of reporters, Aimee toured the city's nightclubs as she had years earlier in Winnipeg and other cities. When a fight broke out a few feet from her at one club, she calmly took a pad and pen from her purse and scribbled some notes about it for her sermon. Later, at the Three Hundred Club on West Fifty-fourth Street, Miss Texas Guinan, nationally heralded "queen of the nightclubs," asked Aimee to speak.

"Behind all these beautiful clothes, behind these good times, in the midst of your lovely buildings and shops and pleasures, there is another life," Aimee told the revelers. There was nothing judgmental about her voice, and she smiled with a sincerity and warmth that had already infected thousands. "There is something on the other side. 'What shall it profit a man, if he shall gain the whole world, and lose his own soul?' With all your getting and playing and good times, don't forget you have a Lord. Take Him into your hearts!"

The crowd applauded her raucously. The next morning, the city's newspapers featured the story.

Two-thirty that Saturday afternoon, trudging through the winter's fiercest blizzard, thousands jammed the Glad Tidings Tabernacle at 325 West Thirty-third Street. Hundreds filled the basement, and a large crowd milled on the sidewalk. To the disappointment of society matrons who had come to assess her wardrobe, Aimee preached in her white temple uniform and blue cape.

Immediately after the first service she preached a second, unscheduled sermon for those who had been shut out. She spoke again that night and twice on Sunday, precisely the same message she always had, in an ever-new way: "I tell you, there is no *alternative* to faith in God!" she cried. "I have looked upon this world with new eyes, and one culminative conviction thunders in my soul: Blessed is that nation whose trust is in the Lord!

"Call me a religious fanatic—call me anything you like; but a few years from now—perhaps but a few short months from now—you will say: 'She was right!' You will send a call echoing through the lobbies of the world: 'Page God. Page God! *Page God!*' "

The applause Aimee received on the dance floor of Texas Guinan's Three Hundred Club echoed clear across the nation to Angelus Temple, and with it fresh accusations: Sister had seemed right at home in those dens of iniquity; she'd been laughing, drinking, even dancing.

Minnie knew the rumors were absurd—yet, they sickened her with humiliation. She telegrammed Aimee, demanding her immediate return to the temple, and when that brought no reply, she sent assistant pastor and choir director Gladwyn Nichols to New York to urge Aimee in person to return.

Less than three weeks after Nichols set out across the country, he was back at the parsonage confronting Minnie as she sat at her desk in the living room.

"Well, sit down, sit down," she ordered. "I can see you're no bearer of glad tidings. You're the spitting image of a bird dog." Indeed, his eyes grew more sorrowful as she spoke.

His report confirmed Minnie's most dreaded fears. Sister was being completely managed by the worldly Ralph Jordan. His cohorts spent each day in her anteroom at the hotel smoking cigarettes and playing cards and drinking whiskey. When dear saints who had helped and befriended Sister in her old barnstorming days stopped to see her, Jordan's crowd rudely dismissed them saying Aimee wasn't seeing anyone.

"They even had the nerve to tell *me* I couldn't see her!" exclaimed Nichols in indignation. "But I told *them*—I said I was Ma Kennedy's own personal emissary—and praise God, I walked through their midst like Moses through the Red Sea!"

He hardly recognized Sister. "She was all made up with lip paint and powder, just like a woman of the world," he said. "It was enough to break your heart. But the worst of all"—He reached across the table for Minnie's hand, which she promptly retracted. "Mother, her lovely long hair, a woman's glory as the Bible says—I don't know how to tell you. She's had it cut. And it's a lighter color."

Minnie gasped. So now Aimee was brushing aside even the most fiercely held tenets of the Church—not merely the Church of the Foursquare Gospel, but all churches teaching the fundamentals of the faith, whether Baptist, Methodist, or whatever. In thousands of pulpits across the land every Sunday, pastors railed against jeweled and painted women, particularly denouncing the new fashion of bobbed hair, flaunting as it did the scriptural exhortation that a woman's hair is her glory and should not be cut.

"I told her what you said," Nichols continued, "that the members were embarrassed by the talk of worldliness, and some might withdraw if she didn't come home. You know what she said? 'Let them walk out of the temple. I'll fill it up again.' She doesn't even *care*!"

While Brother Nichols spoke, Minnie pushed her chair away and stood with arms folded across her chest. Her eyes narrowed into needle-points of intensity, and she pressed her lips so firmly together they grew white. Finally she said, "I think God's calling Sister to a different kind of work now. I think she's finished at the temple."

She stared meaningfully at Nichols. "Are you with me?" she asked. He nodded.

"Okay, run along now."

For a moment, the immensity of her chores seemed impossible. She was fifty-two years old now, had raised a sixteen-year-old granddaughter, and worked with bulldog tenacity in uncompromising service to God, from the Salvation Army barracks in Ingersoll to the great temple in the City of Angels. Now, mellowed and not all that full of pep since the trial, she'd even considered retiring to travel and rest. Instead, she would fight again, for the sake of her life's work, Angelus Temple. Her adversary would be her daughter, whom she loved more than anything in this world. She would have preferred even to die, but her conscience would not allow her to sit by while the Lord's people suffered heartbreak and disillusionment, their hard-earned donations squandered on worldly amusements. She'd march into battle once more, even if it broke her heart.

A few days later, a reporter asked Minnie when Aimee would return. She responded with the guarded suggestion that Sister might never resume the pulpit. "We've heard she's finding work enough to keep her busy in the field indefinitely," she said with a meaningful nod.

Aimee was preaching in Dallas when word reached her through a temple confidant that Minnie was unofficially broadcasting the evangelist's resignation. "Oh, Sister will keep on preaching from time to time at the temple," Minnie was quoted. "But we'll have to get a new acting pastor, and we might as well start looking now." Aimee wired immediately she would be home on April 1, proposing she be met at the railroad station with fanfare every bit as lavish as when she returned from Douglas nine months earlier. Temple workers devoted themselves to hasty preparations, but the grand reception never took place, for, on Friday night, March 31, Aimee stepped out of a limousine before the sweeping facade of Angelus Temple, ran through the lobby and up the sweeping stairs to the Five Hundred Room where the most devoted followers had gathered for the weekly prayer meeting. The crowd greeted her first with gasps, then riotous cheers.

Aimee responded with magnificent laughter. "I missed you so!" she exclaimed, throwing wide her arms as though to embrace them all. "These have been the loneliest months of my life—a day here, two days there, little fellowship with brothers and sisters in the Lord. But oh, how God has blessed! People have come to know Christ who never would have set foot inside Angelus Temple or any other church, beloved."

She spoke briefly of the tour, of drug addicts and prostitutes and thieves converted to holy, upright lives, the impact her ministry was having all over the country through the faithful prayers and support of the saints at Angelus Temple. When she finished, she and Minnie slipped into the hall and started back to the parsonage with Minnie setting the pace.

"Aren't you going to tell me how glad you are to see me?" Aimee cooed.

"Glad to see you!" Minnie fumed, refusing to even glance at her daughter. "I ain't never been so ashamed in my life. First the rumors about Ormiston, then the whole trial scandal, and now this—accused of worldliness by your own people, them that stuck by you loyal while the whole world made its accusations!"

Together they hastened from the temple and along Glendale Boulevard toward the parsonage, Minnie's short, bustling steps keeping her slightly ahead of her daughter's long, graceful strides.

"So that's it," Aimee exclaimed. "That's why you're trying to take the temple from me!" Ignoring passersby, Aimee clutched Minnie's arm, bringing her to a halt. "Well, you listen to me, Minnie Kennedy. I'm *sick* of you and that Gladwyn Nichols and reporters and politicians and every drunk in the *gutter*—just *everyone* thinking they have a right to pass judgment on me. Who are *you* to condemn me? How many people have *you* won to Christ in the last three months? I've won *hundreds*! Never in the history of the *world* has a preacher had such acclaim. I'd think you'd be ecstatic, but no—you *judge* me and *condemn* me. 'Judge not, lest *ye* be judged!' "

Only a growing cluster of the curious kept Minnie's anger in check. Turning from Aimee, she marched toward the parsonage. "You have the nerve to quote Scripture to *me*!" she hissed. "Well, here's some Scripture for *you*. 'Be ye not unequally yoked together with unbelievers: for what fellowship hast righteousness with unrighteousness?' That's Second Corinthians six, fourteen. And the seventeenth verse: 'Wherefore come out from among them, and be ye separate, saith the Lord.' And Romans six, one: 'Shall we continue in sin, that grace may abound? God forbid!' "

Marching through the parsonage foyer and past Emma Schaffer without acknowledgment, Minnie went straight to the living room, waited for Aimee to finish embracing her faithful secretary and follow her, then slammed the door shut behind them.

"Once you counted it all joy to serve God," Minnie stormed, "but now you want to serve both God and Mammon. Well, the Bible says it can't be done. You're double-minded, and the Bible says a double-minded man is unstable in all his ways. You're neither hot nor cold, but lukewarm, and even God abhors the lukewarm—He'll spew you out of His mouth!"

Aimee turned away. "It's been a long trip and I'm exhausted," she said.

Minnie came to stand in front of her.

"I just wish I knew," she said bitterly. "I just wish I knew what's happened to you."

Aimee turned to gaze coldly into the face of the feisty warrior who confronted her, but for all her combativeness, Minnie appeared to Aimee suddenly defenseless, her face not that of a proud enemy but showing the weary carnage of one defeated.

"You'll not make me feel guilty again with talk of my poor, broken-hearted mother, so spare us that, will you?" Aimee said with less vehemence than she'd intended. "Even little Aimee Elizabeth grows up sometime. Even someone as naïve as all that eventually eats of the tree of the knowledge of good and evil—it is, after all the original sin."

Minnie shook her head in bewilderment. "Does it make you happy to mock your poor mother?"

"Is that what you think I'm doing? Then I'll stop and go to bed." She sauntered to the door, then turned back to Minnie.

"Incidentally, I've decided to take complete control of the temple finances," she said. "I want all the books turned over to me and my representatives tomorrow morning." Minnie's face grew ashen, but Aimee continued: "I have a great many bills outstanding because of the trial, more than you could possibly imagine or I would dream of telling you, and I intend to pay them without being harassed by you at every turn as I've been in the past. I'm the one who takes the offering, I'm the one to whom the money's given, and I'm the one who shall control it."

Aimee threw open the door. "And of course we both know she who controls the purse controls the temple," Aimee announced, slamming the door behind her.

"You'll not get the books!" Minnie screamed after her. "You'll not drag this temple down with you into the gutters of filth and sin! I'll fight you, Aimee Semple McPherson!"

With no hint of her intentions, Aimee gathered the children and Emma Schaffer the next day and moved out of the parsonage to an Ocean Park beach house. Although it seemed to Minnie a petulant and impulsive act, Aimee conceived it in far shrewder terms to force Minnie's surrender. Minnie would not long endure newspaper headlines hinting of dissension between them. She would agree to virtually anything to save the temple from such embarrassment, Aimee predicted. And she was partly correct.

First, Minnie discussed Aimee's demand for financial control with several church leaders; they agreed it could do no harm as long as Minnie remained business manager and vice-president of the Echo Park Evangelistic Association. Then she prayed about it, kneeling beside her bed in the parsonage until her knees were sore, then lying on her back and staring up at the ceiling, travailing with God for a sign. She had done well, been a good and faithful servant through all these difficult years; for all Aimee's boasting, Minnie assured herself she was as much the builder of Angelus Temple as her daughter was—perhaps more so.

But perhaps Aimee was right demanding the chance to run the

257

temple her way. She was thirty-six years old, after all, and the temple could hardly be in sounder financial shape, with assets of more than two million dollars, no mortage, and no long-term debts. Even Aimee, with her utterly impractical thinking, could hardly jeopardize the temple's security, especially with Minnie overseeing it.

So she agreed to turn over the temple finances—under the condition that Aimee would dismiss Ralph Jordan, devote herself to managing the temple, and avoid behavior that might be interpreted as worldly.

Aimee responded not to her mother, but to the temple board of managers, most of whom she had appointed in reward for their unswerving loyalty to her.

"Next month I'll be campaigning in Chicago and all over the Midwest," she said. "I'll be taking Ralph Jordan along again as my tour manager. There are certain factions within the temple who oppose Mr. Jordan, but he's proved an invaluable help to me, and I intend to keep him. I want you to take a vote on this matter—was I right to take Mr. Jordan with me on my last tour? Will it be right for me to take him again? If you vote not, I'll take it as a sign from the Lord and hand in my resignation from the temple immediately."

The board gave her their support.

Ecstatic, she circled the table grasping hands and kissing foreheads. "Praise God, it would have broken my heart to leave!" she exclaimed.

Suddenly her face grew somber. "But the fact is, *someone* must leave, for a house divided against itself cannot stand. I say this in confidence—I love my mother very much. She's been of incomparable assistance in the work. But in recent months we've been at loggerheads. She opposes all the Lord is leading me to do in the work. I won't say any more—may you do the wise thing."

She left the room.

The following day, the board released a public statement: "We are shocked and grieved that Mrs. Kennedy should attack her evangelist daughter, as she has been quoted as doing. Mrs. Kennedy has no quarrel with Mrs. McPherson. We are the ones, the church, who want a change of business management of the temple.

"Mrs. McPherson has made no move, we are sure, which would embarrass her mother in any way. But the committee does think that for the good of the work Mrs. Kennedy should let someone else take her place.

"The board of the church and the committee desire that Mrs. Kennedy be cared for in splendid style and would be delighted to assist her in working out any one of the several courses open to her."

Minnie replied haughtily that the board of managers were tin soldiers without authority. "They're not gonna dictate to Minnie Kennedy!" she thundered. "And as for Aimee Semple McPherson, who does she think she is? We're partners fifty-fifty, every bit of it—deeds and all."

At the beach house, Emma Schaffer brought Aimee word of Minnie's response. Aimee pondered a moment, then her face brightened.

"Let her keep the temple if she wants it," she told Emma. "Let her bellow over five thousand empty seats. Let her voice echo through the dusty corridors until the whole thing crumbles around her. Let our friends know I'm looking for some new land, not far from Echo Park. I'll build a cathedral so monumental it'll dwarf Angelus Temple. I'll fill it to the rafters—and this time it'll be in my name alone."

When Minnie heard that, she recognized defeat, for it was no idle threat her daughter had hurled and precisely the sort of challenge Aimee thrived on. She would launch such an undertaking with never a thought as to the consequences, would risk splitting the membership, its loyalties and tithes, threatening the temple's very survival.

The next day, Minnie moved out of the parsonage and into a small house she'd purchased half a block away on Lemoyne Street. She refused to discuss at length with reporters her breach with Aimee, but said, "Ever since Sister went to the Holy Land last year, I've been thinking about retiring to do some preaching of my own. So maybe I will—but only if I get all that's coming to me, fifty-fifty."

With Minnie's departure, the Reverend Mr. Gladwyn Nichols also resigned, carrying with him the entire temple choir and about three hundred members. He told the press the secession was prompted by Aimee's surrender to worldliness—her wardrobe of fancy gowns and short skirts, jewelry, furs, her new infatuation with cosmetics and bobbed hair, all specifically condemned by the Scriptures.

"The God of the Gospels is being replaced at Angelus Temple by the god of materialism," he told the press.

When reporters asked Aimee to comment, she laughed airily. "Mr. Nichols is a sweet, dear man," she said. "I can say nothing about him except that he was *very* loyal and *very* fine to all of us. Of course you know musicians are temperamental. Why should I get into a controversy with a bandmaster? Mr. Nichols couldn't have meant me with his talk of short skirts and bobbed hair—you don't really think my skirt is too short, do you?"

When lawyers finally reached a settlement between the two women, Minnie retained her interest in the deeds to the property on which the temple, Bible School, and parsonage were built and was granted $10,000 annually in interest payments on the mortgage she held on the land. No payments would ever be made on the principal. As compensation for her interest in the buildings and furnishings as well as the temple's business value, Minnie received $106,000 in cash and property. Aimee was given the same amount in canceled checks representing the money the temple had spent for her defense in the kidnapping case.

Thus, Minnie's business interest in the temple was severed, but as Aimee soon learned to her abject frustration, Minnie had not surrendered. With distracting regularity she read of Minnie's comments to the press: Temple expenditures had been shady since a few months before Aimee's case was dismissed; Aimee should make public the names of all people receiving gifts from her before the case was dropped—"everybody should know the truth." Minnie Kennedy, who had always opposed airing temple problems before a worldly throng, now used the newspapers to tell the entire city her views on Aimee's absolute power.

"The board there," she was quoted, "do whatever Sister wants. My daughter has a magnetic personality, and ability to win people to her. When she wants to accomplish something, she tells them about the terrible death of Robert Semple, her evangelist husband who died in China. She moves everybody to tears, and then they hold up their hands and approve anything she asks for."

Minnie's comments about the kidnapping evoked more pride than anger in Aimee, for she'd taken great pains to keep Minnie ignorant of every incriminating aspect of the case, and now, when Minnie might have used it against her, her mother had nothing more than a handful of insinuations to scatter about. Nor did the comments about her ability to sway the board unduly concern Aimee. Rather, she saw that, too, as a compliment of sorts, assuming Minnie secretly envied her persuasive power.

But one of Minnie's attacks struck Aimee with stunning force. "My daughter's like a fish on the beach when it comes to handling money," Minnie declared. "I don't believe if you put an ad in the newspapers you could find anybody dumber when it comes to business. It was me that bailed her out when I came to help her down there in Florida, and it was me that put the temple on its feet. All they got to do is let her have her way for a year, and she'll bankrupt the place, mark my words."

Aimee's anger soared. She would silence Minnie if it took her last breath. After midnight she called Ralph Jordan, demanding he come to the parsonage. An hour later he stood before her sleepy-eyed, his golden curls uncombed.

"I'm going to beat Minnie at her own game if it kills me!" Aimee exclaimed. "She thinks she's the only one who can handle money. She's so *proud* because she pays the bills and saves a few dollars. Well, I'm going to show her what it's like to make *real* money—millions and *millions*! Ralph, come up with some schemes that'll pay off big. We're going to be millionaires, and I want to do it so quick Minnie's *head* will spin!"

CHAPTER XXVII

In January 1928 Aimee announced her "Blessed Home Memorial Park," a fourteen-acre cemetery in nearby Burbank. A large lot in the center was designated Sister's final resting place, and Ralph Jordan and his crew pressured temple members to buy surrounding plots so that, at Christ's return, the entire Angelus Temple fellowship could "go up with Aimee." Burial spaces increased in price in ratio to their proximity to Aimee's.

That project was hardly under way when Aimee announced another, Tahoe Cedars, a summer camp on the shores of Lake Tahoe, the exclusive vacation resort in the High Sierras of Northern California. Mr. H. L. Henry, who owned the lakeside property, donated land on which Aimee was to build a permanent tabernacle. The rest was subdivided in lots and offered to temple followers.

To launch the venture, Aimee conceived a gala Foursquare Gospel Summer Camp Meeting at the Tahoe grounds. On July 20, she told her radio, temple, and "Bridal Call" audiences, she would personally lead thousands from the temple doors. There'd be a mass dining tent, meeting pavilion, and hundreds of sleeping tents the faithful could rent.

Railroad officials added special trains for the mass exodus north, and Mr. Henry and his associates ordered food enough for seven thousand, including two tons of meat, a thousand doughnuts, 490 loaves of bread, and seventy-five gallons of ice cream.

But only a handful departed with Aimee that summer day, and when the entire group assembled at the campsite, Aimee counted hardly more than a hundred. Allowing herself no sign of disappointment, she enthusiastically greeted her people, then climbed aboard a launch and guided load after load around the lake. Later, in a hollow beneath tall pines, she led her vacationers in jubilant singing and preached with great feeling, while the unused food perished on the platform of the Lake Tahoe railroad depot.

A summer-long effort led to the sale of only seven lots, which provided Aimee no capital with which to build a tabernacle. Thus, even the seven purchasers sued Aimee for breach of contract; by September, the legal claims totaled $150,000. Aimee settled out of court, dollar for dollar.

Blessed Hope Memorial Park—or "Sister's boneyard," as Minnie dubbed it—also failed. Only a few purchased plots, and even they rebelled when they learned that the land upon which Aimee had knelt during her solemn consecration was not her memorial park but an adjoining cemetery, and that the Blessed Hope was a weed-ridden wasteland. They sued for a refund, and Aimee plunged further into debt.

Her failures only hardened her resolve to succeed in a business enterprise beyond Minnie's greatest dreams. In September 1929, a year after she settled the Tahoe Cedars lawsuits, she filed papers of incorporation for what she called the Echo Park Hotel Corporation, Ltd., "to maintain and deal in hotels, apartments, restaurants, garages, and real property." She would build a hotel-apartment complex costing between $650,000 and $1 million. She would raise $1.5 million by selling stock in the corporation.

The venture collapsed in another heap of breach-of-contract lawsuits, one for $65,000, another for $216,000, a third for $25,000.

Determined that one success would wipe out all the failures, Aimee plunged into new real estate schemes in San Fernando and the San Bernardino Mountains. One led to an $1,800 claim by real estate promoters, another for $143,000 for time and money spent preparing the properties for sale.

But Aimee's financial debacles until then were minuscule compared to those that tumbled upon her in the next few months. The Reverend Mr. John Goben, assistant pastor of Angelus Temple and general field secretary of the Foursquare branch churches, learned that Aimee was juggling temple funds. The information Goben gave to the district attorney showed Aimee had set up a joint bank account with Ralph Jordan under the names Elizabeth and Edith Johnson in which she'd deposited about $100,000. More than $8,000 donated to the commissary had found its way to that account.

Goben made one more revelation. In March 1928 Aimee had gone before her congregation with a desperate appeal for $25,000. She told her radio listeners and temple followers that she'd just found notes totaling that amount signed by Minnie Kennedy and now falling due. The devoted members of her congregation made sacrificial contributions, and Aimee raised the money.

What Goben learned, and told the district attorney, was that outstanding notes did indeed exist—signed not by Minnie Kennedy, but by Aimee herself—and payable to Ralph Jordan, possibly for his services in squashing the kidnapping trial.

Goben resigned, and the following day Aimee fired him. At their last confrontation, he told Aimee, "Sister McPherson, I've never in my life met anybody so deceitful as you. The single motive of your life is an overriding greed for money."

That night Aimee brooded in the parsonage living room over Goben's departing words. If there was one thing in the world she had never cared about, she assured herself, it was money. Minnie had been obsessed with bank balances, large offerings, and that sort of thing, while Aimee herself had been as happy in a leaking tent as in the temple's palatial manse. What did Goben know of her motives, of the colossal debt of the kidnapping trial, officially at least $170,000 and unofficially—even Aimee had never calculated it—perhaps $800,000. What did he know of the myriad lawsuits?

"Greed!" Aimee exclaimed to herself. She hurried out of the room, intending to tell her daughter of Goben's outrageous accusation, for they had grown much closer since Minnie's departure, sharing as they did the work of the radio station and routine business management. Roberta had even absorbed some of Aimee's preaching responsibilities.

But when she approached her daughter, Aimee said nothing of Goben. Instead, with eyes full of praise, she touched her fingers to Roberta's cheek and said tenderly, "I sometimes forget how beautiful you are."

Roberta returned her smile.

"Mom!" Roberta whispered, throwing her arms around Aimee. "Sometimes I think you're the most courageous person in the world!"

Aimee closed her eyes and pressed her lips together.

"Let's go for a walk," she suggested. "I've got the most exciting idea—I want to tell you about it!" She would organize a motion picture company, Angelus Productions, not a worldly film company like those in Hollywood, but one devoted to producing sacred films. She'd raise funds by selling two thousand shares of common stock at one hundred dollars each, and her first production would be *Clay in the Potter's Hand*, the story of her kidnapping. Aimee herself would play the starring role, and Roberta would have an important part. Aimee had already signed a contract with Harvey Gates, who had written the script for the very first talking motion picture, Al Jolson's *The Jazz Singer*.

"Oh, if I have my way, the devil's crowd won't be able to boast anything we haven't got!" Aimee exclaimed. "All through history, it was the *Church* produced the most beautiful art, the greatest architecture, the classical music and drama—the Catholic liturgy is *incomparable*! But now—we've gotten so *decent* and holier-than-thou. Where's the Christian influence in popular music today, in the motion picture? Why, that's the *art* of the twentieth century—and the Church ought to be in the driver's seat!

"Every week I give my people theater on the temple stage, and it's as good as anywhere. We give them everything the *world* gives them—only it's to the glory of God. And now we're going to give them their movies. We'll make them in the temple—we've got all the space and best acoustics and the radio station equipment."

Aimee's attorneys filed the articles of incorporation for Angelus Productions in October 1929. A few days later, the stock market crashed, throwing great numbers of Aimee's followers out of work and hurling the economy into an unparalleled downward spiral. Aimee had no choice but to call off the project.

One of her few backers, attorney Cromwell Ormsby, immediately filed a $250,000 suit claiming breach of contract and loss of anticipated profits, and demanded $4,500 more in attorney's fees. Harold Simpson, who was to produce the film, sued for $5,000 for screen tests, and scriptwriter Harvey Gates asked $10,000.

The Angelus Productions debacle finally accomplished what Minnie Kennedy had predicted—it pushed the temple to the brink of bankruptcy. The temple needed new money—lots of it—and quickly, and Aimee's first thought was to mortgage the temple. To do it, she would need Minnie's approval, for the deed to the property still remained in both names.

She approached her mother with exclamations of sorrow over the bitterness that separated them, vowed to follow Minnie's wishes ever after, then raised the mortgage issue. Minnie responded in outrage. With Aimee managing the finances, she exclaimed, a mortgage against the temple would lead to certain foreclosure. Aimee could save her breath—nothing in the world would persuade Minnie to agree to a mortgage.

The night Minnie told her that, Aimee walked along Lemoyne

Street toward the parsonage, her hands clasped behind her back, so lost in thought she ignored the Bible School students who greeted her in passing. "It must have been a million dollars you threw away on them crazy schemes of yours," Minnie had said. "I figured it up from the newspapers." And no doubt she was right. They'd been *good* ideas that *should* have worked, and it seemed to Aimee that God Himself must have stepped in to cause such repeated failure. Predestined before the world was formed to preach the Gospel, she had set aside that calling once and reaped failure and unhappiness. But she'd forgotten that lesson of the past, and now once again it confronted her. The temple was in jeopardy, and God was again driving her to His plan for her life.

She would save the temple through another campaign, perhaps the greatest of her life, winning souls to Christ all across the United States, and use income from the tour to pay the temple bills.

Before she left the city, she fired those on her staff whom her critics had denounced as worldly, filling the positions with loyal temple members. As she'd promised Roberta, she made her and Bible School dean Harriet Jordan associate business managers.

But Aimee knew that neither her daughter nor Miss Jordan had the tenacity of a Minnie Kennedy, who could fire unnecessary or unprofitable workers, slash expenses, and beg for free what others paid for. Nor were they experienced and inventive, as Minnie had been, in fund-raising schemes. Without such a business leader, the temple's finances could not improve. Aimee found the one she needed in Giles Knight, a tall, thin man her age, in appearance not a great deal different from Ken Ormiston, although with his tailored suits and gloves and glasses strikingly distinguished. Knight, soft-spoken and diligent, had first served the temple as one of Minnie's bookkeepers.

Before setting out on her campaign, Aimee gave Knight the position of assistant business manager, in charge of reducing expenditures and raising funds. While in theory he was answerable to both Harriet and Roberta, in fact he took orders from no one but Aimee, and with humorless singlemindedness, reminiscent of Minnie Kennedy herself, he began slashing expenditures. He personally lectured every department head on the sinfulness of wasting God's money and ordered substantial budget cuts throughout the temple. He pleaded with the branch churches for special pledges, instituted second offerings during temple services to pay off the debts most threatening the temple's survival.

Aimee toured for a whirlwind five months, covering fifteen thousand miles, visiting twenty-one states, forty-six cities. She preached an average of more than twice a day—336 sermons to more than 2 million listeners, in addition to radio audiences of forty-five stations.

The public seemed never weary of news about her. Writers rivaled each other in descriptions and analyses of her power, assuring their readers that from the instant of her grand entrance each week, the entire temple audience was held hypnotized by her. Beverly Nichols referred to her as the evangelist with sex appeal, Sara Comstock as the producer who "is staging month after month and year after year the most perennially successful show in the United States." Even John Goben offered the sad commentary: "Since the days of Jesus Christ upon this earth, there never has been a religious leader who has been blessed as Mrs. McPherson has. She has had one of the greatest opportunities to do good put in her hands that was ever entrusted in a human to carry on the work of God."

In analyzing Aimee's success for readers of *The New Republic*, Morrow Mayo wrote: "Sister substituted the Gospel of Love for the Gospel of Fear. This doctrine was as strange in Southern California as it is elsewhere in Christendom. No ambassador of Christ in that section had ever thought of it until she introduced it; the others had rejected it at once on principle. Sister substituted the cheerfulness of the playroom for the gloom of the morgue. She threw out the dirges and threats of Hell, replacing them with jazz hymns and promises of Glory. The Gospel she created was and is an ideal bedtime story. It has a pretty color, a sweet taste and is easy for the patients to take. She threatens nothing; she promises everything. . . .

"Mrs. McPherson describes the Holy City literally—the jewelled walls, pearly gates, golden streets, milk and honey. She says she is not sure—she is not *sure*, mind you—but she has a pretty good idea that Heaven will resemble a cross between Pasadena, California, and Washington, D.C. That will give an idea of what may be expected at Angelus Temple. The atmosphere bubbles over with love, joy, enthusiasm; the Temple is full of flowers, music, golden trumpets, red robes, angels, incense, nonsense and sex appeal. The service may be described as supernatural whoopee."

Aimee read such stories with glee—few compliments could brighten her more than a brief report in the Los Angeles *Times* that someone had threatened to distribute photos of Aimee and a friend in the nude if Angelus Temple didn't meet certain unspecified demands. The years of headline making had not dulled in the least the thrill of seeing her name in print. One story, published in the November 30, 1930, *New York Times*, gave her particular pleasure. It read:

Aimee Semple McPherson, titian-haired "whoopee evangelist"

267

has averaged a first page story in the Los Angeles newspapers three times a week for five years. There are reporters working the "Temple beat" who are growing old in pursuit of a single assignment. Mrs. McPherson is still top-hole news even in her home town where the daily goings on are eagerly followed.

On one recent Temple day there were stories intimating that she had been spirited away in a coffin; was being held a prisoner in her own home; had signaled from a barred window in a mysterious limousine driven by a Japanese chauffeur and had received a code reply.

Her business manager was reported to have punched a reporter's nose; there was a thrilling description of "Ma" Kennedy's activities; the prayer plant was to be sold to an Eastern syndicate for a varying number of millions; the pastor was to be married; she was dying; she had reduced too fast to meet the requirements of a movie contract; she was only resting; she was preparing to resume her platform work; a big legacy was ruled out by a court decision. And it wasn't a very busy Temple day at that.

So, it had been no hollow dream that her name would one day stand with that of Luther and Zwingli and Fox and even Saint Peter and Saint Paul. Even as the public had begun to recognize, she had created a synthesis between the world and the Church, had brought to a dying faith a new spirit equal to the times. It had been no simple life, but she had stepped in the breech and had helped save the faith of millions. It was no idle boast that led her to suspend along the entire sweeping facade of Angelus Temple a banner declaring in huge letters, "Aimee Semple McPherson," and in smaller letters beneath, "World's Greatest Evangelist."

CHAPTER XXVIII

Opposition to Giles Knight's stringent economics erupted promptly—from the department heads, the branch churches, the congregation, and even friends of those who had been fired. Aimee answered all complaints with effusive expressions of concern, promising to investigate immediately. But she seemed pleased. Even Minnie had caused no greater ruckus with her penny pinching—a sure sign Giles Knight was doing well. In fact, hardly a month passed before his influence made a profound impression in the temple ledgers. In addition to meeting all operating expenses, Harriet and Roberta paid two thousand dollars toward overdue bills.

The news filled Aimee with such happiness that she offered Knight a bonus—which he refused as an unnecessary expense. The temple would be saved, she knew, and by this most unlikely hero, this reticent lover of ledgers who could have spent his days as cheerfully burrowing through figures in the temple office as stepping into the limelight and rescuing it from foreclosure. Perhaps she had somehow stumbled back into God's will for her life, and He had forgiven her after all, sending Knight to deliver her.

One evening during Knight's second month in office, while Aimee hurriedly dressed for a temple service, Roberta walked into her room.

"Mother, we have to talk about Giles Knight," she announced.

"What about him, sweetie?" Aimee turned to her daughter with tender eyes.

"Oh, I know—I *know*!" she exclaimed. "He's just—"

"He's a dictator!"

Aimee smiled. "That's *just* what he is!"

"Some people say he even tells *you* what to do."

Aimee's eyes flashed anger; then she smiled again.

"Well, there aren't as many flowers around the baptismal tank as there once was, and my bouquets are a little skimpier," she said. "I'm not to charge personal things to the temple anymore—and I won't be getting a new car this year. So—yes, in some ways he does tell me what to do, and it's for my own good. But no, he's not the boss—I am. Giles Knight works for me, and for you, too, my sweet, for, praise God, he's doing a miracle neither you nor I could have accomplished. He's saving our temple—*your* temple someday—we couldn't have done it without him."

Roberta met Aimee's smile with coolness.

"There's more to the temple than money, Mother. There's the service we're committed to—the commissary, the best teaching aids in the Bible School, quality broadcasting in the station, highest quality in the temple productions. And there's something else, too—joy in the work. When the emphasis is always on money, money, money—and that's all you've talked about since Bonnie left—I don't see how you can call that a miracle."

Aimee turned abruptly away. Then, dropping her hands, she turned again to face her daughter. "Oh, I was the *same—exactly* the same!" she laughed. "Minnie was always talking about money, and I was always condemning her. But darling, it *is* true, the temple's in financial chaos. A bandage won't help—we need major surgery, and I just *know* Giles Knight is the surgeon God has raised up."

Thus, Aimee dismissed the subject.

One evening a few weeks later, with preliminary services under way in the temple, Aimee hurried down the stairway into the parsonage foyer to confront Harriet Jordan, Giles Knight, Roberta, and the temple attorney, Jacob Moidel. Told earlier of the meeting's purpose, Aimee tossed her head back and glared into each face.

"I won't tolerate unnecessary problems," she demanded. "We'll settle this matter here and now, and if it means someone has to leave, then so be it." She turned blazing eyes on Harriet Jordan. "Now, just *why* have you refused to follow Reverend Knight's proposals?" she demanded.

"Harriet didn't refuse, I did," said Roberta in a moderate voice. "I've already told you the reason. I think he's going to ridiculous extremes. For example, I'm in charge of the radio station, and I need more help and newer equipment. But Mr. Knight refuses."

Aimee's face grew a shade softer. "You know I'd give you anything on earth, Roberta," she said. "But every department in the temple would be up in arms if I made an exception for you. Perhaps, not long from now . . ." Aimee turned hopeful eyes to the stern-faced Knight.

"But that's not the *problem*," Roberta pleaded. "Mother—Harriet and I are the business managers. I'm vice-president of the association. I'm on all the boards. I'm your *daughter*, and you've always said that someday I'll be pastor of Angelus Temple. He has no *right* to usurp my position and authority!"

"He has any right I give him in my temple, Roberta—and don't forget that!"

Roberta began to speak, hesitated, then said softly, "Perhaps there's something *you* ought not to forget. My mother is Aimee Semple McPherson, my father the sainted Robert Semple, and my grandmother Ma Kennedy. I won't be supplanted—do you want Mr. Knight, or do you want me?"

Aimee's face grew livid and her eyes blazed. "I won't be given ultimatums by *anyone*, not even my *daughter*!" she screamed. "The temple's more important than *any* of us. If you can't realize that, you're not *worthy* to serve it. You or Mr. Knight! Do you think for a second *you* could salvage this hopeless mess? Do you think if I fired Knight there'd even *be* a temple a year or two from now? I'd take Mr. Knight every day for a thousand *years* before I'd leave it in the hands of a child like you!"

Roberta brushed past her mother and started up the steps. "Then I'll leave," she said simply.

"Yes—do!" Aimee screamed.

Jacob Moidel stepped forward. "Well, that's certainly a fine thing to do—throw your daughter out in the street because you're in love with Knight!"

Grasping his shoulders, Aimee shook him violently. "How *dare* you say such a thing, you liar!" she screamed.

Moidel brushed her hands away, and grasping her arms firmly, pressed her back against the stairway. "You may be a first-class bully, Sister, but you're not bluffing me and you're not pushing me around."

Giles Knight pulled Moidel away.

"Keep your hands off her," he warned. It seemed for an instant that Moidel would hit him, but Knight's unblinking stare dissuaded him. Instead he called to Roberta: "Forget your clothes—you can get them later. Let's get out of here!"

Almost immediately Roberta skipped down the stairs, tugging her coat on. As she passed her mother, Aimee grasped her arm.

"No, Roberta—don't go!" she cried. "This is insane, everybody's trying to take the temple—you, Knight, Minnie. I've tried so hard, so hard!"

But Roberta pulled away and ran to the door. "I'll be back when you've calmed down and are ready to behave yourself and talk reasonably," she said calmly. "There's no sense in my staying now."

Moidel followed her out, casting a violent glare at Giles Knight and slamming the door behind him.

"Roberta, Roberta!" Aimee cried.

That night, in her hotel room, Roberta telephoned Minnie, who was now living in her new home at Hermosa Beach. Minnie insisted Roberta stay with her, and the following morning she drove to Los Angeles to pick her up. Before returning to the beach, Roberta stopped at Attorney Moidel's office to dictate an open letter to her mother. It said, simply, that the powers Giles Knight demanded "as necessary to his employment are unreasonable and illegal. Legal action will be taken to protect the corporation from those who wish to create a dictatorship at Angelus Temple. As you know, I have no personal quarrel with you." She signed it "lovingly and sincerely."

Copies of the letter were given to the press, and Minnie Kennedy added the comment: "I refuse to tolerate any abuse of Roberta and will fully support any action taken by my granddaughter."

Later that day, Roberta called Aimee, offering to meet with her alone and talk over their disagreement.

"I see you're in league with Minnie now," Aimee said icily. "You've pulled the press into it, publicly threatened to take me to court—and *now* you think we should talk."

"Mother—"

"I'm just so sorry Roberta, but I'll be busy all day—I'm having my hair curled," and she hung up.

As always, the press badgered Aimee for a comment, and she said, "I propose to direct the spiritual and temporal activities of the temple, which I built up. I will not allow anything or *anybody* to interfere with my work."

For three days, Aimee endured the agony of indecision, praying Roberta would return humble and apologetic, almost certain she wouldn't. Finally she determined to force her daughter's surrender. She formally fired Jacob Moidel, ordering him to turn over all records to her attorney, Willedd Andrews. That same night, she called a special meeting of the board of directors of the Echo Park Evangelistic Association, which consisted of Rolf, Roberta, and herself. In Roberta's absence, the two expunged her from the board. In the same way, Aimee removed her daughter from the controlling bodies of the radio station and Bible School.

272

In a formal statement she explained, "Roberta shall continue to assist me in publicity, radio, platform, and any such reasonable church and social business as I may ask." Her daughter could continue to live at the parsonage and retain her salary for work rendered.

Roberta responded immediately, vowing never to return while Giles Knight was in Aimee's employ, and refusing the virtual surrender Aimee had demanded.

Willedd Andrews immediately issued a statement as Aimee's attorney: "Mrs. McPherson has been intimidated, threatened and blackmailed for the last time. This time she is prepared to fight to a finish. While she regrets that the war will be sanguinary—with her own child—the only course ahead of her is protection of the organization which has consumed the best years of her life."

In response to Andrews' accusations that she had threatened to blackmail her mother, Roberta immediately sued him for slander, demanding compensation of $150,000.

After two months, Harriet Jordan telephoned Roberta urging her to return to her temple chores. Roberta refused.

"It would only postpone the inevitable," she said.

Convinced that Roberta was acting under Minnie's direction in a contest of wills, Aimee took the step of revoking Roberta's every responsibility at the temple. Rolf, Giles Knight, and Willedd Andrews surrounding her, she signed abjectly the necessary documents.

"She'll see I'm not pretending now," Aimee mumbled. "She'll come back, then, won't she—Giles? Rolf?"

But Roberta told a reporter, "When I was a very small child, I was told that I must prepare myself for membership on the board of directors of the Echo Park Evangelistic Association. I devoted my youth not to children's games, but to the church, and I was elected to the board and became an official. Now my mother has seen fit to separate me from my lifework. I didn't believe she would allow herself to be that unfair, but if my own mother doesn't want me associated with her, I certainly don't intend to push myself into her affairs."

Giles Knight opened the limousine door before the Los Angeles Hall of Justice on an overcast spring morning, and Aimee stepped out into a sea of photographers and reporters. Behind them, separated by wooden barricades, the police held back a large crowd.

"Is this your twenty-seventh court appearance this year?" shouted a reporter.

"I've lost count!" Aimee exclaimed, smiling.

"Look this way, please, Sister."

Aimee turned. Flashbulbs popped.

"Is it true Rheba Crawford, your associate pastor, is suing you for a million dollars!"

"*Assistant* pastor," Aimee corrected.

"For slander?"

"She told me she's ambitious—until now I never realized just *how* ambitious!" Aimee laughed. "She's hit on a moneymaking scheme even I hadn't dreamed up!"

Racing up the steps, she turned at the door to wave back to the crowd, allowing photographers a final opportunity. Then, with Giles Knight at her side, she slipped into the building.

The whispering ceased in the crowded courtroom and every head turned toward her.

At the far end of the room sat Minnie and Jacob Moidel, the litigious assistant pastor Rheba Crawford, and Roberta. Aimee turned away, walking briskly to Willedd Andrews' table.

Although the trial was brief, Aimee's thoughts still wandered. Even when she was called to the witness stand, her thoughts strayed. Her answers were alternately swift and trailing. Frequently she asked to have the question repeated. Once, ridden with anxiety, she refused to answer unless the question's purpose was explained. She told the court her daughter was a good girl, that she'd never attempted to blackmail her.

"I love my daughter," she said softly.

The trial ended quickly, and the judge rendered an immediate decision: He found Willedd Andrews guilty of slander and awarded Roberta two thousand dollars and court costs. The announcement brought cheers from Moidel, Minnie, and Rheba Crawford.

"Well, at least it's not much," Knight whispered to Aimee.

Closing her eyes and dropping her chin, she exhaled in a long sigh. "It's everything," she said.

Across the room, as the crowd filed out, Roberta motioned Minnie, Moidel, and Rheba Crawford toward the door. Her eyes met Aimee's and she walked hesitantly toward her. Aimee reached out.

"Roberta," she whispered, "come home."

Roberta grasped Aimee's hand. "Momma, I'm going to New York. I've got a job with a radio station. I . . ." Her voice cracked. "I wanted to say good-bye."

Aimee quickly turned away, clasping her mouth with her hand. Closing her eyes, she waved Roberta away.

After a moment, she took the handkerchief Giles Knight offered.

"Please go," she said. "Take Willedd and Rolf and the others. I want to be alone."

Knight hesitated.

"Do as I say!"

She sat alone. From the hallway came the voices of reporters and Minnie Kennedy. Then Rheba Crawford answered a reporter's query:

"I tell you, Aimee Semple McPherson is the most tragic figure in America, living in mortal fear that the glories of her past will be taken from her. That woman could have been truly great."

At 6:15 the crowd flooded through the doors of Angelus Temple, poured down the aisles, trickled into the first and second balconies. By 6:30 the auditorium was already filled. The great stained-glass windows and side doors were opened wide and the damp breeze rushed through, cooling the building.

From a side door near the platform, the fifty orchestra members entered and marched to their seats on the stage near Aimee's red velvet throne. The chair, bathed in creamy yellow lights, was framed by a backdrop of red roses and crowned with a banner proclaiming, "Sister McPherson."

Still, the multitude surged through the doors, stood shoulder to shoulder along the walls, crowded the lobby, found positions along the grand staircases. Finally they overflowed the sidewalks and began to block traffic in the streets. Hundreds more rushed to the Bible School auditorium to hear the service over a public address system.

The orchestra played Sousa's "Washington Post," Sullivan's "Lost Chord," a waltz-time arrangement of "Mighty Lak a Rose," then a booming hymn, announced by the leader as "Radiant Morn March."

The fifty choir members, clad in scarlet and white robes, moved gracefully along the ramps toward the platform, the Kimberly organ accompanying them in a militant hymn. When they reached their seats, the singing stopped. The clock on the temple's rear wall announced thirty seconds to 7:00 P.M.

Anticipation swept the audience. Temple lights dimmed. "Here she comes!" someone whispered. Necks craned. Eyes focused on the door to the right of the first balcony, where two spotlights played.

Whispers in the orchestra momentarily distracted a few people in nearby seats. The conductor answered the intercom, spoke briefly, and hung up. He whispered a few words, then lifted his baton, and the temple again trembled with music.

The audience grew restless. "Where's Aimee?" cried one woman. "They ain't kidnapped her again?"

The buzz gathered in volume until it drowned the orchestra. Men loosened their ties, women fanned themselves with copies of "The Bridal Call" from the seat racks. Children squirmed impatiently, cried, ran through the aisles, ushers chasing them.

Sitting at her vanity, Aimee ignored the waves of fever jolting her and deftly rubbed cold cream into her face. Emma reached for a comb and began untangling the snarls in her hair. Touching her forehead, Emma exclaimed, "Good Lord, you're burning up!"

"No, no—get me the blonde wig, the short one with the lovely curls. Giles, dear, my shoes."

Frowning, Emma adjusted the wig as Aimee powdered her cheeks, applied the lipstick and eye liner. Giles found her white satin shoes in the closet, slipped them on her feet, then hurried to the kitchen for the roses.

A moment later, Aimee skipped down the spiral stairs and ran to the living room for her notes and Bible. As she turned to leave, the oval-framed picture above the piano caught her attention. She had almost forgotten it, hanging there these several years like all the other taken-for-granted furnishings. She smiled remembering how she'd crammed it into the old steamer trunk and carted it along to Providence, hanging it, of all preposterous things, above Harold McPherson's wedding bed, then to Salford, and through every backwoods town along the Atlantic coast, and finally across the whole great nation to that very wall.

"Oh, Robert," she sighed. "My whole life consumed in the work, and what's left? So much rubble, so few monuments!"

"You'd better hurry, Sister," called Knight.

"She can't go! She's got a fever!" Emma demanded.

Dear Lord, Aimee thought. Dear Robert. If only we'd lived out our lives on that riverbank in China, growing old together and dying like ordinary people. Instead, I've gone the whole way alone—how utterly alone!

She rushed into the foyer and out across the patio, Emma hurrying after her with an umbrella. Crossing the alley, they climbed the fire escape to the temple entrance. A young usher opened the door a crack, smiled and nodded respectfully, turned to signal the conductor. Emma brushed a few strands of hair under the wig.

In the moment before the music died, Aimee turned to look down into the bleak, puddle-ridden alley, then lifted her gaze to the sky.

O Lord, she thought. O Lord, O Lord.

Inside, the audience was singing the old hymn "Give me the old time power, the Pentecostal power. . . ." She hummed along, staring up into the clouds and holding herself tightly in her arms.

The fine mist of rain wafted soundlessly around her like a windless Canadian blizzard. She closed her eyes and, in her rising feverishness, visualized herself dashing through a swirl of snow to the Pentecostal mission. Newsboys were crying, "Aimee Drowned!" and the words echoed from the sea's depths, and were sung in tragic beauty. I am the alpha and the omega, she thought. The beginning and the end. The kingdom of God is within you. And without me was not anything made that was made.

The mist settled on her, and she shivered and again clasped herself in her arms, crushing the Bible against her breast. In her imagination she gazed upon ten thousand faces glowing with the joy of heaven, her name on every lip. Throngs danced on every land, and multitudes walked with hands uplifted across the gleaming waters of the earth. All who had died arose in garments white as snow and praised the name of Aimee. A grand procession split the night with the voice of a thousand trumpets clear as a Salford night. "Glory, glory!" they sang, the jeweled crowns on every head glimmering in rainbow lights.

"Now, Mrs. McPherson," the usher whispered. The door stood open. Aimee took a step, weaved, beads of sweat rolling down her forehead and cheeks.

Giles Knight laid the roses across her arm.

Aimee took Knight's arm and stepped through the door.

Thousands of voices greeted her with cries of adulation. The organ boomed "When the Roll Is Called Up Yonder," while the choir sang, their voices drowned in the frenzied ovation. With head high, Aimee beamed a smile that was almost laughter.

Releasing Knight's arm, she lifted her hand high and swept down the ramp to a crescendo of cheers.

"Oh, my people!" she cried into the microphones. "My precious people—I love you so!"

The multitude rose to cry her name.

It seemed she heard the voice of Minnie shouting, "Glory to Aimee—God's little girl!" "Glory to Aimee!" shouted Marvel White and Mr. Jacobs and George Quinn and Sister Sharp and all and all. "I love you," said Roberta. "I love you," echoed heaven. And Aimee laughed and laughed, for it seemed she heard the voice of Robert saying, "This is my beloved!"

"Hallelujah! Hallelujah!" she shouted with tears and laughter.

277

CHAPTER XXIX

Five hours before the interment, the mourners began trickling into the exclusive Forest Lawn Memorial Park in Glendale. Only 2,500 invitations had been extended, but by midafternoon on that ninth day of October 1944, another 6,000 had crashed the gates, flowing in a steady stream along Westminster Road past the Little Church of the Flowers and up the hill to the mausoleum complex. There the procession turned left onto Valley Way Road, circling behind the buildings and past shrines and sculptured crypts of the great and famous, past rolling, statue-studded terraces and landscaped lawns. Lullaby Land, Rest Haven, Slumberland—by such sentimental epithets were the park's sections designated.

Immediately behind the buildings, across the road from Sunrise Slope, the crowd milled among the grave markers. Others gathered along the roped-off corridor leading from the road up the grassy hill to the large plot which Aimee, after her Blessed Hope Cemetery failed, purchased for a rumored forty thousand dollars in 1934.

No freshly dug grave lighted the landscape, but a great sarcophagus of Italian marble glistened like porcelain against a backdrop of bushes and pines. Pedestaled marble angels knelt in prayer at both ends of the tomb. On it in simple letters was engraved the name *McPherson*.

While the crowd swelled at Forest Lawn, the casket-laden hearse moved slowly along the boulevards from Angelus Temple to the cemetery, six hundred cars in its wake, seventy-five motorcycle-riding police officers in escort. Along the sidewalks, hundreds stood solemnly as the procession passed.

Such sobriety was not part of Aimee's intention when she wrote the detailed script of her funeral and burial. She'd have been gleeful to learn that the London *Daily Mail*, limited by the war to only four pages daily, nonetheless devoted a thousand words to her passing. And the lavish superlatives from every corner would have thrilled her. But not the sorrow. It was she who'd insisted that the final hymn at her funeral be a bouncy rendering of "When the Saints Go Marching In." At the cemetery, she'd envisioned an acre-long cross of white roses, the sarcophagus at the center, her band under one arm, her choir under the other, producing a medley of foot-stomping gospel hymns. Either a lack of space and time (the official explanation) or a sense of impropriety led temple officials to dispense with that final flamboyance.

Still, the tributes would have pleased her no end. Carey McWilliams wrote later: "She believed, with all her heart, in goodness and kindness, and before this fact all else was meaningless. . . . There was not a trace of snobbery in this woman. She conducted no 'vice crusades,' engaged in no snooping, and bated no radicals. She was, as a Los Angeles newspaperman once said, 'Neither a political hellcat nor a scandalmonger.' It is not surprising, therefore, that Los Angeles has already begun to miss Sister Aimee and to wish that she were back at the Temple, chasing the Devil around with a pitchfork, calling the lonely to love in her unforgettable voice."

Concluding that even the finest praise would fall short, the Los Angeles *Times* allowed Aimee to speak for herself in her obituary:

At its peak, the bass horns of a big brass band would boom triumphantly. The "miracle room" at Angelus Temple would open, a museum of crutches and other artificial aids discarded by the halt and the lame after prayer-induced recovery.

The music would soften into a religious appeal. It would sweep in crescendo in martial strains. Then Sister's sermon and the climax:

"Ushers! Jump to it!" her vibrant, far-reaching voice would shout, "Clear the one-way street to *Jesus*."

She would make a dramatic pause in the blinding spotlight. Then her cry:

"Come on, sister! Come on, brother!"

And down the aisle they came, first slowly and haltingly. Then in droves. Sobbing, shouting, on crutches, in wheelchairs and on foot came the faithful followers. They would pray. And Sister Aimee would shout hallelujah for their salvation.

Not all the press coverage was eulogistic, of course. As Aimee herself had told reporters only months before, "Aimee good—that's no news. But Aimee bad—oh boy!" And in her mode of dying she had proven herself, if not bad, then certainly the still supreme champion of headline grabbing.

On September 26 she'd arrived in Oakland, near San Francisco, to begin a four-day campaign marking the dedication of the Oakland Church of the Foursquare Gospel. That evening she rode to the auditorium in a horse-drawn carriage—a publicity raiser she often used—and spoke to a crowd of ten thousand. Later, returning to her tenth-floor suite at the Leamington Hotel, she seemed happy with the meeting's success. The next morning she was dead, having swallowed a considerable overdose of Seconal tablets.

After a lengthy autopsy, Dr. Mary Ruth Oldt of Western Laboratories, assistant county pathologist, said, "In life, Mrs. McPherson was a very sick woman, with a bad kidney condition, which seriously damaged the liver, thus increasing the effect of the drug she took."

At a coroner's hearing later, Dr. Oldt answered the question "Could death have been accidental?" by saying, "It could. A person could get in such a state of forgetfulness that he might not remember how many he had taken of these pills." One of Seconal's first effects is to impair memory.

Dr. Wilburn Smith, Aimee's Los Angeles physician, testified that his answering service had received a call from Oakland early in the morning of the twenty-seventh, but he had been performing emergency surgery and couldn't answer. Another Los Angeles physician who had treated Aimee was also phoned from Oakland, and he referred the caller to a Dr. Palmer in that city. Aimee never made the third call. The implication was that, realizing she may have taken an overdose, she tried to get help, but collapsed first.

The jury ruled Aimee's death accidental, but official decisions had never influenced anyone's opinion regarding Aimee Semple McPherson, and her death was no exception.

The one fact that apparently went unannounced in all those millions of words expounded about Aimee at her death was that she'd succeeded in doing precisely what she'd set out to do. She'd established a denomination, the International Church of the Foursquare Gospel and four hundred branch churches in the United States and Canada, another two hundred mission stations throughout the world. She'd sent three thousand graduates from L.I.F.E. Bible College into the field, most to preach the Gospel as ministers, missionaries, and evangelists. And in the last years of her life, with Giles Knight's help, she'd paid off every temple debt and left it in sound financial condition.

At Sunrise Slope, twenty-five Foursquare Gospel ministers with American flags lined the left side of the corridor from the road to the burial site. Another twenty-five flanked the right with Foursquare banners. Finally, amid sobs and outbursts from the sea of mourners, the sixteen pallbearers began the ascent. The bronze casket weighed almost three quarters of a ton, and every six feet its bearers lowered it to a resting block; still, they almost dropped it several times.

When, surrounded by great banks of flowers, it was set before the marble tomb, the immediate family gathered around. Rolf McPherson, thirty-one now, stood beside his lovely wife, Lorna Dee, his two daughters nearby. So did Minnie Kennedy, seventy-three, weeping. Harry McPherson was there. Although he hadn't seen Rolf in fifteen years, he took a bus from Ocala "to be with Rolf and comfort him in his sorrow," he told reporters. He spoke briefly of the days when he and Aimee had preached along the Atlantic coast.

But Roberta wasn't there. Her young daughter was teething and in considerable pain, and she felt at such times a mother's place is with her daughter. The admirable quality of that sentiment was lost on Rolf, who told the press his sister had been unable to secure an airline reservation.

With sunset, the clutter of autos dispersed and the crowd moved slowly along Valley Way Road toward the gate, leaving Aimee alone in the silence, the shrubs and pines rising behind her grand sarcophagus, Sunrise Slope falling away before it.

EPILOGUE

In her will, Aimee left her mother ten dollars with the stipulation that if Minnie contested it she would get nothing. Roberta received two thousand dollars and Aimee's son, Rolf, inherited the entire financial interest in the temple. A few months before Aimee's death, she had Rolf appointed vice-president and business manager, replacing Giles Knight under whom Rolf had been trained. Rolf became president at Aimee's death.

According to a recent statement issued by the International Church of the Foursquare Gospel, the Pentecostal denomination has grown dynamically since Aimee's death: "Since her demise the number of Foursquare churches in the United States and Canada has risen from four hundred to seven hundred eighty-three; foreign mission stations from two hundred to over two thousand with two thousand two hundred ninety-two missionaries and national workers registered. There are thirty day schools, thirty-two Bible Schools and two orphanages which now dot foreign shores and one hundred seventeen radio broadcasts, daily and weekly, proclaiming Jesus Christ as Saviour, Baptizer, Healer and Coming King in twenty-seven countries outside of the United States and Canada. Over one million dollars is raised annually by the home field to support the worldwide Foursquare missionary program. Foursquare church membership has risen from twenty-two thousand to two hundred thousand with a total property valuation around the globe of fifty-nine million three hundred eighty-one thousand dollars."

At her death, writers by the score felt led to pen Aimee's epitaph. The October 11, 1944, issue of *The Christian Century* said this:

Sister Aimee generally "put on a good show." Well, most churches try to do that, in more dignified ways, and some of the most dignified go to the greatest lengths in clothing the service in spectacular trappings which will appeal to every sense. Mrs. McPherson made her programs cheerful rather than solemn. Her scheme of things was an adaptation of Salvation Army techniques to the tastes of those who were, culturally and economically, of the middle class.

On the other side of the ledger were her fallacious and dogmatic simplification of Christian teaching, her glorification of ignorance, her mouthing of pious slogans and catch phrases, her fraudulent faith cures, her reliance upon the spectacular and the sentimental. An audit of Sister Aimee's account would have to go much farther into both the credits and the debits. These qualities are mentioned because they are those which she shared, in large measure, with many other irregular cults, marginal movements and free-lance enterprises which operate in the name of religion.

In a more complimentary vein, writer Carey McWilliams, long a neighbor of Aimee's in Los Angeles, said: "At different times and by a variety of observers, she was pictured as a misplaced queen of musical comedy; a woman who 'might have been a great actress' (of course she was a great actress); a siren of a magnetism such as few women since Cleopatra have possessed. But such notions are essentially false. She was lonely and sad, as only a person suddenly catapulted into the floodlight of unbearable fame can be lonely; indeed, as only a woman who has lost the talisman of personal happiness, lost it far away and long ago, and tracks it endlessly through troubled dreams and cruel fantasies, can be sad."

But if Aimee were to have written her own epitaph—which she didn't—it would have held not the slightest hint of sadness or self-pity. She may well have selected her trite but sincere and often-repeated declaration, "I only see the sunshine." But the truth, of course, is that she did more than *see* it—Aimee reflected the sunshine into all the dark and fearful places. And that is why so many loved her.

NOTES AND COMMENTS

CHAPTER 1

Aimee's mother has an interesting story in her own right. Born Mildred Pearce in about 1872, she was orphaned as a child and was raised in and around London, Ontario, by an active Salvation Army couple. At age fourteen, in reply to a newspaper ad for a live-in nurse, she traveled to a farm on the outskirts of Salford, Ontario, to care for the wife of James Morgan Kennedy. When the woman died a few months later, young Minnie became the housekeeper. Not long after, her fifty-two-year-old employer proposed marriage.

The two went to Michigan for the wedding, Minnie claiming to be twenty-one, James forty-two. For a while, the wedding was the talk of Salford and Ingersoll, but Minnie soon let it be known that her husband's almost four-decade seniority did not intimidate her. Natives of Ingersoll found her to be "possessed of a strong, determined personality, a fluent speaker, and a self-educated woman." Although her grammar wasn't the best, for she had virtually no schooling, her reading vocabulary was large. A close friend of hers said she acquired an excellent vocabulary by looking up in the dictionary every new word she came across.

And she was a hard worker. When the Salvation Army barracks

needed a Sunday school superintendent, Minnie volunteered. And at Christmas, it was she who headed the fund drive and saw to it that virtually everyone she contacted made a contribution. She hadn't a grain of self-pity in her, but she was not above playing upon the sympathy of others to obtain her ends.

She was tough-minded, shrewd, and penurious to a fault and kept her savings separate from those of the household, dipping into them only rarely, and then usually for Aimee's sake.

James Kennedy was a widely respected man of genuine piety, a member of the Salford Methodist Church choir. He was not only a farmer but also an engineer. He had sons and daughters from his previous marriage, all older than Minnie.

The degree to which James and Minnie pampered their only child is illustrated by this story related by Byron Jenvey, Ingersoll's town historian, who knew the Kennedys well: Aimee originally attended Number Three Dereham School, but at the age of thirteen or fourteen, she had a falling-out with the teacher there. Minnie was so determined that her daughter be fully appreciated by her teachers that she persuaded James to rent land adjoining his, but in another school district. Thus, the Kennedy farm was extended into two districts, and Aimee immediately transferred to Number Two Dereham.

On July 18, 1906, when Aimee was fifteen years old, she published a controversial letter to the editor in the *Family Herald and Weekly Star* of Montreal. It gives important insight into her thinking regarding faith and reality. In it she says:

> As a Collegiate [high school] pupil, I have for some time been an ardent student of the *High School Physical Geography*. All my life I have been trained in unwavering confidence in the teachings of the Holy Scriptures and God as creator of all things, and that man God created in His own image, a living soul. The teachings of the *High School Geography* tend to undermine and destroy this faith in God as Supreme Being and Creator. Its doctrine is at direct variance with that taught in our Holy Bible. It leads us to believe that neither earth nor man were created by God, but by a process of evolution, man being a product of the animal kingdom.

Aimee reveals that her faith was strongly tested by the teachings of this text, but explains she was delivered from unbelief: "Just in the nick of time I had my eyes opened to the awful position one must be in who accepts the teachings of this book. If needs be, I will be willing to sacrifice science rather than religion."

She finishes the long letter with a rousing appeal: "In closing let me appeal to every student, to rally and stand by the sacred old truths which right away through the ages have withstood every storm, and risen triumphant above every blast in spite of all the cold-blooded reasoning of scientists. 'For what shall it profit a man if he gain the whole world and lose his own soul?' "

Aimee's highly articulate letter brought a flood of responses from other readers, many stoutly criticizing what they considered her ignorant approach. Years later, when Aimee recalled her letter, she said it expressed her religious doubts—she ignored completely her rallying cry to the faith. Apparently, the letters published in rebuttal were instrumental in at least temporarily shaking her faith.

The Salvation Army in general, and Evangeline Booth in particular, played a great role in molding Aimee in her early years. Miss Booth, the daughter of Salvation Army founder General William Booth, led the movement in Canada from Aimee's sixth year to her fourteenth. Thereafter, Miss Booth headed the Army in the United States. Minnie, who was actively involved in the work, no doubt had great respect for the young evangelist's leadership and power in preaching and encouraged Aimee to emulate her.

Evangeline was heralded as a great actress. In raising support for the Salvation Army's social works programs, she often used props and special lighting and appeared in tattered clothing for her dramatic presentations. Aimee later utilized the same techniques on a more sophisticated level at Angelus Temple.

CHAPTER III

I have dramatized the romance between Aimee and Robert; some details were not recorded. There is no record of their first kiss.

Aimee and Robert spent a year and a half in North America before sailing to China. In describing the Stratford days, Aimee said (*This Is That*, 1919): "We had three little rooms in the heart of the city where swirling smoke clouds from nearby foundries swept over the roof and tiny backyard where I struggled desperately with my first washing. I would wash and rub and rinse, and as fast as I washed the clothes the soot would black them. . . . The rooms were furnished in an unpretentious way, and even with my eyes filled with smoke from the broken door of the little kitchen range, my first pan of biscuits, hard and brown though they were, were considered a great and triumphant success by the husband who came in, from his toil in the boilerworks, at noon. . . .

"The little assembly was poor in this world's goods, and my dear husband, not willing to lay us as a burden upon them, had accepted this humble position of work, though in other cities he might have commanded a dignified position with a good salary. Like Paul, he was not afraid to work with his hands."

In London, Ontario, they stayed at the home of one of the city's few Pentecostal believers. When they left less than a year later, Robert had built a congregation of more than one hundred.

From there, the Semples felt called to assist Brother W. H. Durham in his work at the North Avenue Mission in Chicago, and Aimee persuaded Minnie to give them enough money for the trip. Aimee writes that it was here God gave her the gift of interpreting the tongues-speaking of others. In her earlier writings, she also claims that God miraculously and instantly cured an ankle she had broken.

CHAPTER VIII

According to Aimee's accounts, she was hospitalized twice during this period—once for a difficult delivery of son Rolf and again for an operation the nature of which she never specified but which later evidence suggests was a hysterectomy. She almost died as a result.

The depression she suffered at this point can hardly be exaggerated—she herself termed it a complete nervous breakdown.

CHAPTER IX

After her rededication to God, Aimee actually persuaded Mack to rent for her a lovely home at 34 Benefit Street in Providence. Much of the money for furnishing it was provided by Mrs. Anna McPherson, Mack's mother. Exactly how long they lived there is unknown, but it was not long, and I have therefore simplified the narrative by allowing Aimee to remain on Claverick Street during her stay in Providence.

CHAPTER X

The road to Mount Forest was not quite as direct as it may seem. Leaving the children at the Salford farm with Minnie, Aimee first went to a revival meeting in Kitchener, where she and Robert had made good friends years before. She attended not as a preacher's wife but as a penitent backslider. Yet, her friends greeted her warmly. When that campaign closed, she attended another in London, where she helped by playing the piano, washing dishes, painting signs. It was there that Sister Sharp invited her to Mount Forest.

CHAPTER XI

Christine and Reuben Gibson became good friends of the McPhersons, offering encouragement and support when the two set out on the sawdust trail, and providing a place for them to stay after they gave up the home on Benefit Street. Later, when Mack and Aimee separated, the Gibsons pleaded with them to reunite and accompanied Mack to Georgia where they attempted to persuade Aimee of her responsibility to her husband. Aimee would not consider abandoning the ministry to return to Providence, and, in despair, Mack and the Gibsons left Aimee in Philadelphia.

Some years later the Gibsons started a small Bible school in East Providence—the Zion Bible Institute. In stark contrast to the flamboyant approach of some, the Gibsons never asked for contributions; they requested prayer for certain needs and nothing more. Today, half a century after its founding, the institute still flourishes.

CHAPTER XII

Aimee writes that she and Mack separated in Miami, but Mack has said she left him in Orlando, where he stored the tents before traveling to Jacksonville to work in the shipyards. He did not stay there long, only until he earned enough money to pay his way back to Providence. When he and the Gibsons failed to persuade Aimee to return home, he returned to Providence for a couple of years, divorced Aimee, then went south again, settling in Ocala, Florida. In 1925 he married Alyce McPherson, twelve years younger than he. Anna McPherson sold the house in Provi-

288

dence and went to live with her son and daughter-in-law in Ocala. After some years, Mack and Alyce were divorced and Mack married his last wife, Pearl. Until her death his mother stayed with Alyce McPherson in Ocala. Harold McPherson died in July 1978.

There is some evidence that, after Aimee moved to Providence, Minnie Kennedy had a rather involved romance in New York City which continued until 1918. When, after the kidnapping episode, she feuded with Aimee, a temple committee publicly recommended, "Mrs. Kennedy might return to her wealthy husband, Mr. W. Whittebeck, who is a well-to-do engineer on a big Hudson River liner. He lives in New York where Mrs. Kennedy resided until eight years ago." The press located the Mr. Whittebeck, who denied knowing Minnie and insisted, "I am married to Mrs. Mabel Archer Whittebeck, we have a home in Catskill, New York, and I am a grandfather."

Roberta, who had lived with Minnie throughout this period, told reporters, "Grandmother married William Whittebeck, an engineer on a Hudson river boat, but I do not know just when." The press never did solve the riddle, but Aimee herself sheds some light on it in her book *The Story of My Life* (1973 edition). During the restless and depressing months after she returned from China, Aimee traveled aimlessly from New York to Chicago and the farm before finally settling in the East. During one of the visits to the farm, she writes:

> One day as we [James and Aimee] were both wielding snow shovels, clearing a path from the door to the front gate, he inquired wistfully, "How long do you think your mother will stay in New York? Did she say anything about returning to the farm?"
>
> "No, Dad. She says that all the money in the world could not induce her to bury herself out here again and that she merely put up with it as long as she did for my sake. When I married, it set her free to go. She loves the city and really seems a part of it."
>
> "Maybe if I get a neighbor to look after the stock, I could go to her . . ."
>
> "No, darling. I'm afraid you'd get run over in the rush." . . .
>
> Poor Dad! He did go to the big city for a visit but only stayed a short time before returning to the farm.

Several who knew the Kennedy family report that James and Minnie were quietly divorced immediately after the visit.

CHAPTER XV

In *Seize the Day*, Saul Bellow describes Los Angeles in the early twenties: "Someone had said, and Wilhelm agreed with the saying, that in Los Angeles all the loose objects in the country were collected, as if America had been tilted and everything that wasn't tightly screwed down had slid into southern California."

Nathanael West describes the city's unique religious movements in *Day of the Locust:* "He spent his nights at the different Hollywood churches, drawing the worshippers. He visited the 'Church of Christ, Physical' where holiness was obtained through the constant use of chestweights; the 'Church Invisible' where fortunes were told and the dead made to find lost objects; the 'Tabernacle of the Third Coming' where a woman in male clothing preached the 'Crusade Against Salt'; and the 'Temple Moderne' under whose glass and chromium roof, 'Brain Breathing, the Secret of the Aztecs' was taught."

It was to this sensation-craving mass that Aimee fortuitously brought her faith healing, tongues-speaking, and gutsy, emotional faith. As Carey McWilliams says, "All America was stepping out on an emotional binge, and Aimee was determined to lead the parade on a grand detour to heaven."

But the "loose screw" mentality that helped bring Aimee success in Los Angeles also presented her with headaches. For example: In June 1924 a fifty-year-old man entered the parsonage and told Aimee, Emma Schaffer, the two children, and a maid to leave—they had occupied the place long enough, he informed them. Carpenters working at the Bible School threw him out and the police took him to a mental hospital.

According to Roberta Semple Salter, one night about that time she and Aimee observed an old lady waiting in front of the parsonage. For hours, the woman stood there until finally Aimee called her to the door. The woman said she'd been "waiting for my husband," but Aimee realized she simply had nowhere to go and invited her to spend the night at the parsonage. Early the next morning, Roberta was awakened by her mother's screams. The old woman had entered Aimee's room and attacked her while she was sleeping. As usual, Minnie came to her daughter's rescue.

On March 4, 1925, the Los Angeles *Times* reported that a fifty-year-old blacksmith threatened to blow up Angelus Temple unless the pastor permitted him to place a "kiss from God" on her lips. Victor Bell Pendelton had written Aimee thirty letters before she finally had him arrested.

Pendelton told authorities a butterfly had landed on his lips with the message to deliver the kiss.

A week later, Pendelton was declared insane. While being escorted to an asylum, he told reporters, "I'm just as much an emissary of God as Mrs. McPherson is!"

In September of that year, a Mrs. Marcie Stannard was also committed to an asylum—for threatening to kill Aimee. She said the evangelist had installed a secret radio transmitter in her home and was broadcasting her family secrets to her neighbors in violation of the Interstate Commerce Commission regulations.

The temple regularly received letters threatening to blow it up or kill co-workers unless ransoms were paid or rather vague demands met. Sometimes these were turned over to authorities, sometimes simply thrown in the trash.

On June 3, 1936, the Los Angeles *Times* reported that someone had threatened to distribute photos of Aimee and a friend in the nude if she didn't meet certain unspecified demands.

CHAPTER XVI

According to Ishbel Ross, Aimee rejected the faith-healing aspects of her ministry the year following the San Diego campaign. Says Ross: "After a series of mammoth outdoors meetings she announced to reporters at the Palace Hotel in San Francisco in the spring of 1922: 'I say very definitely, right now, that I do not wish the lame, the halt, the blind and the crippled to crowd my meetings. I hope they will stay away. . . . That is the portion of my work to which I am least attracted. . . .' " (See Ch. 18.)

But the quote is suspect. For one thing, Aimee continued to have faith-healing services on a regular basis throughout her life. Further, I could not find reference to the quote, beyond Ross. My guess is that Aimee grew to view faith healing in a more mature way—not doubting it, but understanding the mechanisms at play and putting the healing into less sensational perspective. (What's more, I have no reason to suspect Aimee ever turned away any audience, crippled or otherwise.)

CHAPTER XVII

Fundamentalists often criticized Aimee for preaching, since I Timothy 2:11–12 exhorts: "Let the woman learn in silence with all subjection. But I suffer not a woman to teach, nor to usurp authority over the man, but to be in silence."

Aimee addressed that challenge directly in San Diego, saying: "Woman brought sin into the world, didn't she? Then surely she should have the right to undo the wrong and lead the world to the Eden above. Woman's personality, her tender sympathies, her simple, direct message—the woman, motherheart, working over the world, yearning to help its wayward sons and daughters—these are all qualities in favor of her right to tell the story of God's love. . . .

"Women were co-laborers with Peter and Paul in their work. But did not the apostle say, 'Let your women keep silence in the churches'? Yes, but he did not refer to a Godly woman's right to preach the eternal Gospel, for he also gives specific instructions as to how a woman should conduct herself when preaching or praying in public.

"The best reason in favor of a woman's right to preach the Gospel is that God's favor has attended it and blessed results follow. Called into the work at seventeen, I have been in active service practically ever since. I have seen thousands come to the altar laden with iniquity, then rising to their feet changed men and women."

CHAPTER XVIII

Aimee always viewed Angelus Temple as an evangelistic center, not only a church. Her midweek and Sunday morning sermons were usually designed to educate and edify Christians, but the others, particularly the Sunday evening services, were evangelistic. Standing on street corners, temple followers distributed postcards which guaranteed first-nighters up-front seats every Sunday night, and two thousand of the best seats in the house were reserved for them. Aimee actually told her congregation to stay home Sunday nights so there would be sufficient room for the unsaved.

To bring those lost to her meetings, she needed publicity, and she would go to great lengths to secure it. She has been criticized for such stunts as dropping thousands of invitations from an airplane over the city of San Diego, using her faith healing on a lion at a local zoo, standing on the back of a donkey to please photographers—but this was criticism she hardly understood, for it *did* make headlines, and it *did* bring the lost to her meetings, where many were saved. She gave no thought to an ineffectual sense of personal dignity, only results.

CHAPTER XIX

Neither Kenneth Ormiston nor Aimee ever admitted any romantic relationship whatever. The chapters regarding this relationship are drawn not from the testimony of the principals but from the overwhelming weight of evidence uncovered by reporters, the Los Angeles district attorney's office, and detective Herman Kline in the summer and fall of 1926, as well as personal interviews and unpublished correspondence in my file. For an exhaustive account of the published evidence, see Lately Thomas, *The Vanishing Evangelist*.

At this point in her career, as Carey McWilliams points out, "In Los Angeles she [Aimee] was more than just a household word: she was a folk hero and a civic institution; an honorary member of the fire and police department; a patron saint of the service clubs; an official spokesman [*sic*] for the community on problems grave and frivolous."

Aimee's use of the radio in that medium's infancy has not been fully appreciated. She was the first woman ever to preach a sermon over the airwaves—in San Francisco, in the spring of 1922. She established the third station in the city of Los Angeles. Harold Ellens writes, "Aimee understood radio thoroughly and knew that she could make it work as a dramatic medium for her message and her personality." He adds, "Her radio spectaculars were miraculous. Hundreds of thousands of people were electrified with the certainty that the broadcasts represented God's invasion into their personal lives. Thousands believed they were miraculously healed when, at Aimee's urging, they placed their hands on the radio receiver."

In 1925 the Angelus Temple float entered in the Tournament of Roses parade carried radio receivers tuned to KFSG, the temple station. That summer, Aimee used the station even more spectacularly, organizing simultaneous evangelistic tent meetings all over Southern California with two-way radio hookups from each tent to the temple auditorium. She describes the results in "Preaching to Eight Cities Simultaneously," published in "The Bridal Call Foursquare," September 1925:

"When a hymn number was given out in the Temple, the congregation in these various cities opened their hymnals to the same number. . . . When one was told to lift their hands, all lifted their hands. When one congregation was asked to wave their handkerchiefs, they all waved together; all listened to the same sermon, and the leaves of Bibles turned and rustled simultaneously in the various cities; . . . when the aisles of the Temple were choked with men and women coming forward to kneel in penitence at the Savior's feet, the aisles of the tents saw similar lines coming forward to bow at the foot of the cross."

CHAPTER XX

A commonly held but false notion is that Sinclair Lewis used Aimee as his model for Sharon Falconer, the evangelist, in his book *Elmer Gantry*. Lewis' associate Mrs. Birkhead has told biographer Mark Schorer that the novelist derived the idea of a female evangelist who drowns from a dream he had. Later, *after* Lewis wrote the drowning episode, Aimee disappeared into the Pacific. Disappointed, Lewis told Mrs. Birkhead, "We'll have to change that whole section of the book or everyone will think that Sharon is Aimee." Thus, thanks to Aimee, Sharon Falconer perished by fire.

CHAPTER XXI

The name Donald Yoder is fictional. Although at least one witness testified under oath that Aimee was in the company of the Yuma rancher during her disappearance, the friend himself denied it and the investigation was discontinued.

CHAPTER XXII

Actually, Robert Shuler first began attacking Aimee in 1924 when he published a pamphlet denouncing her. All in all, Shuler ultimately fared less well than Aimee did. His *Bob Shuler's Magazine* was less successful, and although he began a radio station in 1926, in 1931 the Federal Radio Commission revoked his license to broadcast because of his propensity to disseminate "private gossip" on public airways. Thereafter, his influence waned.

CHAPTER XXIII

The evidence presented at the kidnapping trial was far more complicated—and more damning of Aimee's position—than I have indicated. For an exhaustive presentation, see Lately Thomas's *The Vanishing Evangelist*.

CHAPTER XXIV

The McPherson trial provided the public with humor as well as drama. When, in November, the state of California held a gubernatorial election, Aimee Semple McPherson received many write-in votes for governor, Minnie Kennedy almost matched her for treasurer, and Kenneth Ormiston received a few votes for lieutenant governor.

The senior member of the Williams team which published "Aimee McPherson—Was She Kidnapped?" said in his foreword that someone, presumably a supporter of Aimee, shot at him through a window and missed. He commented: "We deplore the poor marksmanship of her defenders and venture the remark that she rarely misses anything. If any champion of Mrs. McPherson should find it necessary to shoot my son or myself through the window or elsewhere I humbly beg that it be my son as he is younger and can stand being shot better than I, also he has a wife who would grieve for him while no one cares a hang whether I am shot or not. Of course I love my son dearly but it should be remembered that such a shooting would aid the sale of the book and we need the money."

Many felt the trial itself provided the richest humor of all. The grocery slip in Aimee's handwriting, found in the Carmel cottage, disappeared under what some considered criminal and others entertaining circumstances. One jury member, Mrs. A. E. Holmes, was accused of either eating the evidence or flushing it down a toilet. She didn't deny the accusation and agreed to be dismissed from the jury. However, on the following Monday, when the jury assembled again, Mrs. Holmes was found sitting tight-lipped in her usual seat. The judge under whose jurisdiction the grand jury met was called in and, furious with the whole proceeding, dissolved the entire body. Mrs. Holmes was never prosecuted. Photocopies of the grocery list were used in place of the original.

At this point, Aimee was in no mood for humor, however. When the city park commissioner sent her a formal complaint because the temple's outdoor speakers were drowning out the band concerts in Echo Park, she retorted with a formal complaint against the park commissioner, whose band concerts were drowning out her religious services.

On a highway near Los Angeles, an enterprising businessman had opened a restaurant called Aimee's Shack. He did a thriving business until Aimee heard of it. She immediately obtained an injunction and closed the restaurant.

CHAPTERS XXVI AND XXVII

Aimee began her vindication tour not as a preacher but a lecturer, renting halls, charging admissions, and eliminating the altar call. Attendance was poor, response cool, and Aimee quickly realized few would pay to hear a preacher, no matter how famous. She promptly switched to free-will offerings, with much greater success.

These chapters actually cover a span of ten years, from 1928 to 1938. I have avoided reference to a number of biographically significant events because they contributed nothing to my story. For the interested reader, they're presented in detail in *Storming Heaven*, by Lately Thomas. In brief, they are as follows:

For a while between 1928 and 1929, Minnie returned at Aimee's request to help get rid of "worldly" and destructive leaders at the temple, and to rescue the church from financial chaos. The reuniting of mother and daughter was short-lived; Minnie left the temple once and for all after receiving a broken nose during an explosive argument with Aimee.

For the next few years, Aimee traveled a great deal, as much to recuperate from physical and emotional problems as to preach. Roberta accompanied her on an around-the-world tour in 1931, fell in love with the ship's purser, William Bradley Smythe, and married him in Singapore.

In June of that same year, Ma Kennedy, aged sixty, also married. Then Rolf married Miss Lorna Dee Smith, a Bible school student. By the end of that year, Aimee, not to be outdone, eloped with a thoroughly unlikely match, David L. Hutton, a professional performer she had hired to play the leading role in a biblical oratorio she had written.

Of these four weddings, only Rolf's lasted; the others ended in divorce within a few months or years. Aimee's dissolved in 1934.

During these years, Aimee bought a grand but gaudy imitation

Moorish castle on Lake Elsinore, a secluded and private area east of Los Angeles. She spent much of her time there until the late 1930s, when she was forced to sell it to raise the money for the settlement of the slander charges brought by Rheba Crawford. During this time she also maintained her residence at the parsonage.

Aimee first met Rheba Crawford during the 1916–17 Florida campaign. Driving along the road, Rheba had seen Aimee's tents and had stopped just long enough to give the evangelist a donation and pray briefly for the work. By then, Rheba, a Salvation Army worker who, like Minnie, had been orphaned as a child, had already made a name for herself in New York City. She had become a celebrity of sorts as a street corner preacher of hellfire and repentance, sometimes addressing audiences of as many as five thousand, and once even being arrested for causing a rush-hour traffic tie-up in Manhattan. Damon Runyon modeled his heroine in *Guys and Dolls* after Rheba Crawford.

Married in Florida, Rheba left her husband to preach, as Aimee had done, and her husband, like Aimee's, divorced her. In 1929 she found her way to California and became director of the state's Department of Welfare. With that training, she volunteered to reorganize the Angelus Temple Commissary, the finances of which were under investigation by the district attorney, so that it conformed to the legal requirements. Soon she began preaching at temple services and on the radio. Aimee signed a contract with the attractive "Angel of Broadway," as Rheba had been known, making her assistant pastor.

For all the two women seemed to have in common, Rheba's style was entirely different from Aimee's. She had little interest in glamour and exhibited not the slightest trace of worldliness, but preached a hard, hellfire message. While Aimee spoke of love and joy, Rheba used the temple radio station to attack the city's crooked politicians. She threatened a recall movement against the city's mayor and city council.

Battered emotionally by the stress of endless business failures, the split with Minnie, a second divorce, and vague physical problems, Aimee perhaps exaggerated the significance of Rheba's growing popularity among temple loyalists—or perhaps she accurately diagnosed a growing dissatisfaction with Aimee herself, the frequently absent celebrity pastor. At any rate, Aimee's reaction was, as always, emotional. She had Giles Knight cancel Rheba's contract. Rheba responded by telling Aimee, in effect, that she would have to do the dirty work herself—Giles Knight had no authority to cancel a contract between Aimee and Rheba. Then, listing eighteen specific scurrilous and derogatory statements attributed to Aimee, Rheba sued the pastor for damages of $1,080,000.

The official complaint charged Aimee with calling Rheba a Jezebel, a governor's mistress, a thief, a partner of the devil, a hypocrite, a Judas, another Ma Kennedy, an embezzler, and a blackmailer.

The case would have come to court simultaneously with Roberta's against Willedd Andrews, but Aimee settled it for an undisclosed amount.

Many celebrities came under the influence of Aimee Semple McPherson. According to Norman Mailer's biography of her, Marilyn Monroe was baptized by Aimee at Angelus Temple. Her grandmother, Della Monroe Grainger, was a devoted temple follower.

Anthony Quinn, in his autobiography, *The Original Sin*, says that, although he was a Roman Catholic, he came to attend Angelus Temple as a young teen-ager because temple members prayed for his ailing grandmother and she recovered. He says, "I was fourteen when I met the most magnetic personality I was ever to encounter. Years later, when I saw the great actresses at work I would compare them to her. As magnificent as I could find Anna Magnani, Ingrid Bergman, Laurette Taylor, Katharine Hepburn, Greta Garbo and Ethel Barrymore, they all fell short of that first electric shock Aimee Semple McPherson produced in me."

In the nine pages Quinn devotes to his experiences with Aimee, he has nothing but the highest praise for her. "This was all during the height of the Depression," he says, "when hunger and poverty permeated America. Many Mexicans were terrified of appealing for county help because most of them were in the country illegally. When in distress, they were comforted by the fact that they could call on one of Aimee's branches at any time of the night. They would never be asked any of the embarrassing questions posed by the authorities. The fact that they were hungry or in need of warm clothing was enough. No one even asked if they belonged to Aimee's church or not."

The first time he met her, he says, she smiled as if to say, "I know you. I like you."

Singer Pat Boone and his family are, at this writing, active in the Van Nuys, California, Foursquare Church.

For the seven years she lived after her separation from Roberta, Aimee apparently rededicated herself to the type of spiritual ministry she proclaimed in the early days of her career. Although Aimee conducted a few individual meetings from time to time, she devoted herself almost exclusively to Angelus Temple and the Bible College, and in the late 1930s, a great spiritual revival swept the temple.

TO THOSE WHO HELPED

So many have contributed to the information, research, and production of this book that, although they would hardly be noticed in the immensity of Angelus Temple, they'd make a respectable congregation in their own right. To those who, for obvious reasons, prefer to remain anonymous, and to the others listed below, I extend the deepest gratitude:

Ingersoll, Salford, Ontario

Byron G. Jenvey, Aimee's grammar school teacher and local historian; Miss Ethel Page, schoolmate and friend; George and Gladys (Wert) Quinn, neighbors; Rev. John H. McDonald, pastor of the Pentecostal Tabernacle of Ingersoll; Stanley J. Smith; and Yvonne Mott of the Ingersoll Public Library.

Providence

Miss Alice Stevens Chase, treasurer of Zion Temple and the registrar and treasurer of the Zion Bible Institute (Miss Chase was a teen-ager when Reuben and Christine Gibson allowed Aimee to preach at their little Pentecostal church—she remembers well the marital difficulties between Mack and Aimee and the pain it caused the Gibsons); attorney Francis O'Brien; Joseph O. Mehr, librarian, the Providence *Journal* and *Evening Bulletin*; Robert Whittiker, religion editor, the Providence *Journal*; Dr. William McLoughlin, of Brown University, author of several books. Dr. McLoughlin wrote a brief biography of Aimee for the book *Notable Women in America*, and provided me with his extensive source material, including an interview with Roberta Semple Salter.

Florida

Bernard Watts, editor, the Ocala *Star-Banner*.

Los Angeles

Evelyn Godwin and Edna Splees, temple workers (Mrs. Splees kept a detailed scrapbook of temple affairs); James Vale, Los Angeles City Library, newspapers division; Warren Blaney, businessman.

San Diego

Sylvia Arden, the San Diego Historical Society; Rhoda E. Kruse, the San Diego Public Library.

Others who assisted in the research include Bradley B. Williams; James Peel; Mrs. T. O. Beasley of the Methodist Publishing House in Nashville; Gerald W. Gillette of the Presbyterian Historical Society in Philadelphia; Lori Davisson of the Arizona Historical Society; William M. Roberts, Bancroft Library, the University of California, Berkeley; Linda Ervin, National Library of Canada; and Esther Heillig of the Montreal *Star* Library.

Particular thanks to the entire reference staff of the Allentown Public Library, Allentown, Pennsylvania, and its director, Kathryn Stephanoff.

In the winter of 1973 Roberta Semple Salter generously granted a lengthy interview in her New York City apartment and provided, in addition to invaluable information, her own interpretation of her mother's life.

In the course of this project, Barbara Erich transcribed approximately 4,500 pages of manuscript, of which fewer than 600 survived; Lately Thomas, author of two marvelous books on Aimee, made available all his research and offered useful advice; Jergen Haver patiently endured and criticized the early efforts.

Others who did the same were Nahum Waxman, whose detailed letters crucially shaped this book, and Dr. James Frakes, whose advice helped me develop the style in which it is written.

To all those, and to the many others who would not be named, I am grateful. And to one, my wife, Alice, I owe an inexpressible debt. A professional research librarian, she not only helped pay the bills during the years the book was being written but gathered all the published sources; she wrote letters, proofread the manuscript, critiqued the writing, scolded, cajoled, and flattered the author as required. She listened. She endured. It is her book, too.

Periodicals

Aikman, Duncan. "Savonarola in Los Angeles." *American Mercury*, 21 (1930), 423–30.

"Aimee of the Angels." *Newsweek*, 24 (October 9, 1944), 82+.

"Aimee Semple McPherson." *Liberty*, 69 (Winter 1974), 37–39.

"Aimee Semple McPherson." *Life*, 17 (October 30, 1944), 85–88.

"Aimee's Foursquare Behind the War." *Newsweek*, 22 (July 19, 1943), 64.

"Aimee's Rival." *The Literary Digest*, 123 (March 20, 1937), 32.

Bissell, Shelton. "Vaudeville at Angelus Temple." *Outlook*, 149 (May 23, 1928), 126+.

Bliven, B. "Sister Aimee." *New Republic*, 48 (November 3, 1926), 289–91.

Bretherton, C. H. "A Prophetess at Large." *The North American Review*, 226 (December 1928), 641–44.

Brown, Sevellon. "Another View of Aimee McPherson." *Providence Journal*, 11 (March 1963).

Budlong, Julia N. "Aimee Semple McPherson." *The Nation*, 128 (June 19, 1929), 737–39.

"California Evangelist, A" *The New Statesman*, 28 (November 13, 1926), 134–38.

"Christ in Vaudeville." *The New Statesman*, 31 (October 6, 1928), 785, 786.

Comstock, Sarah. "Aimee Semple McPherson: Prima Donna of Revivalism." *Harpers*, 156 (December 1927), 11–19.

"Court Record, The" *Providence Evening Tribune*, April 13, 1921, p. 13.

"Criticisms of Mrs. McPherson." *Promise*, 1 (March 1922), 17, 18.

Duncan, Ray. "Fighting Bob Shuler—The Holy Terror." *Los Angeles Magazine*, 8 (1964), 38.

"Foursquare." *Time*, 40 (February 16, 1948), 71, 72.

"Has Sister Aimee Been Deposed?" *Christian Century*, 50 (February 15, 1933), 232.

Hedgepeth, William. "Brother A. A. Allen on the Gospel Trail." *Look*, 33 (October 7, 1969), 23–42.

Hynd, Alan. "Sister Aimee—Sexpot in the Pulpit." *Official Detective*, 41 (June 1972), 36+.

"Just a Sick Girl." *Outlook*, 156 (September 3, 1930), 15.

Keatley, V. B. "Siren of the Sawdust Trail." *Coronet*, 42 (August 1957), 52–58.

King, Elisha A. "Mrs. McPherson, Evangelist and Healer." *Congregationalist*, 106 (October 26, 1921), 435–37.

"L. A.'s Celebrated Case of 'Missing' Evangelist." Los Angeles *Times*, May 18, 1969, Section B, p. 2.

Los Angeles *Times*, 1923–44.

Lynd, R. "Hot Gospel." *New Statesman*, 32 (October 13, 1928), 8, 9.

McLoughlin, William. "Aimee Semple McPherson: Your Sister in the King's Glad Service." *Journal of Popular Culture*, 1 (Winter 1968), 193–217.

McPherson, Aimee Semple. "The Crucible of God." *Bridal Call*, June 1920.

——— "How We Were Led to Cross the Continent in the Gospel Auto." *Bridal Call*, December 1918, pp. 10, 11.

——— "Wonderful Downpouring in the Baltimore Churches." *Bridal Call*, March 1920, pp. 7–13.

"McPherson, Rolf. Portrait." *Time*, 51 (February 16, 1948), 72.

Mayo, M. "Aimee Rises from the Sea." *The New Republic*, 61 (December 25, 1929), 136–40.

Morris, B. G. "The Revivals of Aimee Semple McPherson." *Pacific Christian Advocate*, 70 (October 5, 1921), 4+ .

"Newsmakers." *Newsweek*, 84 (July 1, 1974), 42.

New York Times, 1926–44.

"Pentecostal Unit Reports Growth." *New York Times*, April 29, 1973, p. 15.

Philadelphia *Inquirer*, July–August 1918.

"Portrait." *Outlook*, 156 (September 3, 1930), 15.

Providence *Journal*, 1931, 1944.

Providence *Journal* and *Evening Bulletin*, October 4–26, 1926.

"RIP Aimee." *New Statesman*, 28 (October 28, 1944), 28.

Ryder, David Warren. "Aimee Semple McPherson." *The Nation*, 123 (July 28, 1926), 81, 82.

Samarin, William J. "Glossalalia." *Psychology Today*, 6 (August 1972), 48–50.

San Diego *Union*, January–February 1921.

"Sister Aimee." *The Christian Century*, 61 (October 11, 1944), 1159, 1160.

"Sister Aimee in New York." *The New Statesman*, 29 (April 30, 1927), 71, 72.

Smith, R. L. "Has Sister Aimee Been Deposed." *Christian Century*, 50 (February 15, 1933), 232.

"Story of My Life." *Time*, 44 (October 9, 1944), 58+.

"Suicide Doctor's Papers Involve Mrs. McPherson." New York *Herald Tribune*, September 23, 1926.

"1000's Mourn at Famed Evangelist's Funeral." *Life*, 17 (October 30, 1944), 85–89.

Worthington, W. "Healing at Angelus Temple." *Christian Century*, 46 (April 24, 1929), 549–52.

Records and Tapes

McPherson, Aimee Semple. *The Ancient Mariner*. Tape. Los Angeles: International Church of the Foursquare Gospel.

McPherson, Aimee Semple. *The Big Bad Wolf*. Tape. Los Angeles: International Church of the Foursquare Gospel.

McPherson, Aimee Semple. *Divine Healing in the Word of God*. Record. Los Angeles: International Church of the Foursquare Gospel.

McPherson, Aimee Semple. *From Milkpail to Pulpit*. Record. Los Angeles: International Church of the Foursquare Gospel.

McPherson, Aimee Semple. *God Goes to Washington*. Tape. Los Angeles: International Church of the Foursquare Gospel.

McPherson, Aimee Semple. *Heaven Can Wait*. Tape. Los Angeles: International Church of the Foursquare Gospel.

McPherson, Aimee Semple. *Life Begins at Foursquare*. Tape. Los Angeles: International Church of the Foursquare Gospel.

McPherson, Aimee Semple. *Miraculous Pitcher*. Tape. Los Angeles: International Church of the Foursquare Gospel.

McPherson, Aimee Semple. *Pennies from Heaven*. Tape. Los Angeles: International Church of the Foursquare Gospel.

McPherson, Aimee Semple. *Power of Faith*. Tape. Los Angeles: International Church of the Foursquare Gospel.

McPherson, Aimee Semple. *A Tale of Two Cities*. Tape. Los Angeles: International Church of the Foursquare Gospel.

McPherson, Aimee Semple. *Then the Rains Came*. Tape. Los Angeles: International Church of the Foursquare Gospel.

McPherson, Aimee Semple. *This Is My Task*. Tape. Los Angeles: International Church of the Foursquare Gospel.

McPherson, Aimee Semple. *Treasure Island*. Tape. Los Angeles: International Church of the Foursquare Gospel.

Books

Bach, Marcus Louis. *They Have Found a Faith.* New York: Bobbs, 1946.

Bean, Walter. *California: An Interpretive History.* New York: McGraw-Hill, 1968.

Bellow, Saul. "Seize the Day." In *Classics of Modern Fiction,* ed. Irving Howe. 2nd ed. New York: Harcourt Brace Jovanovich, 1972.

Berle, Milton. *Milton Berle: An Autobiography.* New York: Delacorte, 1974.

Clark, Elmer Talmage. *The Small Sects in America.* Rev. ed. New York: Abingdon-Cokesbury Press, 1949.

Cole, Stewart Grant. *The History of Fundamentalism.* New York: R. R. Smith, 1931.

Ellens, J. Harold. *Models of Religious Broadcasting.* Grand Rapids, Mich. Eerdmans, 1974.

Ellis, William T. *Billy Sunday.* Chicago: Moody Press, 1959.

Fass, Paula S. *The Damned and the Beautiful.* New York: Oxford University Press, 1977.

Furnas, J. C. *Great Times.* New York: G. P. Putnam's, 1974.

Gaver, Jessyca Russell. *Pentecostalism.* New York: Award Books, 1971.

Gee, Donald. *Pentecostal Movement.* 2nd ed. London: Elim Publishing House, 1949.

Goben, John D., Rev. *Aimee: The Gospel Gold Digger.* New York: Peoples Publishing Company, 1932.

Hollenweger, Walter J. *The Pentecostals.* Minneapolis: Augsburg Publishing House, 1972.

Howard, V. E. *Fake Healer Exposed: Miracles and Divine Healing.* 5th rev. printing. A Radio Address. Texarkana, Texas: V. E. Howard, 1970.

Hughes, Richard. *Hong Kong, Borrowed Place–Borrowed Time.* New York: Praeger, 1968.

Hurlimann, Martin. *Hong Kong.* New York: Viking, 1962.

Kershner, John J. *The Disappearance of Aimee Semple McPherson.* Published

Link, Arthur S., et al. *American Epoch: A History of the U.S. Since the 1890's*. New York: Knopf, 1967.

Lloyd, Marjory. *A Brief History of Carmel*. Prepared for the City of Carmel-by-the-Sea by the editor of the *Carmel Pine Cone*, 1966.

Lucas, E. V. *A Wanderer in Rome*. New York: George H. Doran Co., 1926.

McLoughlin, William. *Modern Revivalism*. New York: Ronald Press, 1959.

McPherson, Aimee Semple. *Fire from on High*. California: Heritage Committee, 1969.

————. *The Foursquare Gospel*, comp. Dr. Raymond L. Cox. California: Heritage Committee, 1969.

————. *The Foursquare Hymnal*. Los Angeles: International Church of the Foursquare Gospel.

————. *Give Me My Own God*. New York: H. C. Kinsey, 1936.

————. *In the Service of the King*. New York: Boni and Liveright, 1927.

————. *Lost and Restored*. Los Angeles: Foursquare Publications, n.d.

————. *Personal Testimony*. Los Angeles: Foursquare Publications, n.d.

————. *Songs of the Crimson Road*. Los Angeles: International Church of the Foursquare Gospel.

————. *The Story of My Life*. Hollywood: International Correspondents' Pubn., 1951.

————. *The Story of My Life*. Waco, Texas: Word Books, 1973.

————. *This Is That*. Los Angeles: Bridal Call Publishing Co., 1919.

————. *This Is That*. Los Angeles: Echo Park Evangelistic Assn., Inc., 1923.

————, and Charles Lee Smith. Debate. *There Is a God!* Los Angeles: Foursquare Publications, n.d.

McWilliams, Carey. "Sunlight in My Soul." In *The Aspirin Age*, ed. Isabelle Leighton. New York: Simon & Schuster, 1949.

Magee, Charles H. *Antics of Aimee*. Los Angeles: Pacific Magazine Agency, 1926.

Mavity, Nancy Barr. *Sister Aimee*. New York: Doubleday, 1931.

Mencken, Henry Louis. *Mencken Chrestomathy*. New York: Knopf, 1949.

Nichols, Beverly. "Christ in Vaudeville." In *The Star Spangled Manner*. New York: Doubleday, 1930.

Quinn, Anthony. *The Original Sin: A Self-Portrait*. Boston: Little, Brown, 1972.

Ross, Ishbel. *Charmers and Cranks*. New York: Harper & Row, 1965, pp. 252–82.

Schorer, Mark. *Sinclair Lewis: An American Life*. New York: McGraw-Hill, 1916, pp. 460,461.

Sherrill, John L. *They Speak With Other Tongues*. Westwood, N.J.: Spire Books, 1964.

Simister, Florence Parker. *Streets of the City*. Providence, R.I.: Station WEAN, May 31, 1954, III, 1, 2.

Sinclair, Gordon. *Will the Real Gordon Sinclair Please Stand Up*. Toronto: McClelland and Stewart, 1966.

Stagg, Frank, et al. *Glossalalia*. New York: Abingdon Press, 1967.

Story of Aimee McPherson. Was She Kidnapped? Los Angeles: Williams and Williams, n.d.

Thomas, Lately. *Storming Heaven*. New York: Morrow, 1970.

———. *The Vanishing Evangelist*. New York: Viking, 1959.

Weisberger, Bernard A. *They Gathered at the River*. Boston: Little, Brown, 1958.

West, Nathanael. *The Day of the Locust*. In *The Complete Works*. New York: Farrar, 1957.

Whiteman, Luther, and Samuel L. Lewis. *Glory Roads: The Psychological State of California*. New York: Crowell, 1936.

Wisbey, Herbert A., Jr. *Soldiers Without Swords*. New York: Macmillan, 1956.